cities in transition

The Stylos Series

Series editor **Arie Graafland**

cities in

transition

Guest editor **Deborah Hauptmann** With contributions by **Henco Bekkering Stefano Boeri Franziska Bollerey Henk de Bruijn Peter Brusse Paul Drewe Arie Graafland Dieter Hassenpflug Deborah Hauptmann K. Michael Hays Toshikazu Ishida Ben Janssen Ton Kreukels Scott Lash Winy Maas Peter Marcuse Han Meyer Henk Molenaar Michael Müller Hidetoshi Ohno Jan Oosterman Hugo Priemus Saskia Sassen Yorgos Simeoforidis Ignasi de Solà-Morales Rubio Michael Sorkin Haruo Ueno Hajime Yatsuka** 010 Publishers Rotterdam 2001

PART I Rotterdam

PART II Tokyo

PART III Cultural-Urban Criticism

PART IV Urbanism

Contributors

Henco Bekkering Professor of Urban Design, Faculty of Architecture, TU Delft. Partner in Heeling, Krop, Bekkering, office for urban design and architecture, Groningen and The Hague. Projects: a sensitive design for the Netherlands extensions of the inner cities of Zwolle, Amersfoort and Alphen aan de Rijn; revitalization of post-war housing areas.

Stefano Boeri Architect, teaches Urban Design at the University of Genoa and the Politecnico di Milano. He is the Managing Curator of the Architecture Section of the Triennale di Milano. Author of, among other works, **Il territorio che cambia, Ambienti, paesaggi e immagini della regione milanese** (with Lanzani and Marini) and **Italy, Cross Sections of a Country** (with Basilico).

Franziska Bollerey Professor, History of Urbanism, the Faculty of Architecture, TU Delft. Author of, among other works, **Venezia** (1999), **Cornelis van Eesteren, Zwischen De Stijl und CIAM** (1999), **Architekturkonzeption der utopische Sozialisten** (1991).

Henk de Bruijn Head of the Department of Strategic Planning, Port Authority Rotterdam.

Paul Drewe Professor, Urban Planning, Faculty of Architecture, TU Delft. Leader Design Studio 'Network City VROM', a search for new spatial planning concepts – among others – 'mainports' (both seaports and airports) as nodes of logistic networks. In cooperation with the Dutch Ministry of Housing, Spatial Planning and Environment (VROM). Has published extensively on urban questions in Europe.

Arie Graafland Professor Architectural Theory, Faculty of Architecture, TU Delft. He is author of, among other works, **The Socius of Architecture, Amsterdam, Tokyo, New York** (2000), **Architectural Bodies** (1996) and **Peter Eisenman, Recent Projects** (1989). Series editor of **The Critical Landscape Series.**

Dieter Hassenpflug Professor of Sociology, Department of Sociology, HAB Weimar University. Author of, among other works, 'From Utopia to Atopia – Citytainment, The City in Postmodern society' (in **Museumkunde**, 1998) and 'On the creativity of memory, Fictionalization and artificial Apathy' (in **Social Utopias of the Twenties**, 1995).

Deborah Hauptmann Architect, Assistant Professor Architectural Theory, Faculty of Architecture, TU Delft. Recent publications include: 'On Re-reading Kafka' (**The Architectural Annual**, 1999) and **Notations of Herman Hertzberger** (1998).

K. Michael Hays Professor of Architectural Theory, Director of Advanced Studies Program, Harvard School of Design, Cambridge. Author of, among other works, **Architecture Theory since 1968** (1998), and **Modernism and the Posthumanist Subject, the Architecture of Hannes Meyer and Ludwig Hilberseimer** (1992). He is the editor of **Assemblage**.

Toshikazu Ishida Associate Professor of Architecture and Urban Design, Department of Environmental Design, Fukuoka Institute of Design, Japan. He has recently published: **The Netherlands, Space and formal distinctiveness in Architecture, Urban Planning and Landscape**. (Maruzen Tokyo, 1998).

Ben Janssen Director of the NEA University of Professional Education in Transport, a Dutch State recognized private university providing web-based Bachelor and Master courses in passenger transport management, freight transport and logistics management. He has specialized in the relationships between logistics and transport strategies of companies and spatial and infrastructural developments.

Ton Kreukels Professor Urban and Regional Planning, University of Utrecht. Member of the Netherlands Scientific Council for Government Policy, The Hague. He is author of **Planning and Planning processes; an exploration of theoretical bases within the social sciences with special reference to urban and regional planning,** and Planning case studies: 'Planning as a Mirror of Western Societies'.

Scott Lash Professor of Sociology, Goldsmiths College University of London, Director of the Centre for Cultural Studies. He is the author of, among other works, **Economies of Signs & Space** (with John Urry) (1994), **Sociology of Postmodernism** (1990) and **The End of Organized Capitalism** (with John Urry) (1987).

Winy Maas Architect MVRDV, Rotterdam, author of **FARMAX, Excursions on Density** (with Jacob van Rijs).

Peter Marcuse Professor of Urban Planning, Columbia University, New York. Attorney and past President, Los Angeles City Planning Commission. Author of, among other works, **Globalizing Cities: A New Spatial Order? Missing Marx; The Myth of the Benevolent State; The Enclave, the Citadel, and the Ghetto.**

Han Meyer Associate Professor Urban Design, Faculty of Architecture, TU Delft. His recent publications include: **De Stad en de Haven, Stedebouw als culturele opgave, London, Barcelona, New York, Rotterdam** (1996). English edition: **City and Port, transformation of port cities, London, Barcelona, New York, Rotterdam** (1999).

Henk Molenaar Professor Emeritus of Economics, Erasmus University Rotterdam, former Director Port Authority Rotterdam.

Michael Müller Professor Art History, University of Bremen, Germany. He is author of, among other works, **Die Macht der Schönheit, Avantgarde und Faschismus oder Die Geburt der Massenkultur** (with Franz Droge) (1995), **Schöner Schein – Eine Architekturkritik** (1987) and **Funktionalitat und Moderne – Das Neue Frankfurt und seine Bauten 1925–1933** (1984 with Chr. Mohr).

Hidetoshi Ohno Architect and Professor of Architecture, Tokyo University, Japan. Former Research Fellow Architecture Department TU Delft. Publishes extensively on Japanese architecture.

Jan Oosterman Senior researcher at the Rotterdam City Development Corporation, part of the Municipality of Rotterdam. The development and spatial planning of leisure facilities for tourists and citizens is his main task. In 1993 he wrote **The Passing Parade; City, Fun, and Sidewalk Cafes**, a thesis in urban studies on changes in Dutch town centers.

Hugo Priemus Professor of Housing, Faculty of Architecture TU Delft. Managing director of OTB Research Institute for Housing, Urban and Mobility Studies, TU Delft. Recent publications include: **Sustainable Cities: How to realize an ecological breakthrough: A Dutch approach, Social housing finance in the European Union** (with F.M. Dieleman) and **Intermodality and sustainable freight transport** (with P. Nijkamp & D. Shefer).

Saskia Sassen Professor of Sociology, The University of Chicago, and Centennial Visiting Professor, London School of Economics. Her latest books are **Globalisation and its Discontents** (1998) and **Losing Control? Sovereignty in an Age of Globalisation** (1996). Her books, among them **The Global City** (1991) have been translated into several languages.

Yorgos Simeoforidis Editor. Has taught history and theory at the Graduate School of the AA, London and at the Graduate School of Fine Arts at the University of Pennsylvania, Philadelphia. Editor and director of **Tefchos**, founder of **Euromap** and **Transart**. Editor of **Metapolis**, Athens.

Ignasi de Solà-Morales Rubio Professor in the Theory and History Department at the Architectural School of Barcelona. Visiting professor at various Universities both in Europe and the US. Recent publications: **Present and Futures: architecture in cities**, editor (1997) and **Differences: topographies of contemporary architecture**, (1996). He has published many articles and books on architectural history and criticism.

Michael Sorkin Architect and critic, New York, author of **Exquisite Corpse – Writing on Buildings**, Verso, 1991– this is a collection of his own essays written between 1978 and 1991. Editor of **Variations on a Theme Park** (1991) – a collection of essays on the Modern American City. For ten years the architectural critic of the 'Village Voice'.

Haruo Ueno Architect and planner Rainbow Town Development, Port Authority Tokyo.

Hajime Yatsuka Architect and critic. President of Urban Project Machine Co, Ltd, Tokyo. Worked for Arata Isozaki from 1978 to 1982. Series editor of 10+1, **Ten Plus One**. Author of **The Architecture of Russian Avantgarde and Metabolism** (Inax Publishers, Japan). Projects: Media Center, Shiroishi, 1997, the Bunkyo University campus and the Folly of the Ten-Chi-Jin, Nagaoka, 1998.

Preface

Jeroen Mensink,
Stylos representative and conference assistant

Three days of Cities in Transition

The conference **Cities in Transition, The Critical Landscape** II is another step in the series **Context and Modernity**, **The Invisible in Architecture** and **The Critical Landscape**, all of which were initiated or supported by Stylos, the student association. These initiatives arose from interest in the subject matter, but also as a result of certain dissatisfaction with the degree of attention to critical and historical thinking within the curriculum.

Pressured by a decrease in the curriculum's length of study and the time allotted for scholarship funding, students are prepared for professional practice in as short a time as possible. Any space for self-development or time for expanding knowledge has to be found and paid for by the students themselves. It is striking that these extracurricular activities such as **Cities in Transition** see a high participation of foreign exchange students studying in Delft. The meager participation of teachers from the faculty clearly indicates the low level of engagement and interest of many who educate the students at this faculty.

During this interdisciplinary event in 1998, architects, urbanists, sociologists, theorists and historians were present to exchange their insights on the contemporary city. **Cities in Transition**, an event in the Stylos series **The Critical Landscape**, was made possible by the combined efforts of students and staff of the Faculty of Architecture in Delft, editors of **De Omslag**, the Urban

Planning Department of the city of Rotterdam (dS+V) and the Port Authority Rotterdam.

De Omslag 18.5

Preceding the conference, one issue of the student-run magazine **De Omslag**[1] was devoted entirely to the themes of the conference. The subjects to be introduced were prepared by students and the work of guest speakers was discussed. For a full year, a seminar led by Arie Graafland and Deborah Hauptmann offered a platform for debate on the articles of the various conference participants. For each of the weekly sessions, one student prepared a short discussion and led the seminar. Once in a while an extra session was held on topics by various thinkers, when it was deemed necessary for a fuller understanding of the subject matter. One connecting issue throughout the student essays, subsequently published in the above issue of **De Omslag,** was the work of Walter Benjamin. Further, one of the seminars at the conference was devoted entirely to his work.

The same issue of **De Omslag** announced a national student competition examining the relationship between the city and the port of Rotterdam. Students were asked to develop a future scenario for a part of the harbor located in a central area of the city, the Waal-Eemhaven. The disappearance of large-scale port activities in the direction of the coast towards the Maasvlakte, a land reclamation project, will open up vast industrial areas in the heart of the city for redevelop-

ment. Plans for an expansion of the Maasvlakte will strengthen this process further. The question is what should be done with the newly emptied areas.

This problematic is not unique to Rotterdam, as port cities elsewhere in the world are also being confronted with the removal of large-scale harbor activities from the city as a result of the increase in scale and of globalization.

Relationship between practice and theory

One of the recurring themes at Stylos conferences until now has been the relationship between theory and practice in design. The tension between the conceptual side of design and the final realization of a building. As an architect, your head is in the clouds and your boots are in the mud, as Koolhaas once expressed these two extremes. Students wonder what value theory has in terms of design, whether they will actually learn to design better if they study the critical background relevant to the field. They are also curious as to what remains of the academic approach to design once they actually practice architecture. How conceptual can the process be, if a contractor actually has to build the plan?

In the Netherlands there is an excellent architectural climate. Progressive young firms get the opportunity to test their ideas in practice. They receive commissions from housing corporations and are asked to enter into discussion with the government about important, large-scale projects.

1 **De Omslag** is a magazine produced by students of the Faculty of Architecture at the TU Delft.

Just recently, firms such as MVRDV and Mecanoo have been asked to offer proposals for a number of highways running straight through dense urban areas.

In addition, there is much work available because the economy is currently stronger than ever, thanks in part to the lauded 'polder model'. This strong economy allows many clients to spend more money on extraordinary designs, where in times of economic slump a simple, cheap design might have sufficed. Because of this, Dutch architects appear more pragmatic and less utopian in their designs. The number of constructed works in the Netherlands is so big that there is hardly any time left to 'daydream' about utopian plans.

Outside of the Netherlands, progressive architects seem to get fewer opportunities and are mostly commissioned by only a selective group of rich private clients, museums or universities. Aside from this they have to turn to exhibits, publications and teaching positions to supplement their more critical work. More time and attention seems to be paid to the concrete projects in the firm, including the presentation and publication of these projects.

The situation in the Netherlands

As already suggested, there is a very large building boom in the Netherlands, and a large part of these projects consists of housing. The postwar housing scarcity seems to have been solved,

insofar as there is no longer a quantitative housing shortage. The accent has shifted to a qualitative shortage; there are enough dwellings, but not the kind many people are looking for. Families are becoming smaller and the number of single-person households is increasing. More and more people are leaving the city center to settle in the so-called Vinex locations. These building sites were designated by the government in the Fourth Report (extra) on Spatial Planning (Vierde Nota Ruimtelijke Ordening Extra – VINEX) to end this qualitative housing shortage.

In this report, the Netherlands nurses the ambition of building some 800,000 new dwellings between 1997 and 2005, or about 100,000 dwellings every year. In 1995, Adriaan Geuze showed what these 800,000 extra dwellings could result in. He organized an exhibition in the NAi (Netherlands Architecture Institute) and had students place 800,000 scale modeled houses under the arcade of the institute. Seeing this 'model' he stated: 'This demands a plan. I mean, you can't leave it to all those councilors.'[2]

How are the Dutch cities treating this policy? The Hague is characterized, both in the city center and in the suburban developments, as the city where retro-architecture is celebrated. The reconstruction of the most important pedestrian route from Central Station to the city center is indicative of a transformation led by Rob Krier, who is 'resurrecting' a nonexistent traditional 19th-century city in cooperation with architects

---

2 Quoted in the article '800,000 houses in search of a plan' by Hans van Dijk in **Archis**, June 1995. The exhibition organized by Adriaan Geuze/West 8 was accompanied by the publication **In Holland staat een huis** (There is a house in Holland), NAi, Rotterdam 1995.

such as Sjoerd Soeters, Gunnar Daan, Michael Graves, Cesar Pelli and Adolfo Natalini. In the Vinex locations just outside of The Hague, the Frank Lloyd Wright-type of housing is especially popular. These brick dwellings with large can- tilevered roofs, either freestanding or connected, are often sold before they have been completed.

In Amsterdam a completely different approach is apparent. There, virtually no construction is per- mitted within the city center. All building activities, even the smallest renovation, are placed under the strict supervision of the Monument Conserva- tion Department. This attitude has made Amster- dam into an open-air museum where catering and tourism are ousting each other in the city, consequently slowing or stopping every possible development of the city center. The most impor- tant economic activities are departing from the city center to relocate in the southern part of the city near the ring, in part pressured by the impos- sibility of reaching the city center by car, let alone finding a parking space.

Just on the northern border of the center, old harbor areas are being transformed into new res- idential areas. The Java Island has been given new 'canals' by Sjoerd Soeters, and Jo Coenen has divided the KNSM Island into a number of large apartment blocks. The artificial islands Borneo and Sporenburg have been partitioned by West 8, Adriaan Geuze's firm, in small deep ribbons of ground-level entry patio dwellings and a few large apartment blocks called 'big mother- fuckers' by the firm. A little further along the river, a completely new island will be constructed for yet another 8500 dwellings before 2005 in the IJburg plan. After that, the total number of dwellings is meant to continue growing to 18,000. The proposals for the Pampus plan by Van den Broek and Bakema appear to be becoming reality.

Utrecht has been trying for years to develop plans for its station area. Until now, full agree- ment between all parties involved has not been reached. Should the current plans still be imple- mented in the future, here just as in The Hague, some connection will be sought with the historical city center, for example by re-excavating the city canal. The Fourth Report (extra) on Spatial Plan- ning expects a near doubling of the city of Utrecht. This city expansion, Leidsche Rijn, has a size unequaled in the Netherlands since the major expansions of the sixties: not a transformation of previous 'urban wastelands', but agricultural land being prepared for new construction. Ever since the Bijlmermeer, thinking on this scale has been forbidden.

The population of the city of Utrecht will nearly double after the completion of the urban plan Leidsche Rijn, led by the firm Max 2 headed by Rients Dijkstra. One of the many differences with the plans from the sixties is that there is no longer a strictly defined final image as originating princi- ple, but rather a thought process in the form of a scenario for the future, as we have seen before in the work of Rem Koolhaas. The plan also does not even consider the idea of a spacious suburb, but seeks a high density and an explicit connection to the existing city, even going so far as to partially cover a major highway, which forms a barrier between the expansion and the existing city.

In Rotterdam we encounter a completely different situation, as a large part of the necessary postwar construction took place within the city itself. After the center had been heavily bombed, dwellings found a place in the heart of the city during the reconstruction. Even the more recent 'qualitative housing shortage' can be provided for within the city itself, because the harbor activities are shifting out of the center of the city. The most familiar example of this is the project 'Kop van Zuid'. Here, a way of allowing the city and the port to coexist and profit from one another is explicitly being sought. This requires some reflection on the relationship between city and harbor, which is a theme this book will treat in more depth. Until recently, a strong division existed between city and port, institutionalized through a division in their management, namely the Urban Planning Department (the dS+V) on the one hand and the Port Authority Rotterdam on the other. The fact that both institutions are involved with the **Cities in Transition** project already indicates that both are investigating the possibility of a mutual relationship.

The conference

In consideration of the situation as described above, and using Rotterdam and Tokyo as test cases for the debate, architects and critics were invited to come to Delft. Universities from around the world were represented. The younger generation of architects presented their work on the first day, so that it could function as a reference for the presentations and discussions in the days following. Under the guidance of Chris Dercon, director of the Boijmans van Beuningen Museum, the audience was invited to participate in the discussion after these presentations. Adriaan Geuze and Winy Maas represented two firms from the Netherlands who had gotten the chance to investigate their ideas in practice quite early in their careers. Adriaan Geuze is even involved with a number of Vinex locations. The architects Greg Lynn and Alejandro Zaera-Polo, the foreign contributors to this debate, are good examples of architects working very conceptually, building less than their Dutch colleagues, but who spend quite some time on developing new concepts and the presentation of their work.

Following this opening session with architects, the rest of the day consisted of theoretical papers presented by various contributors. Lectures were given by Saskia Sassen, Edward Soja, Peter Marcuse, Michael Hays and Scott Lash.

The second day was divided into a number of workshops, some of which overlapped, necessitating a participatory choice by outside participants and guests. The division into smaller groups transformed the one-way traffic typical of lectures into a discussion forum with the audience. In the morning session, one group examined the 'urban waterfront experiments' in Japan, while another presented papers and opened discussion on the work of Walter Benjamin and its implications for thought on the contemporary city; concurrently there was a session on the future development of the harbor of Rotterdam. In the afternoon session there were three more seminars, the first on urban policy in Rotterdam and Amsterdam, led by politicians who actually made plans for these cities; a second group debated the value of theory for urban planning, while the third group compared developments of international ports such as those of Rotterdam, Athens and Genoa.

The third day began with a closed session for invitees: a boat excursion over the Maas through the harbor of Rotterdam. While lunch was served the Rotterdam harbor activity was viewed from the water. In the afternoon Arie Graafland sensing the mood of the group stepped onto a chair and announced the closing of the final debate, further inviting the participants and students to an informal drink and conversation. Afterwards all the speakers were surrounded by groups of interested students, to the visible enjoyment of the guests.

Alongside the planned activities, the informal moments were of great value. The rides in the bus between the faculty and Hotel New York were platforms for perhaps the most fruitful discussions between the participants. These were then generally continued in the restaurant of the hotel. Imagine what happens when you put for example Edward Soja, Michael Hays, Dieter Hassenpflug, Michael Sorkin and Scott Lash in a single car… the Ford Transit as a cooker full of ideas.

On behalf of Stylos I can state the hope that our conference has been able to contribute something to still the 'hunger' of students at our faculty and all other interested parties. This substantial book is the concrete result of those three days in November, in which many of the issues discussed can be reread, also for those who could not be present at the conference.

We were surprised at the level of attendance and were pleased with all the attention from other countries. This international climate within which the conference took place is inspiring and suggests that it should be as easy to exchange teachers with foreign universities as it is to exchange students.

The opportunity to meet with the authors behind the book clearly stimulated our drive in understanding the work better.

Our thanks to everyone, especially Arie Graafland, without whose enthusiasm this endeavor would have never succeeded.

Introduction:
Cities in Transition Arie Graafland

Synopsis   The following introduction deals with the effects of globalization and internationalization in relation to urbanism and critical assessments. Globalization is tied to capital markets, the rigid markets of the sixties have been replaced by more flexible ones. This new production sphere is based on flexibility in terms of labor force, markets and rapidly changing consumption patterns. This development has had its effects on architecture and urbanism. The introduction discusses the effects in the Japanese and Dutch context regarding urban questions and, in the cases of Tokyo and Rotterdam, as major port cities. Urban questions are principally conceptual constructions of planners and urbanists; however, problem solving depends on conceptual issues as well as pragmatic solutions. I will deal with these problem-posing/solving strategies in regards to the Bay Area in Tokyo and the Randstad (a ring of the four biggest cities in the Netherlands, Rotterdam being one of them). In the last part of my contribution the case of Rotterdam as a major port city is discussed. The theme of globalization and its social impact on conditions in residential areas is queried; and different proposals for the Rotterdam port development are critically assessed.

Globalization   Internationalization is often connected with the more abstract notion of globalization, which is principally linked to economic developments. Globalization is more tied to capital markets than to goods and services. In past decades, international competition has greatly increased, Western Europe and Japan have grown economically stronger, and the USD has suffered devaluation. Characteristic problems have been the rigidity of (long-term) investments and production systems; and as far as labor is concerned we find the same conditions, long-term labor contracts and an inflexible labor market. This rigid market has been replaced by a more flexible one, bringing the curtain down on American 'Fordism', as David Harvey has stated.

This new production sphere is based on flexibility in terms of the labor force, the markets, and rapidly changing consumption patterns. In many cases this meant lay-offs on a large scale; in the USA especially, the number of lay-offs was higher than ever before. More than 43 million jobs, or one-third of all the jobs in the United States today have been extinguished since 1979. After a lay-off many workers find new jobs, but most of them (65%) either work for lower pay, part time, or are self-employed, and 24% remain unemployed or out of the labor force altogether.[1] It is remarkable that lay-offs are not the direct result of bad economical conditions. The opposite is true, as Masao Miyoshi states. The

---

1   Masao Miyoshi, 'Globalization, Culture, and the University', in **The Cultures of Globalization**, ed. Fredric Jameson and Masao Miyoshi, Durham/London, 1998 p.255.

more downsized, the greater the dividends and the executive pay. Every time a company announces a huge lay-off, its stock rises to signal the approval of Wall Street. New industries have emerged, new methods of financing, new markets, and most importantly a rigorous commercial, technological, and organizational 'innovation'. This economic innovation went hand in hand with a cultural and architectural innovation. To survive in this maelstrom, architecture has turned more frequently to the devices of spectacle and event. Architecture is an economic good, investments are high, and commissions are mostly established on the strength of the cultural profile of the office. Bureaus are mostly local, only a few like SOM, Ove Arup, and Foster and Associates operate on an international level.

One of the most obvious questions raised in this book is whether our present day architecture of spectacle and event is the appropriate response to these conditions, and whether or not there are other possible solutions. Post-modern architecture has let go of the idea of utopia and its inherent con-figurability of society. This architecture of spectacle is in fact an a-topia, as Dieter Hassenpflug has observed: atopias are the new form of pseudo-utopias. They are real and at the same time without site: they are potentially everywhere and at the same time nowhere. Whereas the utopias, of which dreams are made, create an image of a better life in the space and time of a nowhere, atopias proliferate in the here and now, creations made of steel, glass, concrete, chlorophyll and water, or hardware and software, bits and bytes, in order to take control of dreams.'[2] His plea for a new moral code in architecture, acting against all the theme parks and Disneyworlds, is currently an extraordinary voice, although, as we shall see, a concrete utopia raises some problems too as in the case of Tange's Bay Project for Tokyo.

Market supply has undergone infinite multiplication and become highly differentiated, creating a situation we usually label postmodernity. Culturally speaking, these developments have opened the borders for other influences. What is new is the universality (or globality) of mass culture and consumption, rather than the exchange of only high culture and luxury goods. This has even had spatial consequences. The London based archi-

2 Dieter Hassenpflug, 'From Utopia to Atopia', in **Social Utopias of the Twenties**, Bauhaus Dessau, Berlin, 1987.

tect Alejandro Zaera-Polo has linked the idea of flexible accumulation to a changing
spatial pattern. Urban structures are required to maintain the flexibility so as to absorb
a continuous spatial reformulation without losing their specificity and centrality. The
production and organization of urban space acquirc within late capitalism an extraordinary
importance, despite the decreasing value of spatial boundaries. [3]

Economic innovation became dire necessity – innovation and increased flexibility
became requirements for (economic) survival. Or, in the words of Zaera-Polo: 'The evolution from an economy of scale to an economy of scope – from industrial to informational
– shows that production is no longer competitive through a good cost/price relationship,
but through its diversification and capacity to adjust to a constantly evolving demand.'
Politically speaking, this runs parallel to the so-called 'privatization' of social securities
and other collective resources and institutions. We are already familiar with the results
of this process: a continually 'tougher' society, where sacrifices to the private system must
inevitably be made. In recent times this phenomenon has been analyzed by Manuel
Castells and Saskia Sassen, among others. This process has had numerous disadvantageous
effects, such as 'junk jobs', poor to no company education policies and the insecurity of
no lifelong job guarantees, a phenomenon that has only recently been felt in the case of
Japan.

The Japanese perspective; economic growth and the Bay Project

As a result of the rapid growth of the Japanese economy in the 1960s the
Japanese business community became particularly concentrated in Tokyo. However,
despite the territorial dispersion of present economic activity, the top-level control management of industry is concentrated in Chiyoda Marunouchi, Chūō, Ginza and
Nihombashi, Minato Roppongi and Akasaka and more recently Shinjuku. Shinjuku,
together with Shibuya and Ikebukuro, has become a sub-center. It was only after the earthquake of 1923 that it obtained new opportunities to develop. Shinjuku station was built in
1885, on the Shinagawa Line. Ginza, Shinjuku, Ueno, Asakusa, Shibuya, Ningyō-chō and
Kagurazaka are mentioned in a 1923 summary of Tokyo's sakariba. Nowadays the last two
no longer belong in this list. Ikebukuro and Roppongi have now taken their place as new
entertainment centers. [4] At present Shibuya is one of the most popular and fashionable
of these centers, closely-knit and very busy. The development of Shinjuku was tackled in
1960 with the construction of a 150,000 sq.ft. plaza, situated both above and below ground,

3 Alejandro Zaera-Polo, **Order out of Chaos. The Material Organization of Advanced
Capitalism**, London, 1995.
4 Edward Seidensticker, **Tokyo Rising. The City since the Great Earthquake**,
Harvard University Press, Cambridge Mass., 1991, p.40.

and with a new street profile, parking spaces, etc. In 1964 a new floor-area ratio (FAR) was introduced in order to limit the detrimental effects caused by the abolition of the building height restrictions, which had resulted in many buildings being deprived of sunlight. The economy continued to grow and the demand for offices increased. In 1982 the present multi-core structure was adopted, with the intention of decentralizing administrative tasks. However the concentration of labor and capital in the metropolitan area was much greater than had been anticipated. Some industry withdrew from the city and the resultant vacant space was taken over by high-rise buildings. This ultimately resulted in one gigantic metropolitan area. The extremely high densities evident in these commercial districts constitute a spatial expression of our present economic language, as Sassen has shown.

The spatial answer to this congestion came, in particular, from the Japanese Metabolism Group. In 1961 Kenzo Tange presented his design for Tokyo Bay, a large-scale plan in the bay comprised of a complex structure of superhighways to which residential areas were attached. Tafuri compares it with Tange's project for Boston that he drew up in conjunction with students from the Massachusetts Institute of Technology (MIT). In 1959 he was a guest at the last CIAM meeting in Otterlo. At this meeting he presented his Tokyo City Hall and Kagawa's Prefectural Office. He also showed a project by Kiyonori Kikutake that had never been realized, which consisted of cylindrical residential towers in combination with floating platforms in the sea for heavy industry. Tange left Otterlo the day before the definitive end of CIAM, as he had to go to MIT. As a result he was the first to announce its closure (he had a telegram in his pocket) to Walter Gropius and Sigfried Giedion. Kikutake's plan played an important role in the assignment he presented to the students at MIT, a plan for the Bay of Boston for 25,000 inhabitants. In this assignment the residential areas were planned not on land but in the water, as in the later Tokyo Bay project.

Tange proposed with his Tokyo Bay project a decisive alternative to the official plan of 1956 for the Tokyo region. The project evidenced obvious affiliations with the Greater London plan designed by Abercrombie and

5   Manfredo Tafuri, Francesco Dal Co, 'The International Concept of Utopia', **Modern Architecture**, chapter V, p.385. As quoted in Arie Graafland, **The Socius of Architecture. Amsterdam, Tokyo, New York**, 010 Publishers, Rotterdam, 2000. Note: Much of this introduction has been excerpted from **The Socius of Architecture**.
6   In 1940 the then Minister of Foreign Affairs, Yosuke Matsuoka, referred to a Greater East Asia Co-Prosperity Sphere, a community that was 'to include southern regions such as the Dutch East Indies and French Indochina'. But much of the New Order was not applicable to the

Forshaw. Tange's argument was leveled against what he saw as an equalizing and reductionist tradition of planning that denied the promise of a city center through the dispersal of such centrality into peripheral satellite towns.[5] Tafuri has linked Tange's proposals to those of the English Archigram Team of Peter Cook, Ron Herron, Dennis Crompton and Michael Webb, for the Plug-In City of 1964 and Herron's later Walking City (as a bestial macrostructure capable of both hovering motion and telescopic displacement). Since any form of social-economic analysis was lacking in Archigram's work, Tafuri considered it to be nothing more than a 'graphic divertissement', an 'ironic nostalgia for the future'. It was the time of 'an academy of the utopian' that was then especially popular in architectural education. The resistance to the unimaginative bureaucratic planners resulted in a particularly graphical design that paid no attention to the ratio of a large-scale scheme, local complexity, or long-term planning. Tange's Tokyo Bay is a more definitive plan that hardly allows for Zaera-Polo's flexibility or conceptual changes in time. Tafuri rightly observed that the plan exhibits great affinity with Le Corbusier's Obus plan for Algiers, which was also a more rigid scheme; it was also revised several times by Le Corbusier because the sociopolitical context in Algiers was unable to do anything with it. However Tafuri's criticism is also one-sided, because Tange certainly did make a conscious attempt to integrate traditional Japanese culture in his plan. The form of the homes in the bay is more akin to a modern example of an ethnic continuity; the residential blocks are given a traditional form, but are executed in a contemporary manner.

Tange wrote a book about Ise, the most sacred of Shinto sanctuaries. He had played earlier with the idea of the shrine in a 'fascist' project of 1943, now detested by everyone. This was for the Greater East Asia Co-prosperity Sphere that was projected at the foot of Mount Fuji. He described his project as a representation of the shrine of Ise in combination with Michelangelo's Capitoline Hill, a reconstruction begun in Rome in 1538. The Mount Fuji project did win him first prize, but it was never carried out. Nor is it 'fascist', but at most an attempt to create something of classical sublime architecture. It was hopelessly monumental and quite suggestive of the Japanese wartime nationalism.[6] However it is striking that the theme of the Ise shrine resurfaces in the Bay. Ise is a holy place where Amaterasu, goddess of the Sun, is worshipped. Every twenty years the temple of Ise is completely destroyed in order that it may be identically rebuilt. This act of recreation can be found in many primitive cultures; its basis is in the belief that the

Co-Prosperity Sphere's 'southern regions', whose relationship to Japan was historically quite different from those between Japan and its closer neighbors, China and Manchuria. Southeast Asia was geopolitically and economically a very different region from Northeast Asia. In 1942 the Intelligence Section of the Ministry of the Navy drew up the document 'On the Greater East Asia Co-Prosperity Sphere' (Daito-A kyoeiken-ron). This document made a distinction between five categories, in which Japan was the 'leading country' and China, Manchukuo and Thailand were independent countries classified in the second category. These latter countries were sub-

act of creation is never absolute but must be perpetuated in action and
continuous renewal. Such rituals necessitate that a class of carpentry artisan
be maintained in order to preserve the ancient and arcane techniques (or
rituals) of building. The site of Ise was once the destination of a pilgrimage
that every Japanese was to undertake at least once in their lifetime. Yet the
interior of the sanctuary was never entered, for the pilgrimage was completed
by visual proximity alone.[7]

Tange's homes exhibit some resemblance to Ise, although his roofs are
curved like the Chinese. There may be continuity with the past, but everything is planned, drawn, and designed. The ten million inhabitants seem
to have found their definitive place. A development in time is rendered
impossible. And that is very un-Japanese, and very much 1930s European
Modernism. The temporary and the provisional in Japanese architecture
are negated. Another example of this respect for the aspect of temporality
in Japanese culture is what is known as the 'flowers of Edo'. As a result of
the predominant use of wood and paper in building practice whole neighborhoods in Edo were regularly consumed by fire; which in spite of the obvious
devastation wreaked were greatly appreciated as a place worth visiting.
Further, as earthquakes ravaged Japanese cities, houses were taken apart
and rebuilt elsewhere. Shintoism and Buddhism emphasize the relativity
of life, everything is temporary and relative. But in the Bay Project everything is permanent in a trivial copy of the urbanism of the 1930s. Japanese
architecture is capable of 'floating on a sea of signs' and is less tailored to
historical continuity and stability than is Western architecture.[8] Tange's
implicit model is 'utopia'. The decision as to what should be specified and
what should be un-specified was decided to the advantage of a concrete
utopia, rendering the plan analogous to the Obus plan for Algiers. Tange's
entreaty for stability within an apparently chaotic structure, though polem-
ically disguised, can be easily read as a modernist appeal towards control
through rationalization of highly populated urban areas. Equally however
it contradicts such utopian strategies through its complicity with traditional
Japanese city planning tactics such as those found in Kyoto (as opposed to
Edo or Tokyo).

ject to the 'mediating leadership' (shido bakai) of Japan. For more details see J. Victor
Koschmann, 'Asia's Ambivalent Legacy', in Peter J. Katzenstein and Takashi Shiriaishi, **Network
Power, Japan and Asia**, Cornell University Press, Ithaca/London, 1997, p.102.
7 Michel Random, **Japan, Strategy of the Unseen, A Guide for Westerners to the Mind
of Modern Japan**, Northamptonshire, 1987.
8 For details refer to Hajime Yatsuka, 'An architecture floating in a sea of signs', in **The New
Japanese Architecture**, p.38.

In Tokyo an orthogonal grid of infrastructure is overlaid upon the entire bay area, while at its center megastructures find their objective identities. Bordering, and set perpendicular to the road system are the remarkable dwelling units, conceived upon the shrine typology borrowed from the WHO scheme. This residential diagram based on the model of Ch'ang-an (Sian), China, thus imitates the plan repeatedly articulated in ancient Japanese capitals.[9] Ch'ang-an had the same pattern as the Western fortified city, a regular grid of roads from East to West and North to South that was enclosed by fortifications. Actually there is no city in Japan with such a singular pattern; the layout is always comprised of a hybrid mixture of different patterns, of which the grid is just one. Although Tange recognizes the changing dynamism of Tokyo's real estate market the answer remains just as utopian as that of the Modernists. Kisho Kurokawa's new Tokyo Plan 2025 is of the same order; it consists of a gigantic island in Tokyo Bay. Kurokawa incorporates just about all of Japan in his plan; the island is plan 5 from a series of 12. His concentric city is the prototype of all utopian cities, and, in fact, runs contrary to his own notion of heterogeneity.[10]

In recent years Tange has done little else than construct enormous projects, of which the latest are in Tokyo's Waterfront Subcenter, the Tokyo Teleport Town. Both the Fuji Television Building and the Tokyo Fashion Town Building are by his office. Both buildings are located in the new land reclamation area, Ariake, district 13. The first plan for this area consists of a landfill about 4 miles south of central Tokyo, and dates from 1987. Since the end of 1989 and the burst of the 'bubble' economy the demand for office space has decreased dramatically. Moreover the 1996 Expo, which was precisely what was needed to vitalize the plan, did not take place. In 1996 the Tokyo Metropolitan Government presented a revised plan. The budget had been cut back, and every five years every aspect of the plan is to be subject to a review. Although the *Japan Architect Yearbook* still describes the area as a 'lively environment' there is virtually no-one to be seen. It is just one more desolate enclave, unassailable for pedestrians, and totally without character. The whole area is strung together by the Yurikamome Line, the 7.5 mile elevated railroad connecting the Subcenter to the existing subway and train lines. The Yurikamome passes over the Rainbow Bridge and makes a loop through the area. The total system is reminiscent of the lines in amusement parks, such as Singapore's Sentosa, although they are on a smaller scale. It is also a residential area, with high-rise housing and stores in the Daiba Area. Daiba Seaside Park is intended for residential complexes. It houses an elementary school

9   David B. Stuart, **The Making of a Modern Japanese Architecture, 1868 to the Present**, Kodansha International, Tokyo/New York, p.182.
10   Kurokawa Kisho, **Intercultural Architecture, The Philosophy of Symbiosis**, The American Institute of Architects Press, London, 1991, p.202.

and a secondary school, and a supermarket stocks the day-to-day necessities. Daniel Buren's Twenty Five Porticos rises from the inside area to the waterfront. Recently the Decks Tokyo Beach was opened, which is comprised of restaurants, bars, stores and the unavoidable amusement park. A Bay-side walkway, the Waterfront Promenade, links the Daiba Seaside Park and the Nikko Hotel. Tange's Fuji Building stands in between. District 13 is an example of what Saskia Sassen calls a 'new form of locational concentration', which means not only concentration in the existing city, but also land reclamation projects such as Tokyo Teleport Town and Yokohama's Minato Mirai 21.

The increased mobility of capital brings about new forms of locational concentration, which are as much a part of this mobility as is geographic dispersal. According to Sassen they do not simply represent a persistence of older forms of agglomeration, but respond more to a new economic logic. The increase in land prices made it impossible to live in the commercial districts. Ten years ago one square foot of raw land in the Chiyoda Ward sold for about USD 4,000, while developed property in Chūō went in the range of USD 13,000 per sq.ft. Prices were somewhat lower in Yokohama, but the difference was not great. The Japanese government recognized the problem of the one-sided development and initiated new residential projects in these areas in order to prevent them being completely deserted at nighttime. However residence in these wards has become considerably more expensive during the past decades. At present Roppongi, Aoyama and Akasaka closely resemble parts of New York and London. The gigantic Ark Hills redevelopment project (*Akasaka Roppongi Kaihatsu*, by Taikichiro Mori) that straddles the border between Akasaka and Roppongi consists of a series of skyscrapers containing the very latest communications and information technology. It has swept away complete hills and has eliminated all local residential forms in the area. Most Japanese cannot afford to live here. Most commute between home and work, usually a journey of an hour or more.

Narita Airport is about 40 miles from the city, located far outside the Tokyo wards. For most Japanese this has become an acceptable distance from their home. Within the city they cannot afford even the tiniest apartment. The per capita floor space in the USA is twice that in Japan (USA 540 sq.ft., Japan 270 sq.ft. per capita dwelling floor space). In Tokyo the cost of a home is 12.9 times a person's annual income, in comparison to 2.9 times in New York.[11] Usually about 20% of the income is devoted to residential expenses, but the percentage is much greater in these areas. Cheaper homes are increasingly to be found far from the commercial districts. There are already mortgages on the market with a term of 99 years, so that whole generations are committed to their house. The picture that has increasingly continued to take shape over the past few years is exemplified in New York where increasing poverty and vagrancy (principally amongst the elderly who have been displaced by gentrification) becomes progressively more salient when witnessed in contrast to the advent of stylish residential and conspicuous commercial development.[12] Sassen has shown that the poorest areas do not lie at the edge of the city, but adjoin the central business district. Arakawa, Taito and Sumida, which border directly on the business district, are extremely impoverished. The demise of traditional manufacturing is the reason for the decline of Arakawa and Sumida. Taito, which is part of the old Asakusa Ward, had housed higher concentrations of the poor and those with lower incomes for a much longer period of time. The different areas are relatively autonomous, for example they have the same closing times for the stores, so that a kind of complex patchwork or mosaic is created. It is precisely because Tokyo is a city with many cores and without a 'city center' that most visitors consider it to be a turmoil of cars and chaotic buildings.

The Dutch perspective: the Randstad as an issue of definitions (or: what is 'urban'?)
The cultural dimension is extremely important to the 'assessment' of our spatial problematic. More and more emphasis is placed on the complexity of space, while the notion of hierarchical structures is disappearing; Tokyo is certainly an example of that. Instead, we are confronted with ideas about networks, streams of information, knots, and space that is no longer to be controlled or planned. In reality, we do not (yet) possess the proper terminology to label this process.

The German philosopher Walter Benjamin seems to have envisioned this problem for the West very early on in this century. In his *Passagen-Werk*, he attempts to describe the phenomenon of the modern metropolis in both a literary and a philosophical manner. The book is built up of short analyses and descriptions rather than chapters. These

11 **Japan Almanac,** Ashai Shimbun Publishing Company, Tokyo, 1997.
12 Saskia Sassen, **The Global City, New York, London, Tokyo**, Princeton University Press, Princeton, 1991, p.27.

compact pieces of text, the *Konvoluts*, offer an impressive picture of the transition from the nineteenth to the twentieth century in Europe. As the complex non-hierarchical structure makes it difficult for an inexperienced reader to follow, this book is not the most accessible of Benjamin's works. However, Susan Buck-Morss has offered a doorway into the book through a detailed reconstruction of it.[13] Even now, Benjamin's ideas offer inspiration and a hint of understanding towards the current situation. M. Christine Boyer, for one, is strongly influenced by his work. Economics, politics and social sciences are all currently seeking terms to describe this process. Even within the fields of urbanism and planning, the vocabulary is undergoing a shift; this is visible in, for example, the definition of the Dutch Randstad (consisting of the four big cities Amsterdam, Utrecht, The Hague and Rotterdam). Years ago, the Dutch sociologist De Swaan already pointed out that metropolitan areas such as the Randstad and the Rhine-Ruhr area are principally 'conceptual' constructions of planners. He especially appreciated urban culture, specifically as exemplified in the city of Amsterdam. The terminology used by De Swaan extended not only to formal statistics such as numbers of inhabitants and density per square kilometer, but also dealt with issues such as functional connective tissue surrounding an urban center. In this sense, he considers the Randstad a metropolis, and one of the most eminent ones in Europe.[14]

In a more recent debate, the Dutch urbanist Willem de Bruin draws a critical view of all the policy guidelines for this area (Dutch newspaper *de Volkskrant* 20 May 1996). He sees the urban centers and rural areas slowly beginning to fade into one another. The treatment of major planning issues such as the HSL (high speed railway), Schiphol, the Betuwe freight line and building schemes in the Randstad, give the impression that we can hardly speak of an overall vision on the planning of Holland. A reaction from a Delft professor in urbanism, Dirk Frieling, in the same newspaper is interesting. He wonders about the nature of the changes becoming visible in urban Holland through the Betuwelijn, Schiphol, the HSL and projects such as the recently announced second national airport and the second Maasvlakte. These changes are to Frieling 'the

13   Susan Buck Morss, **The Dialectics of Seeing, Walter Benjamin and the Arcades Project,** MIT Press, Cambridge Mass., 1991.
14   Abram de Swaan, **Perron Nederland**, Meulenhoff, Amsterdam, 1991.

same symptoms indicated by economists with the term "globalization" and in the social sciences with the terms "multicultural community" and "pluralist society".' He argues that we should adapt the image of Holland to the actual situation and give up myths such as the 'empty' Green Heart and the 'full' Randstad. One of the deciding factors appears to be our judgment of internationalization and economic globalization. In the development of our spatial discipline, these critical judgments play an increasingly important role. In other words, knowledge in a very general sense is more important than ever. Economic flexibility is combined with an accelerated growth and accessibility of knowledge and information, also termed 'reflexive accumulation'. Increasingly, a cultural meaning is contained within this.[15] This increase in knowledge acts on two levels: economic and cultural.

The issue at stake is not just information technology, but also the cultural context within which it takes place. Information in and of itself has no meaning; it is rather what is done with it that matters. This becomes a qualitative, not just quantitative, question, as is apparent in the Randstad debate. In the Netherlands, that question has been asked with reference to the concept of the Randstad. It has also been asked with respect to Paris: Do the five outlying towns belong to the city of Paris or not? The answer is yes when the criteria are length of journey and accessibility. According to Deyan Sudjic, it is wrong 'to see the five Parisian new towns as distinct entities in their own right. Rather, they are essential parts of the city itself. They could not exist without the network of motorways, airports, and above all metro lines that constitute Paris just as much as the picturesque crust of masonry buildings of Haussmann and his predecessors. It is not just that you can get from one part of Marne-la-Vallée to another by train that counts. The fact that you can get to the shopping malls of Les Halles in less than twenty minutes, and on to the other new towns on the far side of the city without changing platforms, had transformed the mental map of the city that Parisians carry in their heads.'[16] In the opinion of Sudjic, 'the Dutch claims for the existence of the Randstad megalopolis – the ring of cities that takes in Amsterdam, Utrecht, The Hague and Rotterdam – amount to a deliberate political statement, an attempt to turn what would otherwise be regarded as a nation of extremely modest size into a very large city. If it actually existed, Randstad would be vast. More than eight million people live amidst its baroque steeples, prefabricated concrete housing estates and bulb fields.'[17] But as he notes, large numbers of people living in close

15 Scott Lash and John Urry, **Economies of Signs & Space**, Sage Publications, London, 1994.
16 Deyan Sudjic, **The 100 Mile City**, A Harvest Original, San Diego/New York/London, 1992.
17 Deyan Sudjic, o.c.

proximity do not in themselves constitute a city, an analysis that led the Dutch urbanist Niek de Boer to conclude that the Randstad does not exist.[18] If we look at the maps, as he suggests, any comparison of the Randstad with the metropolises of London and Paris seems outlandish. The latter two cities are compact agglomerations, whereas the Randstad is a rather arbitrarily delimited set of cities, towns, villages, and farmlands. Moreover, in the latter case, it would be irresponsible to include all the activities that take place in the area and add them all up together as if the Randstad functioned as a single urban entity. The Randstad definitely does not perform as a metropolis of more than eight million inhabitants. It simply does not have the metropolitan quality of a Paris or a London. The functional connections of De Swaan could just as easily be extended to London, Brussels or Paris. Niek de Boer's analysis is much more tempered; if the Randstad is a metropolis, it should operate on the level of importance it claims by virtue of its population level and its being situated in the center of Europe. Since it does not function at this level in cultural, economic or juridical aspects, it should not be considered a metropolis. We find the same questions of evaluation when faced with the Rotterdam harbor. As with the Randstad, the Harbor incites us to consider the consequences of globalization and informatization.

The Rotterdam harbor; a new relationship between city and port

'City and port together form one of the catalysts of the Dutch economy. Rotterdam is the gateway to Europe and still number one on the list of world ports. Most of its income is earned (benefiting the rest of Holland more than the region itself) with taking and passing on, with trade and transportation, and is mostly geared toward quantity (much and more of the same); collecting and delivering containers and delivering and transporting raw materials, petrochemicals, iron ore, and coal for German blast furnaces. The city belonging to this scenario is one of offices and institutions specialized in business and financial services, transport and communication, among which are many internationally oriented headquarters. Thus city and port belong together', the Rotterdam

---

18 Niek de Boer, **De Randstad bestaat niet**, NAi, Rotterdam, 1996.

Planning Bureau stated in 1995.[19] However, this does not mean that it will be the same in the future! In the report *Naar een economische visie voor de Rotterdamse regio, vier scenario's* (January 1996), the observation is made that Rotterdam has been indebted to the port for its growth in the past, but that the relationship between port and city is decreasing. First, the port is geographically shifting toward the sea, and secondly the port no longer offers an adequate share of jobs to Rotterdam with its staggering unemployment rate. In a recent article in the newspaper *de Volkskrant* (10 May 1997 by Jelle Brandsma and Hans Horsten) this relationship between city and port is analyzed. 'The port of Rotterdam is still proudly wielding the title and status of the largest in the world, but behind this facade the city of Rotterdam is struggling with some serious problems. Over the past decade, the number of jobs in the metropolis has been decreasing by 1% per year. The port, once a major source of employment for the city and its surroundings, has been transformed through its extensive mechanization into a fully automatic world where there is no longer any demand for "muscle". The port itself may be flourishing, but the city of Rotterdam is no longer profiting from it directly in terms of employment. The demise of the working city on the Nieuwe Waterweg has extensive social consequences for its 600 thousand inhabitants. Its population has no more slack to offer. In 1996, the average family in Rotterdam had 20% less income than its counterpart elsewhere in the country. The 15% unemployment rate is more than twice the national average. A schism is apparent along the whole front. Twenty thousand families have disconcertingly high debts. Of the sixty thousand Turkish and Moroccan inhabitants, only eight thousand are employed. An additional problem is the poor quality of education: one third of these job seekers have no education beyond grade school or the lowest level of vocational schooling. To the outside world, Rotterdam is an unlivable city where sharp contrasts dominate.'

This image is also solidly lodged in the consciousness of the city's own population. Many employed inhabitants desert the city as soon as they have outgrown a subsistence-level income. They migrate to growing urban centers within a green buffer zone. The main question Rotterdam has been posing is how to give substance to a 'renewed relation between city and port'. Four scenarios were generated to offer images of a possible future. The main point here is not what these scenarios look like; more important is the fact that some very explicit connections have been made with education (importance of knowledge), standards and values, urban planning (how to treat spatial questions) and also with ecology and sustainability as an increasingly important frame of reference. Port and city incite

19   Omzwervingen door het landschap van de toekomst; Rotterdam 2045, visies op de toekomst van de stad, haven en regio, Rotterdam, 1996.

us to reconsider the above-mentioned critical conditions. The vision of the Dutch architectural firm OMA on this problem is very clear: city and port have been (quite literally) growing apart, and have little if nothing to do with one another anymore. Therefore, they need desperately to be disengaged from each other; this is the only way Rotterdam will survive.[20] Together with the Dutch research institute of Nijenrode (NYFER), OMA produced a 'rational vision' of a richer Rotterdam, which involved the construction of a second Maasvlakte. The city of Rotterdam can support the investment of 5 to 12 billion Dutch guilders (app. USD 2-6 billion) in a new port and industrial area off the coast near the Dutch island of Voorne-Putten. The question is how big this second Maasvlakte needs to be. This would depend on the type of transshipment and industry. The Central Planning Bureau criticized the ambitions of the port of Rotterdam, saying an industrial zone of 500 hectares rather than 2000 would suffice. The port authorities accuse the 'number-crunchers' from The Hague of having no guts and no vision, suggesting that whoever does not offer free rein to the business world and its investments, is slowing down progress.

In April 1997, the Dutch employers' organization VNO-NCW organized a symposium about the construction of a second Maasvlakte. This was mainly to address the different visions of the Central Planning Bureau and the Port Authority of Rotterdam about the benefits and necessities of Maasvlakte II. Nyfer was asked to contribute to the symposium, and its director Bomhoff pulled in OMA for an urban proposal. This proposal, now complete, states that Rotterdam needs to be released from its identity as port city, and that the second Maasvlakte will take over the old port activities. If the port completely moves away from its old setting, Rotterdam becomes the first city of Holland to start swimming in its leftover space. 'In the world of globalization, a strong and permanent identity is not an unconditional advantage', as OMA states: The less identity the better. And as is to be expected from Koolhaas, he brings one of the Asian tigers to the floor as an example: Singapore. Not only has Singapore reasoned itself out of quicksand like a Baron Münchausen, but also it continually reinvents

---

20 OMA, **Maasvlakte**, Sdu, The Hague 1997.

and questions itself. Permanently afraid for its survival, it follows a strategy of contra-dictory, varying, successive identities. The city itself hardly belies the presence of a port anymore. The Singapore coastline is being changed radically and reconfigured into an idyllic shore: 140 kilometers of tropical beach. The port is no longer a conceptual theme, but only the financial backer, according to OMA. To my mind the specific contents of this 'idyll' is the island of Sentosa mentioned before: a world where the fun never ends. This is where East meets Disneyworld on a gigantic island just off the coast, an island developed solely for recreation. Underwater World, Orchid Garden, the Dragon Trail (adventure!), Fantasy Island, The Lost Civilization, Asian Village and hotels are all strung together with a monorail. In other words, this is Hassenpflug's artificial world of a-topia. Is this the future for Rotterdam's Waalhaven/Eemhaven? Even aside from the differences in climate, this seems too eccentric to consider. Or not? Dutch museums are introducing more and more 'events', and 'science parks' are popping up everywhere; spectacular build-ings are made to pull in more visitors, and going to a theme park has become an everyday activity. There is no life without events; this appears to constitute our new 'identity'. In other words: the port project offers grounds for a critical view of the livability of the city of Rotterdam.

The four scenarios, referred to above, are structured around the opposing poles of local development and globalization, respectively slow and aggressive administrations. They all address the issues previously discussed. In *Wereldwijd* (Worldwide), the first scenario, knowledge and information are seen as the essential factors of the global economy. Unlike knowledge, information is ephemeral. The speed and accessibility of information determine the competitive level of a company. This has made the control of information a powerful weapon. Of course, we are only talking about a possible scenario, a projected development. But the importance of the infrastructure of knowledge is evident; the Port, as a spatial and organizational unit, requires reflection on urban planning and the concep-tual basis of the city. The July 1995 year-plan of the *Stichting Kennisinfrastructuur Mainport Rotterdam* observes that knowledge and technology are becoming more important to the Mainport; however, the infrastructure of knowledge now present is not adequate. In other words, the agents involved in the Port are not sufficiently aware of current developments. The same problem appears to lie at the root of the relapse of Waalhaven/Eemhaven. Many Rotterdam stevedore companies ran into trouble simply because they did not assess the changes accurately or early enough. The report of the Port Authority indicates that many companies fell into a downward spiral: less cargo shipped resulted in lower revenues, which meant fewer investments were made and an even lower productivity ensued. 'The causes of the disappearance of these companies are usually similar: aside from low productivity, there were high operations costs (especially cost of labor), a poor work environment, decreasing quality of leadership, a poorly functioning SHB, a terrain layout that did not fulfill current demands and an over involved government.'[21] The question of quality is very prominent in the report *What port for the future* by the Dutch urbanists Drewe and Janssen (1995). Precisely because changes are occurring in the supply of cargo and the infrastructural possibilities of road transport, the problem needs to be redefined. Quantity alone will not save us; this is especially true for Waal/Eemhaven. The report, *Toekomstvisie* (future vision) for Waal/Eemhaven notes that radical changes are hovering on the horizon. This is not only the result of strengths, but also of weaknesses. Certain segments of the container sector have simply outgrown Waal/Eemhaven and have moved to the western port areas, where they can be handled appropriately. This migration in itself is not a problem, but many of the general cargo activities have also moved to the competing port of Antwerp.

Not all wagers should be placed on a large-scale shift to containers, for 'just-in-time' delivery flourishes in a small-scale area. Waal/Eemhaven should offer possibilities for the continuation and reinforcement of these small-scale activities. This should also encompass new possibilities for living in Charlois, the adjacent residential area, especially since the current governmental policy on large urban areas opens up numerous opportunities. Within the structure of the Dutch Large City Policy, Rotterdam has chosen a full-scale regional directive. Charlois is one of the targeted areas, and has a clear relation with the future development of Waal/Eemhaven. An integrated neighborhood proposal has been created for Charlois; the main objective stated in the plan is to develop the area into an 'outer skin of activities', encircling an attractive residential area. This will be attained through proposals on the level of infrastructure/accessibility, housing,

---

21   Port Authority of Rotterdam, **Toekomstvisie Waal/Eemhaven, Ruimte voor initiatieven**, Rotterdam, 1995.

social facilities and exterior space. The relationship between the city and the port is to be explicitly developed here, in terms of street furnishings, signage and lighting. Also, a tourism/recreational structure is being considered. The relationship between water, cargo transfers and dwelling is a good starting point. The shift to containers has not benefited Waal/Eemhaven, but this same development should now be used to allow for the importance of just-in-time delivery and to enhance the options for living and working in Charlois. The port of the future is especially dependent on logistic networks, and the transition from a large-scale turnover to a logistic conception. This was already a policy resolution formulated by the Alberda Committee in 1987.[22] In the rat race against other ports of Western Europe, these added potential benefits of a port are beginning to take precedence over its primary functions. The motto of the *Nota Kennisinfrastructuur* (Report on Knowledge Infrastructure) is: 'A world-class port needs world-class knowledge.' The same motto should be applied to the field of urban design in Holland; it certainly applies to the theme of the conference, as well as to the intention of this book.

22 Alberda, **Rapport Nieuw Rotterdam; een opdracht aan alle Rotterdammers, Adviescommissie Sociaal Economische Vernieuwing**, 1987.

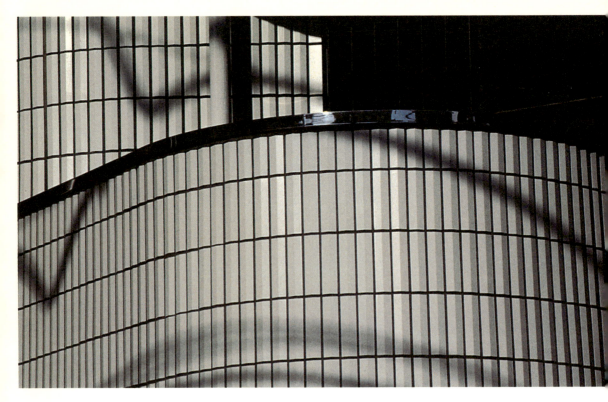

Part I

Rotterdam

Rotterdam, Ports and Port Cities in the Netherlands
Anton M.J. Kreukels

Summary   This contribution offers an institutional study of the most recent dynamics of Rotterdam as the most pronounced port and port city of the Netherlands. The starting point of this analysis is the complex of changes in technology and economic markets with their impact on ports and port cities, as well as on the interaction between the two. Part one opens with Rotterdam as illustrative of the pronounced tradition of maritime transport and distribution in the Netherlands, given its geographical position at the mouth of the River Rhine and situation between the world and the European hinterland. The second, and central part of the study, presents the recent dynamics in Rotterdam as first Dutch port in a changing world. Part three is devoted to the potential positioning of Rotterdam in the near future. This goes together with a positioning of the Dutch maritime transport and port system, with an international comparative approach throughout.

The main issue presented regards the interface between the port on the one hand and the city and city region on the other, in functional, cultural and physical terms. Therefore I'll refer first to a number of economic/technological, institutional/political and societal/cultural trends and finally to urbanization and urbanism, decisive for the evolution at the interface of port and city in Rotterdam, but also manifest in other Dutch ports, especially that of Amsterdam.

Economic/technological trends

The Netherlands can be characterized as a country with a long and outstanding tradition of sea and river trade. This national history manifests itself in a great number of ports, spread over the country and related to accessibility with regard to waterways. In the golden age of Dutch trade in the seventeenth century, the capital city, Amsterdam, was the outstanding center of international trade (Konvitch, 1978; Rotterdam 1340-1940-1990, 1990). Amsterdam long retained this outstanding position in Dutch history, while Rotterdam was little more than a small fishing harbor.

From the nineteenth century onwards industrialization, technological progress and changing international trade formed the start of an ongoing selection process, which resulted in a relatively small number of ports functioning as trade centers in the industrial production of goods and profiting from new technological innovation in transport such as steamships. Rotterdam became part of this category of industrial ports. In 1870 the 'Nieuwe Waterweg' – a reconstruction of the waterway from Rotterdam to the sea – opened Rotterdam and with it the Rhine river to the North Sea. The previously small fishing port profited from the advantages of its natural location: the opening to the North Sea of the main European river, the Rhine. However, one must be aware of the fact that in the nineteenth century other European ports such as Hamburg and Antwerp had a much more pronounced position than Rotterdam.

The real growth of Rotterdam as world port took place in this century, especially after the Second World War. The main impetus came in the inter-war period from a coalition of entrepreneurs in the German Ruhr region and industrialists in Rotterdam. This coalition had a vested interest in guaranteeing a speedy passage of coal, ores and grain to the Ruhr area and to Germany. Even today, this coalition with the Rhineland/Westphalia region in Germany is an important factor behind the ongoing strong position of Rotterdam as an international European seaport.

In the period after the Second World War, especially in the fifties and sixties, the selection process of ports with a strategic function in industrial production and trade continued. Finally, only three to four main seaports were left, operative between the international sea trade and the European hinterland connections by waterway, road, or railway. Rotterdam re-strengthened its position as world port in such a way that Antwerp and Hamburg would only follow at a distance as second and third rank ports in Europe. In the Netherlands itself, besides Rotterdam, one could only register some relatively small but well functioning ports in a national and international perspective, like those of Amsterdam and Vlissingen.

Looking back one must admit that this selection process from the nine-teenth century onwards and particularly that of the post-war period passed without great problems, resistance or social and economic turbulence. One can characterize it as a smooth continuous process of adaptation to the requirements of a modernizing economy. Apart from a limited group of ports, which function within industrialized production and commerce, there is a group of Dutch ports with a lively fishing function. With regard to fishing, the port of IJmuiden (at the sea-opening of Amsterdam) is the principal port, though one must note that there are more fishing ports spread over the country. Furthermore, there is an even greater group of ports that function principally for leisure and sport. Often these ports combine their recreation and tourism function with scenic historical waterfronts. Many Dutch cities and villages with access to rivers or sea fall in this category. The Netherlands has an extended network of waterways: sea arms, rivers, lakes, canals, and channels. This network connects towns and villages and urban and rural areas. It also easily opens the country to other parts of Europe. It isn't surprising that this 'nation of land and water' developed a chain of inland ports and a vital inland navigation, which functions relatively well nationally, but also internationally (for instance the traffic along the Rhine river).

In this way the functional differentiation of Dutch port cities and villages represents a long and continuous process, in which the reduction (to only a limited numbers of ports functioning in the first ranks of national and international trade and commerce) did not cause serious trouble or conflicts. This smooth adaptation process is also manifest where traditional fish ports are losing ground, especially after the introduction of the national quotas for fishing by the European Commission. This is also the case in those places in which population and the workforce were very dependent on the fishing industry and trade where these communities often sought and quickly found economic alternatives in addition to, or instead of, fishing.

The geographical location in the Rhine/North Sea estuary, the focus of Rotterdam on the natural qualities of this location and the powerful Rotterdam/Northern Westphalia business complex are important factors behind the outstanding position of Rotterdam as a port. However, all this seems insufficient and even indecisive in explaining its success. Strategic for Rotterdam's success are the concentrated and combined efforts of port and city, both as a strong coalition and with support of the national government investing structurally over a long period in the port and port infrastructure and in port-related trade and industry. Worthy of mention are investments that aim at an enduring optimal accessibility of Rotterdam to the sea, and in optimizing the specialties of the Rotterdam port: oil distribution in Europe and the chemical sector related to the refineries. A strong coalition between the municipal port authority and the city administration of Rotterdam in close connection with the so-called 'harbor barons' (i.e. the group of the most mighty entrepreneurs in the port of Rotterdam) was the motor behind the expansion of Rotterdam, first as Euro port and subsequently as modern world port in the late fifties and sixties. During the sixties this structure was symbolized by the two-man team consisting of the socialist mayor of Rotterdam, W. Thomassen, and the dynamic chairman of the Municipal Port Authority, F. Posthuma (Plan 2000 +, 1969; De Goey, 1990; Van der Laar, 1991; Van Walsum, 1972).

However, this strong tradition of port and sea trade did not continue. Rotterdam experienced a break, as many urban areas in Europe and the United States did in the late sixties and early seventies. It was the time of the student movements and parallel to it of actions throughout the population in Berkeley, Paris, Berlin and Amsterdam etc. Instead of an ongoing focus on technology and economy, in an increasingly congested and polluted Rotterdam region as elsewhere pleas were heard for a better living and working situation for the common man and a more healthy environment for all (Welters, 1969; Boender, 1985). The mega-proposals for expansion of the port and the region of Rotterdam, in the southwestern part of the Netherlands (the Delta region) in the Plan 2000 + at the end of the sixties were rejected as a symbol of the doomed technocracy. The new era of the Dutch welfare state in its heyday, mirroring itself in a strong coalition between government and social-issue organizations, lasted from the early seventies well into the mid eighties.

Even when the feelings, culture, and mentality of the people and authorities in the city region of Rotterdam remained focused on the port and port economy, the longstanding symbiosis between port and city disappeared. The emphasis on the welfare state resulted in a neglect of the interests of the port and of the port economy. The lively formal and informal contacts between port economy and city administration dwindled. From the seventies onwards the municipal administration and the municipal port authority functioned more at a distance from each other. Besides, in the seventies Rotterdam lost, in an increasing international competitive markets for shipbuilding, its contribution to maritime construction, and with that followed a devastating loss in employment. From the time of the loss of shipbuilding onwards Rotterdam experienced the problems related to high unemployment, concentrated in inner city areas.

However, in the period between 1970 and 1990 Rotterdam also proved to possess a safety net, a buffer from the most negative effects of the 'retreatism' of city and population with regard to the economic development of the port. Particularly the strategic agreement in the eighties between unions and employers concerning the port economy, guaranteeing stability in the workforce of the port, must be mentioned here. Also the goodwill of the Rotterdam port and port economy in circles of the national government made it possible to safeguard the smooth functioning of a world port. The most important factor here seems to be the solid association between the harbor barons and captains of the port economy as well as with the strong municipal port authority. This Rotterdam port establishment didn't erode in that period and was also the impetus behind the new strategic investment plans for the port in the eighties. The international and national economic recession of the 1975-1984 period naturally had a serious impact on the main Dutch urban centers including Rotterdam's city and port. The statistics of the transshipment in that period illustrate clearly the decrease in the functioning of the Rotterdam port, even if it maintained its first rank position.

This formed the drive behind the restoration of strategic thinking and acting in the port of Rotterdam (from 1984/1986 until 1991), for the first time after the boom period of the fifties and sixties, with the expansion of the port towards the sea with Botlek, Euro-poort, and the Maasvlakte (Van Schaick, Dekker, and Dietze, 1984; Poeth and Van Dongen, 1985). In the second part of the eighties the port authority and especially the city administration finally became committed to this new investment program and strategy. The resulting Port Plan 2010, and the related Overall Plan for the City Region of Rotterdam (Ruimtelijke Ordening en Milieubeheer, or ROM), were politically settled no earlier than 1992/1993. Now, there is again a climate of expansion gradually revealing itself as 'managed growth' of the port, the city and the region of Rotterdam. Here it is enough to state that Rotterdam's port and city again have a strategy and on this basis are coordinating actions to keep Rotterdam ahead as a strong world-class port as well as an attractive urban area in which to live and work.

Institutional and political trends
We will not address the perceptions and reactions of Dutch society, local and regional communities, and political circles regarding the port and the city region in the declining years of a hypertrophic welfare state, and as well, their reaction to the economic recession and unsound public finances.

In the eighties and early nineties Dutch society and politicians opted for a steady recovery on a sound financial basis and for an economic re-strengthening of the country; especially manifested in the national government under the three successive Dutch Cabinets of Prime Minister Ruud Lubbers, which resulted in the early nineties in a sound basis for competing in an international economy. Besides these positive features of a restored solid public sector there were also characteristics with negative undertones.

The first of these characteristics – seen in an international context and in comparison with other European countries – is the limited inclination of the Dutch political system to provide the business sector with specific and strategic financial and policy support. There is a hesitation for across-the-board investment after several financial disasters that resulted from various large scale business support schemes in the seventies. Besides, the Dutch culture of corporatism with a mass of different lobbying institutions and vested interest groups, functions as a pressure element, preventing national and local/regional authorities from focusing on one-sided economic positions, at the same time forcing politicians to give credit to other interests. This results in hesitation on the part of the authorities to commit themselves with clear and timely action to economic investments and infrastructure works.

This was illustrated in the eighties and nineties in the course of events surrounding the expansion of the national airport of Amsterdam and in the decisions on the new railway for goods traffic between Rotterdam and Germany: the Betuwe line. In the Port Plan 2010 reference is made to this. It states that the Dutch government's involvement in the Port of Rotterdam is predominantly oriented towards business economics. According to the report, this forms a contrast with the orientation towards the socio-economic structure of the ports and specific support for this aspect in countries such as Belgium, Germany and France. A further factor here is that in a policy concerning a single European market of the European Community, the Dutch political culture is inclined to conform strictly – in theory at least – to the principles of equal competitive relationships, particularly where these could be affected by selective government support in the countries of the European Community. In this context it may be mentioned that, depending on the economic sector, there are major differences between the countries of the European Community with respect to the degree of restraint regarding direct or indirect forms of this support. With regard to the requisite infrastructure works, the amount of support by the Dutch government is modest and restrained in comparison with other European countries (particularly larger countries such as France or Germany), although there has been some greater commitment since 1988, using for these investments extra revenue from natural gas that the country has at its disposal (Netherlands as a Country of Trade and Distribution, 1992).

The second of these characteristics is that since the early seventies a vigorous increase in policy coordination and planning within the Dutch administrative system has taken place. This has, together with an endeavor to give the general public a voice, resulted in decision-forming procedures becoming exceedingly long and complex. This makes fast reactions to new developments in economic, technological and infrastructure fields extremely difficult. The Netherlands is clearly at a disadvantage in the case of strategically and nationally important projects in an international context, even though similar problems exist in a number of other countries (Decision-making about Infrastructure Projects in a number of European countries, Part 1. A Comparison of countries: Analyses and Issues, 1992).

The third of these characteristics is the marked political and governmental commitment in the field of physical planning and environmental protection. The Netherlands is held by many to be one of the leading countries with regard to a powerful national land use planning. In Dutch physical planning this implies a national programming of locations and space requirements, especially of expansion and growth areas, on the basis of an aggregation of prognoses for each region in the country. This leaves little room for responsibility and risk at the local and regional level. Subsequently, it is the national planning agency which decides – after negotiation and bargaining with the local and provincial authorities – about the so-called strategic development areas and schemes in the main cities and in the expansion locations nearby the main cities. In this way the redevelopment of the waterfront, the 'Kop van Zuid' area in Rotterdam, is a nationally strategic urban development program. On this basis Rotterdam gets financial and administrative support for this strategic development.

In the Dutch administrative system these strategic schemes wouldn't
be possible without this dominant role played by the national government.
Since the first National Environmental Policy Plan, environment policy
has become a strong national policy category. Also in the sector of environmental protection the national government is making every effort by
drawing up standards, systems of permits etc. to both clean up the existing
situation and to ensure that new developments will conform to strict
regulations. In this context, one should include the Environment Impact
Statements (MER procedures) laid down by law and obligatory in specific
cases. A spin-off of all this involvement is that where expertise, data and
analyses are concerned in the Netherlands, there is an impressive amount
of cooperation between the Government, research institutes affiliated
with the government, university research centers for environmental protection and finally a number of influential associations active on behalf
of the environment. In comparison with other countries, the Netherlands
has in this respect established a largely national and provincial tradition
in environmental protection. Local and regional involvement has so far
been mainly confined with a few exceptions to the two largest cities:
Amsterdam and Rotterdam (Kreukels, 1993b).

The fourth and last of these negative characteristics is related to the
previous point: the tradition of centralization, and consequently the high
degree of dependence by local-regional government, by the national government from a financial and procedural point of view. This is particularly
expressed in physical planning and environmental policy. In these policy
fields the final decision ultimately lies with interdepartmental agreement at
the national government level. In addition to having advantages in an international context, this centralization also has a number of clear disadvantages
particularly in the case of the large cities and their development policy in a
regional context. With regard to urban revitalization it is essential, given the
dynamics of the international competition, to be alert to and respond in a way
adapted to the prevailing situation. This refers to the necessity of strategic
alliances between strong local/regional units and the national political/cor-
porate system (Institutions and Cities, 1990; Kreukels and Salet (eds.), 1992).

Societal and cultural trends The Netherlands has a long history as a trade and distribution economy. This economy is related to the strong position of Dutch firms in transport by water and road, nationally and internationally. In this respect Rotterdam is an example of a long national tradition of business acumen, trade, distribution and transport orientation, characteristic of the Netherlands and most particularly manifest in the Golden Age of the 17th century, with Amsterdam at that time the most important trading city.

Behind the targeted investment and effort over a long period that resulted in Rotterdam becoming a dynamic world port and city, one observes a social and administrative culture specifically geared to this dynamism. Up to this very day, Rotterdam is distinguished for its down-to-earth approach and awareness for opportunity in trade, distribution and transport economy at an international level. The port of Rotterdam is the main symbol and real representation nowadays of this tradition.

However, one finds after the break of the seventies and early eighties nationally and regionally a shift in orientation in Dutch society and in the political machine. There is no longer the intensive and strong focus of the population and the work force of the Rotterdam region on the port and the port economy. This reduction of port culture and port mentality has become reinforced by a port economy in which, in general, the work force is reduced, the shipyards for constructing and repairing ships have disappeared and in which the new port areas (Botlek, Europoort, and especially the Maasvlakte) are an isolated phenomenon; vital only for some internationals, a group of strategic shipping companies, and finally a variety of small and medium size port handling enterprises with their related work force.

This reduction of the immediate reality of the port in Rotterdam and elsewhere in the Netherlands, parallel with a diminishing direct interest for many in working and dwelling, results in a fading away of port culture and mentality. The future port of Rotterdam is dependent not on the traditional societal/cultural backing, but on a relatively small inner circle of vested interests in the Netherlands and internationally. Assuming, however, that these groups are economically and politically strong enough to offer openings for this port option in Dutch society and politics. Only when new investments result in undeniable advantages and in a variety of spin-offs, will it be possible again for a new civic and political port culture to develop as a motor for continuous restructuring of the Rotterdam Mainport.

Urbanization and urbanism The development of what was originally a fishing village into a world port has been erratic. There have been three major waves of expansion. The first occurred in approximately 1600, the second around 1900 (forming the basis for present-day Rotterdam) and the last after 1945 (the reconstruction of the city following the bombing of the inner city during the Second World War). Rotterdam is part of a long Dutch tradition of urbanism (Mumford, 1938). This manifested itself in the adaptation of the city to industrialization during the nineteenth century. From the inter-war period onwards Rotterdam and Amsterdam were champions of a strong civic culture with a competent liberal and left-wing city administration. Harbor barons, bankers and captains of industry contributed enormously to modern Rotterdam in the period 1920-1960, through initiatives, financing and leadership with regard to urban design, building schemes and infrastructure works (De Klerk, Moscoviter (eds.), 1992). Rotterdam can be regarded in this period as one of the exemplary cities in the international movement of modern architecture and urban design as represented by J.B. Bakema, M. Brinkman, J.H. van den Broek, J.B. van Loghem, H.A. Maaskant, J.J.P. Oud, M. Stam, C. van Traa, W. van Tijen, L.C. van der Vlugt and W.G. Witteveen. In the period of the Congrès Internationaux d'Architecture Moderne (CIAM)-1928-1932 – some of these architects were prominent participants in the international Modern Movement (Rebel, 1983; Wagenaar, 1992).

In stark contrast to this was the swing in the second half of the sixties. The number of inhabitants stopped increasing, as did the level of employment. After 1970 a pronounced decrease actually set in. This change in the city's structure at the beginning of the seventies – fewer residents occupying more accommodation, taking up more space (linked with a general decrease in the city's importance) – found its complement in the region around Rotterdam (Institutions and Cities, 1990; De Klerk, 1990). The region became relatively stronger and more important. In this way the city and surrounding municipalities became more functionally involved with each other, as in the Rijnmond agglomeration. This was expressed during the seventies in the form, unique in the Netherlands, of a special administrative provision: the Rijnmond council. In the eighties this council was, however, dismantled during a period of government cuts and a deregulation process. Now, there are again attempts to have a separate administration for the city region of Rotterdam. However, the population did vote recently against these proposals in a referendum held in the city of Rotterdam.

Since the second half of the eighties, the city has managed to recover somewhat. The population is no longer on the decrease. There is even some evidence of growth. The economic decline has been converted into a slight recovery, even though the city does remain rather fragile and unstable and keeps its huge unemployment rate despite the pronounced real-estate boom and urban regeneration. The upheaval in Rotterdam from approximately 1984 onwards, as described here, is representative of the urban (economic and later also cultural) revitalization manifest in other European countries and in the USA from 1975 onwards. In the Netherlands Amsterdam, Rotterdam, The Hague and Utrecht shared this urban revitalization (Institutions and Cities, 1990). In these cities unemployment had become a serious problem. The tackling of the economic recession and the accompanying unemployment at that time manifested itself especially in the major Dutch urban centers.

With respect to the composition of the population, there has been a pronounced increase in the number of immigrants over the past twenty-five years (migrant workers and their dependents and Surinamers entering the country following independence of this former Dutch colony). This influx into the city, plus the fact that the poorer among the indigenous population were the ones who tended to stay, created a rather one-sided picture. The middle and higher income groups became concentrated in the surrounding municipalities of the Rijnmond agglomeration. Recently, one can even note out-migration from the Rijnmond agglomeration towards other Dutch regions, especially among firms and higher income households (Atzema, Hooimeijer, and Nijstad, 1995). This process, whereby the population became increasingly one-sided, was reinforced to an important degree by a housing policy catering primarily to the public housing sector. Also, the policy of urban renovation kept more lower-paid inhabitants in the inner city and neighborhoods than would otherwise have been the case.

A similar shift can also be seen in employment. From 1973 (the year of the oil crisis) onwards, a change occurred in that Rotterdam began to lose some of its status as industrial and trading city, which it had acquired at the beginning of the century. The city lost much of its industry and became more of a business and a commercial and non-commercial service center. This was further reinforced by the second oil crisis in 1979. This period also witnessed the end of the shipbuilding industry in the city. This alone meant the loss of some 20,000 jobs. Unemployment climbed drastically until 1984, after which there was some evidence of an increase in job opportunities. The level of unemployment, however, remained high as new vacancies tended to be filled by the better educated from the surrounding cities. In addition, from 1971/1975 onwards much of the service industry, but also support facilities such as stores and other businesses tended to follow the consumers into suburbia. Again, this migration from the city was encouraged by a policy originating from the former city council, which did not feel called upon to preserve these economic functions within the city (Institutions and Cities, 1990; De Klerk, 1990; Atzema, Hooimeijer, and Nijstad, 1995).

In the course of this century even the exponential growth of the port up to the seventies made relations between port (particularly with regard to surface area and significance) and city disproportionate. Observers from abroad therefore considered Rotterdam, as a city, far inferior to its port with respect to scale and significance. On the other hand, the bombardment of the inner city during the Second World War made it easier for post-war Rotterdam to keep adapting to new activities and functions in relation to the port, as compared with other port cities. Even now, this affects positively its accessibility to reserves of land for building and infrastructure.

This situation is beginning to change, with the evolution of the port on a regional scale, as referred to above. The port as independent unit with its related activities, services and transport and traffic flows, is becoming less part and parcel of the city and more part of the broader agglomeration of Rijnmond. This region is encompassing more and more areas. The latest developments in the port mean more intensive activity and transport flows, particularly on the scale of the Rijnmond region. This broader port area is increasingly becoming a distinguishable residential and labor market. It is continuing to branch out further into the neighboring countryside and is, at the same time, acquiring offshoots into the main international transport axes to the European hinterland with the relevant domestic transshipment centers. In the Netherlands, Arnhem/Nijmegen (particularly with respect to road transport) and Venlo (with relation to rail and road transport) are examples of such domestic junctions (Van den Berg, Van Klink, 1995; De Klerk, 1990; Kreukels, 1992; Kreukels, 1993a).

The stronger relations between the port and the broader region do not imply that the city of Rotterdam itself hasn't had to adapt as an urban center in line with the port of the future. In particular, the new mix of logistics, distribution and production in the Port Plan 2010, requires both regional expansion and a restructuring of the city itself. As in many cities nowadays, in Rotterdam the master plan is no longer the most decisive vehicle of urban planning. In contrast to the past, with Rotterdam's famous example of Van Traa's postwar master plan, the development of the city is now guided by strategic projects and plans for particular areas and locations.

The scheme of the Kop van Zuid is the most important example of the revitalization of Rotterdam nowadays. This concerns an area on the southern banks of the river (the New Maas), parallel with the city center on the northern banks. This waterfront area no longer forms part of the port structure as a functioning entity. The restructuring of this central-city waterfront area in favor of city functions was possible because of the gradual shifting of the port to the west beyond the central zones of the city. The only competition in the central waterfront in line with the city center is that between offices, houses, accommodation for leisure and culture on one hand, and the quayside for inland shipping, only possible in the central and eastern parts of the waterfront, on the other. The Kop van Zuid area has been chosen for important restructuring within the city of Rotterdam to offer additional office space and other facilities. The chief of the planning department of Rotterdam, the initiator of this scheme, has defended the choice of this location, with a reference to the weak links between the southern and northern banks of the New Maas. The argument that the southern part of Rotterdam failed to score positively when compared generally with other parts of the city, besides its relative isolation, also played an important role. The new Erasmus Bridge provides the connection between the city center and this southern area. The area will be developed as one unit, as in the docklands project, but with a phased development of different sections. The city of Rotterdam is the leading actor in the development of this area. However, for the implementation of the plan, the city has to negotiate with the private sector: financiers and builders. Given the reticent real estate financing nowadays, this causes a lot of uncertainty about the implementation of the Kop van Zuid as a whole. To guarantee the desired professional standards an international steering group of outstanding urban designers and architects has been formed, that includes Joan Busquets, who originally was working for Barcelona. The resistance to this plan, that emerged in the city as a result of fears regarding the negative consequences for the inhabitants of the area, was neutralized when the city council granted a spin-off of employment and residential opportunities in favor of the resident population. This area, together with the new architectural profile on the northern banks of the New Maas, is supposed to provide Rotterdam with a more metropolitan profile.

The Kop van Zuid project is part of an axis along the new Erasmus Bridge across the New Maas running through the center of Rotterdam with its booming sections at the northern banks, with one eastern section (the Weena) concentrated on new offices and one western section (the Museum Quarter) concentrated on new cultural institutions, for instance the Kunsthal by Rem Koolhaas and the Netherlands Architecture Institute (NAi) by Jo Coenen, and finally arriving in the Noordrand, the northern edge of the city and location of Rotterdam Airport, also of new offices and housing areas. The second strategic restructuring and expansion project is this Noordrand project. However, because of a negative outcome in the national and local decisions about enlargement of the airport, this project is now shifting into a plan aimed primarily at new housing. With regard to this axis concept one can conclude that the Kop van Zuid development is part of a master plan (be it implicit) for the city of Rotterdam with a strategic choice for bridging the southern and northern bank of the

New Maas and for a pronounced connection of southern and northern Rotterdam. This tactical choice results in an emphasis on the revitalization of the waterfront in line with the center of Rotterdam. The two strategic projects – Kop van Zuid and Noordrand – relate well to a previously realized, new city profile, which was created in the vicinity of the old port area along the northern banks: the Overblaak area and the section of the

Boompjes with its new, eye-catching buildings and facades and the revitalization of the so-called Water City – a Maritime Museum and a Tropical Swimming Pool – are examples of new urban attractions on the waterfront at the northern banks.

The urban revitalization of Rotterdam in the second half of the eighties was aimed at restoring the city to a central position within a strong region. This was a counter-reaction to the policy of urban renewal in the seventies and early eighties, when attention was focused exclusively on the urban housing areas, thereby neglecting the quality of the city center and the city's economic functions. This social-orientated urban renewal of the seventies can be seen, in turn, as a reaction to the reconstruction schemes for highways and the port economy in Rotterdam in the fifties and sixties. With this sketch of post-war 'dialectic' urban policies in mind, one will not be surprised that the emphasis on economic regeneration in the eighties caused again a counter-reaction from 1989 onwards, in which there were pleas for 'social renewal' in the city of Rotterdam. Even though this program was paid a lot of attention, not only in Rotterdam but later also in a national setting, its focus and impact seem limited as yet, even if there were a number of surprising initiatives.

In the meantime, Rotterdam ranks in the Netherlands as a champion among other cities and regions such as Amsterdam, The Hague, Utrecht and Eindhoven in terms of its growth strategies and success. Rotterdam shows a surprising 'facelift' in terms of real estate and infrastructure as well as urban design. The totally new Rotterdam skyline remains impressive, to say the least. There are new urban landmarks, remarkable new facades at the northern bank of the New Maas river; the old port-related area of the Kop van Zuid at the southern bank is being redeveloped in a mixture of port functions, institutions and offices and housing with much care for amenities and architectural and urban quality such as the revitalization of the old Holland-America Line passengers terminal – a symbol of the trans-Atlantic steamship era – into the 'Hotel New York' restaurant and hotel; and the magnificent new structure – the Erasmus Bridge – designed by Ben van Berkel. Subsequently, after this real estate expansion and the infrastructure works in the center of Rotterdam and in the waterfront areas, Rotterdam also invested in programs of cultural and social importance, as mentioned above. However, as of yet one does not find a workable balance between economic, social and cultural qualities of the city in relation to the port (Harding, 1992). One must be aware of the fact that the policies for economic development have a low profile. Until now, even while paying lip service to these policies, it seems that economic development has been put on a par with the building boom and the facelift of the physical structure of Rotterdam. Certainly, there are initiatives for economic development, stimulated especially by the late Council for Economic Development (Rotterdam Ontwikkelingsraad or ROTOR). However, the city of Rotterdam has still to develop an explicit and consistent strategy for its economic restructuring, combined with new facilities for training and education related to the port economy of the period ahead. This contrasts with the policy view taken by the Port Authority, which in the Port Plan 2010, indicates the necessary economic profile and strongly suggests that economic policy should serve as a foundation on which other interests (e.g. social and environmental) can rest.

Perspectives and options with regard to Rotterdam as an example for Dutch ports and port cities

In this section I will present the new agenda of the port and city of Rotterdam. This suggests insight into the main options and positions with regard to this new agenda as they relate to the manifold interests in the daily functioning of port and city, in recent investments, and finally in the strategic choices in the public sector and the public/private partnerships.

In preparing the Rotterdam port for the next decades three positions have emerged. The first is the lobby intent on keeping Rotterdam strong as a world port and as an economic/technological system. One finds the representatives and advocates of this position in the port and in the port economy, and – to a limited degree – within the Municipality, and further within the Ministry of Economy, the Ministry of Transport, Rivers and Sea in the National Government, and to some degree in the Cabinet itself. The second position is likewise in favor of the port and port economy of Rotterdam, or at least has no arguments against it. However, at the same time it expresses that such a development needs absolutely no strategic support from the outside: neither from the government, nor from other institutions. In this second position the port and the port authority are seen as the only responsible and self-sufficient units – and what is more, they are seen as bound to the same conditions and regulations as those holding for other economic units and sectors. There is no reason in this 'laisser faire' scenario to offer privileges to the port, not even if mainports in other countries become backed by their national governments. One finds representatives of this position from the seventies onwards spread over a variety of institutions, in the political spectrum from the left to the right wing and at the local, regional and national levels. In the third position, Rotterdam – though an outstanding port – is considered as an example of an economic and technological infrastructure that has already had its day. Especially if one pays tribute to the preferences of people and organizations nowadays and if one bears in mind the new economic and technological dynamics, regionally, nationally and internationally, then continuation of the Rotterdam port profile is not a matter of course. One finds this position in the Green Movement and left-wing political groups. It is also manifest among technological and economic experts.

In the period from 1988 until the present, national politics have exhibited intensive debate around the required balance between economy, environment and comfortable living and working conditions. The political confrontation over these issues was demonstrated in the national decision-making processes with regard to the expansion of the airport of Rotterdam, the expansion and restructuring of the port of Rotterdam and the construction of the Betuwe railway. These debates and decisions mirror the institutional and political forces at stake at the moment, nationally, regionally and locally. It should result during the period ahead in strategic choices with regard to either a monolithic economic port profile, a mixed profile of port business and other economic sectors, or a profile in which Rotterdam shifts to an economic, working and living area, liberated totally from the port (the port and its economy are viewed here as a relic of the twentieth century late industrial complex).

At this moment one can observe – parallel to the three positions – three options for the interface of port and city in terms of economy and technology (Den Blanken et al., 1995; Boeckhout, Haverkate, 1995). The first is the option, still dominant in the city and to a lesser degree also in the Port Authority, proceeding from the observation that the city and the region as an economic system are dependent on the port. In this option the port and the port-related economy are decisive for the economic profile of the city and region. This option is manifest in the Port Plan 2010 and in the Overall Plan of the City Region of

Rotterdam: the so-called ROM program, mentioned above. Here one sees a call to strengthen the economy of Rotterdam by investing in spin-off activities originating from the international trade and transit operations of the port. This is rendered in the slogan of the Port Plan 2010: *added value instead of tonnage*. This strategy hopes also to strengthen employment in Rotterdam; this being an important target because of the extreme unemployment in the city.

The second option is manifest in the most recent discussions about the port and the economic basis of Rotterdam. This proposes a scenario in which investments are also made structurally in other sectors of the economy that are not at all related to the port, even though the port economy is still considered an important part of the economy as a whole. In this way the economy and also opportunities for employment in Rotterdam become more differentiated and at the same time to a degree less vulnerable, compared with a scenario that emphasizes the mono-economy of the port. This option especially has adherents among economists, urban planners and other experts in the city administration.

The third option is a derivative of the welfare state culture of the seventies. This option originates from an unfavorable attitude towards the port and the port economy, emphasizing the serious negative impact on the environment and on the quality of life, living and working in the Rotterdam region. Particularly the awareness that the modern port of Rotterdam is more and more an entity that operates geographically as a unit isolated from the city (the modern port of Rotterdam is now concentrated outside the city on the coast) and also economically functions more and more apart from the Rotterdam region, with profits and spin-offs not automatically favoring the immediate region, but extending to enterprises throughout Europe. Particularly technical experts, economists, members of various political parties and the green movement support this option.

It is evident that a strategic choice of one of these three options has serious implications not only for the economic relations between port and city (the first dimension of the interface) but also for the morphological interface of port and city (the second dimension of the interface). In the first option the economic relations between port and city are intensive and so is the morphological interface. In the second option the interface in both dimensions is more indirect and slack, while in the third option the interface is almost non-existent, at least that is what this option suggests. One can clearly observe at this moment traces of all three positions. Also the perspectives and motivations behind these positions are demonstrated nowadays in political discussions about the port in local, regional and national arenas.

An assessment of the future of Rotterdam as an illustration of the interface between Dutch ports and port cities

I will conclude with an assessment of the prospective conditions for making and keeping the port and city of Rotterdam strong for the next decade and well into the new century.

At the moment both the city and the port of Rotterdam are simultaneously involved in an important process of redevelopment. This is unlike the pattern in the past, when each demonstrated more its own cycle of expansion and development, even if related to the other. The relation between city and port is changing. The port is becoming more of an entity in its own right, specifically linked to international networks of trade and transport, in which new technology and related new dominances play an important role (Van den Berg and Van Klink, 1995; Bukold, Deecke, and Läpple, 1992; Hayuth and Hilling, 1992). At the same time any links with the direct surroundings tend to be made more with the Rijnmond region and less exclusively with the city of Rotterdam. With a view to successful development of both city and port – each with its own demands in this wider regional perspective and linked with increasingly strategic hinterland connections – a policy is needed whereby long-term economic, social and environmental interests are better coordinated at various administrative and policy levels (Kreukels, 1992; Kreukels, 1993a; Kreukels, 1993b).

There seems in the case of the port and city of Rotterdam – as in other functioning international ports such as Antwerp and Hamburg – no problem at all for the city itself in losing its port locations and functions. The expansion of the port of Rotterdam is either a redevelopment of inner city waterfront areas for inland navigation and sea transport, or a new development scheme in the new port areas of Botlek, Europoort, and the location in the sea: the Maasvlakte. This means a correction of the proposition that the modern mainport is a phenomenon of new isolated complexes outside and at a distance from the urban centers (Hoyle and Pinder, 1992). This proposition by Hoyle and Pinder seems to apply to a number of ports which are losing their international trade function and not, per se, to port cities with a functioning port, such as Rotterdam, Antwerp and Hamburg (Krekt, 1995; Charlier, 1992). However, in the strategies of both the port and city of Rotterdam one missing element is registered with regard to the interface of port and city. The necessity was not foreseen for locations providing for the 'spin-off' economy related to transshipment, with a preference for functioning nearby the port areas. With regard to these related economies, Antwerp, Hamburg and Ghent show a more balanced land use planning (Charlier, 1992). At the moment the Port Authority of Rotterdam is correcting the Port Plan 2010 with regard to economic activities in and near the port areas bounding the city. The schemes for Waalhaven/Eemhaven currently contain locations for this 'spin-off' economy.

In general with regard to the port, the new plan for the port of Rotterdam – 2010, drawn up by the Port Authority – appears to provide a well-balanced approach to the confrontation between all these interests. It is a well-founded program, based on an analysis of both the long-term opportunities and threats facing the port, rather than concentrating on short-term economic success. It does not offer a blueprint for the port with fixed targets, but instead guarantees the necessary capacities for change. This also means suggesting solutions for structural problems related to pollution and congestion. The strategic concept of emphasizing added value, instead of tonnage, in relation to distribution and production provides a strong backbone to the program. Finally, the plan mirrors the awareness of the importance to the Port Authority, representing the port economy, of being the initiator and participant in public and private networks at different levels. One can imagine that in this perspective the Port Authority of Rotterdam is beginning to operate increasingly as a relatively independent unit mainly in an international context, characterized by strategic alliances with other units of transport and trade by way of financial and managerial cooperation (such as that with the Dutch port of

Vlissingen and with other national and international seaports, inland ports and terminals such as Duisburg, the German inland terminal, connected with Rotterdam by a rail and barge shuttle) (Kreukels, 1992; Kreukels, 1993a; Kreukels, 1993b; Kreukels, 1995; Naaykens, 1995; Zacher and Sutton, 1996).

The city of Rotterdam is faced with a more challenging task. It must redevelop those qualities befitting a center in a region of basically strong satellites which form one residential and employment market. To complicate matters, the city is characterized by a serious one-sidedness with respect to population composition (many immigrants, many people on welfare, many unemployed) and economic profile (a commercial structure which itself is becoming increasingly one-sided). On the other hand, the city of Rotterdam, when compared with other port cities, has had ample, longstanding opportunities to adapt to the dynamics related to the port. At this moment too there are latent reserves for restructuring and further expansion; this is all thanks to the devastation by bombing of the city center in 1940. The choice of combinations in distribution, logistics and production in the new port plan in particular, offers the city and the Rotterdam agglomeration challenging opportunities following a long period from the mid seventies onwards when a lot of ground was lost, especially economically. With regard to this profile, port and city are again pointing in the same direction.

As was suggested in the paragraph on institutional trends, an unavoidable precondition for the success of a city policy equal to that of the port, demands more effort on the part of the city's commercial sector and social groups acting in close collaboration with active city politics. This is only likely to succeed if there is sufficient autonomy at city level for the responsibilities and risks involved to be adequately distributed. In order to make this possible in such a centralized welfare state system as the Netherlands, a modification of the financial relationships linking the various parties involved in the city and the city council is necessary. With such a modification of the Dutch institutional system it is also quite possible that the national authorities will offer the port and city more of the necessary strategic backing than is the case at present. This support will be indispensable in an international context, in which the outcome of competition between cities and between ports will be largely determined by such strategic national support, be it veiled or evident. It can be in the form of financial aid, expertise or political influence in international organizations (Institutions and Cities, 1990; Kreukels and Salet (eds.), 1992). In their strategic policies, both port and city will become more and more confronted with responsibilities on the regional scale of the agglomeration and even the Randstad conurbation. This implies, among other things, necessary agreements with the province of Zuid-Holland, with different departments of the national government, and with regard to the European Union when it comes to policies in the context of the European Commission (Kreukels, 1992; Kreukels 1993a; Kreukels, 1993b; Kreukels and Doe, 1994).

This strategic backing does not alter the fact that port and city will both have to become more proactive themselves in various circuits and at different levels of government, in the European and global context. The Port of Rotterdam is already alert in this respect and has been operating within the European Community/Union, besides its relations with other mainports all over the world. The city has also – often in connection with the port – invested in these relations over the past few years. However, this needs to be further reinforced, considering the initiatives of comparable cities elsewhere. If it becomes possible for enterprises and interests groups in the city, together with the city administration, to again play an important role in the development, using their own assets, they will be able to join hands where necessary and free each other when it is a question of specific responsibility. Then port and city can meet each other on more equal terms than is possible at present.

Literature

O.A.L.C. Atzema, P. Hooimeijer, and R. Nijstad, **Niet met woning-bouw alleen; Verstedelijking en selectieve migratie in de provincie Zuid-Holland** [Not only housing construction and housing policies. Urbanization and selective migration in the Province of Southern Holland], Utrecht, Universiteit Utrecht, Faculteit Ruimtelijke Wetenschappen, Werkdocumenten STEPRO, 1995.

L. van den Berg and H. A. van Klink, **Van Havenstad naar Havennetwerk. Een nieuwe toekomstvisie voor mainport Rotterdam?** [From Port City to Network of Ports. A New View on the Future of the Mainport Rotterdam?], Rotterdam, Erasmus University, ECTAL Erasmus Center for Transport and Logistics, 1995.

R. den Blanken, J. van Boven, W. Hamel, K. Machielse, and A. Verkennis, **Naar een economische visie voor (de stads-regio) Rotterdam. Vijf thema's voor de scenario-workshops** [Towards an Economic Vision for the (City Region) Rotterdam. Five Issues for a Workshop on Scenarios], Rotterdam, Ontwikkelingsbedrijf Rotterdam, 1995.

S. Boeckhout and R. Haverkate, **Port development in the Netherlands: engine for economic growth or creating overcapacity?**, Contribution to European congress by the Regional Science Association, Odense 22-25 August, Rotterdam, Netherlands Economic Institute, Department of Regional and Urban Development, 1995.

S. Bukold, H. Deecke, and D. Läpple, **Der Hamburger Hafen und das Regime der Logistik. Zum Strukturwandel im Güterverkehr und seinen Auswirkungen auf die Hamburger Hafenwirtschaft** [The Port of Hamburg and the Regime of Logistics. About structural change in the transport of goods and its impact on the economy of the port of Hamburg], Hamburg, Reidar Verlag, 1992.

J. Charlier, 'The regeneration of old port areas for new port uses' in B.S. Hoyle and D.A. Pinder (eds.), **European Port Cities in Transition**, London, Belhaven Press, 1992, pp.137-154.

Concept Havenplan 2010, Toekomstbeeld van Mainport Rotterdam [Concept Plan for the Port 2010; Image of Mainport Rotterdam], Rotterdam, Gemeentelijk Havenbedrijf Rotterdam, August 1991.

Besluitvorming over infrastructuurprojecten in andere Europese landen), Deel 1. Een vergelijking van landen: analyses en overwegingen [Decision-making about Infrastructure Projects in a number of European countries. Part 1. A Comparison of countries: Analyses and Issues], Rotterdam, Kolpron Consultants B.V., 1992.

F. de Goey, **Ruimte voor Industrie. Rotterdam en de vestiging van industrie in de haven 1945–1975** [Opportunities for Industry. Rotterdam and the start of industry in the port 1945–1975], Rotterdam, Stichting Historische Publicaties Rotterdam in association with Uitgeverij Eburon, 1990.

A. Harding, 'Rotterdam, croissance ou développement?' [Rotterdam: Expansion or Managed Growth?], in J.L. Bonillo, A. Donzel, and M. Fabre (eds.) **Métropoles Portuaires en Europe: Barcelone/Gênes/Hambourg/Liverpool/Marseille/Rotterdam**), Les Cahiers de la Recherche Architecturale 30/31, Paris, Editions Parenthèses, 1992, 4ème trimestre, pp.147-162.

Y. Hayuth and D. Hilling, 'Technological change and seaport development', in B.S. Hoyle and D.A. Pinder (eds.), **European Port Cities in Transition**, London, Belhaven Press, 1992, pp.40-58.

B.S. Hoyle and D.A. Pinder, 'Cities and the sea: change and development in contemporary Europe', in B.S. Hoyle and D.A. Pinder (eds.), **European Port Cities in Transition**, London, Belhaven Press, 1992, pp.1-19.

Institutions and Cities; the Dutch Experience, Netherlands Scientific Council for Government Policy, Reports to the Government No. 37, Revised Edition, The Hague, 1990.

L. de Klerk, 'Hoe groot is Rotterdam?' [From city to city region of Rotterdam] in **Geografisch tijdschrift**, special issue Rotterdam, Vol. XXIV, No. 3, 1990, pp.200-210.

L. de Klerk and H. Moscoviter (eds.), **'En dat al voor de arbeidende klasse.' 75 Jaar Volkshuisvesting Rotterdam** [And this all for the working classes. 75 years of social housing in Rotterdam], Rotterdam, 010 Publishers, 1992.

J.W. Konvitz, **Cities and the Sea. Port City Planning in Early Modern Europe**, Baltimore/London, The Johns Hopkins Press, 1978.

A. Krekt, **Rotterdam, de haven of de stad. Een studie naar de ruimtelijke ontwikkeling van de haven en de stad van Rotterdam** [Rotterdam, city or port. A study about the spatial planning of the port and city of Rotterdam], Rotterdam, Port of Rotterdam, Utrecht, Universiteit Utrecht, Vervolgdoctoraal Planologie, 1995.

A. Kreukels, 'Ville, port, region; la rupture d'échelle; Rotterdam', in J.L. Bonillo, A. Donzel, and M. Fabre (eds.), **Métropoles Portuaires en Europe: Barcelone/Gênes/Hambourg/Liverpool/Marseille/Rotterdam**, Les Cahiers de la Recherche Architecturale 30/31, Paris, Editions Parenthèses, 1992, 4ème trimestre, pp.163-177.

A.M.J. Kreukels, 'Rotterdam. Le port englobe la ville' Rotterdam. The scope of the port is surpassed that of the city in **Les Annales de la Recherche Urbaine**, 'Grandes Villes et Ports de Mer', 55-56, September 1992 – Diffusion: March 1993a, pp.23-34.

A.M.J. Kreukels, **Environment, Economic Development and Administration**, Organization de Cooperation et de Développement Economiques OCDE/OECD, Document for Expert Meeting on the Ecological City, Paris, OCDE/OECD, Château de la Muette, 1993b.

Anton M.J. Kreukels, 'Glasgow and Strathclyde Region (Scotland, United Kingdom)' in Michèle Collin (coordination), **Les Politiques Urbaines d'Accompagnement des Développements Portuaires en Zone de Reconversion Industrielle et Sociale**, Rapport Final, Programme d'Action pour Les Collectivités Territoriales (PACTE), géré pour le Compte de Commission Européenne, Le Havre, Edition Association Internationale Villes et Ports, August 1995, pp.6-31.

A. Kreukels and A. Doe, 'Un nouveau plan portuaire' in **Villes Portuaires. Acteurs de l'environnement** [City and Port, partners for the environment, Port Plan 2010 and the environment], Quatrième Conférence Internationale Villes et Ports, Montréal, Québec, Canada, 10 to 13 October 1993, Association Internationale Villes et Ports (AIVP), Secrétariat a la mise en Valeur du Saint-Laurent, Le Havre, 1994, pp.207-220.

A.M.J. Kreukels and W.M.G. Salet (eds.), **Debating Institutions and Cities. Proceedings of the Anglo-Dutch Conference on Urban Regeneration**, The Hague, Netherlands Scientific Council for Government Policy, The Hague, SDU Uitgeverij, 1992.

P.Th. van de Laar, **Financieringsgedrag in de Rotterdamse Maritieme Sector 1945–1960** [Financial Behavior in the Rotterdam Maritime Sector 1945–1960], Ph.D. Thesis, Rotterdam, Erasmus Universiteit Rotterdam, 1991.

L. Mumford, **The Culture of Cities**, Jovanovich Publishers, San Diego, New York, London, Harcourt Brace, 1938.

E. Naaykens, De intermodale bereikbaarheid van Rotterdam over land. Onderzoek naar de mogelijkheden ter verbetering van het functioneren van railshuttle- en binnenvaartlijn dienstverbindingen vanuit Rotterdam [The accessibility of Rotterdam by intermodal forms of terrestrial traffic. A research project on the optimization of the functioning of the rail shuttle and inland navigation routes throughout Rotterdam], Rotterdam, Port of Rotterdam, Utrecht, Universiteit Utrecht, 1995.

Plan 2000+; Ontwikkeling Noordelijke Delta [Plan 2000+. The Expansion of the Northern Section of the South West Dutch Region: The Delta region] in opdracht van het Gemeentebestuur opgesteld door het Havenbedrijf en de Dienst Stadsontwikkeling en Gemeentewerken, Rotterdam, Gemeente Rotterdam, 1969.

G.G.J.M. Poeth and H.J. van Dongen, **Rotterdam of de noodzaak van een infrastructuur voor informatie** [Rotterdam or the Necessity of an Infrastructure for Information], Rotterdam, Interfaculteit Bedrijfskunde Erasmus Universiteit Rotterdam, 1985.

B. Rebel, **Het Nieuwe Bouwen. Het Functionalisme in Nederland 1918–1945** [The Movement of the New Building. Functionalism in Dutch Architecture 1918–1945], Utrecht, Universiteit Utrecht, dissertation, 1983.

ROM – Ruimtelijke Ordening en Milieubeheer – Project Rijnmond. Plan van Aanpak. Beleidsconvenant [ROM – Land Use Planning and Environmental Quality – Project Greater Rotterdam Area, the so called Rijnmond Area. Start Document and Commitment Package], Stuurgroep ROM – Rijnmond, Rotterdam, 1993.

W. L. van Schaick, T.C. Dekker, and P.M. Dietze, 'Europoort – Maasvlakte; Besturen met visie' [Europoort and the Maasvlakte – the Expansion Area at the Sea Coast. Management with Vision] in **Openbare Uitgaven**, Vol. 16, No. 4 August 1984, pp.180-200.

C. Wagenaar, **Welvaartsstad in wording. De wederopbouw van Rotterdam 1940–1952** [The first start of the welfare city. The rebuilding of Rotterdam 1940–1952], Rotterdam, NAi Publishers, 1992.

G.E. van Walsum (ed.), **Rotterdam/Europoort 1945–1970**, Rotterdam, Ad. Donker, 1972.

L.A. Welters, **Wonen, leven, werken in Rijnmond; beleidsaanbevelingen van het bestuur van de Stichting Onderzoek Arbeidssituatie in het Rijnmondgebied** [Dwelling, living and working in the Greater Rotterdam Area, the so called Rijnmond Region. Recommendations for the Regional Authorities by the Board of the Foundation Research Conditions for Working in the Rijnmond Region], Rotterdam, Universitaire Pers Rotterdam, 1969.

M.W. Zacher and B.A. Sutton, **Governing Global Networks. International Regimes for Transportation and Communications**, Cambridge, Cambridge University Press, 1996.

The Port of Rotterdam: Synthesis between Rotterdam City and Mainport Henk de Bruijn

Introduction   Expansion of scale, globalization, containerization, clustering, added value, environmental awareness – these are the watchwords and trends in the development of Rotterdam Mainport. Conversely, the same issues are relevant for the city. Eventually, because of the scope offered by the creation of Maasvlakte 2, this world-class port and city will be able to integrate more where once they were divided. Rotterdam is planning a retake on the river.

Rotterdam today is a long way from the port it once was. The typical exotic aromas that could once be sensed there can no longer be detected; shipbuilding activities have decreased drastically, and the squeaking of cranes and the clanging of steel have been replaced by the whirring of computers. Although the distance between Maasvlakte and Rotterdam city center is virtually the same as that between Amsterdam Airport and Rotterdam, the present relationship between city and port is as strong as ever.

During a process that has been going on for over a century now, the border between the actual port and the city has shifted westward. The development to Mainport commenced towards the end of the nineteenth century with expansions on the south bank, continued westwards in the sixties in the shape of Botlek (Rotterdam's petrochemical area) and Euro-poort, and was later completed by the Maasvlakte. These expansions were a more or less autonomous process for the port, with separation of functions as a central theme. The city was not so much in transition as undergoing a one-track change. A recent and logical step in this process that is causing plenty of commotion is the planned construction of Maasvlakte 2. There is one important difference, however: the global economy allows the city to play a much greater part in maintaining the port's competitive position. Rotterdam should be offered the chance to do so; and it will be, because of Maasvlakte 2.

The large European market share of the port of Rotterdam should no longer be taken for granted. The present expansion of the port should enable the city to better meet the port's demands. In other words: the city should be an active part of the port and not just function as a labor pool. In its competition with other ports, Rotterdam no longer focuses merely on matters such as the depth of waterway, number of terminals and speed of transshipment, but also on the quality of life and attractive living and working conditions for its inhabitants.

Reflection   To prosper, port and city must be able to expand, and must have at their disposal a stable labor supply, extensive port-related knowledge centers and, as mentioned, plentiful high-quality housing, a flourishing cultural and entertainment center, and 'green lungs'. A port that is of global importance is in continuous flux – as is Rotterdam. Although the office blocks on the Weena, the Erasmus Bridge and Erasmus University, the call centers, and the World Port Center may all be mirrored by the depth of the New Waterway, the chemical cluster, and the computerized terminals, the position and the image of Rotterdam as a residential city are still quite underdeveloped. The type of housing is far from diverse and mostly consists of cheap, rented houses and apartments.

As a result, those with a higher income move to areas outside of Rotterdam. A great deal of money and attention is being spent on restructuring the old districts: better quality housing, 'greening', better schools. Nevertheless, the attraction of suburbia remains strong, and can only be mitigated if the city can find the space to create a better housing and living environment. At the moment, there are few suitable possibilities for those with middle to high incomes. Although Rotterdam is trying its utmost to catch up, the Wassenaar of Rotterdam is still… Wassenaar.[1] Moreover, the question of where to find work is becoming secondary to the one of where to live, especially for earning couples. In short, Rotterdam will have to increase its residential attractions, especially for professionals.

Primarily, the focus should be on drastically improving the quality of life – in every sense of the word: a 'happening' inner city, excellent living conditions, recreational possibilities in parks and by the river, extensive facilities, more leisure functions, plenty of activities and, especially in the city center, attractive public architecture, exploiting the waterfront to its full potential: the scope is endless. The lure of places other than Rotterdam may also be strong for the port: if companies – especially international ones – cannot find ideal sites in Rotterdam, they are likely to relocate to areas where they can. City and port: one cannot exist without the other. Each is subject to constant change, all the while sounding out the other's potential. The greatest number of opportunities arises when city and port meet.

1 Wassenaar is a small town just north of The Hague. Originally developed as an elite country villa retreat area, it now provides residences for upper and upper-middle income families.
2 Reallocation space refers to the space needed for the port's continued flexibility. A bookcase cannot be rearranged without a few extra shelves; urban renovation cannot be carried out without space for temporary housing and facilities; a port's industries cannot be clustered further if there is no physical room for new developments.

Space and reallocation space   At the moment, a great deal is going on in spatial planning. One government amendment will just have been printed when the next is already being written. Everybody seems to be frenetically planning the future. It goes without saying that the Netherlands has a rich tradition in spatial planning. Because of the limited available space, every square yard of Dutch soil has at some point been redesigned. Within the Netherlands, Rotterdam may be called the champion of planning, 'aided' by the Second World War, when its center was destroyed by bombs. On a national scale, the Fifth Bill of Amendment for Spatial Planning is published. It will determine the look of the Dutch landscape for the next 20 to 30 years. Decisions must now be made about the future of the Netherlands, not least about that of the Randstad. Will the Randstad's 'Green Heart' remain green, will Amsterdam Airport be allowed to continue to expand, and what is the best way for that other hub of transport, the port and industrial complex of Rotterdam, to develop?

In its recent *Spatial Plan 2010*, Rotterdam has drawn a picture of its near future as a city, in which the relationship between port and city is one of the spearheads. 'Reallocation space'[2] is the key phrase for every urban and port-related development, in the sense that changes within the Port are likely to result in new opportunities for the city. Urban renovation such as that in Kop van Zuid, where prime locations but outdated docklands were transformed into an extension of the city center, was only possible because of additional space available to the port. This, by the way, is not a novel phenomenon; the first phase of urban renovation in the seventies was itself made possible by the relocation of companies.

What made these relocations easier is the unique and fortunate fact that Rotterdam is, and always will be, 50 kilometers from the sea. The land between the river estuary and the city allows for a relatively large amount of freedom in spatial planning. However, after Europoort was completed the land became scarce there as well, and for its only alternative for expansion, the port had to look to the sea. Real expansion areas are limited, making reallocation space hard to come by. The desired quantity of expansion sites (for instance land reclamation) and the necessary quantity of reallocation space (for instance, optimizing the use of the existing port and industry complex) are now on the agenda. The need for both is mainly determined by the dynamics prevalent in ports and in the economy.[3]

3   Space is also one of the most important site selection factors in the so-called knowledge economy. This knowledge is certainly not limited to the inside of offices; nor does 'knowledge economy' simply refer to Information Technology. Moreover, in Rotterdam, further logistic development does not conflict with development in IT. On the contrary: IT is used relatively often by the transport cluster. For this sector, IT leads to efficiency: goods flows are programmed in such a way that lorries are half-full less often; also, the distribution network becomes increasingly fine-meshed as a result of, among other things, e-commerce. Companies' site selection

Trends It is hardly useful to philosophize about the relationship
between port and city if it is unclear which direction the port is heading in.
One of the prime tasks of the Rotterdam Municipal Port Management
(RMPM) is to occupy itself with this issue. Policy is always based on future
expectations. In the *Port Plan 2010* (written in 1993), the port is no longer
described as a separate entity, but as part of the complete logistic chain.
The starting point was that Rotterdam's favorable position in and of itself
will not be sufficient for helping it maintain its competitive advantage.
The quality of the total service package connected to the transshipment
and forwarding of goods (with all the necessary information systems) is a
very important factor in the competitive battle between ports. Rather than
being simply a huge goods depot, above all, a Mainport is a high-tech
industry.

Rotterdam is not just concerned with the quality of its logistic services.
Too little attention is often paid to the fact that, first of all, its port is an
industrial complex in which the chemical sector in particular has been able
to develop over the past decades into the third largest chemical complex
in the world. In this time, a shift has taken place 'from tonnage to added
value' – the slogan of the *Port Plan 2010*. When the *Port Plan 2010* was
being written, a number of trends within the port's industry and logistics
became increasingly prominent.[4]

Projections 2020 For the past few decades, the Rotterdam
Municipal Port Management has been making a Cargo Flows Model every
six years, in which estimation is made of the amount of cargo in its various
shapes and forms (bulk, containers, roll-on/roll-off, etc.) that is expected
to come Rotterdam's way. In the last edition, *Projections 2020* (1998), a
wider, more integrated approach was opted for, in which the possible
development of industry is accounted for, as well as of distribution, traffic
and transport, the environment, employment, added value and space

factors are far less subject to change than is often supposed. Good accessibility will always be vital,
no less so in the future. Industrial sites will always be needed, even in a knowledge-intensive economy,
for example to ensure that expanding companies will remain in the area.
4 Trends in industry and logistics. It is impossible to have globalization without the availability of
(relatively cheap) transport. It is therefore expected that there will be a huge expansion in scale,
particularly in the container industry. The large shipping companies with their mega-ships (that will
possibly hold as many as 15,000 containers – as opposed to the present 4000) will put in at just
a few ports. Per continent, only a limited number of Mainports will have the capacity to deal with the
growing cargo flows and keep up with the latest industrial developments. At the same time, market
parties will have greater freedom to select a port, especially the container and general cargo indus-

requirements. In *Projections 2020*, the Port Management's starting point is the trends in two different economic scenarios.[5] The presuppositions of the Global Competition Scenario are that the European economy will develop itself favorably, whereas the guiding principle of the Divided Europe scenario is a stagnating economy. In Global Competition, all Europeans have jobs, the market mechanism is prevalent and international competition will develop freely. There is a strong growth and fast circulation of knowledge, as well as a significant increase in private spending. The Europe of Divided Europe – 'nomen est omen' – is internally divided, with a failing market mechanism and minimal growth of private spending, and the knowledge potential is hardly disseminated at all.

In *Projections 2020*, the development of every element of the two scenarios has been calculated and compared. In the Global Competition scenario, it is expected that the total transshipment for 2020 will amount to 480 million tons; in Divided Europe, it is expected to come to a 'mere' 379 million tons. This is not to say that either of these scenarios will necessarily come true. Disregarding unexpected disasters, actual transshipment figures will in all likelihood be an average of the two predictions. Generally speaking, the transshipment trends in both scenarios are quite similar. The main difference is that the developments in Global Competition will be a great deal faster and more violent than in Divided Europe. Rotterdam will develop from a bulk cargo port into a modern container port and from a refinery port into a chemical port. In both scenarios, the number of containers and amount of ro-ro (roll-on/roll-off) will increase greatly, with bulk cargo stagnating or increasing only minimally.

Containers: even in the Divided Europe scenario, the number of TEUs in transshipment is predicted to have redoubled by 2020; in Global Competition, they are expected to quadruple to 17.6 million TEUs.

From the early nineties onwards, there has been a rapid development of distribution activities as a result of the growth in container transshipment and the creation of Distriparks. Roughly 15% of transshipped containers are opened in Rotterdam, stored there, processed if necessary, and then transferred on; this percentage is unlikely to change much. As the number of containers is expected to increase, there will be a large or possibly enormous rise in activities as well as in related employment, depending on the scenario.

tries. One of the reasons why companies will continue to opt for Rotterdam is the presence of cargo-binding industries such as refineries, 'distriparks' and 'industribution'. As far as bulk goods – ore, coal and oil – are concerned, the present prime position of Rotterdam will not change much. What is relevant, however, is that often, chemical companies belong to international concerns (such as ICI, Eastman and ARCO/Lyondell) – hence, Rotterdam is unable to directly influence decisions about location, expansion or closure. In this market, Rotterdam's main competitors are Antwerp, Houston and Singapore. More cargo and more types of cargo are being transported by means of containers. As a result of this containerization, the traditional general cargo industry is suffering. The few sectors that are not are more specialized, as is for instance the case with steel transshipment firms and those dealing with forest products.

Distribution is a real growth industry. Especially in the Global Competition Scenario, the chemical sector – as compared to the refining business – is becoming more and more prominent within the Rotterdam industrial complex. Rotterdam is gradually turning from a 'refinery port' into a 'chemical port'; hence, the advantages of clustering are becoming more and more obvious.

Projections 2020 earmarks container transshipment, distribution and the chemical sector as growth industries. Viewed in this light, the chapter on space in *Projections 2020* is very interesting. As space requirements increase with fits and starts, there should always be a reservation of strategic areas. Scope for optimization of space is limited, after all, because of technical reasons and environmental restrictions. According to the Global Competition Scenario a shortage of space is expected between 2002 and 2004; according to Divided Europe, it will not arise until the year 2020. In terms of averages, then, the shortage will arise some time between 2002 and 2020.

It will not come as a surprise to anyone that the RMPM is convinced of the economic necessity of constructing Maasvlakte 2; certainly if one considers that the figures of the past years are indicating that the Port is living its own Global Competition Scenario right now.

Space – the essential factor
For decades, the creation of space has been part and parcel of Rotterdam's policy. This can be achieved by optimizing the use of the existing port and industrial areas, both by co-operating with other ports, such as those of Moerdijk and Flushing, and through land reclamation. The latter is the projected method for Maasvlakte 2, which is expected to become an ultramodern 1000-hectare industrial site, accessible to even the largest sea vessels. Trends such as expansion of scale and clustering call for a drastically different and more efficient

The size and variety of the petrochemical industry has resulted in certain 'cluster advantages' (meaning that partners and competitors/colleagues make use of each other's produce and waste as well as joint facilities). Clustering is not just economically sensible but is also beneficial from spatial and environmental points of view: after all, it results in decreased distance between suppliers and buyers and their customers. Examples of recent favorable clusters are the recycling and agro industries. Rotterdam's scale could be of particular benefit to the general cargo industry by the creation of dedicated terminals that would result in more efficient transshipment. After dedicated terminals for cars, scrap metal, fruit and forest products, there will be others for various cargoes.
Mainport industries that are not based in the Port itself, such as office activities, R&D/knowledge, suppliers, etcetera, will be of increasing importance. More and more, the Mainport will transcend its

rearrangement of the port and industrial areas. This will only be possible if there is sufficient free space, as well as sufficient reallocation space (about 10% of the total acreage). Maasvlakte 2 will directly provide that much-needed room for expansion and, indirectly, the necessary reallocation space. In the event of it not being realized, there will be a fierce struggle for space in which Rotterdam will be unable to comply with the demand for industrial sites. This will be especially detrimental to the growth industries, and also to, for instance, the added value that is created near factories and terminals (industribution).

Having sufficient expansion and reallocation space will also be advantageous for the environment. Companies with a high nuisance factor could be located far from residential areas, and clustering could be stimulated, both of which will lead to a decrease in traffic – not to mention the opportunities that will be created for 'greening' the areas in and around the port. With this in mind, the idea to move companies from the old docklands to the port areas to the west of Rotterdam gains in interest, offering scope for new entrepreneurs and for residential or green areas. In this way, Rotterdam will get the extra reallocation space it needs to restructure the city center, the most relevant old docks in this scheme being on the south bank: the easterly part of Waalhaven/Eemhaven.

Waalhaven/Eemhaven

Waalhaven/Eemhaven is a complex of old docks on the left bank of the Maas that were constructed in the course of 80 years. As a consequence, their aspect is extremely varied, with sites and basins ranging from small to large. The area measures 540 hectares, making it ten times the size of Kop van Zuid, and far larger than the actual city center. Nearly all port-related activities are represented there. As far as transshipment is concerned, Waalhaven/Eemhaven easily stands all comparison with any other medium-sized Western European port. It houses deep-sea and short-sea container transshipment, homogeneous general cargo (wood and wood products, iron, steel and nonferrous cargo), and heterogeneous general cargo (on pallets and in sacks). A large part of the container transshipment, namely the deep-sea trade on the northwesterly route, has recently been relocated to the present Maasvlakte. The empty space this left behind has been taken up by the terminals of Hanno and Uniport, two medium-sized container transshippers. Incidentally, by relocating Hanno to Waalhaven, space was returned to the city. On the former Hanno site in Katendrecht, a new central residential

traditional boundaries. Spatial adjustments will be inevitable if Rotterdam wants to make the most of these trends. Flexible use of space is obviously going to be an extra business requirement.
5   How crucial is the Rotterdam Port to the city and to the Netherlands as a whole? 110,000 people – working in industry, transport, the wholesale business, the building and construction industry and for the council – are directly employed in the port and industrial complex. 50,000 people are employed by the liquid bulk industry, and a further 60,000 by firms based throughout the region. There is a concentration of banks, insurance companies, consultants, classification societies, shipping companies and suchlike in the city. In total, 315,000 Dutch people earn a living thanks to the Port of Rotterdam. The total added value comes to 18 billion Euros, roughly 7% of the Gross National Product. In both scenarios depicted in Projections 2020, the added value increases. Naturally, the increase is

district has now been built. Because of Uniport's relocation, space became available to the present 'Fruit Port' on the north bank.

In 1996, in *The Revitalization of Waalhaven/Eemhaven*, the RMPM drew up the future plans for this area, in which the opportunities for small-scale port-related entrepreneurs are especially highlighted. The port's 'breeding ground' function should be cherished and stimulated. Young companies, although they often need the support of their larger colleagues, create a dynamic innovative atmosphere that is beneficial to all. Suitable site selection conditions are particularly important to them: firstly, the general quality of life, secondly, sufficient space for entrepreneurship of this kind. Small-scale companies will eventually become more common in the traditional port industries, too, co-existing with their large-scale competitors.

In the light of present trends (expansion of scale, clustering, relocating of companies that cause nuisance), however, it is expected that many activities that are now carried out in Waalhaven/Eemhaven will eventually – between 2010 and 2030 – be moved to westerly port areas in spite of any redevelopment plans. Should new room indeed be created to the west of Rotterdam, then Waalhaven/Eemhaven may well become the pre-eminent 'additional space' location of the future, where city and port will once again meet. Several researchers are now looking into the area's possibilities.

Dreaming about the borders between city and port

Tentative speculations are now being made about the question as to what will happen to the borders between city and port once Maasvlakte 2 has been built. These speculations are made on various levels: nationally, in the Fifth Bill of Amendment for Spatial Planning; by the council in the *Spatial Plan Rotterdam 2010*; and by several boroughs on the south bank in the Zuid Gallery. Maasvlakte 2 will only offer space for large-scale industries such as the chemical sector, recycling, containers, and distribution. The industry in Waalhaven, however, is mostly small-scale and labor intensive. For alternative possible locations, then, it would look to existing sites vacated by larger firms moving to the west of Rotterdam.

greater in the Global Competition scenario: by 2020, a rise is forecast from 38.6 billion to 104.1 billion Dutch guilders, an average yearly increase of 4%. In Divided Europe, the rise is a mere 1.7% to 59.5 billion guilders.
In both scenarios, especially in the Global Competition one, the share of the Port in the Gross National Product will increase. Clearly, the economic impact of the Rotterdam port cluster is bound to grow further still.

Supposing that recycling were to really take off, having a plant on Maasvlakte 2 would make sense. This would result in reallocation space in the Botlek and Europoort areas. The large-scale developments in the container and roll-on/roll-off sectors would also pre-suppose relocations to either Maasvlakte, resulting in vacant lots in Waalhaven and in the Fruit Port on the north bank. In all likelihood, distribution will go wherever the container industry goes, so there will be space in Distripark Eemhaven for port-related and other industries. In this scenario, the Botlek Noord area could take over Waalhaven/Eemhaven's old role as 'stepping stone' port.

In both the Waalhaven/Eemhaven area and the Fruit Port, many general cargo companies are beginning to concentrate on containerized transport; alternatively, they are specialized in general cargo in its purest form. After all, there will always be a need for this type of small and flexible firm. All in all, the growing tendency for the urban economy to become intertwined with that of the port could be demonstrated by the Waalhaven's eventual make-up: dry bulk goods firms will be housed there, too. Companies that com-bine production with services would be particularly suitable – high-tech firms that carry out port-related as well as general commercial activities. Apart from these, there should also be purely services-directed companies, such as engineering and software agencies. In this way, Waalhaven could become the 'Brainport of the Mainport'.

This will entail a partial change of function in the easterly area of Waalhaven, which will require the necessary spatial adjustments. There will be definite advantages for the bordering districts in the Charlois district of Rotterdam: less environmentally damaging nuisance, more jobs, more facilities, easier accessibility and more 'greening' of public spaces. By 2030, most of the larger transshipment companies and port-related industries will have disappeared from the city's ports as a result of this trek westward. The city will benefit, as old docklands may be redeveloped in favor of a knowledge infrastructure, services, housing and tourism. This urbanization of Waalhaven may cause a considerable reduction in the pressure that is being put on Holland's 'Green Heart' at present by the construction of housing estates. Because of the area's varied layout, there are also plenty of tourist opportunities (water-based theme parks, marinas). An obvious idea would be to gradually start mixing functions. Waalhaven/Eemhaven is where the seeds will be sown for 'Rotterdam, Port of global importance', should the Global Competition scenario – as depicted in *Projections 2020* – be realized.

From then on, there will no longer be any boundaries between city and port and Rotterdam's two faces will merge into one. The new economy will bind the city to the port and vice versa. Knowledge will have become both the most important and the most profitable production factor. Rotterdam will remain up to date by means of the global exchange of information networks. The economy keeps on rolling, 'Open for Business' 24 hours a day, and its constant innovation will keep Rotterdam ahead of its competitors.

Transformation   In different ways, the construction of Maasvlakte 2 will bring about a transformation of the city of Rotterdam – a much-needed transformation at that, because the high-quality, high-tech port on the west coast should have its counterpart in the city. This transformation will show in the different spatial planning, in environmental benefits, in the different types of employment that will arise. Logistic knowledge, for instance, will be a unique selling point and a binding factor for cargo.

It goes without saying that the investments in Maasvlakte 2 must be economically sound. At the same time, the economy should not determine all. Other equally important factors are idealism, social commitment and responsibility and, above all, a belief in a better world. Social realities have an impact of their own on the development of the economy. In other words, investments should not necessarily be made where they are most profitable; they should be judged for their social benefits. Maasvlakte 2 is needed, to provide new incentives to both port and city. Rotterdam in transition will prove unstoppable!

The Port of Rotterdam

Kop van Zuid Spoorweghaven

Kop van Zuid Wilhelminakade

Rotterdam

Caland Canal

Eemhaven

Maasvlakte, ECT

Pernis

Brielse Maas

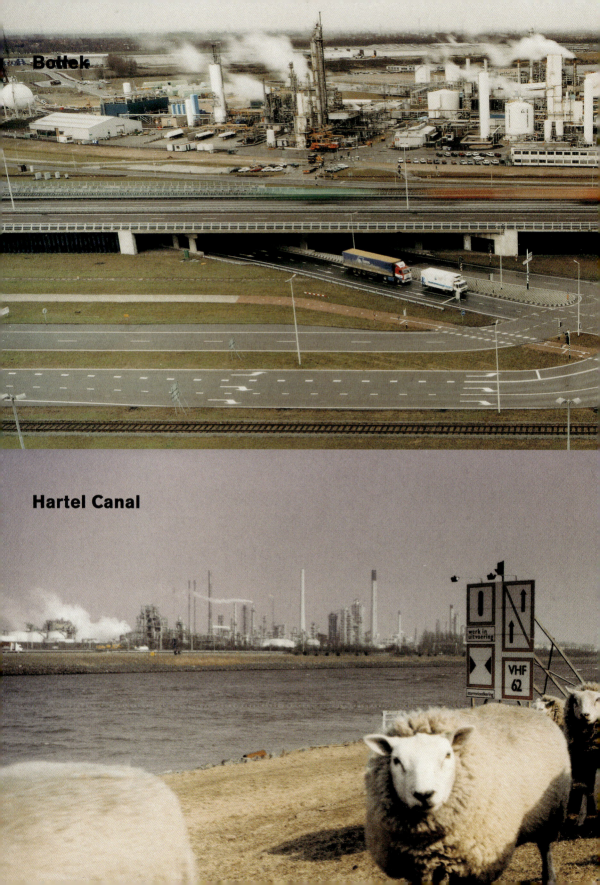

Bottek

Hartel Canal

Traffic Centre Hook of Holland

Rotterdam port

Mississippi Harbour

Maasvlakte

Planning in a Complex Environment: the Spatial Plan Rotterdam 2010

Jan Oosterman

Introduction The spatial development of Rotterdam has until now been characterized by different periods, each with its own specific emphasis. In the seventies, the main priority was urban renewal (the so-called building for the neighborhood) and in the eighties and nineties it was large urban projects. The period ahead of us, until 2010, appears to be becoming a time in which both issues will feature prominently on the city agenda. Moreover, for the first time now, the policy fields of recreation and tourism will receive a distinct position within the spatial policy alongside the issues of housing, working and transportation. In other words: the urban question is now more multi-faceted than ever. To be able to coordinate this project of the future and accommodate the different components, the city of Rotterdam has developed a new spatial plan for the city: the Ruimtelijk Plan Rotterdam 2010 (RPR 2010), or Spatial Plan Rotterdam 2010; this should be established as a formal plan within a year. The plan defines the spatial development of the city in broad strokes. Within the plan, the city also defines a number of large projects that should form new impulses for the desired spatial development.

'Actions speak louder than words' is the motto of the Rotterdam soccer club 'Feyenoord'. This is a saying that many people from Rotterdam identify with. The Rotterdam resident has great mettle, and it has been said that in the port city of Rotterdam, shirts are sold with their sleeves already rolled up. 'Actions speak louder than words' also typifies the planning history of Rotterdam, a history that has until now been characterized mainly by large strategic projects rather than comprehensive schemes.[1] Rotterdam has virtually no tradition of comprehensive plans. That time has come now, though, at least if the local authorities of Rotterdam have their way. This has everything to do with the complexity of the issues currently facing the city. There is a need for an integrated perspective and a framework with which to consider the priorities of one spatial project over another. At the same time, the local government does not wish to undermine its project-oriented, high-powered manner of working. On the contrary, with the RPR 2010, they wish to offer the necessary order and prioritization to the vast number of ambitions and desired projects being placed on the municipal agenda by different parties.

The rest of this article will describe how the municipality of Rotterdam plans to design its future in a spatial-strategic sense. First it will be important to know a little more about the history of the city's spatial development, as well as a few important trends and figures.

---

1 Rotterdam does have a tradition of structural planning for specific districts, such as the Basis-plan by Van Traa for the reconstruction of the city center and the structural plan for the Water-weg region. However, formal structural plans for the entire urban area of Rotterdam have never been established. The most recent formally established structural plan for a large part of Rotterdam was the 1982 revision of the Structural Plan Rotterdam within the tangential highway system around the center (Centrumruit).

Rotterdam: a short history of city development

From phased city development to simultaneity The development of
Rotterdam is marked by different phases of intensity, interrupted on occasion by abrupt transitions. Sometime in the middle of the eighth century,
the first inhabitants settled in the swampy delta of a little river called the
Rotte, which flows out to the wide Maas River. They lived off the land
and their fishing. In the twelfth and thirteenth centuries, when the sea
became increasingly tempestuous and the land was flooded more and more
often, the first dikes were built to protect smaller parcels of land from the
salt water. Slowly but steadily a continuous sea wall was formed along
the northern bank of the Maas, separating water and land. Part of this wall
was a dam in the river Rotte, which gives the city its name.

In the sixteenth and seventeenth centuries, thanks to its strategic position
near the mouths of the Rhine and Maas, Rotterdam grew into one of the
most important mercantile cities in the Netherlands (and even in Europe),
with shipping, trade and industry. The number of inhabitants in Rotterdam doubled during this period. The city built prestigious buildings such
as the Koopmansbeurs (Merchant's Exchange), the Korenbeurs (Grain
Bourse) and the City Hall. The area outside the dikes became the bustling
trade center of this mercantile city. In 1615, when the city had some 17,000
inhabitants, a linden-lined promenade was created along the river:
the Boompjes. This promenade completed the new 'waterstad': a lively
area full of harbor and trade activities.

At the end of the 19th century, a second stage of growth was completed.
Influenced by the industrial revolution and a general depression in the
countryside, an enormous migration from the country to the city took
place. Between 1850 and 1900 the city grew from 90,000 to 318,000 inhabitants! At the same time, the strong growth in world trade provided for
an increase in the number of ships. Coal and steel, but also coffee, tea and
tobacco accumulated, awaiting transport onward to the German hinterland. The railway was also established, creating direct connections with
Amsterdam and Antwerp. Considerable expansions were made to the

docks along the southern bank of the Maas and in the direction of Schiedam. New railroad and traffic bridges established the important connection between the residential right bank of the Maas and the left bank with its new docks. The strong increase in the number of inhabitants and economic activities led to plans for large-scale construction on the left bank – still an agricultural area with small villages at the time – of housing for the dockworkers, close to the docks and shipping wharfs. In the bowl-shaped polders behind the harbor basins, various working-class residential districts and garden cities developed, such as Feijenoord and the still much-loved Vreewijk.

A third development stage of the city consists of its emergence as a modern city. This stage still provides Rotterdam with its identity, but has been deployed since the thirties. The thirties saw the realization of the Blijdorp district, Feyenoord Stadium and the enormous Waalhaven. The sand from Waalhaven was used for the layout of the Kralingse Bos (a recreation area) in accordance with an employment-opportunity project. These were also the years that saw the conception of the ambitious plan for the Maas Tunnel: a long tunnel for car traffic between the north and south bank of the Maas using a revolutionary building technique. Earlier, work had already been started on a new city hall and a new post office along the Coolsingel. This *singel* (or watercourse) was to become a prestigious city boulevard, following the example set by Paris. The Merchant's Exchange and the new department stores were also situated along the Coolsingel. The Passage, between the Coolsingel, the Blaak and the Old Harbor, became an important shopping area. Since the conceptions about the modern city considered the old city center inappropriate to modern city living, plans were made for demolitions, infills and redevelopments.

The bombardment of Rotterdam by the Germans in May 1940, forcing the Netherlands to surrender, proved the most abrupt transition in the spatial development of the city. The massive bombardment, which lasted only a few minutes, caused the wholesale destruction of the city center. More than 80,000 people lost their homes. Thousands of stores, workshops, offices, schools, churches, restaurants and cafes were destroyed. The city had lost its heart. Months were needed to clear the debris and to tear down the remnants of broken buildings.

After the liberation of the city in 1945, the reconstruction of the harbor received first priority, due to its crucial role in the reconstruction of Europe. From 1949 onwards the reconstruction of the city was taken up with every endeavor. Although the bombardment temporarily dampened the spirits of the city in its process of renewal, modernization gained momentum after the war as a result of that bombardment. The reconstruction proceeded in accordance with the ideology of the decentralized city, with its American-style separation of functions. Following the American grid or matrix-model, large thoroughfares were constructed such as the Weena, the Blaak and the Maas Boulevard. At the edge of the city, conforming to the latest insights, were mono-functional city expansions and rustic-style garden cities. The national port became a world port and adapted to the demands of a world economy and the latest technological advances. This increase in scale shifted the harbor activities toward the west. In the city proper, one saw less and less of the hustle and bustle of harbor activities.

The seventies introduced yet another stage of the city's development: that of urban renewal. The nineteenth century neighborhoods, which at the time were constructed at an extremely rapid pace to help house the quickly increasing populace, showed a poor quality of construction. In the sixties, those involved with spatial planning presumed these neighborhoods to have fulfilled their life spans. Moreover, a number of thoroughfares were planned through these areas, which caused the leveling of some properties. The year 1970 however marked a complete reversal in attitude toward these neighborhoods. Toward the end of the sixties inhabitants of these districts had begun to protest heavily against the large-scale plans of the municipality and pleaded for a totally different approach focusing on the desires of the occupants. Due in part to the changing spirit of the times, their plea was quite successful.

Wielding the slogan 'Building for the Neighborhood' the city of Rotterdam began an extensive process of urban renewal, renewing or replacing older dwellings in consultation with the occupants. The physical renovation of the buildings was successful, but often little was left of the previous vitality and activity of these neighborhoods. Emphasis was also placed on cheap social housing, leaving both the housing supply and the social structure of the area one-sided.

In 1985 the urban development of Rotterdam changed direction once again. Under the motto 'The New Rotterdam', a period of construction started on metropolitan projects, where the scale of the city as a whole became important again. The final gaps in the heart of the city were requisitioned for prime-site urban projects and the river was rediscovered as a potential vehicle for urban development. Various urban projects along the river and in the city center were added to the agenda, with the wholesale urban development of the disused harbor area, Kop van Zuid, at the top of the list. The Rotterdammer has a right to be proud of the results: a new Museum Park with five new or renovated museums, among which OMA's Kunsthal and the NAi – Netherlands Architecture Institute; developments along the riverbanks, and the new Erasmus Bridge. Exemplary was the renovation of the former office of the Holland America Line on the Wilhelmina Pier. For many decades this pier was an important point of departure for many cruise ships between Europe and America: a place where tens of thousands of Dutch and other European migrants set off to begin a new life in 'the New World'. As part of the total development of the pier, this monumental terminal has been renovated as a grand hotel-café-restaurant, bringing in thousands of visitors. In the city center, a number of projects and squares were also redeveloped to give the city greater distinction.

Now, at the end of the nineties, Rotterdam has become the kind of city appropriate to its position as a world port. The relationship between the city and the river has been reinstated to its former glory. Along the city's riverbanks an impressive number of new districts and urban projects have either been completed or are being developed at present.

The development of the Randstad and the south wing Aside from the city's development in Rotterdam there was also a strong dynamic occurring on a larger scale. Rotterdam is part of a densely populated agglomeration built around the four largest cities of the Netherlands: Rotterdam, Amsterdam, The Hague and Utrecht. The story has it that KLM president Plesman could see a 'ring of cities' from the sky as far back as the thirties: he called this the 'Randstad'. Since this observation, the four large cities and their environment have increasingly begun to show the characteristics of a single city: a spatially and functionally coherent complex, positioned around a green central area, the 'Green Heart', cherished by both planners and politicians. The concept of a single metropolis that could measure up to other European centers thus became more realistic. The Dutch currently tend to consider the Randstad as an area with its own metropolitan identity, differing from the rest of the Netherlands. The Randstad not only has some six million inhabitants, but also has a large international airport and a world-class port.

Topographical maps show how the cities of the Randstad have grown towards each other. The urban projects currently approved and being implemented and the creation of new infrastructure will further strengthen the development of a single metropolis. An important project in this context is the construction of a high-speed rail system between Amsterdam and Rotterdam. Though the travel time by rail is currently over an hour, in a few years it should take no more than 30 minutes to travel between the centers of the two cities. The Amsterdam international airport, Schiphol, will then be a mere 20 minutes from Rotterdam!

In February 1998 the officials of the spatial planning departments of the four major cities issued a joint statement with the title 'Deltametropool' (Delta metropolis). In this statement they declare that the western area of the Netherlands should become a single urban network of international stature that can compete in an increasingly strong European market. Meanwhile ten smaller Dutch cities in the Randstad have joined this initiative.

In the Randstad, two distinct subdivisions can be perceived: the North Wing and the South Wing. The South Wing comprises, besides the Rotterdam agglomeration, Leiden, The Hague, Delft, Zoetermeer, Gouda and the Drecht cities, and has some three million inhabitants. By now, the South Wing has become a single urban entity with numerous core areas and nodes.

The economic circulation and exchange of people and products within this South Wing is increasing. Various facilities (theaters, museums, hospitals, schools) no longer obtain their clientele only from within their own city, but also from within a large area of the South Wing. It has become increasingly difficult to distinguish which of the large new housing sites between Rotterdam, The Hague, Delft and Zoetermeer belong to which of the existing cities. The same holds true for the new Rotterdam district of Nesselande, which is closer to the center of Gouda than to the center of Rotterdam. The strong intertwining of the city with the greater urban networks of the Randstad and the South Wing necessarily leads to new projects and intentions more appropriate to this position.

Rotterdam: some important trends and figures What are the special characteristics of Rotterdam, opportunities that the city can utilize toward its spatial development? And what are the threats and weaknesses the city must beware of?

The figures on population growth show a positive trend. The city's population is growing and, even more importantly, the city is rejuvenating. According to forecasts, the border mark of 600,000 occupants will be crossed again soon. In the rest of the urban region the population is also growing. While the population of the regional municipalities is on average growing older, the center of the city is becoming younger. This labor potential offers important opportunities for the future economic development of the city. It will, however, become even more important for Rotterdam to retain the younger, affluent, two or more person households in its city populace. Many of these people currently leave the city proper when they move into larger or more expensive dwellings, simply due to a lack of appropriate housing.[2] Most take up residence in the suburbs of Rotterdam. Newcomers are predominantly young households consisting of one or two people who settle (temporarily) in Rotterdam either for schooling or as a newcomer to the labor force. The influx from other countries consists mainly of refugees and immigrants joining their families. Consequentially, the Rotterdam populace is becoming more colorful but not more prosperous.

As far as the housing supply and different residential environments are concerned, Rotterdam occupies a relatively weak position. The housing supply generally lacks variety, with a surplus of cheap dwellings, rental units and multiple-family dwellings. There is a meager supply of top-end dwellings. There are precious few villa districts and even the possibilities for chic urban dwellings are limited. These conditions make it more difficult to cater to the wishes of those in the middle and upper-middle income brackets. Since they can find something suitable in the surrounding vicinity, many of them leave the city. A more comprehensive supply of up-market yet urban living environments could alleviate this problem.

Although Rotterdam, like the rest of the Netherlands, is profiting from the current economic growth, the unemployment rate is still particularly high compared to the national

2 **Komen en gaan. Een onderzoek naar sociaal-economische kenmerken en verhuis-motieven van vestigers en vertrekkers** (Comings and goings. An investigation of the socio-economic traits and motives for moving of new residents and ex-residents), Centrum voor Onderzoek en Statistiek (COS), October 1997.

average. In 1998 Rotterdam had 25,000 unemployed, which amounted to 10.2 % of the labor pool. Continued economic growth will therefore be necessary in the coming years.

An important quality of the Rotterdam economy is the presence of its international port. Although the port still offers a fair share of the economic activity in the Rotterdam area, related employment opportunities have been steadily decreasing for years. The positive growth in employment rate is to be found in the city regions, which include the dry business districts. Sectors such as the service industries, telecommunications, the audiovisual sector, personal services, recycling, graphic industries and the media have particularly contributed to the positive growth in employment rates and appear favorable for further development. Businesses currently tend to leave the major cities because of the lack of space and the congestion, among other reasons; most of those leaving are companies requiring a lot of space. In the past, industrial companies accounted for most of the departures, but now the sectors of transport and distribution, wholesalers and even business services are following suit.

Recreation opportunities, greenery and surface water Recreation spaces and parks are seen as an increasingly important part of a vital city. Not only to offer local residents sufficient space to play, stroll and generally relax, but also to attract new businesses and affluent inhabitants. To this end, both the greenery in the immediate residential environment and that in the direct vicinity of the city are important. People do not always leave the city for open-air recreation; facilities within the neighborhood such as parks, playgrounds and gardens or other urban greenery, are used intensively, especially by the young and by immigrants, both of which groups are heavily represented in the Rotterdam population. Rotterdam has to contend with a 'qualitative' problem with greenery. There is an acceptable quantity of green, but it is often poorly accessible, offers little choice in usage and is hardly accommodating. Links in the network of recreational routes between residential and business districts and squares, parks and the clusters of facilities are also missing. The improvement of the existing green areas is a crucial task in the future spatial development of Rotterdam.

Another area that needs improvement is the management of the rivers, harbors, canals, ponds and lakes in Rotterdam. Located some meters under sea level and containing the lowest point in the Netherlands, Rotterdam has long had an extensive system of dikes, locks and pumping stations to sluice away rainwater and to brave threats from the sea and the rivers. Even so, the water in Rotterdam is not managed in a sustainable manner. Some areas regularly suffer shortages of water, while other places in the city are sometimes flooded. This imbalance occurs for several reasons: In some parts of the city there are not enough *singels*, ponds and lakes to retain the extra water after a heavy rainfall or to hydrate the area during dry spells. Also, the system of ditches and *singels* that pump the water through is not always optimal.

The environment and its eco-system has become an important theme in the spatial structuring of the Netherlands. In Rotterdam the profuse traffic, which is in part attributable to the harbor, causes most of the environmental and health problems. By clustering through-traffic along a few main routes wherever possible, the trouble should be minimized. The main thoroughfares, however, which sometimes cut through densely populated areas, continue to cause environmental and health problems that are difficult to solve, especially regarding the noise pollution and exhaust fumes. In the future solutions must be found for these main thoroughfares through urban areas, for example by moving them below ground level or fully underground.

Three ambitions on three scales

What are the main guidelines for the spatial policy set out by the city of Rotterdam? In any case, the Spatial Plan Rotterdam 2010 (RPR 2010) will need to adapt to the trends and spatial developments as described above. By now it should be clear that this is a multi-faceted project, covering various scales as well as various areas of policy. In contrast to earlier phases, when the emphasis continually shifted to something new, the city must now play its spatial development game simultaneously on different chessboards. Not only is there a daunting task in the renovation of neighborhoods and districts, at the same time the scale of the city, as a whole, requires interventions. Not only the port but the city too needs to be renovated and expanded. As stated above, the greenery inside as well as outside the city requires attention.

Many issues are situated on a higher level than that of the city itself. In other words,

Rotterdam cannot decide everything alone; sometimes the city has hardly any control over what crosses its path. At the same time, these external influences are important motives for its spatial development. If the city does not take these factors into account, it will risk losing major investments. To be able to focus on the issues for Rotterdam in 2010 demands a common long-term policy. Thus the RPR 2010 offers three ambitions as a guideline. Rotterdam harbors these intentions on three different scales.

The three scales are:

- Rotterdam as an independent city
- Rotterdam as part of the South Wing of the Randstad
- Rotterdam as part of the Randstad on the map of international European cities

The first ambition: Rotterdam as a diverse and attractive city This ambition focuses on the livability of the city. This comprises not only the dwelling environment, but also the possibilities for work and recreation. Although this applies to everyone in Rotterdam, special attention will be given to realizing this intention for people with middle-class and upper-middle-class incomes, visitors, employers and employees.

This aspiration should take shape in the existing areas of the city, the districts and neighborhoods. This revolves around more than decent housing. Equally important, if not more so, are decent living environments, pleasant public spaces, good connections in terms of bicycles and public transport, ample greenery and sufficient connections beyond the city. This implies an improvement and diversification of the surroundings within which one lives, works and finds recreation. If districts and city regions have different qualities, then those differences should be emphasized. A city also becomes attractive through the conveniences it offers, such as various shops, museums, nightlife and educational and care facilities. Attractive corporate environments should also be offered – not only in the center and in industrial or corporate zones, but also within the neighborhoods. This aspiration goes hand in hand with an improvement in livability and consideration for the environment. Among other things, this implies lightening the burdens arising from motorized traffic and encouraging the use of bicycles, both for commuting and for recreation.

The second ambition: Rotterdam as center of the South Wing The position of Rotterdam in the South Wing of the Randstad should be reinforced. This requires improvement of the connecting network and a broad scope of facilities, workspaces, recreational opportunities and exceptional residential environments.

Crucial to this intention is the accessibility from Rotterdam of the most important centers and facilities in the South Wing and a sufficient accessibility of Rotterdam from the vicinity. This especially applies to public transportation and commuter traffic. Prerequisite is an extensive and properly functioning traffic and transportation network, in which Rotterdam Central Station occupies a crucial position. Park and ride facilities (transferia) should also be created. The 'green' and 'blue' networks are of great significance for the South Wing. The most important ones are the so-called 'major landscape elements' such as the Dutch Coast and the Rhine-Schelde Delta. These elements must be emphasized. The major green areas that are of importance to the rest of the South Wing should also be developed further.

Rotterdam has a large number of facilities serving the whole of the South Wing, such as the academic hospital, the Erasmus University and a number of higher vocational schools, a much frequented zoo, the most important shopping area of the South Wing in the heart of the city, three soccer stadiums and an enormous sports and events complex. This collection of facilities should be reinforced and expanded. Because the city center is easily accessible and still has sufficient space – and because a concentration of facilities ensures a valuable spin-off – the center is the most preferable site for any new facilities.

This does not preclude new facilities outside of the city center. Easily accessible places on major crossings of traffic and railway infrastructure, such as the environment of Alexander and Lombardijen stations, are especially appropriate locations. These nodes have good connections to the rest of the South Wing and the Randstad. Furthermore, they are excellent sites for a transferium (a transfer hub from car to public transport). One of the methods to limit the increase in motorized traffic is to increase the density of urban functions (offices, shops, facilities, dwellings) around comparable nodes of public transportation and highways. Beyond this, exceptional residential environments are still a possibility in Rotterdam. Opportunities for living environments that are scarce in the vicinity are to be found along the Maas river, at the coast (Hoek van Holland), in the Green Heart (Rotterdam-Northeast) and in the city center.

The third ambition: Rotterdam as European city with a world-class port
The Rotterdam port needs to retain its position at the top. Furthermore, the identity of the harbor can help strengthen the service economy and tourism. The landscape around Rotterdam, with its unique ecological and cultural value, forms interesting surroundings for both dwelling and recreation. Within Europe, Rotterdam must present itself, together with the other cities of the Randstad, as part of the 'Deltametropool', alluding to the development of the Randstad as a metropolitan environment. This aspiration implies that Rotterdam wants to develop as a 'European city', from world-class port to world-class city. The festivals, museums, architecture and sports accommodations offer the cultural climate necessary to such an international city. Another essential ingredient is the position of Rotterdam in the international traffic network, with Central Station as the stopping place for the high-speed rail line to London, Brussels and Paris.

Not enough use is made of the port in the economic development of the city. It could give a boost to tourism, which would result in an expansion of the urban economy. Moreover, Rotterdam is not only the 'port to Europe' for sea containers and bulk transport, but also a center of knowledge and experience related to the harbor. In other words, the port is also an important foundation for Rotterdam as a service economy.

Finally, the surrounding landscape should be used toward the realization of this third aspiration. The river delta has a unique ecological and cultural quality in Europe, with the characteristic Dutch peat-bog landscapes of Alblasserwaard and Krimpenerwaard (with the row of windmills on the Kinderdijk as a UNESCO monument on the World Heritage list) and the natural development in and beyond the delta. These qualities offer many more possibilities for further development, in terms of both ecology and tourism.

The New Maas River has been a determining factor in the development of Rotterdam. Even now the river is the most important spatial element that distinguishes Rotterdam from other cities. Still, the leading role the river plays in the city is no longer visible in many areas. The lively harbor activities are barely noticeable in the city center. Also, traffic has seriously damaged the situation along the river, such as the former promenade along the Boompjes.

The New Maas will play a prominent part in the realization of the three intentions of the RPR 2010. In the RPR 2010 great value is attributed to the river towards the spatial, economic and recreational development of the city. Vacated harbor and industrial areas offer plenty of space for future developments in terms of dwelling, working, tourism and recreation. A pleasant environment with attractive pedestrian routes along the river will play an important role here.

The integral spatial structuring policy

The elaboration of the three ambitions has resulted in a 'spatial structuring concept', among other things. This structuring concept shows how the space of the city should be used in 2010. It determines which functions should be located where in the city. Since the RPR 2010 is a plan for an existing urban area, the structuring concept shows how existing areas (parks, residential, traffic, industrial) should develop and improve. Most of the city areas will retain their current primary function (dwelling, working, parks, traffic). Emphasis will be placed on developing and improving these existing functions. In this process of development and improvement, 'differentiation' and 'quality' are key notions. Also, beneficial combinations of the different functions have been sought, so that businesses and parks, residential and recreational areas reinforce each other wherever possible.

The Rotterdam structuring concept contains many more legend-units than is common to a 'standard plan'. For example, there are four different types of legend-units for green areas. For residential areas, there are even six units. In this way, the desired differentiation is emphasized and elaborated upon.

The legend-units of the integral spatial structuring concept are divided into three categories: environments, networks and nodes. For each category there are one or more projects. These are shown in the following diagram:

Category	Project
environments (city districts, parks, industrial areas, etc.)	■ more hybrid forms of dwelling, working and recreation ■ differentiate, distinguish ■ increase quality
networks (infrastructure, water and green)	■ intertwining ■ reduce barriers
nodes (of infrastructure)	■ increase density with intensified dwelling, work and recreational functions ■ quality of public space ■ identity or theme

The category 'environments' indicates distinct regions in the city, such as residential, green and industrial areas. The RPR 2010 seeks to introduce more mixed forms of living, working and playing in these areas. Also, the differences should become sharper and clearer. We can thus prevent Rotterdam from becoming too uniform, and the city will become attractive to many different people.

The connections to and within Rotterdam are part of the category 'networks'. The most important ones are the main traffic arteries, the railway lines and other rail connections, such as trams and subways. But the recreational network (for bicycling and water sports) is also a part of it. These networks need to be more attuned to each other. For example, there will be more opportunities to transfer from one mode of transportation to another. Another important issue is the problem that railway lines and highways often still create barriers between city neighborhoods. 'Nodes' are to be found in places that are most easily reached with different modes of transportation. The most important node is Central Station. Outside the city center, nodes are located near train and subway stations near a highway exit. Because they are so accessible, they offer ideal high-density areas for dwellings, offices and other facilities.

Projects: integral approach

The RPR 2010 concludes with a chapter in which the many desires are positioned in a concrete plan of action. It is clear from the outset that not everything can happen everywhere at the same time. A number of 'strategic urban areas' are distinguished in the plan. These areas are particularly appropriate to the aspirations and the program of the RPR 2010. For example because they will allow successful combinations of dwelling, working and recreation. These are regions where the municipality will put in extra effort. Also, these areas are seen to have a high potential for successful private investments. In the strategic areas, all three ambition-levels of the RPR 2010 can and should be fulfilled. To this end the plan proposes some crucial projects, called 'extra impulses'.

Center on two banks An important strategic area is the 'center on two banks'. There are many opportunities to make the center on both banks of the Maas River even more lively and attractive. There is still available space for more housing, shops, facilities, tourist attractions, offices and businesses. The most important assets are Central Station, the 'Cultural Axis' and the river.

The Central Station is already an important junction for local, regional, national and international transportation. In a few years it will also become a full-fledged station for the high-speed rail, with high-speed connections to Brussels, London, Paris and Amsterdam. Above and below the tracks there is enough space for a new station, offices, dwellings and facilities. The Central Station area is one of the 'extra impulses' of the RPR 2010.

The second extra impulse in the center is called 'The River Central'. The New Maas should become the Rotterdam logo. There are still numerous possibilities for connecting the city's activities with the waterfront. Facilities for tourism and recreation in particular should find a site along the river. The Boompjes should develop into a boulevard, allowing people to stroll along the river.

The third and final 'extra impulse' in the center is the Cultural Axis. This is the zone between Central Station and Veerhaven, where most of the cultural institutions are to be found. The extra impulse is geared towards more investments in the organization of this area, improving the green areas and the connecting pedestrian routes.

Time and money – translating ambitions into concrete projects After a great number of desires and their corresponding projects have been contributed by the various sectors, some coordination is needed on the use of space and the list of priorities. For one, an even distribution of these projects over time is a prerequisite for a balanced development of the city. For example, not all the residential areas should be completed at the same time.

By distributing them over time, undesirable peaks in the housing supply are prevented and there is less danger of the dwellings remaining unoccupied and of excessively low market prices. The same goes for office sites.

In determining priorities, financing is also important. In this case, private or semi-private parties will expressly be invited to invest alongside different local governmental institutions, and thus fulfill the ambitions of the local authorities together with the city of Rotterdam.

Decision With the RPR 2010, the municipality of Rotterdam hopes to have an important instrument with which to approach the development of the city in a well-founded and gradual manner. The coming years will prove whether the RPR 2010 is indeed a tool with which the many ambitions and plans of the city can be properly channeled and intelligently attuned. No effort has been spared to offer the best possible conditions for the plan to fulfill its task. The level of involvement with the plan of the authorities and various civil services has only increased further.

Under these circumstances, it can be shown that official structural plans can be handled another way. The conditions are present for creating, instead of a thick and impenetrable document, a structural plan in true Rotterdam fashion. A plan that recruits both investors and entrepreneurs; a plan characterized by flexibility, ambition and daring, and of course, by action.

1 a-f Rotterdam's phases
of development.

[1a]

[1b]

[1c]

[1d]

[1e]

[1f]

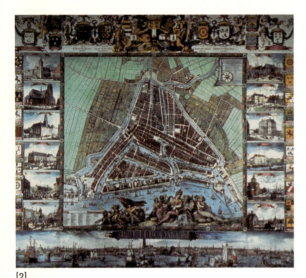

[2]

[4]

[3]

▲[6]
◄[5]

[7]

2 Rotterdam in the 17th century: The city is clearly oriented towards the water, as exemplified by the riverbank promenade the 'Boompjes'.

3 Garden community, Vreewijk.

4 The Maas Tunnel was constructed circa 1940, utilizing, at that time, a very modern connection with a revolutionary construction method. The image shows the entrance for pedestrians and bicycles, the vertical element in the background is the ventilation shaft.

5 Already in the thirties the Coolsingel was intended as a prestigious boulevard, at a scale not unlike those found in Paris.

6 With massive aerial bombardments of Rotterdam in May of 1940, the Germans forced the Dutch surrender. The inner city was all but leveled, its character destroyed completely.

7 'Actions speak louder than words' as the famous slogan goes: Rotterdam is continuously in the process of building.

[8]

[9]

[10]

[11]

▲[14]
◄[13]

8 Post-war reconstruction of the inner city took place in the fifties and sixties according to the latest ideas of modern city planning.
9 From the 70s forward the slogan was 'building for the neighborhood' while the play of forces between citizens and local authorities resulted in drastic reconstruction of the traditional living quarters.

totale bevolking	1999	2014

700,000

600,000

500,000

400,000

300,000

200,000

100,000

0

0 t/m 24 jaar	1999	2014

200,000

180,000

160,000

140,000

120,000

100,000

80,000

60,000

65 jaar en ouder	1999	2014

200,000

180,000

160,000

140,000

120,000

100,000

80,000

60,000

The population of Rotterdam is expanding and according to projections the average age per capita of its inhabitants is decreasing.

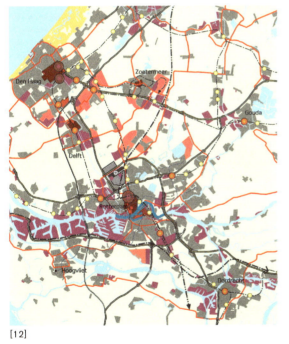

[12]

10 From 1985 onwards there was much attention paid again to the city center and the river. One of the effects was the reconstruction and adaptation of the old terminal and offices of the Holland America Line into a grand hotel and café-restaurant.
11 The four big cities in the Netherlands (Amsterdam, The Hague, Rotterdam & Utrecht) together form what was named the 'Randstad': a coherent complex of cities enclosing a 'green heart' with a world-class port and a major international airport.
12 Rotterdam is the center of the South Wing of the Randstad.

13 Some of the greenery and pubic space in Rotterdam is not very attractive or vital, remaining in need of drastic improvement.
14 The first ambition is to improve the vitality, the 'livability' of the city. Attractive living domains with a pleasant public space are one of the first objectives.

[15]

[16]

[17]

[18]

[19]　　　　　　　[20]

Enviroments

██	City centre
██	Edge of the centre districts
██	Pre war residential areas
░░	Shopping streets
░░	Garden city
	Suburb
░░	Village / garden village
░░	Villa-park
██	Parks and gardens
░░	Woods and lakes
	Landscape
██	Concentration of sports facilities
░░	Industrial and businessparks

Networks

——	main roads
‑‑‑	High speed rail
——	Main railway lines (national)
-----	Underground line / lightrail
░░	Water

Hubs

—○—	Highway exits
■■	HST station (high speed train)
—●—	NS station (national rail)
--●--	Underground / lightrail station
██	Mixed offices and amentities centres
----	Municipal bounder
——	Plan bounder
★ ⤹	Option
⬚	Urban area outside municipal boundary

[21]

15 View of the strategic center on the banks of the Nieuwe Maas.

16 The Nieuwe Maas has ample opportunity for further development as a tourist center.

17 Model of the center.

18 Rotterdam seeks to keep its position as center of the Randstad's South Wing. The inner city has amble opportunity for developing urban facilities as the reconstructed 'Schouwburgplein' with theater, cinema and concert hall illustrates.

19 The windmills in the landscape of Kinderdijk are considered a cultural monument that enhances Rotterdam's position.

20 In the Spatial Plan Rotterdam 2010 (RPR 2010), the Nieuwe Maas plays a central role. Along the urban banks of the river, a large quantity of housing and civic projects are either already realized or under development.

21 RPR 2010: Integral Urban Plan.

Project: PORT CITY, 1999

Winy Maas, MVRDV

Megacity Holland   In the Johan de Witt lecture on 5 November last year, Mr A.W.H. Docters van Leeuwen made the following noteworthy statements: '... The Netherlands is a Megacity. We should therefore also plan the Netherlands as a Megacity. A well-ordered city, in which not necessarily everything is prohibited, but where, per region, the landscape takes central place ... A free city focused on trade, intelligence, industry and nature, with a huge well-ordered dynamism. If Hong Kong and Singapore can achieve this under much more difficult circumstances, why can't we?'

He went on to point out the management implications that are at stake: 'In my opinion there is room for no more than two levels of administration. You would even have to dare to take on suggested experiments with only one administrative level ... We need a strong megacity administration, where we have to decide, amongst other things, about nature and infrastructure. And therefore not 600 (number of municipalities) × 12 (number of provinces) × 14 (number of departments): That amounts to at least 98,800 smaller decisions, where it could also have been one big one...

'Everyone does his best, but on striking points such as safety, nature, infrastructure and area planning the Netherlands evaporates because there are too many decision-makers...

'What would it be like to live in a megacity, where the Asian dynamism buzzes around your ears, but where the deep peace from authentic landscapes is also to be found? Would it not be sensible to develop a framework in which pluralism can develop as a positive force? ...'

Can Rotterdam become a port city again?   Recent developments have led to an almost strict division between harbor activities and the remaining urban developments of Rotterdam.

On the eve of new large-scale investments in the ports, it seems fitting to question the possibility of using these investments in such a way that port and city can be combined so that a genuine mixed port city is achieved, one that connects the city with the North Sea: Rotterdam on Sea. By applying new navigational routes to the northern and southern areas of the 'Nieuwe Waterweg' the existing harbor domain can be extended. The length of embankment is significantly increased, thereby providing an address for port, urban and ecological functions along the large channels, with their maritime assets: the spatial quality of Rotterdam pur sang!

By connecting to existing navigational channels and sparing such areas as the dunes of

Voorne Putten an archipelago emerges in which the various islands can be alternatively used for port, urban and park functions. The channels serve as ecological dividers of the different functions.

Through a trade-off of less capital-intensive areas such as bulk storage with newly required residential areas, the possibility of a mix within the existing port can also be achieved.

The series of water pathways causes ecological and recreational domains from Delfland to Haringvliet allowing for an imaginable multi-usage of the port. Surrounding the main navigational channel, a chain of smaller inland shipping routes and aquatic recreation domains can be found. A Dutch Sydney or Stockholm then comes into existence. By reusing and depositing the excavated sand during the formation of the islands, hills resembling Loreleis can appear in the archipelago, in turn forming spectacular places of settlement. By 'creeking' specific islands, Miami-like residential districts are born.

The archipelago forms a fully fledged 'cushioned' alternative to the contemporary 'hard' coastal defense, and in which some parts – for instance Hoekse Waard – can be used as retention or spill-over areas, keeping Rotterdam as a relatively 'shallow' city and where wide open spaces can be found at relatively short intervals.

The ambition of realizing a mixed port city can be combined with an increase in population: There is room for 3 to 4 million residents. This relieves the green areas of the Netherlands and delivers a remarkable urban area: Port City.

PORT CITY, 1999
Concept for a mixed-use port city, in the framework of the research project
Denkrichtingen Bestaand Rotterdams Gebied

Client:
Samenwerkingsverband Bestaand Rotterdams Gebied (SBRG)
Rijks Planologische Dienst (RPD)
Project team:
Samenwerkingsverband Bestaand Rotterdams Gebied Irene Houtsma
PHAROS (port & hinterland advice, research, organization services) Jan Willem Koeman
Rijks Planologische Dienst (RPD) Willem de Visser
MVRDV [Winy Maas, Jacob van Rijs, Nathalie de Vries] with Ronald Wall, Arjan Harbers and Bas van Neijenhof
H+N+S Lodewijk van Nieuwenhuijze
Design:
MVRDV [Winy Maas, Jacob van Rijs, Nathalie de Vries] with Ronald Wall, Arjan Harbers and Bas van Neijenhof

[1]

[2]

Port City

[3]

[4]

[5]

T = 0

STAD
HAVEN
NATUUR

[6]

T = 1

[7]

T = 2

STAD
HAVEN
NATUUR

[8]

T = 3

STAD
HAVEN
NATUUR

Port-city 2050

Lorelei II.
Reservering Maasvlakte II
Golden Gate
Hoek van Holland
Dam-city
Droge bulk
Fruit-port
Chemiestad
Maasvlakte I
Euro-Miami
Maassluis
Vlaardingen
Oud-Rotterdam
Oostvoomse duin
Oostvoome
Den Briel
Groot Rozenburg
Schiedam
Zeevrachtoverslag
Lorelei I
Pernis
Waalhavenzwin
Chemiestad
Ahoy a.d. Maas
Containerstad
Hoogvliet
Hellevoetsluis
Biesbosch
Groot-Spijkenisse
Chemiestad
Zuidland
Supergriend

[9]

1	New Maassluis	4	Rotterdam centre	7	Phase 2: new islands
2	Rotterdam on Sea	5	Existing situation	8	Phase 3: further connections
3	Den Brielle-sur-lac	6	Phase 1: second river	9	Waalhaven swamp

Future Developments of Seaports. Lessons for Rotterdam?

Paul Drewe & Ben Janssen

1 To set the stage   Recently, the Dutch government has decided to build a new rail connection for the transport of goods, the Betuwe line. This is to link Rotterdam, Europe's premier seaport, to its German hinterland. A critical evaluation of the planning and decision making process (Drewe and Janssen, 1996) has revealed a major flaw of a strategic nature. Why there is a need for the Betuwe line has not been sufficiently explained. Referring to the seaport of Rotterdam as needing the new rail connection to secure its position as 'mainport' evidently has tended to clinch any fundamental debate. *Mainport* has been used as a slogan. The danger with slogans is that they keep us from penetrating to the heart and essence of the problem. Of course, expertise has been provided, even a large amount of it. It boils down to assuming that the predicted growth of containers, cargo and bulk – to be transported along the East-West axis – meets with infrastructure bottlenecks and therefore asks for additional capacity. This turns out to be rail capacity, in order to strengthen the multimodality of the port (also anticipating the possible political pressure for rail transport of goods). The future mainport function of Rotterdam seems to imply continued growth of flows of goods along the axis at a rate of 93% over a period of 25 years (Table 1: Commissie Betuweroute, 1995). Not all the goods transported along the East-West axis originate from or arrive in the port of Rotterdam although the position of this seaport is a dominant one. The table also shows that container flows are expected to be the fastest growing category of goods. Bulk will 'only' grow by 57% until 2015 according to the experts, but will still remain the 'bulk' of the goods transported.

Without transport growth, no mainport, as a closer look at a scenario reveals; the Port Authorities are mainly focusing on containers. This is not only expected to be the fastest growing category of goods, Rotterdam is also Europe's number one container port, compared with Hamburg, Antwerp, Bremen and Le Havre (some 45 million tons of containers in 1993). It is the fourth largest container handling port in the world, too, scored over only by Hong Kong, Singapore and Kaohsiung. According to the Rotterdam Port Authorities, the number of containers is expected to grow by 232% between 1989 and 2010 (Gemeente Rotterdam, 1990). The modal split shows that the roads to and from the seaport have to cope with a growth of 182%.

So there are shifts ahead both with regard to the mix of goods to be handled and transported and the modal split. However, the underlying model of extrapolated growth

Table 1 Total flows of goods along East-West axis by category (in millions of tons)

	1990	2015	% Change
Containers	10	32	+220
Cargo	66	177	+168
Bulk	174	274	+57
Total	250	483	+93

remains unaltered. The answer to the question 'What future for the port?'
is further growth, measured in terms of tonnage. To simplify a problem in
this manner, might lead to a wrong solution, as the mainport slogan might
distract from the alternative question of 'What port for the future?' Is it
not heroic to assume that the world will not undergo substantial changes
up to the year 2015, to assume that we are not living in an uncertain world?
What about new ways of coping with supply and distribution of raw
materials and goods, called product channel logistics? And doesn't the port
for the future therefore appear as a node of logistic networks? The interest
in these developments is not purely academic, but rather dictated by both
socio-economic and environmental reasons.

1/1 The socio-economic perspective
The origin of
the growth model, referred to above, can be traced to the late 1960s when a
plan had been set up for the Greater Rotterdam area aiming at maximizing
the volume of tons shipped. Some critics at the time pointed out that the
authors of the plan had glossed over the production of value added in the
area requiring a different use of land. Amazingly, it took decision makers
in Rotterdam more than 20 years to recognize this fallacy. The development
plan for the port of Rotterdam in the year 2010 stresses the urgency of creating more space in the port area for activities that generate value added.
But critics have pointed out that there may not be enough space left for
locating these activities, which moreover tend to further increase the existing congestion (Van Klink, 1993). Anyway, the Greater Rotterdam economy
needs a new impulse. Its overall vitality in the years 1986-93 was relatively
low, with vitality being measured in terms of turnover, investment and net
profit (Louter and De Ruyter, 1995). Incidentally, the province of South
Holland, to which Greater Rotterdam belongs, has a Gross Domestic
Product per capita just above the average of the European Union: 106.3%
in the period 1989-91 as against 109.3% in the years 1986-88. The GDP per
person employed has dropped from 126.2% in the period 1986-88 to 105.7%
in the more recent period (European Commission, 1994a; Commissie van
de Europese Gemeenschappen, 1991).

1/2 **The environmental perspective** The second reason for dealing with an alternative future for the port of Rotterdam is an environmental one.

The area is already highly congested which causes delays in the journey-to-work as well as in the transport of goods. In order to transport 800 TUEs, about 580 (automatic guided) vehicles are needed with a total length of 6.8 kilometers.

Can the Greater Rotterdam area really handle an increase in the road transport of containers of 182% between 1989 and 2010?

'Traffic jams are not only exasperating, they also cost Europe dear in terms of productivity' – this according to the White Paper of the European Commission. Indeed, in 1994 the economic damage caused by congestion in the Netherlands has been estimated at 1.4 billion guilders. But will investment in transport infrastructure automatically bring relief (even when combined with improving alternatives for cars and a better utilization of the existing infrastructure by traffic management)? Does the Netherlands need a Betuwe line? In the final analysis, the success of the line largely depends on limitations to be imposed on road transport, which in turn, depend on measures to be put into effect at a European level. Without these limitations, however, i.e. with an unchanged policy in the Netherlands, emissions (NO_x, CO_2, VOS, SO_2), and energy consumption will augment markedly.

To pollution one has to add, among others, various hazards linked to the transport of dangerous goods as well as industrial hazards in the port area which has a high concentration of petrochemical complexes. Even without a nuclear power plant (as in the Antwerp port region), the Greater Rotterdam area, densely populated with some 1000 inhabitants per km², qualifies as a potential environmental disaster area. The environmental problems tend to grow worse under a continued growth regime. This is not only detrimental to the quality of life in the area, but may also thwart attempts to create a new impulse for the Greater Rotterdam economy. Note that the European Commission has warned against 'the rising costs of congestion in the central areas of the Community' – delays, pollution, etc. are '... likely to act as an increasingly powerful deterrent to new investment in these areas' (Commission of the European Communities, 1991).

To set the scene, we so far have used Europe's premier seaport as an example. The question 'What port for the future?', also applies as a matter of course to other ports, both in and outside Europe, though the ports of the Hamburg-Le Havre range are our primary concern.

In section 2, product channel logistics will be explained in a nutshell. With the rise of this kind of logistics, the positioning of ports is about to change. Section 3 deals with the transition from a competitive world of ports to a strategic cooperation of ports. If this is to be more than just a wild-goose chase, one has to search for complementarities. The future of ports, however, is embedded in an uncertain world. Hence, the necessity of managing uncertainties. 'The art of the long view' will be broached in the final section.

2 Product channel logistics and port development

We witness today some important, interdependent, trends in freight transport (Ruijgrok et al., 1991):

- globalization: the market produced for and transported to is getting more and more diversified, covering a growing geographic scale (alongside a globally networked production);
- the rise of buyers' markets: the development of a less-standardized production entails smaller, varied product series and hence smaller batches in transportation (economies of scope tend to become as important as economies of scale);
- flexibility: the flexibility of production and labor processes is increased in order to cope better and faster with market changes;
- dematerialization: less traditional bulk goods and more lighter and smaller products (with a high value density) requiring flexible and varied means of transport;
- integration: transport is increasingly integrated with production chains and networks;
- computerization: the rise of far-reaching management and control of production and transport flows, using computer techniques and information engineering.

2/1 Product channel logistics in a nutshell

Logistics is basically concerned with the movement and storage of goods in the supply chains to customers. In the past decade we have been witnessing a transformation in the ways the movement and storage have been managed by companies. In the 1970s, companies began to implement the concept of 'integrated distribution' which brought together transport, warehousing and inventory management. As the benefits became evident, this approach was extended to become 'channel integration' in which there was coordination of the management of materials and finished goods, from the sourcing of raw materials through to the point of final consumption of finished products: integrated supply chain management or product channel logistics (NEA and Cranfield, 1994).

Product channel logistics provides a means to cope with the trends referred to above by evaluating cross-functional trade-offs to maximize overall (chain) profitability, rather than managing supply, production or distribution activities individually (Anderson, 1989). Product channel logistics differ from traditional approaches to logistics. There is a shift from managing assets (such as warehouses, trucks, inventories) towards managing processes (product systems, transport systems, product flows and information flows). This requires a new way of handling linkages between a firm and its suppliers and distribution channels by new intra-company and, above all, inter-company transport and information systems.

Inbound and outbound traffic is no longer 'just transportation', based on minimum cost or similar 'hard' criteria. Shippers and transport firms must redefine transport as a critical factor in product channel and value chain management. The chain's critical linkages involve transportation companies as well as suppliers, distributors and customers seen from the vantage point of a production company. By using new communications and information technologies, firms are able to rearrange activities in physical space in such a way that the time involved in production and distribution is drastically reduced.

A study dealing with the development of product channel logistics in six industry sectors relevant to the Dutch economy, has shown that companies in the automotive and business

Figure 1 Logistics integration by industry sector

Internal Integration	Channel Integration	Geographical Integration	
			Automotive (Inbound)
			Automotive (Outbound)
			Fmcg (Inbound)
			Fmcg (Outbound)
			'Channel Management' Retailers
			Fap (Inbound)
			Fap (Outbound)
			Chemicals
			Business Equipment (Inbound)
			Business Equipment (Outbound)

equipment industries are most advanced in the logistics integration process – especially with regard to inbound logistics. Food and agriculture production companies are still in the stage of linking (internally) their separate logistic activities. Most companies, however, are engaged in restructuring their logistic systems in order to reap the significant benefits accruing from economies of scale in purchasing, manufacturing, warehousing and distribution. They are not yet in a position to integrate their operations geographically, simply because they have not yet reached a European span of activities. Nevertheless, many companies remain committed to the transformation and integration of their logistic systems because they are anxious to capture the potential advantages, both in terms of cost and service. See figure 1 (NEA and Cranfield, 1994).

2/2 A new positioning of ports   What implications does the rise of product channel logistics have for the positioning of ports?

First of all, a rethinking of the 'tonnage approach' is called for. The conventional positioning approach can be summarized by the following equation:

M.Ce	$= Co.Q$ (Equation 1) where:
M	= mass of goods to be transported per port
Ce	= centrality index of port
Co	= transshipment/transit costs in port in relation to competing ports
Q	= quantity of goods transshipped in port

The central index measures the infrastructure access of ports to their hinterland by rail, road and inland waterway. Another way of positioning ports in terms of accessibility is by calculating the so-called market distance (Roodenburg, 1989). The higher a port's multimodal physical accessibility, the higher the mass of goods it attracts and the higher the transit of goods – provided the costs can be kept relatively low. The left-hand side of the equation 'explains' why port authorities today fixate on multimodal, physical infrastructure expansion: seaside, in port, and landside.

The impact of product channel logistics on this kind of reasoning is two-fold. On the right-hand side of the above equation, 'tonnage thinking' is replaced by 'chain and value-adding thinking'. And, as far as the left-hand side is concerned, the emphasis is shifting from physical accessibility to controlled and dedicated logistic accessibility and hence to facilities and services.

2/2/1 **From tonnage to chains and value adding** Let us first take a closer look at chains and value adding. As a first step, freight volumes are to be divided into segments and the (gross) value added per segment per ton is to be calculated.

A rule of thumb (Winkelmans, 1991) can be applied to illustrate that it is possible to create the same amount of value added or even more value added by shipping lesser volumes of goods:

1 ton cc = 3 tons ul = 6 tons db = 15 tons lb   (Equation 2)

In the year 2015, one expects 274 million tons of bulk to be transported along the East-West axis of the Netherlands (see table 1). Assuming that the goods are transshipped in the port of Rotterdam and that the bulk is dry (DB), then the same amount of value added can be earned by transporting 46 million tons of conventional cargo (cc). In the case of liquid bulk (LB), the equivalent volumes of conventional cargo amount to 18 million tons. Similarly, equivalent volumes of containers or unit load (UL) can be calculated. As far as containers are concerned, it is also important to distinguish between 'Full Container Load' (FCL) and 'Less than Full Container Load' (LCL). The latter can generate a value added about five times as high as the former (either in the port or elsewhere, dependent on where the regrouping takes place). And, as a large part of continental container flows in Europe consists of 'empty boxes', this has to be deducted from the gross value added – unless better ways are found to handle the logistics of empty containers.

cc, UL, DB and LB or similar segments are still transshipment categories. It is preferable to use a classification more apt to deal with product channel logistics (Janssen, 1991). First, a distinction can be made between producing activities, referring to the production of goods in an industrial process, and service providing activities. The latter include other goods-handling activities (storage, transportation, distribution and trading of goods) and other producer services, especially in knowledge-intensive services essential to strategic design, planning and execution of the entire production process.

Next, the producing-activities group is subdivided into four types of activities:

- continuous processes: the production of large series of standardized products, in general the processing of raw materials;
- discontinuous processes: medium-sized series of different standardized products (semi-finished products, components, consumer products);
- product groups: small to medium-sized series of heterogeneous products such as fashion-sensitive, ready-to-wear clothing or consumer electronics;
- project situations (single and multiple): small series or 'series of just one product', manufactured by the piece following consumer specifications (e.g. buildings, ships, airplanes etc.).

This typology is two-dimensional. Variety in products relates to the ever-increasing market (consumer) demand for a broad range of products stressing the importance of economies of scope or flexibility of the production process. Standardization of production, on the other hand, refers to the way in which a variety of products can be produced as efficiently as possible, building on one or more standardized modules – a matter of economies of scale.

Different products or markets imply different lead times, the time intervals between the placing of an order and delivery. This brings us to the topic of controlled and dedicated logistic accessibility.

2/2/2 From physical to logistic accessibility

With the rise of product channel logistics, either centrality or market distance changes into:

closeness in lead time $\dfrac{\text{density of population}}{\text{quantities/times}}$

Population density and quantities of goods, preferably should be weighted respectively according to the wealth of the population and the values of goods.

Logistic accessibility involves networks and platforms. In the channels connecting units of production to points of sale or final destinations, platforms (terminals) intervene in different ways. Logistic platforms are not only material platforms for the consolidation as well as the deconsolidation of flows of goods, but increasingly turn into platforms in data-flow networks. They are also hierarchically positioned, ranging from international main logistic centers down to city/local distribution centers.

Where do the ports come in? They are mainly cast as inter(national) nodes of logistic networks. Seaports are just one type of node among others (airports, border nodes of infrastructure, inland terminals). Seen from a different perspective, the port is the focus of two divergent types of logistics: 'product logistics' and 'transport logistics'.

Product logistics focuses on the individual product moving through a logistic chain, along which a range of activities is performed, adding value and tailoring the product to consumer needs. Transport logistics, on the other hand, refers to the efforts of transport firms to optimize the utilization of their equipment and networks while maintaining the required level of service.

With regard to ports, the latter implies a strategy of standardization and massing of flows and services. Paralleling this strategy often is a move toward 'mainporting'. The aim is to establish (global) transport pipelines in which the port no longer constitutes a breakpoint in the transportation of goods. Ports consequently become 'ship-oriented', with increasing economies of scale. Returns measured in terms of value added and employment per ton of goods handled in the port, however, tend to diminish.

The strategy of product logistics, on the other hand, requires a broad spectrum of logistic services and facilities. This type of logistics calls for a 'cargo-oriented port', marked by more value adding and customization of activities and less technology-driven port development. Today, it is still an open question whether ports like Rotterdam, Antwerp or Hamburg will develop according to both types of logistics or just one, the mainport strategy which is, essentially, a strategy of transport logistics.

With the emphasis shifting from physical to logistic accessibility, the provision of logistic services becomes of vital importance: 'The choice of a port is less determined by the facilities of a port, but more and more by the logistics facilities offered. Hinterland connections and telematics facilities of a port have become essential elements of these logistics facilities' (Haven van Rotterdam, 1986).

Logistic service providers may be companies that, in collaboration with a shipper, offer services concerning the control and operation of goods-flow processes in order to achieve an optimal exchange between consignor and receiver. They may also be physical distribution companies that provide, at the request of shippers, transport plus warehousing and distribution services. In both cases, the services provided may either be shared by many different customers or tailored to the needs of one specific customer. Within the European Union, complementary logistic organizations and networks of producers and their suppliers, wholesale and retail companies, and logistic service providers are emerging. They tend to internationalize (europeanize) as well as to concentrate spatially.

The integration of shippers and logistic service providers can take different forms. These depend on the choices and management approaches of shippers and the degree of logistics integration they have achieved (which, in turn, differs from one industrial sector to another and may even vary within the same sector).

Apart from shippers' logistics, logistic service providers have their independent strategies geared to the logistics of transport. Strategies can be developed in four directions:

- the geographic scale of independent networks (ranging from local to pan-European presence, though the latter does not yet exist);
- the complexity of independent transport networks (referring to the modality in networks);
- the number of activities in independent networks (ranging from general haulage to high value-adding logistic services, i.e. assembly);
- the number of specializations (focusing on type of products, conditioning, size of shipment, volume of transport).

Hence, as far as possible future developments are concerned, there are different options for the actors of logistic service provision as shown in figure 2 (Janssen, 1994). Every logistic service has to combine successfully the two concepts of product and transport logistics. The same holds for the ports of the future. As a node it represents the physical and functional link between logistic and transport networks. The degree to which the ports are prepared for the future is an empirical question. Compare the requirements to be met in the case of an international main logistic center (table 2). They can serve as a checklist.

3 Ports: from competition to cooperation

The rise of product channel logistics, combined with transport logistics, implies a new way of structuring trans-European networks (TENs). A guiding principle is that of corridors. Once the corridor principle has been adopted, different modes of transport and types of infrastructure will be approached in an integrated manner, not separately as in the present practice of planning trans-European networks. Apart from road, rail and inland waterways, one also has to look at pipelines, airports and telematics. Infrastructure planning in cross-border regions calls for special attention. Insufficient coordination creates problems as in the case of the Betuwe line where the decision of the Dutch government regarding the cross-border link does not concord with the decision of the government of Nordrhein-West-falen. The new way of organizing TENs leads to the planning of inland terminals, logistic platforms, distribution centers and the like at appropriate locations along the corridor, both in the country of origin and abroad (asking for an efficient coordination of both transport and spatial planning). This kind of development can lead to a de-concentration of port-related activities. This trend can hardly be expected to stop at the border. But problems may arise if the policy stances of different member countries of the EU are not compatible. Take for example the Dutch-German case of the provinces of Limburg and Noord-Brabant, favoring locations of logistic activities, which meets the opposition of Nordrhein-Westfalen and of certain municipalities in particular. Among the negative arguments are a low value added and environmental risks. But how about links between corridors originating in different ports, say, Rotterdam, Antwerp or other ports of the Hamburg-Le Havre range? One may consider sea-sea links, in special cabotage. Of greater importance, however, would seem to be strategies of cooperation.

3/1 The competitive world of ports

Seen from a distance, the Rhine-Scheldt Delta may appear as one coherent port region. In reality, however, there is a lot of competition among its constituent ports. Even recent strategic alliances like those between Rotterdam and Flushing, Antwerp and Zeebrugge or Ghent-Terneuzen are rather intended to strengthen the competitive position of the larger ports of each pair vis-à-vis the rest.

Figure 2 Possible future developments/actors in the market of logistics service provision

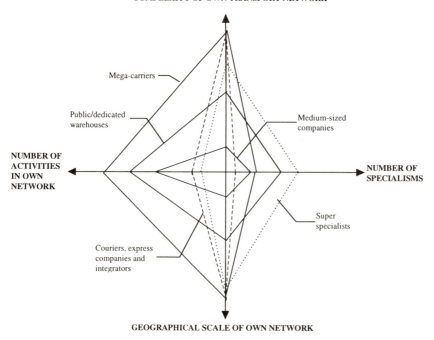

COMPLEXITY OF OWN TRANSPORT NETWORK

Mega-carriers

Public/dedicated warehouses

Medium-sized companies

NUMBER OF ACTIVITIES IN OWN NETWORK

NUMBER OF SPECIALISMS

Super specialists

Couriers, express companies and integrators

GEOGRAPHICAL SCALE OF OWN NETWORK

Table 2 New hierarchy of distribution centers

Type Of Node	Characteristics
International main logistic center (mainport):	Located at main economic development and transport axes
	directly linked to intercontinental flows
	technically advanced combined loading/unloading facilities for road and rail
	intermodal facilities for road/rail and water transport
	sophisticated information exchange facilities (EDI)
	capacity and space to handle/store large quantities of different types of goods for different customers to different quality levels
	availability of vacant space for logistic platforms of all different kinds of logistic/producers services
International logistic center	located at main European transport axes
	active on various international networks and flows
	functions as logistic platform for consolidation/de-consolidation of nearly all types of products
	various logistic and producer services
	dominant mode is truck, but also accessible by rail and combined rail/road transport
International transport & distribution center	located at important international transport axes to and from the mainports
	function primarily as favored locations for transfer, transshipment, storage and/or distribution activities of internationally operating carriers and shippers
	dominant mode is truck. Many are also linked by another mode of transport, rail or water
Regional transport & distribution center	located at junctions and others platforms in infrastructural networks and/or platforms for the distribution of goods within about 50 km.
	predominant location factor is size of the market (population), degree of competition for space
	spatial clusters of transport companies

Especially Rotterdam and Antwerp see themselves as competitors rather than as partners. There are firms operating in or from both ports, but the port authorities and municipalities in question do not seem to be inclined to cooperate. Despite the fact that both seaports possess certain complementarities and that the two cities might even constitute a potential intercity network (Drewe, 1994).

The problems rising from the competitive attitudes can be illustrated by the recent plan to build the Betuwe line. Each of the two ports, located at a distance of some 100 kilometers from each other, favors its own rail connection for the transport of goods to the German hinterland. In the case of Antwerp the link, the so-called IJzeren Rijn, already exists, but needs upgrading. The existing rail line for freight that could connect the two port areas stops at the former Dutch-Belgian border (not too far from Antwerp). The case of the Betuwe line demonstrates that a trans-European network between the Netherlands and Germany may foster competition instead of cohesion between the ports of Rotterdam and Antwerp. Competition is not limited to infrastructure projects; witness, for example, the concern about terms of employment, recently expressed by transport unions from Belgium, Germany and the Netherlands. See also the frequent complaints about 'unfair competition' caused by different national regimes of subsidization.

Considering the amount of capital investment needed to equip a port region and its related infrastructural hinterland networks in line with the latest technology, competition may be a costly strategy. How about, for example, Le Havre's 'Port-2000' plan, a mega-container project aiming at strengthening Le Havre's competitive position especially vis-à-vis Hamburg and Rotterdam? What is at stake here is the causal link between public investment in seaports (transport infrastructure) and long-term employment as well as value added (Debisschop et al., 1995).

3/2 In search of complementarities

The socio-economic cohesion of the Community may be served by a strategic cooperation of ports rather than by unchecked competition. This, in turn, could help to improve the competitive position of Community ports vis-à-vis the 'rest of the world'. It asks for further study, which in the first place, could cover the ports of the Hamburg-Le Havre range. Lessons from cross-border cooperation or intercity networks for that matter teach us that complementarities is a key factor in co-operation. In search of complementarities, it is important to position potential partners.

How to position the ports of the Hamburg-Le Havre range?

Let us first take a look at recent research focusing on flows of goods between four seaport regions and their hinterland (NEA 1995a). The four regions selected for study are:

■ Netherlands (Zuid-Holland, Noord-Holland),

■ Belgium (Antwerp),

■ Northwest-Germany (Hamburg, Bremen),

■ Northwest-France (Nord-Pas de Calais, Haute- & Basse-Normandie).

Their distribution function has been analyzed per mode of transport, i.e. road, rail and inland waterways. The main results are that the Dutch ports excel in inland-waterway distribution of basic, agricultural and oil products (covering the river basin of the Rhine, Main and Moselle, among others). The German and Belgian ports have a strong international position as far as sea-road transport is concerned. In Germany there is a strong North-South orientation whereas Belgium has considerable influence in Eastern Europe, especially in Poland. And, finally, sea-rail distribution is a specialty of the German ports, mainly oriented towards Central and Eastern Europe. The exploratory study also deals with the cost-efficiency (least costs) of different modes of transport, measured in guilders per ton-kilometer. The main reason for commissioning the study has been to identify both opportunities and threats with respect to the present position of Dutch ports as a European distribution center. It has been shown clearly that the function of the Netherlands in Europe is far from unique. Once again, the larger ports in Northwest Europe are revealed as competitors. But it has also been indicated that they are, to some extent, complementary to one another, as to modes of transport and their cost-efficiency. Even if the method applied is still a classic one that does not yet take into account the impact product channel and transport logistics might have on the positioning of ports. The study results also lend credence to the Hamburg-Le Havre range as a multiport-system notwithstanding the dominant position of the Dutch ports distributing more than 149 million tons of goods as against some 140 million tons of the Belgian, Northwest-German and Northwest-French ports taken together.

Trends in (international) freight transport, however, seem to favor mainport development: a concentration of flows of goods in one port only; trends like economies of scale in shipping, 'global transport', regrouping of flows, specialization of carriers and door-to-door integration of transport services. Only the increase in the number of small consignments seems to work in favor of multiports (provided that a regrouping in the port is not possible). But these trends do not alter the fact that mainport development is still open to empirical questions. Empirical evidence (Knaapen, 1993) suggests that a multiport system should at least not be discarded hastily. A large majority of us shippers of forest and food products, for instance, reach their European destinations via a number of European ports and do not intend to change this pattern. This is also related to the fact that their European clients (producers and importers) are dispersed over Europe and prefer the port nearest to their country (which determines the choice of the shipping company to be contracted). Multiport-shipping companies include several ports in their regular service in order to reach the largest possible hinterland in accordance with their clients' preferences. Moreover, choosing a mainport strategy causes feeder costs that exceed the costs of calling at an additional port (nevertheless, the number of European ports of call is expected to be reduced to three or four as far as regular services are concerned).

What about complementarities in the light of product channel and transport logistics?

It is generally expected that platforms or terminals will be hierarchically positioned. This also holds in essence for future ports as nodes of logistic networks. Compare table 2 for a new hierarchy of distribution centers (Janssen, 1993).

Is not the main problem today that all ports of the Hamburg-Le Havre range (or elsewhere) more or less aspire to the rank of an international main logistic center? Many ports may be candidates, but only a few will most probably be chosen, because not all ports are able to meet the requirements. Unchecked competition only causes excessive costs. Finally, the main maritime centers are likely to take the form of a multiport system.

The 'Gateway to Europe' can hardly be monopolized by one mainport. But a multiport system, consisting of a limited number of mainports, implies that a number of existing ports will have to settle for a lower rank in the hierarchy of international, national or even regional and local reach (the 'maritime' equivalents of the 'terrestrial' hierarchy of distribution centers still need to be defined preferably as constituent parts of logistic networks). From a container-port point of view, a reshaped market may be divided into three major categories: major deep-sea hub terminals, secondary feeder locations and smaller ports where limited container handling was a function of a broader multi-purpose facility. To implement such a new hierarchy of ports is another way of achieving complementarities.

As we said before (in section 2.2), there are two ways in which the conventional approach to the positioning of ports is changing under the impact of product channel logistics. On the one hand 'tonnage thinking' needs to be replaced by 'chain and value-added thinking' and on the other, emphasis must shift from physical accessibility to controlled and dedicated logistic accessibility and hence to the complimentary relationships between services and facilities. In searching for complementarities and – subsequently – cooperation, both sides are to be examined.

But the search should go beyond the economics of port development. Advocates of product channel (transport) logistics may claim that the very essence of this kind of economic-technical innovation is to foster sustainable development, as it provides an alternative to the dominant tonnage-growth model. Big, today, may be bad when it comes to the environmental costs of port activities. Among the priorities are: dangerous goods, water pollution, problems related to dredging operations, port-city relations & restructuring of derelict areas, air pollution, wastes, land/soil contamination, industrial plant regulations, visual contamination, stench and noise. Note that these 11 priorities, listed in decreasing order of importance, are a result of research carried out among 218 ports/port organizations/terminal operators covering 51 maritime nations worldwide. See also the checklist of port-related environmental impacts, developed by the World Bank as an aide-mémoire both for port planners and developers and for World Bank staff engaged in the appraisal of lending operations related to port development (Dankfort, 1995).

Hence it is essential to also consider the specific environmental and spatial setting of ports in the search for complementarities. This in relation to key indicators such as population density. The Hamburg-Le Havre range of port regions, covers a variety of population densities.

Among the most urgent environmental problems are those emanating from the present modal split relating to the transport of goods. In the period 1970-1990 road transport has increased by almost 100% whereas rail has lost about 15% (transport by inland waterways has roughly remained constant and pipeline transport has grown by more than 10%). Hence road transport obviously presents the biggest problem. Searching for solutions, four avenues can be distinguished (Verhage, 1994):

■ reduction of total number of ton-kilometers: through changes in the spatial structure and internalization of external costs;
■ technical improvements of vehicles (green technology): improvement of existing modes and of driving and sailing habits, using the potentials of telecommunication technologies;
■ optimalization of transport logistics (green logistic): telecommunication technologies, trip planning techniques ('fuller', 'less empty', 'bigger'), introduction of sophisticated logistic transport concepts, improvement of the use of intermodal transport;
■ shift to more environmentally sound modes of transport (green transport): sophisticated logistic transport concepts, intermodal transport, change of modal split.

Each avenue is not only described in terms of types of intervention, but comprises physical and regulative measures, too.

It should be noted that internalizing the environmental costs of transport should not be limited to road transport, but rather cover all modes of transport.

4 Future ports or 'the art of the long view'

Cooperation still appears to be a far cry from the way port authorities view their business. Research has shown that the authorities of seaports in Western Europe are mainly interested in increasing their market share at the expense of range competitors, as well as in diversifying their activities. Growth rates remain the foremost indicator of port efficiency which unfortunately implies a very limited concept of efficiency. Any attempt to develop a strategy of cooperation must take this into account (even if the prisoners' dilemma suggests that cooperation pays off). Port authorities are business firms sui generis. Maybe there are lessons to be learned from the experience of 'ordinary' firms with strategic cooperation, preferably firms operating in or from ports. In sectors like sea transport, road transport and distribution, some firms have already embarked on a cooperation course. In general, strategic cooperation often is only sought when other strategies are not feasible, say, mergers, take-overs or go-it-alone strategies. Of course there are both advantages and disadvantages involved in cooperation. The advantages include cost sharing, risk reduction, gain of time, synergy and economies of scope, opportunities for specialization, increase in flexibility, access to markets and the like. Some disadvantages are inherent: cultural differences, a lesser degree of freedom, opportunism, instability and so forth. Other disadvantages (control, undesired dependence etc.) can be met.

In an uncertain world it does not suffice to simply extrapolate present (growth) trends into the future as they are most likely to break in the next 25 years. Scenarios may help to scan alternative futures (Schwartz, 1991). In a recent study in the Netherlands, three scenarios have been elaborated dealing with structural change in world-trade flows:

- 'global village' (the worldwide liberalization makes it easier to export from one location to the rest of the world);
- 'global crisis' (an economic crisis leads to a regionalized production, but may also cause its centralization in the most productive locations);
- 'greening of business' (a stronger emphasis on the environment will probably lead to less transport and hence 'globalization'; some production processes, however, from a global environmental policy point of view, might also be served by worldwide centralization) (Junne et al., 1993).

These scenarios have different impacts on the transport, trade and distribution function of the Netherlands (in which the port of Rotterdam holds a pivotal position). If one measures the impact in volume of goods, different estimates emerge.

The Netherlands loses most in the greening of business scenario, more or less maintains its position in the case of the global recession scenario and only wins in the case of the global village scenario. It can be concluded from this that the 'mainport' ambition stands or falls with the global village scenario. In fact, the Port of Rotterdam (1995) has also developed four scenarios only one of which depicts the future of the port as mainport. As the future, alternatively, may have in store: a 'controlport' (subject to far-reaching European regulations), a 'leanport' (optimizing the existing facilities with a minimum amount of new investment) or – finally – a 'serviceport' (focusing on logistic services and environmental innovation).

Moving up the Hamburg-Le Havre range, one also runs into scenarios for the (port) region of Hamburg (Läpple et al., 1994). This time only two alternative futures have been elaborated: a competitive location scenario (Standortkonkurrenz) as opposed to a 'milieu policy'-led scenario (Milieupolitik). The former mirrors the traditional growth-oriented regional policy, dominated by 'economics of scale'-thinking (combined with lean production and global sourcing) and marked by an 'Eurogate' ambition for the region. The 'Milieupolitik' scenario, contrastingly, stresses the use of endogenous development potentials and a strengthening of regional production and innovative milieus or environments. In order to assess the regional impact of the two scenarios the Hamburg economy has been split up into eleven clusters of economic activities ranging from 'port, storage, transport' to the public sector.

Two kinds of impacts have been singled out for analysis: employment and land use. The overall results in terms of employment are rather negative, except for producer services and urban (public) consumer services. Only the milieu policy-led scenario offers possibilities for extenuating employment losses in the urban industrial cluster and for stabilizing the employment situation of city-district and neighborhood firms. The competitive location scenario, in general, demands more space, especially the 'port, storage, transport' cluster (but with the exception of seaport industries), the urban industrial cluster, the insurance cluster, city-district and neighborhood firms, and the public sector. A lesser growth of land use overall is to be expected in the case of the Milieupolitik scenario. The demand for space only slightly increases, remains constant or even decreases (except for trade, producer and urban services).

The port region of Hamburg, in the period 1989-1991, has been the most prosperous region of the EC out of 179 NUTS 2 regions, according to its level of GDP per head. The scenarios, however, teach us that even Hamburg has to arm itself against an uncertain world.

Scenario planning is a tool that can help to understand the implications of alternative futures. Whenever scenarios are developed, this is a sure sign of uncertainty related to

Table 3 The transport, trade and distribution function of the Netherlands, three scenarios: 1990–2015 (a synthesis of 10 groups of goods at world level)

	1990 (×1 million tons)	Global village (1990=100%)	Global recession (1990=100)	Greening of business (1990=100)
Transport	130.2	125	99	69
Trade	146.5	122	105	72
Distribution	71.3	129	108	67
Total	348.2	124	103	70

processes, objectives and means. But how to manage these uncertainties
(Drewe and Janssen, 1996)? They might be reduced in several ways:

- further research (as far as processes or the operating environment is concerned);
- clearer objectives (particularly in the case of conflicting interests);
- more or different means (in order to achieve the objectives);
- a more coordinated approach (involving relevant parties or even competitors).

A more coordinated approach – this is where a strategy of cooperation
among ports comes in, as an antidote to unchecked competition. Cooperation may go a long way towards reducing uncertainty, but most likely not
the whole way. So it may also be necessary to accept uncertainties to some
extent. Then one can only resort to flexibility, to be achieved by an intelligent phasing of the implementation of plans; distinguishing immediate
actions, delayed actions and contingency plans. Of course, one can also opt
for a risky laisser-faire.

The different ways of coping with uncertainty all belong to the strategic
planner's toolbox. In recent years another way has emerged, referred to as
innovative environment (milieu) and/or knowledge infrastructure. It is
closely related to technology and know-how which – according to UNCTAD
(1991) – are decisive factors to third-generation or value-adding ports
whereas first-generation traditional ports and second-generation industrial
ports depended on respectively labour/capital and capital. In other words,
the port of the future must be continuously innovative. The port of Rotterdam, for example, has created a foundation charged with the mainport
knowledge infrastructure (Stichting Kennisinfrastructuur, 1995). Three
spearheads have been selected, i.e. mainport strategy, transport and logistics, and the (petro)chemical industry.

The foundation's activities cover interrelated projects such as:

- a round table (with two pilot studies, one dealing with value-added dry bulk logistics, the other with a simulation model for logistic chains);
- a center for simulation and training;

■ a regional college dedicated to vocational training in the field of process industry;
■ an educational electronic highway.

A knowledge infrastructure has a supply and demand side. In order to turn into an innovative environment for the port and its region, it is vital that supply and demand become tuned to each other. Do the foundation's organizational structure and functioning provide sufficient guaranty for that? As a matter of fact, the demand side often has to set up its own research projects because it either does not know who to turn to or does not expect to receive adequate answers to its questions. Suppliers of knowledge, on the other hand, are willing to work for the firms in question, but often formulate the topics themselves before 'the market' has had its say. This conclusion is drawn from research with regard to the transport and distribution sectors' knowledge infrastructure in the Netherlands as a whole (NEA, 1993b). See also the related research topic of innovation in the transport sector (NEA, 1995b).

A milieu – as assumed in the case of Hamburg's milieu policy-led scenario – is characterized by:

■ a collective of actors (entrepreneurs, research and training institutions, local authorities and so forth) that are relatively independent in their decision making and in their formulation of strategic choices;
■ material elements such as firms and infrastructures as well as immaterial (know-how) and institutional elements (different forms of local authorities and decision making organizations);
■ a synergetic interaction and cooperation between actors: the whole of the know-how of the actors being more than the sum of their individual know-how;
■ a learning process (apprenticeship) in which the actors in the course of time develop the capability of modifying their behavior and of implementing new solutions reacting to a changing environment (Maillat, 1994).

A milieu qualifies as an innovative environment if it fosters innovations such as new or improved products, processes and services that are commercially successful or non-market goods and services that are socially accepted. The European Research Group on Innovative Environments (GREMI), from 1986 onward, has provided ample empirical evidence of this kind of milieu. Its current research program focuses on urban innovative environments. The Regional Technology Plan, a pilot action of the European Commission (1994b), looks as if it has been modeled upon the GREMI research experience or as if it has at least been inspired by it (especially after having been re-baptized recently as 'Regional Innovation Strategy').

The final question, however, is whether ports will be able to practice the art of the long view and, in doing so, will cope successfully with uncertainty. According to a Dutch writer, 'tomorrow was written yesterday'. As the example of Rotterdam has shown, the growth model was written in the late 1960s. There are good reasons for rewriting tomorrow today.

References

Anderson, D., **Product channel management. The next revolution in logistics**, Temple, Barker & Sloane, Lexington, Mass, 1989.

Commissie Betuweroute, Report, The Hague, 1995, 29.

Commissie van de Europese Gemeenschappen, **De regio's in de jaren negentig, Brussel & Luxemburg**, 1991.

Commission of the European Communities, **Europe 2000, outlook for the development of the Community's territory**, Brussels & Luxembourg, 1991, 14.

Dankfort, J.M.M., **Chain analysis as a tool for value-adding port planning, with special reference to Brazil**, OPB, Bouwkunde, Delft University of Technology, 1995.

Debisschop, K. et al., 'Problematiek van de causaliteit tussen overheidsinvesteringen in infrastructuur en duurzame toegevoegde waarde', **Tijdschrift vervoerswetenschap**, 3, 1995, pp.253-277.

Drewe, P., **The towns of Benelux faced with the challenge of transborder cooperation**, Regions of Europe, no. 9, 1994, pp.29-33.

Drewe, P. and Janssen, B., **The Betuwe line: an evaluation**, EUREG, European Journal of Regional Development, 3, 1996, 44-49.

European Commission, Competitiveness and cohesion: trends in the regions, Brussels & Luxembourg, 1994a; European Commission, Regional Technology Plan Guide Book, CM International, Vélizy-Villacoublay, 1994b.

Gemeente Rotterdam, **Delta 2000-8, naar een grootschalig containeroverslag- en goederendistributiecentrum op de Maasvlakte**, Rotterdam, 1990.

Haven van Rotterdam, **Spoorweghaven Rotterdam**, Rotterdam, 7, 1986.

Janssen, B.J.P., 'Product channel logistics networks and a changing spatial organization, conceptual issues and empirical results' in M. Savy and P. Veltz (eds.), **Flux logistiques et organisation du territoire**, CERTES–ENPC, Paris, 1991.

Janssen, B.J.P., 'Product channel logistics and logistic platforms' in P. Nijkamp (ed.), **Europe on the move, recent developments in European communications and transport activity research**, 1993, pp.173-185.

Janssen, B.J.P., **The spatial behavior of logistic service providers**, NEA Zuid, Tilburg, 1994.

Junne, G. et al., **Eindrapport structuurverandering in wereldhandelsstromen**, Faculteit Politieke en Sociaal-culturele Wetenschappen, Universiteit van Amsterdam, 1993.

Knaapen, M., **Mainport versus multiport, een onderzoek naar de trend tot het concentreren van goederenstromen in één haven**, Buck Consultants International, Nijmegen, 1993.

Läpple, D. et al., **Strukturentwicklung und Zukunftsperspektiven der Hamburger Wirtschaft unter räumlichen Gesichtspunkten, Clusterstruktur und Szenarien**, second revised edition, Technische Universität Hamburg-Harburg, 1994.

Louter, P.J. and De Ruyter, P.A., **Ruimtelijk-economische ontwikkelingspatronen in Nederland**, INRO/TNO, Delft, 1995.

Maillat, D., 'Comportements spatiaux et milieux innovateurs' in J.P. Auray et al. (eds.), **Encyclopédie d'économie spatiale, concepts-comportements-organisations**, Economica, Paris, 1994, pp.255-262.

NEA Transportonderzoek en -opleiding, **De transport-, handels- en distributiefunctie van Nederland**, Tilburg, 1993a.

NEA Transportonderzoek en -opleiding, **Voorverkenning kennisinfrastructuur in de transport & distributiesector**, Tilburg, 1993b.

NEA, Transportonderzoek en -opleiding, **Verkenningsstudie ter bepaling internationale transportketens; kansen en bedreigingen voor de Nederlandse distributiefunctie**, Rijswijk, 1995a.

NEA Transportonderzoek en -opleiding, **Innovatie in de transportsector**, Rijswijk, 1995b.

NEA Transport Research & Training and Cranfield School of Management, **CLT, Future logistics structures, the development of integrated supply chain management across 6 industry sectors**, synthesis report, Tilburg/Cranfield, 1994, pp.11-12.

Port of Rotterdam, **Rotterdam dàn... een scenario-verkenning; Mainport, Controlport, Leanport & Serviceport**, Directie Haveninnovatie, Rotterdam, 1995.

Roodenburg, H.J., **Central locations in the European Common Market**, Research Memorandum, no. 59, Centraal Planbureau, The Hague, 1989.

Ruijgrok, C.J. et al., **Sustainable development and infrastructure**, INRO/TNO, Delft, 1991.

Schwartz, P., **The art of the long view, scenario planning: protecting your company against an uncertain future**, Century Business, London, 1991.

Stichting Kennisinfrastructuur Mainport Rotterdam, **Jaarplan 1995, begroting en meerjarenraming, concept**, Rotterdam, 1995.

UNCTAD secretariat, **Port marketing and the challenge of the third generation port**, United Nations, Geneva, 1991.

Van Klink, H.A., **De Rotterdamse haven als schakel in transportketens**, Economisch Statistische Berichten, 78, 1993, pp.268-271.

Verhage, R., **Goederenvervoer, ruimtelijke ordening en milieu, naar een ruimtelijk inrichtingsconcept voor een minder milieubelastend goederenvervoer**, Rijksplanologische Dienst, The Hague, 1994.

Winkelmans, W., **Een strategische positionering van de zeehavens in het Scheldebekken**, Zomer Universiteit Zeeland, Vlissingen/Middelburg, 1991.

The Port of Rotterdam: Mainport and Brainport

Henk Molenaar

Introduction In general the conference on *Cities in Transition* deals with the subject of how social and economic alterations affect the spatial shape of cities. To elucidate that general picture in more specific terms, port cities have been chosen as the focus for the alteration process. And to bring the problem even more to the 'real-life level' the experiences in the port city of Rotterdam are used as an example of this special category of port cities.

This contribution works towards the insights relevant at the mezzo level: the port cities as a group. Simply phrased, what trends can be recognized that steer the spatial needs of port cities.

The first danger here could be to suppose that the functional reduction in the row cities-in-general>>port-cities>>port-city-Rotterdam implies a like reduction in the extent to which the environment effects the process. Big ports like Rotterdam are world ports and the technological and economic changes that influence them are of a global nature. But the second danger could then be to assume that on the mezzo level the consequences of these global technological and economic changes are similar for all ports and port cities the world over. The 'translation machine' in between the global trends and the actual spatial requirements for a given port is composed of complex social, financial, ecological, political and cultural interactions. The generating phenomena, like technology and economy, are global and 'hard'. So is the final local outcome: space. The decision-making process to translate the 'hard' global trends into 'hard' local space is almost always regional and 'soft'. But decisive! The great variety in ports is not only a matter of differences in geographical conditions, but also of the capability to make use of those conditions. Comparing ports means in essence comparing complex 'translation machines'.

Development trends Port comparisons are most commonly executed by simply quantifying the number of tons of cargo handled, based on the most obvious definition of a port being a place where ships are loaded and discharged.[1] According to this definition a big port is almost by nature a port where great amounts of raw materials, like crude oil, grains and ores, are transshipped. That is to say, commodities with a low value per ton were deemed sensible for lowering the costs of transportation to the extreme, resulting in economy of scale in the form of larger vessels.

But larger vessels require the port to deepen its fairways, to broaden its basins and to lengthen the booms of its cranes. Meaning money, time and space consuming adaptations

---

1 This paper refers only to ports handling cargo; activities in the field of passenger traffic are not taken into account.

or even – in the 'soft' translation process – a fall hurdle. It must be realized in this respect that for most raw materials the growth in volume will at best be restricted to only a few percent per year. In this more or less mature market the competition is severe and the possibilities to increase the port dues, so as to cover the costs of the necessary adaptations, are in fact non-existent, leaving as a final argument for spending yet more money and space, that doing nothing will result in even worse effects. The unavoidable conclusion must be that for many ports, particularly large ones, their position on this vessel-related playing field is difficult, requiring more space while profits are gradually melting away.

Making use of the facilities for handling cargo, a port is an attractive place of settlement for certain industries. Especially for the high-volume low-cost industries, involved in the first steps in the production columns. But in the developed countries these types of industries are also mature and here, too, emphasis is put on constantly improving efficiency and cost reduction by means of 'de-laborization' and outsourcing the non-core activities. The generated added value, measured either per ton of cargo or per square meter of port area, is higher than for loading and discharging vessels, but because of modernizations and process improvements, shows a tendency to decrease. As a result, the general long-term trend in the industrial segment of the settlement is downward too, both in growth-potential and in generated added value.

The total picture for the longer-term development is rather gloomy. Especially for the big industrialized ports in the developed world profitability is under pressure, and employment and generated added value are decreasing, whereas at the same time more space is required. In this respect the smaller ports are better off as compared with the big ones.

Escape routes Many big ports have, however, done extremely well in the past decades. Their 'golden tails' permit them to carefully consider possible escape routes so as to obviate the described downward trends. In principle there are two such escape routes possible – growing 'horizontally' and growing 'vertically'. A brief description and listing of several consequences runs as follows:

Growing horizontally: More of the same; still larger volumes and thus growing income; familiar social configurations; proven performance. But also: the necessity to extend the port area; the necessity to improve hinterland connections, increased environmental burden, increased traffic congestions.

And thus: growing public resistance.

Growing vertically: Increased viability with the cargo that already flows through the port (value adding production); increased activities in the non-physical sphere (value adding services); more organization, more knowledge, more information, more relations.

But also: the obligation to extend education; the necessity to reframe organizational and managerial configurations; additional 'footloose' activities; further uncertainty about competitive position;

And thus: growing social division and instability.

Big ports are especially important providers of employment and welfare in their 'catchment areas'. On the other hand they also bring about hindrance and congestion for the population living around them. As explained, the positive effects tend to decrease (in particular for those ports that aim to grow horizontally), whereas the negative effects tend to increase.

Moreover the ports are looking for more land and deeper water and are as a result literally and figuratively moving out of sight of the city they belong to. The voters are losing their emotional attachment to the port and as a consequence the local and regional politicians are losing interest. This is strengthened by the fact that the ports need ever more capital and ever more space. The ultimate result being that the big ports are – in terms of both their governance and their spatial extension – being brought under the most 'remote' control possible. New port areas planned along the shore or even extending into the sea are being administratively privatized, or at least corporatized and commercialized under the national umbrella. Increasingly, the big ports and their port cities are growing apart. Thus, the transition of the port cities is following completely new tracks, and the traditional 'translation machines' are getting stuck. To stay alive and

The port of Rotter-
dam: Mainport and
Brainport

remain competitive both the port and the city are obliged to adhere to changing circumstances. But what emerges is increasing difference not only in the respective sets of influencing circumstances, but also in the way the port system and the city system are adapting themselves to those changing circumstances.

The shift from horizontal growth to vertical growth in a port does not offer an immediate solution. Such a shift takes not only a long period of time, but also creates its own new difficulties. The external spatial problem and the internal financial problem belonging to the path of horizontal growth is, when switching over to the path of vertical growth, replaced by the external uncertainty problem and the internal problem of social division.

'S-world' and 'F-world'
Big world-class ports show a dominant presence of global players. As explained earlier this statement should in fact be reversed; because of the interests of the global players ports can grow big. Global players are valued for their ability to make standard products with as high a quality/price ratio as possible. Standard products need standard procedures, long-term strategies, and scale, proven structures, security and above all stability. In short this world of the global players is indicated as the S-world. Emotional and changeable relations, so often encountered in the local or regional translation-machines, do not fit in this S-world. The S-world seeks 'hard' relations; contracts, long-lasting (if stringent) permits, a stable political climate, a hard currency, a site large enough to allow for any future extension plan. The market is already extremely difficult to predict and the 'law of maximum manageable uncer- tainties' forces the players in the S-world to maximize the certainty of the 'internal' system, ranging from 'passive' employability of their personnel, variable working hours and flexible functions to depersonalized relations with both the port and the port city.

At the other end of the spectrum as compared with the global players in the S-world are the players who are not avoiding uncertainties but making use of them. The utmost efficiency of the process is not that which is at stake, but the instantaneous effectiveness of the product. The market is not served by them, but surprised. Fashion, future, flexibility, fantasy: the F-world. In this F-world all relations are personalized, creative individuals, forming temporary groups of friends.

If a port chooses horizontal growth as the escape route towards the future, it should act according to the rules of the game valid in the S-world. Acceptance of relatively large parts of the sites not yet fully occupied, timely availability of completely new sites in port extensions, timely improvement of hinterland connections for all models of transportation, European environmental regulations, the presence of even playing fields in all respects. But also: not much understanding for the 'soft' games that are played within the 'translation machines' and more interested in docile workers and apprehensive unions.

If a port, on the other hand, wants to bend its future development in the direction of vertical growth, it should respect – or at least accept – the rules of the game in the F-worlds. Friendly gestures, personal favorites, a growing distinction between the haves and the have-nots, uncertainties about the duration of presence, high demands regarding the personal environment, availability of 'experiment parks', where new activities can be tested without being hampered by all kinds of restrictive ruling. But also: less population, less space, less traffic.

Mainport/Brainport
To sum up, what we have observed so far is that for the world-class ports the distinctive use of their capabilities is to a large extent determined by the functioning of the 'translation machine' between the requirements the port generates and the final effects in the form of money and space. It was also explained that the more recent development in many big ports is accompanied by negative trends regarding employment, generated added value, hindrance and availability of new sites. This means not only a moving away from predominantly local and regional translation machines to national and continental translation machines, but also that the ports and their cities are becoming more loosely coupled than they were before. Two 'escape routes' were described for the ports to improve their position: vertical growth and horizontal growth. The horizontal growth is mainly related to the existing players in what was called the 'S-World'. The vertical growth requires relations (in most big ports) with new players in the F-world. Both ways to the future have their own advantages and disadvantages, also with regard to the space required. Most big ports are not very clear about their choice between the two main directions for their development. The changing patterns for the translation

The port of Rotter-
dam: Mainport and
Brainport

machines have no doubt to do with this hesitant behavior, both as an
explanation and as an excuse. The unexpressed approach of most big
ports seems to combine the two main directions. Not a mainport *or* a
brainport but a mainport *and* a brainport.

Of course such an attempt will not result in canceling out the disadvantages of the two directions. Combining the two growth paths means that
all inherent advantages and disadvantages of both approaches are to be
envisaged, be it to a somewhat lesser extent.
The differences between the players in the S-world and the F-world as an
external problem for the ports is then transferred into an internal problem:
within the same port the port players are not only to speak the language
of their relevant configurations outside, but also with each other inside. It
points to the personal capabilities of the port players. Not only an obedient
servant of the global players externally and part of a strict hierarchy internally, or in the other social configuration, externally a personal friend
and internally a self governing person, but somehow via a double inclusion
involved in both networks.

Only if the big ports are prepared to consider themselves as participants
in complicated networks, is there a chance that they may succeed in
combining the two mentioned main directions for the future development.
According to the network paradigm each individual acts both as a trans-
mitter and a receiver of information. Everyone is personally willing to
influence the others, but is also prepared to pay the price for that in the
form of willingness to be influenced by others. And it is of no significance
whether the relationship between the individuals is on the basis of the
classical organizational structure, vertical or horizontal, from outside or
from inside. In this distant perspective it is likely that new relations
with the 'city world' will appear. Not any longer with the port city as an
institution, as was the case in the past period, but with the key players
in the city network.

In the transition of port cities the direct role of the port will vanish
gradually, as will the institutional influence of the city on the port. Port

and port city will more and more follow their independent courses. The indirect effects of a port on its city will greatly depend upon the way the port succeeds in shifting or intensifying its playing field. On the longer term the contacts between port and port city may be strengthened again, but as part of network configurations and far more on an individual basis.

The Port as Public Domain **Han Meyer**

The relation between port and city is a matter of significant discussion these days. This fits within a general trend to consider the relation between the development of large-scale infrastructure and urban fabric as an important task for urban design. In the recent past we have made ourselves familiar with the idea that large scale infrastructure is a necessary evil: on the one hand we consider highways, ports, airports, and railways as inconvenient elements, which cause physical barriers and planning troubles; on the other hand we can't live without the mobility given by these supporting systems.

During the last half century we have tried to live with this paradox by organizing duties and assigning responsibilities: on one side we erected the institutions which are responsible for the design, construction and management of the large infrastructures, on the other the institutions which are concentrated on the design and management of the spatial qualities of city and landscape. Current developments on the relation between city and port are nothing more than an illustration of this organizing tendency, but a very sharp and clear illustration. In Rotterdam the assignment of duties between port development and city development started officially in the 1930s, with the foundation of the Port Authority and of the Department of City Planning. Both departments specialized in different works that had previously been combined in one department: The Department of Public Works. Both sectors have been developed into autonomous entities, each with its own institutions of management, design and planning (with their own methodological logics), and each with its own economic and cultural laws and characteristics. Between these sectors broad buffer zones were organized, which served to obscure, both literally and figuratively, any physical and visual contact between them. Furthermore, this self-sufficiency process was accompanied by a strong belief in 'planning'. The specialization and separation of the municipal territory into a port area and an urban area was founded with the conviction that it was possible to plan each of these environments, port and city, autonomously. During the post-war period this segregation acquired the character of a true battlefield. It is also true that during the post-war reconstruction of the city center, development has tried to propose a new relation between city and port. The 'Window on the River' was a beautiful concept; nevertheless city and port each developed in another way.

During the fifties and sixties interest in the port was dominating the development of the city and its surrounding landscape. Landscapes were destroyed, urban settlements were annexed. A decade later, during the seventies, the priorities changed to the contrary: the political precedence shifted to urban renewal and Port Authority profits were used to

finance this huge operation. Obsolete docklands were converted into residential districts in a fast-track process. The controversy between port and
city became untenable during the eighties. Two important events took place
in the second half of the decade: The development of the urban design for
the Kop van Zuid and the decision to maintain the garden village of Heijplaat. The new design for the Kop van Zuid was an important sign: for the
first time in decades, port activities were no longer considered as troublesome
and inconvenient, but as desirable and attractive elements of the cityscape.

The maintaining of docks, of facilities for river vessels, the renovation
of a cruise-terminal, the construction of office buildings for the Port
Authority, etc., were important elements of the plan. Originally the development of the Kop van Zuid resulted in the relocation of harbor concerns
to the Waalhaven-Eemhaven area. The beautiful village of Heijplaat, an
original example of a Dutch industrial garden village, was to be destroyed
as a result of this development. Thanks to the resistance of its inhabitants
the village was preserved. It became clear that the port could be developed
and reconstructed without destroying all the urban settlements in the area.

Since then we witness port and city attempting to cooperate more and
more. In this cooperation all kinds of motives play a role: nostalgic motives
of people who desire the historic image of big ships in the city, aesthetic
motives of those who are fascinated by the new architectonic configurations
of the port area. The most important motive, however, is the disappearance
of trust in the very idea of planning. We realize more and more that it is
impossible, and also undesirable, to completely control economic developments, as we believed during the sixties and seventies. We are able to create
conditions that provide the basis for new and desirable developments, but
that is something quite different from planning as it has been traditionally
practiced. We can hope that these conditions will generate positive developments, but we have to accept that it might be possible that other quite
unexpected developments can occur. It is especially due to this increased
notion of uncertainty that the question of the significance of the port as a
public work becomes important again. By this I mean the physical infra-

structure of docks, piers, quays, peninsulas, etc: we have forgotten to consider this enormous infrastructure financed by public investments and managed by a public authority, as a part of our public domain. The actual appearance of the port infrastructure has acquired the character of a private domain, including big billboards proclaiming 'NO ENTRY'. How then is it possible to consider and to treat the port infrastructure as a public work? Not just by removing the NO ENTRY signs, nor merely by cultivating some beautiful harbor buildings, nor by developing a tourist route through the port area, nor by attracting some port activities to the city center. These things might be important, but they are still insufficient to critically inform development. Also it is not always useful to look to the developments in Southeast Asia, as the OMA office suggests. Inspired by developments in Singapore OMA has proposed to increase the separation between city and port and to concentrate the port on and around the extended Maasvlakte. As a matter of fact, this proposal is a continuation of the idea of planning that is still very viable in the totalitarian regimes of Southeast Asian countries. In the Netherlands however this political model is not a desirable option.

I believe that there is still much to be gleaned from the period before the institutional separation of port and city, the period in the late 19th and early 20th century in which the design and construction of port infrastructure was an integral part of the work of the Department of Public Works. Even though the nature of port activities and the scale of port infrastructure have changed dramatically, some principles from this period still have value for the present situation. Essential, for instance, was the combining of uncertainty and stability: uncertainty concerning the future use of port accommodation (and equally the city), and the desire for stability by designing public works in such a way that the city could take enduring benefit from them. It is not my intention to plead in favor of the re-integration of the Port Authority and the City Planning Department back into one Department of Public Works. My plea concerns a renewal of the cultural and political attitude that considers port development as a 'public work'.

How did people manage this in earlier days? I will mention three principles, which still have significance for the contemporary situation.

1 The structure of the city plan   During the late 19th and early 20th century several city plans were proposed which produced different types of relations between cities and their ports. Usually these designs were founded on a cultural idea concerning the relation between city and port: the port was either considered as a symbol of urban identity

and independence, or a harmful and abominable element, or just as a neutral part of everyday city life. The 19th-century city plans of New York and
London represent two contrasting paradigms. The so-called Commissioners
Plan for Manhattan, 1811, expressed the idea of a complete equality of city
and port. The port economy as part of the city, just as other types of economy are part of the city: the port integrated in the basic urban structure
of the city. Piers formed, as a matter of fact, the continuation of the street
system stretching into the water. Some piers were used for shipping activities, other piers for urban facilities. There was no distinction, no hierarchy,
and no separation. This principle has been developed in most North-
American cities, such as Boston, Baltimore, San Francisco, and Seattle.

The opposite tendency is evidenced by the development of London in
the 19th century. Here we see, in an early phase of development, a sharp
separation between city and port. The port was concentrated in the East
End of London, with its own specific spatial typology of closed docks. The
legacy of each independent system remains visible. The almost self-evident
relation of the city with the surrounding water as developed in American
cities contrasts sharply with the very troubling relation of the city of London
with the renewed Docklands. In short, the complete system of public
streets in the modern port area should be evaluated not only with regard
to its serviceability for the port economy, but also with consideration to
the potential significance for urban developments.

2 Specific design, neutral possibilities of use

In the modern port area the system of public streets is mostly characterized
by an absence of any well considered design, while the use and the image
of the urban components, the parcels, are very specific. It is interesting to
recall that many of the 19th century designs for port extensions are founded
on exactly the opposite principles: For instance, the urban components are
neutral isles, allowing for a variety of use and architecture. Again, this is
expressed very well by the 19th century city plans of American cities. The
design by De Jongh for the South of Rotterdam, 1899, is another good
example of this approach. The urban components in the design are strictly

neutral, as are the elements located alongside the new docks. Of course the designers hoped and expected that port companies would use these plots, but there was no certainty about it. So the possibility of other kinds of use being present for the future of the port economy was uncertain as well. The system was so general that parts could be used 100 years afterward in the design of the Kop van Zuid. In other words, the current transformation of the Wilhelmina pier is largely founded on the ground plan that was designed by De Jongh in 1899. In the near future we will find at this pier a special mix of old harbor buildings with new uses, renewed and new harbor buildings still with port facilities, and new buildings with urban facilities. This development might be considered as a 'pilot project' for other parts of the port area.

Another relevant point is that in this earlier period, much attention was being paid to the design of public space. The large structural elements, very important for the increasing amount of traffic, were designed not just as traffic routes, but also as distinguished and luxurious avenues and boulevards. Due to this specific design the system of avenues and boulevards attained surplus value, so that it maintains its importance in the present situation of Rotterdam.

3 Considering the port infrastructure as a part of the morphology of the urban landscape
In present times the port infrastructure, like any large-scale infrastructure, is mainly judged on its performance as it relates to the port economy. In the meantime the development of the port infrastructure means an enormous transformation of the urban landscape, with new excisions (the docks) and new elevations (the dikes) in the landscape. This system may have its own spatial and architectural quality, independent of the functionality for the port economy. This spatial quality of the port landscape was especially discovered (or 'recovered') during the design process of the Kop van Zuid, when a new city boulevard was designed as a new type of urban parkway, alongside the water elements of docks and river. Also during the design of new port areas, as well as during the reconstruction of existing port areas, more attention should be paid to these kinds of considerations.

These three aspects exhibit an approach that is very relevant to present-day development regarding the relation between cities and their ports. A pertinent case study might be the city of Seattle, on the North American West Coast. Here we see a port development where the system of public space in the port area is designed and functioning as urban public space. Though the port activities dominate at one side of the city, they are integrated in a structure that is an essential part of the urban landscape. The largest grain silo in the United States happens to be located in an urban park that is intensively used by city dwellers. The granary and the arriving and departing ships contribute to a fascinating spectacle, but we can imagine that the view would be fabulous too if the granary were to be changed into an apartment building or office tower, and the grain ships replaced by yachts. At the other side of the city, nearby downtown, we see a combination of urban facilities and port activities. Ferries to different destinations are continuously coming and going. From Pike Place Market, an important facility for the everyday needs of the city dwellers, the shopping public enjoys a beautiful view of the modern harbor island. At other locations of the urban waterfront too, special facilities are placed to make possible the visual connection between city and port. The design and management of port and city do not interfere with each other, but both elements, city and port, are so interwoven that urban elements and port elements are interchangeable.

A similar strategy in this sense is also needed in Rotterdam. One of the most interesting areas to start with is the Waalhaven/Eemhaven area. This is an area that represents very well the untenable separation between port and city where a sharp demarcation line defines the two different worlds. The docks are, as it happens, outdated, but they are still interesting as a port area. A complete transformation into a new urban neighborhood, like other outdated docklands, is not a realistic future for this area. The Rotterdam Port Authority wants to stimulate new small-scale shipping companies here. But it is unclear and uncertain if this development will be successful. In the same time the neighborhoods of Charlois and Pendrecht, at the other side of the demarcation line, need an extension of public space and also of residential and economic activities. No wonder that designers of the City Planning Department are looking to these docklands. In short, the redevelopment of this area is a fantastic challenge to develop a relationship between city and port.

▲[1]

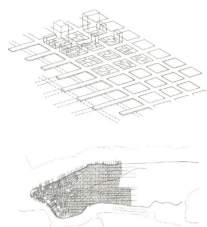
[2 a+b]

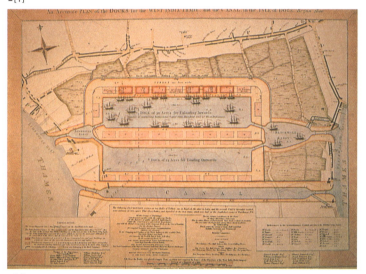
▲[3]

▲[4]

1 Rotterdam Delfshaven: residental quarter alongside the working port, 2000
2 a+b New York according to the Commissioners Plan: integration of street and pier systems
3 London Docklands in the 19th century: the docks as isolated enclaves in the urban landscape (engraving William Daniell, 1805)
4 Seattle 1990: symbiosis of dockside grain silos and urban park

Part II

Tokyo

The 1960 Tokyo Bay Project of Kenzo Tange **Hajime Yatsuka**

After the 1869 Meiji restoration, Japan began to seek new territory to expand her Lebensraum[1], a response to earlier problems deriving from the small size of the country relative to its large population.

Imperialistic colonization of Taiwan, Korea, Manchukuo and the South Pacific islands continued in the early twentieth century, driven by the need for new land. However, after World War Two, which resulted in the total liquidation of the colonial structure, Japan's oceans became the only possible realm for expansion; the waterfront became the water frontier. In the 1960s, avant-garde Japanese architects were making proposals for the future city on this new and singularly viable frontier. Among members of the Metabolists, Kiyonori Kikutake was particularly energetic in this area. He produced many ocean city projects from 1959 onward, eventually realized in the construction of the Aquapolis, a floating model community built for the 1976 Ocean Exposition in Okinawa. Another Metabolist, Kisho Kurokawa, also launched visions of Helix City, a proposed city on Lake Kasumigaura in northern Tokyo, as well as another Metabolist project for a production center on the ocean. Arata Isozaki, who was often associated with the group, but was not actually a member, also made a proposal, Computer-Aided City, in Chiba's Makuhari district on Tokyo Bay. Makuhari actually would become a sub-center of the metropolitan area, an agglomeration of media industry offices and research laboratories two decades later, if not in such dramatic way as Isozaki had conceived.

These projects marked the most radical and systematic challenge by architects for future development of human settlements on this water frontier. However, it is the 1960 Tokyo Bay Project by Kenzo Tange and his team that still holds by far the most profound significance among projects from that period. It is not only important as a project itself, but it is one of the most striking renditions of the crystallization of the ideas and philosophy of certain trends in urbanism during the 20th century.

Before discussing this project by Tange, we need to mention briefly its history, referring to one of the core ideas that characterizes the ideology of this century; constructivism. Of course, architects are quite familiar with the notion of constructivism as an avant-garde art movement. There is also another definition of constructivism, proposed, rather negatively, by Friedlich Hayek, the Nobel Prize-winning economist. For Hayek, constructivism was belief in the capacity of technocrats to control the total economy of a country. These two types of constructivism, conceived independently, were united in the attempts of Russian avant-garde architects and planners, called 'disurbanists', around 1930. In the

---

1 'Lebensraum' is a 'biotope', that is the space which is appropriate for trees, birds, etc., while animals have adapted to these Lebensräume. The word was used in 1870/71 in Germany in order to justify an extension of the 'Deutsches Reich' and then was particularly used in the fascist period in the field of geopolitics to characterize the limited life zone for the German people in order to give an ideological justification of the imperialistic politics of extension of the Nazi regime. Japan's war time activities are an Asian correlative to the German Lebensraum.

philosophy of the Russian disurbanists[2], the linear, open network of a transportation-communication infrastructure – on which productive/administrative centers and human settlements were attached – was to be scattered throughout the vast territory of the USSR. This almost infinite expansion into the Russian frontier of the units of a new social and economic system was envisioned as making up one part of the Five Year Plan inaugurated in 1928. In this conception, constructivism in architecture was integrated with a constructivistic scenario for the national economy.

Another example of integrated constructivism is the work of Le Corbusier in the course of the 1930s. His ideology was never called constructivism, but included a tendency toward syndicalism and regionalism. However, in his vision as well, the socio-economic network of infrastructure and what he called human establishment was envisioned as permeating throughout the frontier of the new Mediterranean community of France, Italy, Spain and North Africa. The titles of periodicals by the intellectuals surrounding him well illustrate the object of their constructivist enthusiasm. These avant-garde works were motivated by aspiration; planning took command.

In part from 1905, and then totally after 1931, the north-east part of China, then called Manchuria, became a new frontier for the expansion of Japanese imperialism. It was the South-Manchuria Railway Company, known as Man-tetsu, established in 1906, which acted as a driving force for the development and successive colonization of the region. It played the same role as the East-Indian Company of Great Britain in India or the North Borneo Company of the Dutch in Indonesia. This substantially state-owned company undertook the development not only of railway lines, but also of a network of productive centers and cities. The first president of the company, Shinpei Goto, a typically enlightened colonialist, was originally a medical doctor and was among the pioneers of public hygiene in Japan. After his great success in the prevention of epidemics among soldiers at the front in the Japanese-Russian War, Goto became Chief Officer of the Bureau of Civil Administration of Taiwan, in 1898. He amassed an enormous body of research on the geography, social customs, land ownership systems,

---

2 The word 'disurbanists' refers to those intellectuals who, in 1930s Russia, promoted the idea of breaking up major cities in favor of decentralization.

and conditions of public sanitation in the region and then introduced modern infrastructure to Taiwan. He was also responsible for the city planning of Taipei.

After Taiwan, Goto moved to Manchuria in 1906 and became president of the Man-tetsu Company. One of Goto's most important achievements during his brief tenure in office was the establishment of a research department. This was a sort of think-tank, its scope of work having no precedent. Ultimately, Goto returned to his homeland, and became Mayor of Tokyo, in charge of the reconstruction of the city after the great earthquake of 1923. But even after his departure, the Man-tetsu Company's research department drew many excellent analysts, planners, and economists. As Manchuria was a front between Japan and Russia, research on the manifestation of the newly established Soviet Union was exhaustive. The amount and the quality of their information on the Soviet Union is said to have superseded that of the American government at that time.

In the brief period between 1931, the year of Japan's occupation of Manchuria and the outbreak of total war between Japan and China in 1937, there was an intention to establish Manchuria, then Manchuko, as a site for an experimentally controlled economic plan. For this purpose, the research department of Man-tetsu was expanded to be more closely integrated with the organization of the Japanese Military Services. The newly established Man-tetsu Economic Research Institute was headed by Shinji Sogo, previously in the Railway Ministry. He had been in charge of the reconstruction of Tokyo after the earthquake in 1923, under Goto.

Another important person working on post-earthquake reconstruction under Goto was Toshikata (also known as Riki) Sano, a professor of architecture at Tokyo University. Sano played a dominant role in the development of many city planning and building laws in Japan. Both Sano and Sogo became involved with development on the Manchurian frontier; Sano in the field of architectural administration and city planning and Sogo in the field of regional economy and national land development. In 1937, the military headquarters launched a Five Year Plan for the region, based on the program produced by Sogo and his staff, including Masayoshi Miyazaki, a specialist on the Soviet Union. Miyazaki incorporated the ideas of not only the Soviet Union, but also of Nazi Germany and Fascist Italy. For at least this moment and in this idea, Manchuko approached closest to the 'command of planning'. However, despite the intentions of the authors of this program, the China front was extended to the whole country in the same year and the Plan degenerated into a system for providing the means to wage war.

Urban planning for Manchuria, first established by Goto and carried on by the architectural department of Man-tetsu, was also extended in terms of territory and scope of intervention after 1931. In particular, the planning of the new capital city for the pseudo-empire of Manchuko, Shinkyo (now Changchun) was greatly amplified to cope with the new socio-political order. This plan, together with plans for other Manchurian cities, including Harbin and Dalian, the former Russian colonial cities, provided unprecedented occasions for experimentation with large-scale town planning, to a degree never realized on the Japanese mainland. However, the basic style of these plans was that of the European (and especially Russian) town planning of the latter half of the 19th century, characterized by immense urban layouts with axial boulevards, vast roundabouts, and monumental buildings, and the technology of sanitary and electrical utilities and rationalized traffic was introduced. A professor at Tokyo University and a young colleague of the more bureaucratic Sano, Hideto Kishida, insisted that the planning of Shinkyo represented the most advanced ideas and leading technologies in city planning throughout the world, but in spite of this, it was rather outmoded, compared to the contemporary ideas of the Russian disurbanists and Le Corbusier. The ideas had been relatively new in Goto's day, but were never modified or updated; the architectural department of the Man-tetsu and the new imperial government did not match an innovative tendency to constructivism with the ambitions of the economists belonging to the same organization.

However, there was one exception found among the urban planning schemes for Shinkyo. This was a plan by Junzo Sakakura, proposed in 1939 for a residential quarter in the southern area of the city, facing the vast artificial lake called Nan-ko (South Lake). Sakakura had been working for Le Corbusier in Paris between 1931 and 1936. In 1936, he returned to Japan, although he was soon to return again to Paris for the construction of the Japanese Pavilion for the World Exposition there. That pavilion would be awarded the Grand-Prix, along with the Finnish Pavilion by Alvar Aalto and the Spanish Pavilion by Jose-Louis Sert. Sakakura's design represented a new direction for modern architecture, transcending the internationalism of German modernists in the 1920s such as Walter Gropius. It goes without saying that this coincided with a shift in Le Corbusier's own ideas, toward a new Mediterranean order and a concern for regionalism.

In the Japanese context, Sakakura's pavilion represented another challenge. It was advocated as a Japanese design to replace an old fashioned nationalist and traditionalist design of the period. Sakakura's building aimed at being modern and Japanese (regional) at the same time. In the text written for this building, Sakakura noted, 'From small residential buildings to large cities, all should be designed as one organic creature.' In criticizing the functionalist theories of Bauhaus architects, Sakakura emphasized the biological state of human beings. This biological emphasis was characteristic of many discourses on colonialism, influenced by the natural selection theories of Charles Darwin. (Goto was also an ardent supporter of these ideas.) And Sakakura's thesis was also very similar to the treatise of Le Corbusier's co-editor, Hubert Lagardelle, in his discussion of 'homme réel'.[3] The biological state of humans was also critical to Lagardelle. Apparently, Sakakura must have been familiar with the syndicalist nexus of Le Corbusier when he returned from Paris to Tokyo in 1939 and then quickly became involved in the planning of Manchuko.

His Shinkyo-Nanko project was remarkably similar to urban work by Le Corbusier, almost a literal copy. It is a fragment of the Ville Radieuse, montaged on the traditionalist framework of the larger city plan of Shinkyo. It would appear that Hideto Kishida introduced him to this project, because Kishida was influential in the imperial government of Manchuko and also in charge of the Japanese Pavilion in Paris. On the new frontier of Manchuko, there had been little opportunity for independent architects like Sakakura, most of the work being undertaken by those belonging to the bureaucracy. At that time, when Manchuko (as well as areas such as Shanghai) appeared to be a new frontier for experimentation, independent and modernist architects became increasingly interested in these areas and grew critical about practice there. They found most of the execution of Manchurian plans either too outmoded and monumental (in the case of public buildings), or too seedy (in the case of temporary residential works). As Kishida was regarded as a supporter of the modernists, he might have found the Nanko project a good opportunity to present more innovative ideas for architectural and urban practice on this frontier. And for Sakakura as well, the project must have been more than a normal commission, judging from his contemporaneous discourses and their romantic, even nationalistic tone.

However, it was too late. As the Five Year Plan soon degenerated into a plan in sup-

3 'Homme réel' is one of the key concepts Hubert Lagardelle developed in his articles: 'L'Homme réel est l'Hommes du Métier. L'expression de l'Hommes du Métier est le Syndicat integré dans l'Etat' and 'L'Homme réel est l'Homme de la Région. L'expression de l'Hommes dans la Région n'est pas seulement l'urne principle; mais, essentiellement l'Assemblée régionale.' Lagardelle was an ex-socialist and had ties to Italian Fascism through a long-standing relationship with Mussolini. He advocated 'L'Homme réel' as a counterpart to man in democratic (and capitalist) society.

port of the war, Sakakura's Ville Radieuse was never realized. Architectural constructivism never united with economic constructivism on this frontier of the Chinese continent. However, this presented not ultimate failure to achieve integration, but only a prelude to events that took place much later.

In Sakakura's office in Tokyo, it is said that intellectuals and military officers were frequent visitors during this period. So were young architecture students, who found in Sakakura an alternative to the more materialist-modernist architects of Japan. Among them was a young Kenzo Tange, who participated in work on the Shinkyo-Nanko project. Young Tange never concealed his distaste for the architecture of older modernist architects in Japan, referring to these buildings as 'sanitary fixtures'. For him, only Le Corbusier among the Western architects showed the new way towards an architecture full of poetic inspiration. In the same year as the Shinkyo-Nanko project, Tange wrote his well-known *Ode to Michelangelo; Introduction to Le Corbusier*, composed with gallant prose. Tange regarded Michelangelo and Le Corbusier as poet-prophets of their time. However, he himself was interested in becoming something more, the organizer of the nation. After briefly working for Kunio Maekawa, another former employee of Le Corbusier's, he returned to Tokyo University, where he took graduate courses on urban planning.

In 1942, Tange won a competition for what was called the 'Greater Asian Co-Prosperity Sphere Monument', a dramatic debut for the young genius. This was a competition geared towards propaganda, to show how architects could contribute to the Japanese task of achieving the Greater Asian Co-Prosperity Sphere and liberating Asia from colonization and exploitation by the West. The program and the site were not fixed, but could be chosen by participants. Tange chose the foot of Mt. Fuji, where he conceived of a funeral sanctum for fallen soldiers. He deliberately avoided referring to sculptural monuments in his design, as he saw western characteristics in them. For him, the sanctuaries and precincts of temples, more emphasis on the environment than on sculpture, was more authentically fitting with Japanese sensibilities. The location of his project, at the foot of Mt. Fuji,

4   The idea that Fuji symbolizes Japan, however, was initially established in the book titled **Nihon Fukei-ron** [Discourse on the Japanese Natural Landscape] by a geologist, Shigetaka Shiga, published in 1897. In this book, which became one of the bestsellers of the period, Shiga tried to give a structure to the image of the nation's landscape, which had earlier been no more than an agglomeration of fragments. He established the highest mountain of the country as a focus for decoding national geography. Shiga, known as one of the most ardent nationalists of the time, succeeded in instituting the people's image of their own country, something which had not existed before the restoration. From

also seemed quite typical, because Fuji is now regarded as a sacred symbol for all of Japan.[4]

Tange's project was not merely a city for the dead; he conceived of it as an alternative capital city. He noted that it should be connected with Tokyo by an axial route representing the Greater Asian Co-Prosperity Sphere, which made it possible to move between the two cities very quickly. For this infrastructure, he proposed combining a city for administration and economy with a cultural city, to reduce concentration in Tokyo. Tange's futuristic enthusiasm for speed, combined with his concern for regional structure, was one that no other Japanese architect had ever articulated. The super-express 'ASIA' of the Man-tetsu Company, the fastest train in the world at that time, might have been a counterpart to Tange's traffic-based cult.

In 1948, after the war, Tange wrote an essay, 'Problems Relating to Architecture' for a periodical published by the Japanese Architectural Academy. In this article, his emphasis drastically shifted, from a previous romantic and even chauvinistic enthusiasm to criticism of the pre-modern structures of land ownership and building industries in Japan. He regarded the achievement of economic stability as the most urgent problem of the period and noted that provision of 'reproductive means' as well as productive ones should become a focus for a new approach to capitalism within a controlled society. Citing the theories of André Siegfried, a French political philosopher and historian, Tange concluded that the world was now faced with two alternatives; freedom or planning. He also referred to the American Tennessee Valley Authority as a possible model for planned economic policy within capitalist society. His interest in the 'commanding of planning' was evident.

It goes without saying that the rebuilding of cities and the national economy was the most important task of this period. Among those who joined the effort were Shinji Sogo and Masayoshi Miyazaki, who had been responsible for the Five Year Plan in Manchuko. While Miyazaki died before achieving any substantial contribution, Sogo played one of the major roles in Japanese post-war society. As ex-bureaucrats of the Manchuko empire such as Shinsuke Kishi (Prime Minister from 1957) and Etsusaburou Shi-ina (co-president of the Free Democratic Party from 1972) attained political power in post-war society, supplanting the Five Year Plan for Man-tetsu and modifying it to meet with the new reality of total warfare, Sogo restarted his career, being involved in the rebuilding projects, and eventually becoming president of the Japanese National Railway. The Tokaido Shinkansen (bullet train) between Tokyo and Osaka, which was later extended to other

then on, Fuji became a focus for the nation, presented as if it had been so since ancient times.
Tange only complied with this reading.

parts of the country to form a network, was inaugurated by Sogo. It was unmistakably a successor to the Man-tetsu 'ASIA' super-express noted earlier.

Tange was also busy working on the reconstruction efforts of many
Japanese cities. Among them was a project for Hiroshima on which he had
worked since 1946. For that city, a special construction plan for the 'memorial peace city' was adopted. Before Tange and his team undertook the
project, plans for roads and the park system were almost settled. Tange's
team modified part of the predetermined plan for the Nakanoshima district,
the epicenter of the atomic bomb's explosion. This district, conceived as a
memorial peace park, was addressed in a architectural competition in
1949, won by Tange himself. Among the judges was Hideto Kishida, a
mentor to Tange at Tokyo University and also a chief juror in the 'Greater
Asian Co-Prosperity Sphere Monument' competition. Kishida, in his
remarks on the competition, found the Tange project notably urbane,
combined with a bold spatial conception. Tange's main idea was again
a dramatic axis, set perpendicular to a broad boulevard in front of the park,
with the dome that had survived the bomb as a focus
and memorial in the background. As an architectural project, it was a great
success and achieved a world-wide reputation for the architect. Tange had
been building so many important public projects in the course of the fifties
and sixties, he had become a sort of architect for the nation. However, this
project was still too limited in scale to cope with Tange's ambitions for
the 'command of planning'; the Nakanoshima district was too small for his
ideas.

In 1961, Tange published his plan for the Tokyo Bay area, developed in
his studio at Tokyo University. It is unlikely that the project was commissioned by anyone, rather, it was a volunteer effort. I have already noted that
this coincided with the contemporary argument that reclaiming the bay
appeared as the only possible frontier for Tokyo. Even at that time, the
capital city had grown enormously, both in size and in population. The
megalopolis was surpassing the city's administrative borders and the traditional geographic borders, the rivers. Tange's earlier arguments on expansion of the megalopolis now appeared to face a crisis. Unlike in pre-war

times, the expansion of the Lebensraum abroad was totally impossible. The sea was the only possible alternative. In this sense, the project became a sort of attempt at inner colonization.

It is possible that this project was initially developed for presentation to the World Design Conference in Tokyo, held in 1960. The young architects, critics and designers who worked as a preparatory committee on this occasion eventually established the Metabolist group. They were directly influenced by Tange, in that Takashi Asada, previously Tange's chief assistant, acted as chair of the committee and brought the group together. Tange was staying in the US in the fall of 1959, teaching at MIT. Thus, his study for the Tokyo Bay Project had already started, but work was suspended while he was abroad. However, Tange produced a preview of the project while at MIT, a project for an ocean community in Boston Bay. This was a megastructure to be built on the sea, in which 25,000 inhabitants were to live.

It is possible that Tange was influenced by Kikutake's project for an ocean city in the same year, because he showed Kikutake's design at the CIAM meeting in Otterlo, to which Tange made a presentation before moving to Cambridge. At any rate, the project for a residential community of 25,000 for Boston was, together with Tange's unsuccessful competition entry for the World Health Organization in Geneva in the same year, to provide the archetype for the residential units for the Tokyo Bay Project.

The substantial part of the Tokyo Bay Project was eventually completed in the fall of 1960; Tange had to be content with presenting the Boston project to the Design Conference in May. This delay was caused partly by the Design Conference itself, but also supposedly because of the upheaval caused by mass demonstrations related to the Security Treaty between the US and Japan, in which most progressive architects, including Tange and his staff, participated. There was historical irony to this event; the Japanese prime minister at that time, in charge of the Security Treaty, was Shinsuke Kishi, whom I mentioned earlier.

Tange's initial idea for the project was again an axis, traversing Tokyo Bay. The axis, which connected the capital city with Mt. Fuji in his pre-war project, was now extended toward the opposite side of the bay. In this sense, the Tokyo Bay project was a negative picture of his 'Greater Asian Co-Prosperity Sphere Monument', just as the political background had reversed from a totalitarian regime to a democratic one. By adopting an axial composition, Tange argued that limitations on the scope of expansion in the existing radial-concentric structure of Tokyo would be greatly alleviated. This is reminiscent of the linear city projects by Russian avant-garde architects and planners around 1930. In the place of the vast field of Russia, the Bay area provided a new frontier. The city could be extended in successive stages, each planned to be built in five-year periods, retaining the same basic composition.

The axis was conceived as a repetition of the highway unit (3 kilometers in length), which was called a 'cycle transportation system'; it was a three-dimensional system that was designed to require drivers to make minimal choices in terms of speed and destination. Kisho Kurokawa, the youngest member of the Metabolists and still a student in Tange's studio, was in charge of this area. The idea of a system based on the principle of minimum choice is said to be his. On this spine, the monorail system was also super-imposed. At the inland periphery on both sides of this main axis were two airports, one of which was Haneda International Airport, in its contem-porary location (now moved toward the sea) and the other being a domestic airport. These were to be connected by a railway on a bridge. At the cross-ing of the railway and the main spine, the new Tokyo station was located. On the next ring cycle transportation unit, moving from the station toward the sea, was the Tokyo New Port.

On this axis were a Royal Palace and the Harumi district, then the only reclaimed land in the bay. In the opposite direction on the axis, further south, the central government buildings and business districts were planned on the sea. This was to be the new city center of Tokyo. Arata Isozaki was in charge of this section and the design was a variation of his own city in the air project, which he called the 'Joint core system'. The joint core idea, in its turn, came from Tange's notion of gathering all the vertical elements, circulation and mechanical equipment in the core of a building, which would then also work to resist to earthquakes.

Isozaki bridged these vertical cores by multi-floor (10 to 20 story) office spaces, liberating the ground level. This was apparently an extended idea of pilotis at a megalomaniac scale. On the ground level were facilities corresponding to the human scale; shopping centers, auditoriums, and plazas. These horizontal skyscrapers are reminiscent of the Wolkenbügel project by El Lissitzky. Tange later developed this scheme in his Tsukiji district project, designed between 1960 and 1964. The idea was also realized in two office buildings for media corporations, one in Tokyo for the Shizuoka Press and Broadcasting Center and another in Kofu City, the Yamanashi Press and Broadcasting Center.

On both sides of this new city center were groups of residential megastructures on the sea, derived from the Boston scheme and the WHO project. These were autonomous communities with public plazas, schools, shopping centers, and parking garages, all of which were connected with the central axis by monorails and highways. They were located in a random pattern to present the idea of indeterminacy within the modern megalopolis. Hiroshi Kamiya was in charge of this section. Tange was relatively indifferent to the problem of production centers. They were to be located, as they were and still are, in the peripheries of the inner bay areas. It was only in later stages, when industrial production shifted from the classic heavy-industry types to more modern types based on electric media that Tange became interested in this district. These details show us that individual parts were rather ad-hoc agglomerations of his previously developed ideas and that the axis structure was by far the most significant part of the project. This is also illustrated by the fact that the project was subtitled 'Proposal for the Restructuring of Tokyo'. For him, structure was more essential than anything else. It was the manifestation of his constructivist will to control the city and society.

Among the sketches for this project is a study for the extension of the axis inland. One sketch shows the spine was curved to be connected with the Shinjuku district, instead of Ikebukuro as had been suggested in Tange's original plan. Farther west, the axis was extended to reach to Mt. Fuji. This is the very idea Tange planned in his Greater Asian Co-Prosperity Sphere Monument of twenty years before. In the accompanying paper on this project, his major emphasis was that restructuring of the capital would induce investment from the growing Japanese economy. Dr. David Stewart has pointed out that this was sent out in a press release against the background of new economic programs announced by the Japanese government.

From 1967 to 1970, at the request of the government, Tange had been working on a study of Japan in the 21st century. In this vision, the axial structure was extended throughout the country to form a networked rapid transportation system, then realized partly in the Tokaido Shinkansen. Tange's megalomaniac belief in societal control finally met with what had been conceived in Manchuria some thirty years previous. This was the outcome of Japanese modern society and its strong inclination towards the 'command of planning'.

Postscript At the same time that he was working on the study 'Japan in the 21st century', Tange had been drawing up the masterplan for EXPO'70 in Osaka, for the Ministry of Trade and Commerce. For Tange and his team, this was the first occasion of experimentation with their ideas for the future city on a real site. Tange designed a Festival Plaza with a megaroof 300 meters long, conceived as a future public zone. The event was quite successful in mobilizing unprecedented numbers of people, but they participated in the event as popular entertainment, without regard for the architects' serious intentions. In turn, the architects were faced with the indifference of the masses. Since then, large expositions that were and still are hailed as effective events to stimulate regional economies are governed not by architects but by advertising agencies; advertising now took command. This marked an unveiling of Japanese postmodern society. As if to illustrate this change in Japanese society, the Tokyo Bay Area is now viable only as a future site for theme parks.

1 Kenzo Tange, Greater Asian
Co-Prosperity Sphere Monument, 1942.
2 Sketch showing the idea to connect
the capital with Mount Fuji.
3–4 Junzo Sakakura,
Shinkyo Nan-ko Project, 1939.

▲[1] ▼[2]

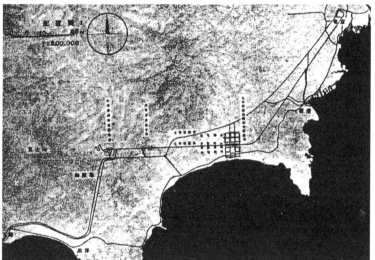

◄[3] [4]►

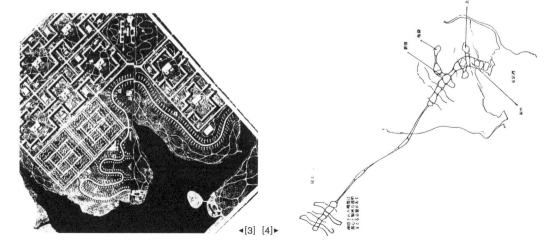

Tokyo Waterfront Development Project: Its Location in the Context of Tokyo Urban Formation

Haruo Ueno

Tokyo's waterfront development has its roots in the Edo era (400-100 years ago), where the feudal lords had their own quays and warehouses on the rivers and canals of Edo. During this era the main transport of commodities was by waterway. After the Meiji Restoration, when the Edo feudal system was changed, Edo's population was decreased and the feudal lord's quays also declined, but waterways were still used for domestic commodities transport.

After the Meiji era, with the development of modern industries, a new reclamation scheme started in the Tokyo Bay area for industrial usage. Especially after World War II, the heavy industries were located on the waterfront by the large-scale reclamation lands; at that time the traditional use for fisheries and resorts had to be abandoned.

In Tokyo, unlike other areas on the waterfront, they located the urban infrastructures such as sewer disposal, garbage disposal and energy plants (rather than the factories) along the waterfront, under the heavy pressure of continuing expansion of the urban population. At the same time, the port area was dedicated to the warehouses, which were to serve commodity transportations for the people of Tokyo and its industries. This land use policy inevitably made Tokyo's waterfront very unpopular with the citizens by denying them easy access to the waterfront. Most of Tokyo's inhabitants, even now, exhibit little notion that they have the sea in the immediate vicinity of the central district, within a distance of just a few kilometers.

In the 1970s, Tokyo's industry was shifted from the secondary sector to the tertiary sector, but still the expansion continued to increase to a population of 25 million in the Tokyo urban area. In the 1980s, with the internationalization of Japanese industries, the activated economy forced a serious shortage of office space in Tokyo. The Tokyo urban area population expanded to more than 30 million. That phenomenon ignited the bubble economy that skyrocketed land prices to an unrealistic level. The housing community area was sometimes invaded by the speculative actions of the developers looking for space for office development. The shortage of office space was serious in the Tokyo urban area generally and it was also difficult to develop the needed amounts of space within the short term. By then the waterfront area had drawn the attention of developers as a result both of its vacancy and its proximity to the central area.

In the Tokyo urban area the local authorities had already started new waterfront development projects. Tokyo, Yokohama, and Makuhari were the major cities where waterfront projects were simultaneously initiated. But without a coherent relation to each other, they subsequently competed by planning similar characters for their new urban space.

It should be reiterated that the Tokyo waterfront development project was originally planned because of the office space shortage, rather than the revitalization of the derelict port area. The aim of the original development plan was to make Tokyo port the information port in the coming international telecommunication era. The idea of the teleport was already in practice at Rotterdam and New York. The teleport plan, with the area of 40 hectares, was enlarged to 448 hectares in 1987 in the Tokyo waterfront project, with the original distribution of 60,000 – residential population, 110,000 – business population.

At that time, Japan was bustling with its economic boom and the Tokyo urban area was one of the most active regions with its high concentration of business activities. Tokyo Metropolitan Government introduced the multi-nucleus urban center plan with seven sub-centers placed around the central business district. The Tokyo waterfront sub-center, the newly reclaimed land, was allocated as the 7th sub-center in order to ease the pressure of urban concentration. The other 6 sub-centers were located within the existent urban area, which was already developed to considerable density. During this time of economic boom, the financial scenario for this development was very optimistic with a 25 year term of financing. The construction cost was estimated at 25 billion dollars for urban infrastructures, such as a multi-purpose tunnel, a district heating & cooling system, garbage and sewer plants and anti-seismic structural measures.

Characteristically, the new scheme for the reversion of profits accruing from the development was introduced at this time to cover up to 50% of the major public investment capital. Yet this was only possible because the Tokyo Metropolitan Government was both the owner/landlord of the area and the local administrative body. There was little private ownership involved.

The ex-governor of Tokyo, very much in favor of the expansion, attempted to incite development by taking the so-called 'event-locomotive' method, announcing plans for a World Expo. He had been a supporter of this catalyst method in the sixties when the Olympic Games were used to push the whole political and social system to collectively work towards the deadline of opening day. This time he invented the 'World Cities Exposition' with the theme of 'growing urbanization'. By setting the deadline for the event as well as for the new waterfront project within a very short time frame (5 years), development started buying time at a very high cost.

There were also high expectations for this area as regards experimentation with the new urban ideas which would result from the exposition event. But this method had serious consequences in that it drastically inflated construction costs, which in turn, suffocated the whole program. The first project-competition began in 1990, 77 plans and 394 firms applying for only 18 sites. It was really the high tide for the Japanese economy, raising investments and profits to an unsustainable level. But soon after came the break in the bubble economy. At this time 5 sites were left open and the collapse forced the development revenues to plummet. The new governor of Tokyo was elected in 1995, claiming that he would cancel the event as well as put a stop to the waterfront development because the project had been implemented without public consent. The expansion development had obviously become an intensely critical political issue and continues to remain so under the current economic recession.

When the sudden fall in the economy occurred, consensus was that the desirability of the area would also suffer a decline. But events proved quite different. As this area offered new scenery of urban waterfront spaces set away from the citizens' gaze, it drew new attention. Further, it became one of the most popular tourist attractions in Tokyo, even competing with the Tokyo Disneyland. Last year alone there were 22 million visitors, which makes this area more of an urban-tourist spot than the global business zone for which it was originally intended. Subsequently, commercial and entertainment projects are presently under way at a very large scale. These kinds of customer-orientated projects require constant renewal in order to maintain interest and assure a returning clientele. The character of the buildings, therefore, tends to be light and temporary, because they concentrate the budget in the economically return-relevant part of the program while the architectural product has little more significance than that of a container.

Temporality and novelty of Tokyo waterfront space have been the key factors for this area's popularity. Looking at the city from across the waterways was a totally unexpected and new experience, people sensed and foresaw a new cultural phenomenon. It could be said that the people of Tokyo suddenly noticed the charm of the water-front, when before they had remained indifferent to it.

Compared to the rigid existing urban space, the new waterfront gave them a new feeling of urban comfort they could enjoy. The Tokyo waterfront development project was originally aimed at the creation of new urban comfort by experimenting with new ideas. To do this, as stated above, the exposition used to promote a new urban system in the area of the water-front as opposed to the existing urban fabric. The new experience of the waterfront area in Tokyo was considered to be the vital factor for the new urban space. To keep the development struggle moving forward it was necessary to augment development with huge loans. Ironically, it was the expo-sition, in the end, that carried ideas forward as regards the invention of new forms of urban space, while the continuing residential and commercial development followed rather ordinary methods of town planning.

Tokyo's waterfront development project still suffers from the economic recession, which inevitably brought a variety of land management, from short-term land leasing to land sales. And temporary usage of land was also new, and, as mentioned above, led to many 'temporary architecture' ideas. To cope with the physical environment process, Tokyo metropolitan gov-ernment, as the key developer, set design guidelines in addition to the ordi-nary legal town-planning restrictions and building codes. The guidelines were first set to outline the frame of the projects at the time of the expand-ing economy; however currently there is little left of the earlier pressures to expand. The guidelines themselves have come under the pressure of revi-sion in order to ease strain from the earlier, very optimistic, projections.

There is also the tendency to propagate the temporal character of the space, because the time-cost factor is very crucial in a consumer-orientated society. As discussed, the Tokyo waterfront area was originally dedicated to the experimental urban project of the cities exposition, and the exposition was also the temporal product itself. From the point of view of temporality, we could re-examine the rigid frame of the existing regulations and the notions of public space in regard to new concepts of comfort in urban design. By disclosing and stimulating examinations of this new facet of urban space, Tokyo waterfront development could be a good counterpart to Tokyo's existing environment across the waterways by virtue of its new openness. And it is precisely this characteristic that continues to attract people to the Tokyo waterfront area today.

▲[2] ▼[1]

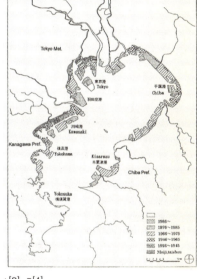

▲[3] ▼[4]

▲[5]   ▼[6]

▼[7]

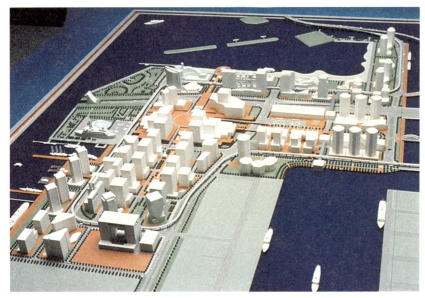

▲[8]   ▼[9]

1 Tokyo waterfront development project.
2 Reclamation lands along Tokyo
Bay showing the abandonment of the
traditional use.
3 Urban infrastructure located in the
Bay area.

4 Teleport plan, 1987.
5 World Cities Exposition site.
6 Example of the light and temporary
architecture which resulted in the Bay area
developments.
7 Tokyo Disneyland.

8–9 World Cities Exposition after 1995.

Two City Center Models   Hidetoshi Ohno

The purpose of this essay is to offer an evaluation of the seaside urban subcenter built on reclaimed land in Tokyo Bay, popularly known as 'Teleport Town' or 'Rainbow Town', in relation to the question of Japan's long-term urban growth strategy. At the same time, I will examine the influence that the kind of urban design we see in Rainbow Town has upon architecture.

Hong Kong – The embodiment of the modern city ideal, or a heretical city

Hong Kong is a non-Japanese Asian city, which like Singapore, has emerged as an economically successful city with a strong nation-city character. From the viewpoint of urban planning, Hong Kong's special characteristics give it an equivocal nature. It is an exemplar of modern urban planning ideals, and yet it has certain heretical characteristics, for it violates many of the taboos of modern urban planning. Hong Kong's features are summarized in the following eight points. Although this analysis is based on an investigation we undertook in 1991,[1] Hong Kong retains these characteristics even after the Chinese takeover in 1997.

Three-dimensionality In examining the three-dimensional use of space in Hong Kong one finds a clear indication of its adherence to the canons of modern urban planning. This functional three-dimensionality includes transportation networks such as the harbor, expressways, subway systems, and elevated pedestrian ways, as well as skyscrapers designed for a variety of uses. All these elements were presented in the futuristic cities envisioned by Europe's architectural and urban planning avant-gardes at the beginning of this century.

High density At the same time, Hong Kong's density violates canonical planning policy. In modern urban planning a transaction is usually implied, in that when the three-dimensional use of space occurs, the amount of green space should increase correspondingly. This is due to the desire to avoid the kind of unfortunate residential environments which occurred in the 18th and 19th centuries in high-density industrialized cities. In Hong Kong, however, both the building density and the population density are extremely high.

Adjacency It is inevitable that with high density comes adjacency. The proximity of objects to objects, people to objects, and people to people means that close contact occurs

---

1 H. Ohno and Ohno laboratory, 'The University of Tokyo, Hong Kong: Alternative Metropolis', **Space Design**, no. 330, March 1992.

at all times. High population density creates a demand for increased floor space. In Hong Kong, many residents have achieved a minimum amount of expansion by attaching boxes or cages outside their apartment windows. In many places, the spaces above the narrow public streets are in danger of being filled in by these cages. One important condition of space in modern planning is the maintenance of distance between objects. In this regard, Hong Kong is anti-modern: its adjacency condition is akin to that which existed in medieval cities.

The emergence of individualism

Apart from the new suburban areas and the luxurious condominiums on Hong Kong Island, a large percentage of the facades of high-rise apartment buildings have also been covered by illegal cages. The outside appearance of each apartment varies according to the character of its resident. The high-rise apartments of canonical modern architecture were often scorned because none of the units made any concession to the individuality of its occupant. The high-rise apartments of Hong Kong, however, are an opposite extreme. The idea of a free, ad hoc architecture which reflects the will of the resident, paying homage to his or her individuality, is one which many architects keen on reforming Modernism's rationality have argued for. Hong Kong, however, has surpassed all of their proposals. Hong Kong is super-modern.

An omnipresent green The provision of parks is one of the important aims of modern urban planning. I would argue that the essence of modern urban planning was the adoption of the features of the suburbs in the planning of urban areas. The iconic image of the modern city is that of a high-rise building rising out of a forest. Modern urban planning presents a compromise between the social and economic benefits of city living and the atmosphere of country life. In contrast, Hong Kong is like a walled medieval city, in that it makes hardly any attempt to introduce the natural landscape into the man-made environment. Greenery is present, but in the form of plants placed in the cages, so that plants pervade the three-dimensional space of the city.

Ambiguous forms and eloquent cages Although Hong Kong's new architecture is striving to emulate the forms of modern architecture, unless a building's height allows it to loom over its neighbors, as with I.M. Pei's Bank of China, then the building will be buried between adjacent buildings. Even Foster's Hong Kong Shanghai Bank, with its distinctive contours, recedes into the cityscape. Extreme density renders the individual contours of Hong Kong's buildings ambiguous. This is not to say, however, that the architecture of Hong Kong lacks symbolic meaning. Architecturally, Hong Kong is a huge composite structure, and the cages hung from the apartment facades are its most eloquent statement. Each cage presents the street with its own gesture of independence. Under the weight of this individual expression, architectural form is completely overwhelmed.

Transparency The cage enclosures apparently became popular in order to prevent children from falling out of apartment windows. But the experience of looking out through the cage is not unlike peering through the lattices found in traditional Japanese townhouses. A visual transparency, achieved without the use of glass, is something both situations have in common. Modern architecture is often termed the architecture of steel and glass, and transparency in architecture is increasing. Glass is transparent to vision, but to other senses it is opaque. It can be argued that glass is responsible for a trend in modern society, that of a heightened visual quality which denies other sensorial experiences such as the olfactory. In cities, though, there are special smells and sounds. Hong Kong smells of Chinese anise as does Florence of cheese and olive oil. While riding the commuter trains of Tokyo, you can detect the faint smell of pickles. So while Hong Kong's cages are not as visually transparent as glass, they are transparent to the nose, to the ear – to the Cantonese language, and to everything else that spills over into the public space of the city. Hong Kong is either far ahead of, or far behind, modernism's desire for transparency.

Market city

One other special characteristic of Hong Kong is that it is one extended marketplace. According to my research, small retail shops may be usefully classified into either the prestige type or the marketplace type.[2] The prestige shop is characterized by its long-standing structure, by the deference of its staff, its subdued display, and the absence of discounts. As can be understood by observing prestige shops, such as premier department stores or fashionable boutiques, their architectural design is of great significance, and

2   H. Ohno, **A typological study of the Transitive Layer of the buildings in Tokyo**, Doctoral Dissertation, University of Tokyo, 1997.

architects are often engaged for this work. The value system of the prestige shop has its foundations in class consciousness and consumer mythology. The marketplace type, on the other hand, has as its origin the temporary tent-covered stalls located in town plazas, and even shops located in permanent structures can be classified under this type because they share its characteristics: an overabundant and colorful product display, competition between shops on product price and freshness, the shop assistants calling out to customers, and the casual informality of their service. In the marketplace type, the entire shop structure can be obscured by a tent, a curtain, or by signage, since the physical structure of this type of shop is regarded as mere shelter, and thus is a negation of architecture. The value system of the marketplace type has its foundations in community life and practical ideals.

At the center of many large cities, a hierarchy of prestige shops can be found lining the main thoroughfares, with smaller, back street boutiques aspiring to these better positions. But in Hong Kong most of the shops are of the marketplace type. It is perhaps rare to find a predominance of marketplace type shops in a city as large as Hong Kong. Although one of the most basic ideals of modern urban planning is equality, in real cities there is a variety of means by which class distinctions are maintained, for the character of a city is revealed in both subtle and overt ways. Hong Kong, saturated with marketplace type shops, is in this regard an exemplar of modernism, much like the cities of socialist countries. But Hong Kong surpasses even the socialist city's diligent modernism because of its vibrant urban space.

Hong Kong is either the embodiment of the modern city ideal, or else it is a city steeped in heresy.

Tokyo Rainbow Town – classic modern city planning in the post-modern age

Tokyo's seaside urban subcenter is a development project on reclaimed land that began in 1987. This development is similar to the reclamation projects taking place in the other big cities surrounding Tokyo Bay,

Yokohama and Chiba (Minato Mirai 21, Makuhari New City Center), which together with Tokyo form an extended metropolitan area. These are large-scale developments intended to expand and complement the existing city centers through complex land use. In other words, they consist of commercial and residential buildings and are centered on Tokyo's business districts. These developments also include large-scale luxury facilities, such as Japan's highest building and huge convention centers. The characteristics of urban planning in seaside urban centers on reclaimed land, such as Rainbow Town, are as follows.

Diligent modernity As an example of modern urban planning, Rainbow Town gets top marks. First, the elements of the transportation system have been vertically layered, with high-rise buildings forming the core. Like Hong Kong, it is in this way a correctly executed modern urban plan, but Rainbow Town surpasses Hong Kong in that its design ensures plentiful green areas and plazas. Its land use includes residential, commercial and business facilities. However, there is no three-dimensional zoning, as there is in Hong Kong, where upper floors are zoned as residential and lower floors as commercial. Zoning is horizontal only, the town being divided into separate residential, commercial and business zones. Rainbow Town has been erected according to a comprehensive urban plan.

Baroque urban symbolism While not as extensive as the avenues of Brasilia, the city's modern infrastructure has been laid over a system of axial boulevards and vistas, concealing a Baroque urban structure.

Building profiles

In basic terms, this area has been designed as a series of superblocks, each block consisting of a large-scale building. Since large spaces have been left between these blocks, the outward forms of the buildings are the protagonists of the view. In other words, where Hong Kong's condition of adjacency resulted in each building being buried, here each individual building stands out on its own as an object.

Theme park As the development was nearing completion, Japan's bubble economy was threatening to burst. Many buildings became difficult to lease, so even now it is difficult to assess effectiveness of the overall management of the town's planning. However, secondary commercial facilities were the first to be completed, and the area began making a

name for itself as a weekend gathering place for young people. The shops of the area were of a quasi-marketplace type, upheld by the myth of a fashionable contemporary lifestyle. In other words, it became a theme park. Rainbow Town's site is isolated from the streets of Tokyo by the Sumida River, and is connected to the city center only by a computer driven train on an elevated line, known as Yurikamome. This small-scale transportation system reinforces the area's geographical isolation from the existing urban center, rendering the relationship between the two places ambiguous. Moreover, there is an element of fantasy present. In contrast to Minato Mirai 21 and Makuhari New City Center, this project has reanimated the city's relationship with the bay and introduced the element of entertainment, causing a confrontation with the existing city center across the water, and offering a new viewpoint from which to re-evaluate it. Gazing at Tokyo from Rainbow Town's wooden decks, lined with shop windows and restaurants, parasols and chairs, the Manhattan-like skyline in the background with windsurfers and large boats moving in the foreground, makes one feel as if one is somewhere other than Japan. This feeling of being in some hard-to-pinpoint place is the very essence of a theme park.

Rainbow Town is a textbook example of modern urban planning, but it has advanced into the theme park realm of the post-modern city.

Existing urban areas versus newly developed land

Behind the impulse to plan a seaside urban subcenter is the recognition that the expansion and growth of Japan's existing urban areas has reached its limit. The same factor also motivates the development of the semi-rural or suburban land surrounding existing urban areas – both situations present a challenge to the existing urban areas. But what is it that is limiting the growth and expansion of Japan's historical cities? In most cities, the existing urban areas have numerous problems, and are suffocating both economically and socially. The problems Japan's cities face, whether large or small, are essentially the same. They can be summarized as follows:

Narrow roads The roads are narrow as are building sites, meaning not only that urban planning must be strictly regulated, but, due to the vested interests and rights of neighboring landowners, many buildings are difficult to build.

Shortage of parking facilities Small sites and narrow roads create a lack of parking space, so that many places are unable to accommodate cars adequately. Small cities find it particularly difficult to deal with this problem.

Lack of historical attractiveness Most of Japan's cities have suffered bomb damage, and the majority of post-war buildings were not built in traditional architectural styles, but in the popular styles of the day. Because of this, places where one can feel a historical attractiveness are limited, and many of Japan's buildings simply look dated.

Decreased night-time population In large cities, there is a tendency for residential areas to gradually be taken over by commercial enterprises, with houses being replaced by corporate buildings, causing the night-time population to decrease.

Lack of enterprise

Many central city shop owners do not have very much capital and many are conservative, and they often lack the economic or organizational capabilities necessary to meet the changing demands of the consumer.

In spite of the fact that Japan's city centers possess the dignity of tradition, and are complete as regards their infrastructure (with the possible exception of insufficient housing), it was believed that there was little potential for investment in the development of existing urban areas because of the problems cited above. As a result, major investors sought large tracts of land in the suburbs of big cities, seeking investment-efficient developments. Then, during the seventies, together with a major shift towards a car-based society, there was a development boom in suburban shopping malls, a tendency that continues to this day.

Aside from this suburban development, during the period of economic growth, which lasted until the sixties, reclamation was considered important for the creation of good harbor facilities, and as land for heavy-industry and housing facilities. However, with the advent of the information age and the maturation of consumerism, the constitution of

Japanese industries and the role of the big cities changed. Reclaimed land was re-evaluated as a potential substitute for the existing city centers. Reclaimed land was often close to the existing city centers, but had avoided most of the above mentioned problems, and so was seen as a favorable location for large-scale investment. In other words, reclaimed land presented large easily obtainable blocks of land without complicated restrictions or histories. While the main use of reclaimed land during the seventies was for factories, in the eighties new projects with complete urban infrastructures were developed, intended to serve as substitute city centers. A fundamental feature of reclamation work is that, since it requires the use of public waters, the cooperation of municipal governments is essential. Echoing a worldwide tendency, in the eighties municipal governments in charge of the reclamation and sale of land took a businesslike approach. In order to guarantee the sale of their product, they adjusted to meet the demands of the big investors who were interested in buying large lots.

In this manner, large amounts of both corporate and government investment capital began to be invested outside the existing urban areas. This led to a rivalry between the new developments and the existing city centers, a situation which occurred in cities throughout Japan. There are a number of factors behind this phenomenon. The suburbanization of Japan's cities started at the beginning of the 20th century, at a time when apartment-block style housing was not at all popular. The public had a strong preference for single-unit housing, a factor that accelerated the outward expansion of the suburbs. Also, Japan's municipal governments failed to exert successful control over urban expansion. District plans and urbanization controls were established by civic planning and administration authorities, and zoning laws were created to prevent unlimited urbanization, but they were not rigorously enforced. The reality is that many city governments in outlying areas found it easy to acquire and develop land in the zones in which they themselves were responsible for enforcing urban planning controls, including the designated rural areas surrounding the cities, and that an easygoing approach to civic government meant that the clear overall vision needed to ensure controlled growth was missing.

Evaluation of urban development strategy in the periphery of Japanese cities

Having outlined the drive toward urban expansion, and toward large capital investment in suburban and reclaimed land, I will now evaluate the future effect of this phenomenon on Japanese cities.

Urban expansion does have a positive effect on the economy as it serves to motivate development. This provides increased opportunities for developer and construction company investments, which keeps the large construction companies active. As competition is created between existing and new development areas, the redevelopment of non-competitive industries and less-effective (or less profit motivated) land use cost in the existing urban areas is also stimulated. Consequently, one can anticipate that the long-term rejuvenation of urban facilities will be encouraged.

On the other hand, urban expansion has a number of negative effects. First, the economic feasibility of low-density suburbs is poor. Population density in new developments is low, creating a reliance on private cars for transportation, and meaning that the area's fuel needs must be conveyed over greater distances. Other transportation, infrastructure and maintenance factors also contribute to a level of energy consumption which exceeds that of a high-density city. This increased energy consumption is, of course, detrimental to the environment. Also, areas such as these are not easy places to live for people who are physically challenged, so that the level of necessary public welfare funding is higher.

While the stimulation of existing urban areas created by the competition between existing and new development areas is described above as a benefit of urban expansion, the reverse could also occur, the outward expansion extinguishing whatever is left of the life in the city center. (Thus, strength turns into a weakness in a blink of an eye.) If this happens, urban expansion accelerates the 'hollowing out' syndrome, in which the existing city's facilities decline and the city loses its appeal, leading to a further decline in facilities, and the establishment of a negative cycle. The result is the collapse of the community, and at the same time, the emergence of difficulties in maintaining the city's historical inheritance of both material and immaterial nature – its culture and traditions. Even now, in some city centers there is absolutely no effort towards urban renewal. This is a particular problem in many small and medium sized provincial cities. Having lost their status as important centers when developments in the transportation system allowed their populations to expand their activities, a drop in the economic vitality of the centers of these cities is inevitable. In these provincial cities, the outward expansion must perhaps be acknowledged, and the urban cycle of prosperity and decline must in some way be accepted. The development of suburbs or of reclaimed land can not be totally denied, but understood as one type of urban strategy.

Even so, we cannot accept this unreservedly, because this type of development is the sole domain of large investors. Since urban infrastructure is scarce in the areas where suburban and reclaimed land development is taking place, the costs include those of the urban infrastructure, so a certain degree of magnitude is necessary for the development to be profitable. To attempt these large-scale developments, a great deal of investment money is required.

The history of a city is the history of authority. At the same time, it is the city that gives individuals with initiative and ability opportunities. This has always been an attraction of the city and it remains so to this day. These are questions to do with human relations and economics, and at the same time are questions to do with the form of the city. In existing cities, when one decides to quit the company and establish a small business of one's own, it is possible to find a small and inexpensive place in the small lanes or on the fringes of the downtown area. Although this is common knowledge, Sony, the large international company, during the fifties was but one small business among many in a Tokyo area populated by small-scale machine shops. A similarly small and inexpensive unit, however, is impossible to find in suburban or reclaimed land developments, since their leasable offices and shops are built on a much larger scale.

The benevolent and stimulating environment of a city is based in part on its formal variety, and individual business people with only a small amount of investment capital can take advantage of this; the only basic necessity is that a small site or building be available. These business people become the protagonists of the city. Naturally, among them there can be found the type of businesses that the average citizens will not want around, but this is something that cannot be helped. At the urban strategy level,

Rainbow Town must find a means of providing small sized lots, so that small investors can participate in and contribute to its urban life. If urban strategy allows only big business to prosper on suburban or reclaimed land, not only does this endanger the existing urban areas, it also jeopardizes the continuing vitality and creative energy of Japan's citizens.

Evaluation of the influence of urban development strategy on architectural design, and the significance of Hong Kong

Now, just what do these new tendencies in urban development mean for architectural design? One of the morphological attributes of modern architecture is the emphasis that is placed on the external form of the building, such that the architect's originality is expressed in the contour of the building, this principle being applied to all buildings. In previous urban architecture, building contours were a device for social distinction. A unique shape was limited to buildings in the realm of privileged public architecture – it was, in other words, limited to monuments of power. All other urban architecture formed parts of blocks, in which a building was sandwiched between its neighbors, leaving the architect very little freedom. These social distinctions were rejected by the architecture of the modern movement, which can be interpreted as establishing a form of democracy. In this way, the architect joined other plastic and fine artists in their dream of becoming free, egalitarian 'modern artists'. This democratic architecture was outlined in the Athens Charter and Le Corbusier's 'La Ville Contemporaine' of 1922, and was closely related to the development of the 'International Style'. Eventually, the democracy of the building contour came into alignment with the principles of consumerism. The illustration 'Captive Globe', found in Koolhaas' *Delirious New York*[3], can be interpreted as a caricature of this situation (but which, in actual fact, does not reflect Manhattan's real condition, in which each block is partitioned into a number of sites). However, whether we look at the Captive Globe, Rainbow Town or Minato Mirai 21, we see the superblock being adopted, with urban planning reinforcing the democracy of the building contour.

Therefore, while Rainbow Town may be an architect's paradise, it is a paradise containing danger. Since a building's envelope represents, sociologically, possession of a site, its shape will eventually be perceived only as an overstatement on the part of the owner. Although the possession of a lot or building is only one of the many related aspects of a city, any architect assigned this type of lot will find it extremely difficult to escape its

3 Rem Koolhaas, **Delirious New York**, 010 Publishers, 1995, pp.294-295.

constraints. The architect is completely involved in the postmodern situation of struggling to achieve differentiation, and is thus reduced to being a mere gadget designer for the city.

Within this context, what are the possibilities suggested by Hong Kong's cityscape? The extreme adjacency and the anarchy of the cage additions overturn the spatial relationships crucial to the generic city form, which defines the monument as figure and nameless other architecture as ground. In other words, it is the openings in Hong Kong's buildings which acquire relevance as figure instead of the outlines of buildings, which due to their ambiguity have been robbed of the authority inherent in their use of the monument's superior contour. As opposed to the authority established by the use of outer contours, the independent, individual nature (or self identity) of inner contours becomes Hong Kong's emblem. This is in contrast to modernism's urban planning, which, being based on the use of the superblock, can only express itself through outer contours.

However, Hong Kong is a very atypical situation. Until 1997 Hong Kong had a privileged role as the economic window into China, which assured its growth. As it developed into a giant city, it received a steady stream of destitute immigrants, which kept it in a state of constant renewal. The cages which characterize its cityscape originated in its severe shortage of housing space, and are not necessarily something to be glorified. Thus, as a modern city, Hong Kong is miraculous. However, this miracle reminds us of the importance of the role played by the individual within the city's construction and evolution. I believe that the problems that Rainbow Town faces are common to all recent large-scale urban redevelopment projects the world over.

1 Three dimensionality/elevated highway, Hong Kong Island
2 Three dimensionality/elevated pedestrian way in the fishing village of Lantau Island
3 Adjacency, trams, people and stores in Kowloon
4 Adjacency, cages and boxes, Hong Kong Island

5 The emergency of individualism, apartment with various cages, Kowloon
6 Omnipresence of green, Kowloon
7 Transparency or eloquent cages, Kowloon
8 Omnipresence of green, Kowloon
9 Diligent Modernity, model of Rainbow Town

10 The building as object, exhibition center Big Site
11 Theme park, Odaiba Park
12 Market city, Kowloon
Photo credits Hidetoshi Ohno Laboratory, The University of Tokyo

[5]

[6]

[7]

[8]

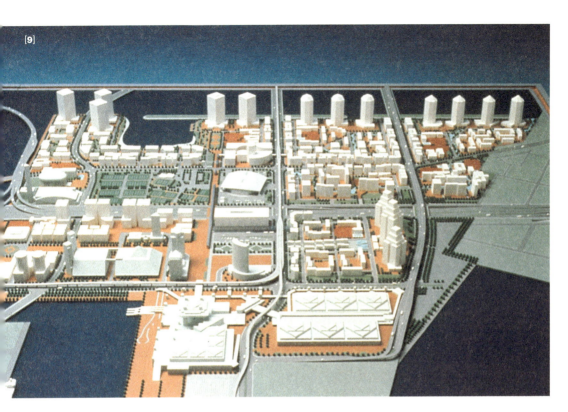

[9]

[10]

[11]

[12]

Japan's Waterfront Experiments – Edo/Tokyo, Hakata/Fukuoka: The Formulation and Evolution of Japan's Metropolis on the Alluvial Horizon

Toshikazu Ishida

Historical background

When we think about the formulation process of habitable land in Japan, broadly dividing it into highland and lowland, the so-called waterfront was often artificially reclaimed land that shared an unstable or rather trans-figurative character in contrast with the highland, considered permanently stable ground. Historically speaking, this stable/unstable relationship in Japan also broadly corresponds to its administrative landscape in general. In other words, apart from a few exceptional cases such as Hakata city (currently known as Fukuoka) and Sakai city (nearby current Osaka) which have been developed as autonomous major trading port cities throughout the medieval period, we seem to be able to apply a hierarchical diagram of domination in terms of the geographical landscape of highland – lowland.

As the urban landscape of the feudal city Edo (now known as Tokyo) demonstrates, a habitable area for the administrative class called Buke (Samurai families) monopolizes the hill-top and its nearer upper area: and on the other hand, the governed class called Chonin (townspeople) were concentrated in the lowland – in between the highland and the reclaimed ground in the current Tokyo Bay front. In this respect, it is possible to point out that the land area reclaimed before the pre-industrial period is recognized as a mass/production field that is controlled by the immutable privileged/consumption highland.

However, this polarized scheme of highland/lowland or privileged/mass is perhaps too simple to characterize the real formulation and varied potentiality of Japanese waterfronts throughout the centuries. Here, I will address two examples that show contrasting backgrounds in terms of the pre-history of current waterfront developments. The city examples are Edo and the western part of Hakata city. Both are known as typical waterfront cities with reclaimed land; however the developmental processes, the metropolitan city vision and their experiences are rather different.

Edo/Tokyo Generally speaking, for the emergence of a so-called metropolis where one's territorial jurisdictions are often diluted and the nomadic heterogeneous elements have overflowed, the alluvial horizon in the mouth of a major river used to provide a suitable area for expansion, given a favorable bay front; as history suggests with examples such as late medieval Venice, 17th century Amsterdam, or New York's, extremely prominent, Manhattan of this century.

Not only do both Edo and Hakata share these geographical characteristics regarding

the origins of their urban establishment, all major Japanese urbanization is
to be found in these kinds of inland bay waterfronts including Osaka,
Nagoya and other coastal cities. In other words, the artificially reclaimed
waterfront as habitable ground is indispensable to Japanese urbanization
when compared to the undeveloped steep mountain areas. Thus the history
of reclaiming land in Japan is quite old, reaching back to ancient periods.
Edo – the original name used for present-day Tokyo until the Meiji restoration in the mid 19th century – developed on just such a typical inland
waterfront. Judging from cityscape paintings of the feudal period, the geographical character of higher and lower, or stable and unstable, precisely
coincides with the socio-political landscape, that is, the highland dominates
and the lowland is dominated. The higher land, on the diluvial ground, was
monopolized by a few privileged groups of the feudal structure. In contrast,
the anonymous mass, or the nomadic minority, were kept on the lower
alluvial reclaimed land. This relationship could be found typically in Edo
where the population strongly increased during the Tokugawa-Shogunate
Era with significant inflow of labor from neighboring villages.

It is often pointed out that the city of Edo developed in a spiral-like structure. The Tokugawa Shogun was located in the center of the biggest lot
of the Edo Castle. The social order follows the spiral diagram: the more
elaborated street pattern (for defense reasons) indicates higher ranked
zones, and the smaller lots with more legible patterns (for administrative
reasons) indicate lower social locations. The proportional distribution was
that approximately 80% of the (mass) population was confined to 10% of
the lowland region, while 10% of the (privileged) population occupied 80%
of the high ground area. The cross section follows the unfolded spiral
structure: the territory occupied by the Shogun's major staff is rather static,
centric and homogeneous, in contrast to the lively and heterogeneous
periphery inhabited by merchants, workers and the nomadic. Free circulation between these two zones was not permitted. However, the attractive
urban flavor of the Edo metropolis, with one million inhabitants, was not
to be found in the western highland or purely concentrated on the produc-

tive field of the bay front, but in the city edge of the peripheral eastern lowland called Kawamukou (meaning 'across the Sumida river' in Japanese).

This lowland area held not only the so-called 'dark places' such as brothels, gambling spots and provisional Kabuki theaters, but also generated a kind of regulation-free frontier where visitors were released from the daily feudal order. This rule-free periphery did not remain bound to one place but shifted its location, following Edo's geographical expansion, from Fukagawa, to Ryogoku, Asakusa and then Tamanoi; all on the eastern periphery of town and therefore remaining always on the outskirts. Although the location itself was detached from the central highlands, those regulation-free zones formulated the place for encountering the unexpected, heterogeneous and real metropolitan activities. The water flow in Edo's lower waterfront area simultaneously connected the Meisho landmarks (attractive city spots) and segregated the town blocks. Based on the features of its natural landscape, Edo was well designed for administrative and productive control in the area between the hilltop and the bay front. However, the truly radical metropolitan environment, and its attractiveness, has always appeared not in the defense-oriented central power of the highland, but on the centrifugal periphery's alluvial horizon.

Hakata/Fukuoka Hakata was the original medieval name of the city now called Fukuoka, which is rather unknown to westerners in comparison with Tokyo. However, it is in fact the oldest trading port city in Japan. Because of its proximity to the Korean peninsula and the Southeast Asian region, the influence from China and the rest of the continent has been quite significant, and its overseas relationships extend back to ancient periods. Evidence of such exchange was discovered at Shikanoshima Island (located at the top of the Hakata bay peninsula), where a golden stamp, originally given by the king of the Han Empire (ca. 1st century AD) to the local dependency of this region as a political and military support treaty, was found.

The waterfront developments of Hakata/Fukuoka bay are broadly divided into three periods: medieval, early modern, and post-industrial. In ancient times, Hakata was apparently developed as an outer port of Dazaifu, the old capital of Kyushu Island. There was an institution called Korokan Guesthouse, where foreign missions from China and Korea visited frequently. Also in medieval times many of the imperial envoys departed from Hakata to the continent for advanced studies in engineering and trading.

However, the connection with the continent was not always constructive. In the late

13th century, after the destruction of the Son Empire on the continent, Mongolian invaders twice attacked Hakata and Dazaifu. The defense dikes built at that time still remain symbolically present along the coast. Actually the famous word 'Kamikaze' originated here, the 'divine wind' which helped counter-attack the Mongolian war ships in Hakata Bay, sinking them into the sea.

In contrast to Edo, which experienced extensive growth in the 17th to the 18th century under the feudal social structure, Hakata was in quite a vulnerable position, both politically and culturally, due to its proximity to the continent and relative detachment from the central government during a period when Japan's centralized governmental body was not completely stabilized. As a result, the city was continuously under threat of being absorbed by the Continent or, conversely, abandoned by the central government. Hence, an independent mercantile spirit evolved even before the feudal Shogunate system was implemented in the 17th century. Consequently, from the late medieval to the early modern period, before a feudal structure was implemented, this rather autonomous mercantile city took advantage of a comfortable degree of independence from the central government's control. After the Shogunate's policy was implemented in the 16th and 17th centuries, the name of Fukuoka first appeared as the name of the city's new main castle. Simultaneously, the polarization between Hakata and Fukuoka became apparent: the former as the autonomous merchant area, and the latter as the Shogunate's territory.

While Hakata's merchant area remained on the existing reclaimed land to the east, the Shogunate's policy brought a sort of highland-lowland model similar to that of Edo in the western part of the city. By the time the Shogunate implemented its policy in this region, Hakata's autonomous citizenship structure was already strongly established, therefore a polarized coexistence began to take shape. Special festival costumes, called Happi, from Hakata districts remain even today. The individual costume patterns each represent a specific quarter, as defined by the seven parallel avenues in the city's reclaimed land area. Huge portable shrines designed by each community are carried around inside old Hakata during the festival week. The whole event still celebrates the strong independent spirit of the quarter developed by its historical process.

As mentioned before, in Edo the feudal government implemented a model for the waterfront land as a productive anonymous mass field and the so-called 'dark side activities' were kept aside on the detached reclaimed land of the city's periphery. There, a sort of segregated minority generated a rule-free place for encountering metropolitan attractions that would liberate them from daily social order. This way, the feudal administration that was based on the dynamics between central highland and peripheral lowland remained well balanced during Sakoku (closed country period). The waterfront was never open to any external envoy until the mid 19th century. For different reasons from Edo, Hakata itself had a peripheral position from the central government, due to significant influence from the Continent; therefore it developed as relatively detached, autonomous and open, and to some extent as an obligatory gateway (since medieval times) to overseas. Even after the feudal government settled regulations in the region, this autonomy was kept based on the predominance of its trading tradition, thus Hakata/Fukuoka functioned as a dualistic center, a condition that has remained apparent even today.

If we regard the polarization between central-highland and peripheral-lowland in Edo as a 'vertical hierarchy' ruling the alluvial reclaimed waterfront, Hakata/Fukuoka's case might show a 'horizontal hierarchy' in terms of a dual coexistence within a strong heterogeneous center. This explains not only the link between the landscape and politics but also the two distinctively different city characters.

Current situation

Tokyo 1960 – Kenzo Tange Generally speaking, typical cross-sections of waterfronts in Japan (after the industrial period in the mid 19th to the mid 20th century, or the so-called Westernization age) have been mostly monopolized by military utilities, trading ports, huge markets or heavy industrial facilities. If we focus on Tokyo's waterfront development after the Second World War, we find that Kenzo Tange's Tokyo 1960 project was undoubtedly the most striking and comprehensive planning proposal. In Tokyo during the sixties post-war recovery process, a sort of chaotic condition had emerged both with the enormous population increase and the heavy infrastructural damage left after the war.

Edo was really well designed in its usage of the natural landscape for administrative control, however it was suitable only for the metropolis population of one million from the feudal period. In the sixties Tokyo already had ten million inhabitants, which made the entire infrastructure obsolete. Additionally the Korean War in the 1950s provided an unexpected economic boom creating a demand for a radical revision of future development plans for Tokyo. Tange criticized the spiral-like Edo development structure as a 'too closed' system, and proposed a contrasting type of linear extended model called an 'open structure'. It was designated mostly to the Tokyo Bay area in a direction from South to North, and was meant to be detached from the existing chaotic condition and offered suggestions of possibilities for the future Waterfront city. This scheme became the initial idea for the soon-to-follow Metabolism Group's evolution: typical mega-structured office blocks connected by three-tiered highways named Cycle Transportation. The residential area was laid out perpendicular to this transportation axis, resembling a gigantic tree structure, instead of the vertebrate animal that Tange had intended as the formal metaphor in his proposal.

This mega-structure project was really epochal after the Second World War's urban planning development. However, the clear division of functions by a transportation infra-axis and low density housing tower blocks full of sunlight still reminds us of the late interpretations of the authentic CIAM paradigms. It should be pointed out that Tange's proposal did create a blueprint for the urban development models of contemporary Japanese Waterfronts such as Yokokama MM21, Makuhari Newtown, and Kobe Portopia Island. In other words, the time for relinquishing the paradigm of the functional city of the 1930s interpreted by Tange has not yet arrived in the field of Japan's urban planning theory even today. After Tokyo 1960, Tange proposed the Tsukiji Project where the original idea was partly realized. This proposal, consisting of megastructure and superblocks, summarizes the destination of the technooptimistic urban vision held in the 1960s. In this project, all of the Tsukiji town quarters originally reclaimed in the Edo period were covered by systematic megastructures, except for the Honganji temple, which was located in the center. The outskirts of the Tsukiji central market's shopping district, called Jogai (or 'outside'), where a lively confusion and the unique flavor that characterized its town identity once existed, were utterly gone, replaced by a hygienic metallic and gigantic urbanscape.

It is a rather significant fact that we can no longer encounter such a heterotopic and random ambience as Tsukiji-Jogai in any major Japanese waterfront development plan after Tange's, mainly because it derives from the accumulation of secondary small capitals based on private investment. Tange's blueprints today, however, cannot help but evoke a kind of doubt regarding the possibility of their re-implementation due to monopolization by dominant capital for the sake of seeking both profit and efficiency with a rigid megascape. Today's Tsukiji district is confronted with a redevelopment plan that includes the relocation of its Central Marketplace to a neighboring quarter. This should be a unique chance to re-examine possibilities other than the sixties model, in order to allow a newly renovated vision for the alluvial horizon in Tokyo.

Fukuoka 1990 – Nexus Project Despite the repetition of high-rise mega-scale projects, it is worth touching upon another epoch-making model that occurred in the 1990s. The so-called Nexus project built in Kashii, on reclaimed land, gets its name from Manyoshu (a famous ancient Japanese anthology of poetry); it is located on the northeast bank of Hakata Bay. Architect Arata Isozaki (who was a student of Tange) was the general client for this project of six collective housing wings and one housing tower designed by six foreign architects and one Japanese. Rem Koolhaas, Steven Holl, Christian de Portzamparc, Mark Mack, Oscar Tosquets and Osamu Ishiyama were commissioned for the low-rise housing design and Arquitectonica for the tower.

Koolhaas' own remarks on his design – 'this courtyard house is surrounded by walls that protect the housing from an excess of information, excess of incidents, and the excessive architecture of present day cities, and creates its own uniquely quiet environment in the midst of this turbulence' – might summarize the architect's attitude of the nineties which has evolved as rather individualistic and autonomous, different from the more socially focused projects in the sixties. Furthermore, he emphasizes the heterotopic character of the units, assembled with various differentiations in details in the three floors facing their individual courtyards, such as etched or colored glass on the uppermost floors, uneven roof shapes and the mix of western and Japanese styled elements. He adds that these co-existing heterogeneous elements of the design vocabulary correspond to the existing Japanese context: 'These details make this compact building fit well with the hybrid land which is a mixture of European block concept and the contemporary city of objects.'

It is perhaps no coincidence that the Nexus projects could introduce a new type of collective housing model for the 1990s. Other facts, such as introducing a new counterpart to the usual high-rise model repetitions, and the possibility of undergoing this level of urban experimentation all at once, were conditions more appropriately implemented in Hakata/ Fukuoka rather than in Tokyo or any other Japanese city. Hakata/Fukuoka is often seen as a vital city because of its quick acceptance of all things new. The city is considered a sort of experimental ground for Japanese market research. All brand-new fashion lines, both domestic and imported, first open their shop in Hakata/Fukuoka in order to test consumer demand and acceptance. In general they branch out to other Japanese cities, including Tokyo, only afterwards. Broadly speaking, because of this city's dynamic mentality, one cannot illustrate a single image of it without encountering a huge hyper-modern fashion building next to a small family enterprise next to a row house left over from a feudal period, or an Americanized entertainment and shopping center right next to a small enclave for illegal activities.

Roland Barthes remarked that the metropolis, which represents the central position in a socio-political space, should exist not in a location-bound establishment but in a place that tends to disregard old customs, decentralize political power, and generate a differentiated vector for any fixed value...the place where human beings encounter strangeness in the ordinary environment. Thus the origins of the metropolis might derive from the field that allows the interaction of heterotopic elements and where value exchanges are freely possible. Throughout the history of Japan's Waterfront, the alluvial ground provided a distinctive horizon where one could encounter something yet unseen, either spontaneously or with the higher administration's consent. With regard to the significance of this potential, it should never cease to advance its prospective by examining future urban development models and avoiding any more repetition of the 1960s visions.

In this context the reclaimed land permanently supports the characteristically potential-based features that continuously reconstruct the fixed social hierarchy and metaphorical periphery.

Currently the so-called Rainbow Town (a huge waterfront project in Tokyo Bay), and 'Island City' (a more than 400-hectare artificial island project in Fukuoka Bay) are under construction with projected schedules for completion within the next few decades. However, with all the concern for the future habitable land on the alluvial horizon, the much smaller Nexus project at Kashii beach should not fail to act as a significant milestone, not only for gaining renewed insight regarding housing concerns, but also for its redefinition of the relation between the metropolitan and the waterfront city vision for the 21st century.

[1]

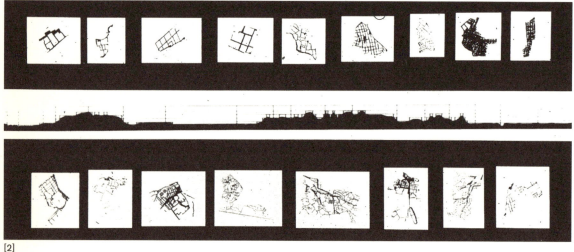

[2]

1 Edo/Tokyo developed on a typical inland waterfront environment – Mt. Fuji, an almost sacred symbol of Japan is illustrated as background to the view of the highland enclosing the reclaimed lowland waterfront below.

2 The unfolded spiral section shows Edo's characteristic geographical landscape and its socio-political zoning between the highland/administrative class and the lowland/governed class.

3 a+b Analytical diagram of spiral development of Edo. The sign shows their family symbol mark.
4 Golden stamp from the Han Empire.
5 a+b Two cityscapes of the lower waterfront.

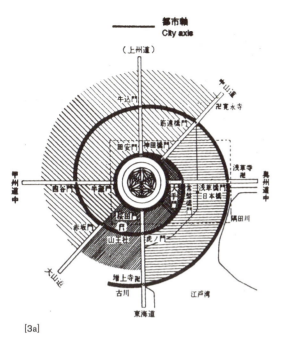

都市軸
City axis

（上州道）

牛込門
牛込門
水道橋門
田安門 神田橋門
淺草寺
江戸城
半蔵門 大手門
四谷門 淺草橋門
赤坂門 日本橋
山王社 虎ノ門
隅田川
大山道
増上寺
古川 江戸湾
東海道

[3a]

[3b]

[4]

[5a]

[5b]

[6]

[7]

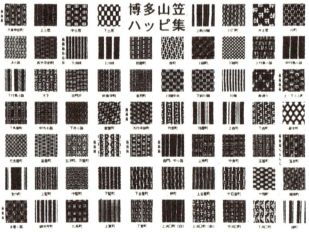

[8]

6 The Nexus project 1990/Koolhaas, and Steven Hall.
7 Arquitectonica's tower.
8 Graphic pattern of special festival costume called Happi.
9 Tokyo 1960 project/Kenzo Tange.
10 a+b 'Canal City'/John Jerde 1996.
11 Tsukiji project/Kenzo Tange.

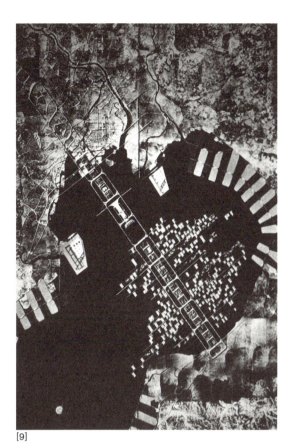

[9]

[10à]

[10b]

[11]

Part III

Cultural-
Urban
Criticism

Informationcritique   Scott Lash

Introduction

How is critical social science, or critical theory or critique possible in the information society? I shall ask the question if it is possible. I shall consider the very strong possibility that it is not. Moreover, that oppositional thinking in our global information order needs to take a different form than critical theory or critique. Critical theory in Germany in the sixties, seventies and eighties was often and largely understood as 'Ideologiekritik'. This is critical theory so expanded as to encompass Adorno and Habermas and Marxism. But what happens in an age in which symbolic power is no longer ideological, i.e. an age in which symbolic power no longer takes the forms of the systems of ideas that constitute ideologies. What happens when symbolic power instead is largely 'informational'? Ideologies were extended in time and space. They claimed universality. They were extended often in the temporal form of 'meta-narratives'. They entailed systems of belief. They incorporated reflection and indeed needed time for reflection. Information is compressed in time and space. It makes no claim to universality but is contained in the immediacy of the particular. Information shrinks or compresses metanarratives to a mere point, a signal, a mere event in time.

There is an immediacy to information that has little in common with systems of belief like Christianity or the Enlightenment. The very speed and ephemerality of information leaves almost no time for reflection. The question then becomes what sort of future is there for critical theory in an age in which there is little time for reflection? Critical social science grew up in an age of 'Ideologiekritik'. What will happen to critical social science in an age of 'Informationskritik'? Indeed is such a thing as informationcritique possible? Can critical thought operate in an information age?

Information

What is information? Let me start by discussing what might be the main parameters of the information age. Technological change has influenced me to rethink a lot of what I've been writing in social theory. So much so that I now would understand contemporary times very much in terms of the information society, rather than postmodernism or the risk society, late capitalism, etc. Information society is preferable to postmodernism in that the former says what the society's principle is rather than saying merely what it comes after. Postmodernism primarily in this sense comes after modernism. Second, postmodernism deals largely with disorder, fragmentation, irrationality, whilst the notion of information accounts for both the (new) order and disorder that we contemporaries experience. Indeed as we will see below the disorder (irrationality) is largely the unintended consequence of the order (rationality). Third, architects such as Venturi understand postmodernism in terms of 'complexity' and 'contradiction', and in particular from the contradiction of juxtaposition of elements of style, and of the contradiction of decoration and structure. Information is preferable and more powerful as a notion because it operates from a unified principle. Thus an 'informational architecture' is an architecture of flows, of movement, encouraging real-time relations over distances; it is an architecture of disembedding. Of the compression of time and space.

What is key in how we should understand the information society (in contrast to other ideas of it from say Bell, Touraine and Castells) is a focus on the primary qualities of information itself. Here information must be understood sharply in contradistinction from other, earlier socio-cultural categories such as narrative or discourse or monument or institution. The primary qualities of information are flow, disembeddedness, spatial compression, temporal compression, real-time relations. It is not exclusively, but primarily, in this sense that we live in an information age. Some people have called some of these qualities 'late modern' (Giddens), others 'postmodern' (Harvey), but these concepts are so amorphous. Information is not. In any event the place to go to grasp these qualities of the information age is for me, not so much Giddens and Harvey or Beck or even Castells. But rather Virilio, Deleuze, Haraway, McLuhan, Benjamin and the architect Rem Koolhaas.

I would understand the information society somewhat differently than it usually has been understood by sociologists. (I haven't yet had the time to benefit from Frank Webster's new book *Theories of the Information Society*.) The information society has often (say Bell, Touraine, Castells) been understood in terms of knowledge-intensive production and a post-industrial array of goods and services that are produced. This needs to be broadened out. First and foremost perhaps is to look at the paradox of the information society. That is, how can such highly rational production result in the incredible irrationality of information overloads, misinformation, disinformation and out of control information. What Josef Esser calls the 'desinformierte Informationsgesellschaft'.

The key to understanding this is to look at what is produced in information production not as information-rich goods and services, but more or less as out of control bytes of information. This is indeed a theory of unintended consequences, but one that greatly differs from Beck and Giddens. For one thing it is not reflexive in their sense. There is little time for reflection. It is perhaps reflexive in an ethnomethodological sense; but, in an ethnomethodological sense in which objects too take on powers of indexicality.

Information production involves an important compression, indeed several important compressions. The most important one for me, I'm ashamed to say I've learnt from McLuhan, read, of course, as a thinker more of the information than the media age. In this context I think it is useful to understand 'the medium is the message' as the paradigmatic cultural form of the information age. Previously the dominant medium was narrative, lyric poetry, discourse, the painting. Now it is the message: The message or the 'communication'. The medium now is very byte-like. It is compressed.

The newspaper already gave us the model for the information age. Only now it has become much more pervasive and has spread to a whole series of mostly machine-like interfaces. Unlike say narrative or discourse or painting, the information in newspapers comes in very short messages. It is compressed. Literally compressed. Traditional narrative as in the novel works from a beginning, middle and end. There is intentionality on the part of the protagonist and events follow from one another as causes and effects. Discourse – as in say philosophic or social scientific texts – is comprised of conceptual frameworks, of serious speech acts, of propositional logic, of speech acts backed up by legitimating arguments. Information is none of these. Once the medium becomes the message, or the byte (quite short but still of various lengths) of information, we are in a different ball game. The value of a discursive book will last 20 or more years. The informational message in the newspaper will have value for only a day. After a day we throw it in the garbage. The message, as German sociologist of science Knorr-Cetina has shown, for international currency traders, has validity (or value) for a mere twenty seconds, at that point your interlocutor is free to change the price spread on the currency deal at issue.

Discourse or the narrative novel or painting is produced with great time for reflection, say 3-4 years for a social science discursive text. The message, the information byte, the article that is written for *The Sun* after Manchester United v. Arsenal must be ready for transmission in about ninety minutes. No time for reflection. Produced pretty much in real time, a time contiguous with the event, separable with difficulty indeed from the event, and in this sense indexical. This is another way in which time is compressed in informationalization. It is very different from narrative or discourse. The bit of information has its effect on you without the sort of legitimating argument that you are presented with in discourse. Information here is outside of a systematic conceptual framework. Without propositional logic. But with an immediacy of symbolic violence.

Power I've just alluded to the non-discursive, illegitimate, preconscious nature of informational power. In this sense I think it fair to say that Foucault may have once been right but no longer is. Power was once largely discursive, but it now is largely informational. Power is still very strongly as Foucault suggested tied to knowledge, but informational knowledge is increasingly displacing narrative and discursive knowledge. Power is indeed still very importantly tied to the commodity, in an age that is more than ever capitalist. But in a very important way it may no longer be commodification that is driving informationalization, but instead informationalization that is driving commodification. Information explodes the distinction between use value and exchange-value as Mark Poster suggests in *The Second Media Age*. But is then recaptured by capital for further commodification. Fast moving consumer goods and branded consumer products are also informational in their quick obsolescence, their global flows, their regulation through intellectual property, their largely immaterial nature in which the work of design and branding assumes centrality, while the actual production is outsourced to Malaysia or Thailand.

Power in the manufacturing age was attached to property as the mechanical means of production. In the information age it is attached to intellectual property. It is intellectual property, especially in the form of patent, copyright and trademark that put a new order on the out of control swirls of bits and bytes of information so that they can be valorized to create profit. For example in biotechnology, patents on genome techniques and forms of genetic modification, allow specific firms exclusive rights to the valorization of genetic information (Rabinow, Franklin, Lury and Stacey). In the IT sector itself, copyright (again the right to keep everybody else out) in for example operating systems software allows firms to realize super profits. In fast moving consumer goods and designer goods, the trademarking of brands, which are already in the public domain, such as McDonalds, Nike, but also Versace and Boss establish other monopolies and re-configurations of power around the otherwise anarchy of information.

To summarize, there is a sort of twisting dialectic involved in the information society. It moves from order to disorder to new order. Highly rational and knowledge-intensive production results in a quasi-anarchy of information proliferation and flows. This disorder of immediacy of information produces its own power relations in the immediate power/ knowledge of bytes of information on the one hand. And in the re-ordering of information in categories of intellectual property in order to accumulate capital on a world scale in the information age on the other.

Inequality: from exploitation to exclusion In the information order inequality tends to be less and less defined by relations of production between for example a German corporation and a production workers' plant there or an Indian plant owner and the worker in his factory. This is the paradigm for inequality in the industrial order. In the information order centrality is less exploitation than 'exclusion'. And exclusion is first and foremost something that is defined in conjunction with the information and communication flows, with information and communication structures. What emerges here is a 'loop' of relatively disembedded (hence increasingly global) elites. The information order is a society of 'the and' connected by networks. These networks have mobile human-machine interfaces for terminals connected by lines of communication. They are relatively disembedded or lifted out. Through these interfaces flow finance, technology, media, culture, information, communications and the like. There is something generic (i.e. not national, a-contextual and non-identity) about being in the loop of such networks. The main machine interfaces at issue here are communication interfaces, including perhaps above all regular air travel for business purposes facilitating the face-to-face communication that is necessary for trust and recognition. Also, the occupation of expensive space in the central districts of the increasingly generic global cities, again opening up the array of face-to-face communications and transactions. In the global city you can face-to-face without flying, and partake of one generic network that regularly interfaces with the others.

The consequences here are the emergence of a generic global elite, whose point of identification is the global elite in other such cities. Thus our research at Goldsmiths College into the global culture industries, the elite in São Paulo of journalists, television hosts, curators, architects, film distributors, pay-TV producers, advertising, pop music sector, etc. have a lot more in common with their counterparts in Tokyo, New York, London, Paris, Milan and LA than they do with their own compatriots in Brazil. Their identification tends to be outward; they compete increasingly in international or transnational labor markets. Now, to self-include and self-identify in the context of the 'global' information and communication flows is to self-'exclude' and dis-identify from the 'national' flows. Additionally, the result in say Britain is what Will Hutton calls 'overclass self-exclusion'. Here, where there was social health care, schooling, pensions and security now there is an overwhelming presence of 'contracting out' into private schools, health insurance, pensions, and policing. Ulrich Beck calls this 'Brazilianization'. Everything held equal, the closer the country is to the core, like Germany, France, Japan, the less this self-exclusion will happen. The less it will lead to vast inequalities. The greatest inequalities are produced on the periphery.

If what Samir Amin called accumulation on a world scale led to surplus exploitation, then 'informationalization' on a world scale leads to a massive surplus of exclusion. In the core, US, UK, Japan, Germany, the Netherlands, especially in highly branded and informationalized firms, the work of design is carried out in the core, the work of production increasingly contracted out to Indonesia and Thailand. In the core the previously exploited, yet unionized ethnic minority and white working class becomes increasingly irrelevant to informational accumulation, which now takes place not on their backs but behind their backs. Self-excluding overclass leads to forcibly excluded underclass. Such is the way of the global information order. So power and inequality are if anything nastier and more violent in the global information order and informationcritique must deal with this.

But a critical theory in the information age must also be affirmative and not just negative. This is the crux of post-colonial theory. Post-colonialism goes beyond the simple dualism of earlier notions of world system and development. At issue is never simple 'roots' on the one side versus domination on the other. Instead these roots are at the same time 'routes' (Gilroy, Clifford). At issue in post-colonial theory are 'third spaces' (Bhabha, Spivak, Soja) that are diasporas, of performativity and not pedagogy, whether this is a pedagogy of simple domination or a counter-pedagogy of resistance. Yet there is something fixed to these ideas of a third space, something that has to do too much with a culture perhaps without origins, but that is still a sort of static layering. It is this sort of 'layering' at issue in the layering of ethnicities that we are given in us-American multiculturalism. (Stuart Hall) Even if these layered ethnicities occupy a third frontier or border space of hybridity, and are performing this space, we still have a layering of hybrid ethnicities. The problem is the fixedness, the staticness. This is much more representative of the third space of critique of the older critical theory, of ideologycritique not informationcritique. Informationcritique is much more based on movement. On diaspora rather than hybridity, because the latter entails movement. But a radicalized diaspora where terminus is not fixed, which is shot through with contingency, with accident, with spaces to dis-identify as well as re-identify, for multiculturalism as radical individualism. This is the post-colonialism of informationcritique. It is a postcolonialism of movement, of contingency, of flows (Appadurai), disjunctures and junctures, of objects as well as subjects, of communications. Hence the booming phone-card business in London in areas of recent immigration of black Africans, Turks and North Africans. It is an information order which is at the same time disordering, a chronic dialectic of disordering, re-ordering and again dis-ordering. Of the violence of Kosovo, but the emergent new international regimes of human (but also non-human) rights (Santos) – cf. Pinochet, Bosnia and the like. Regimes, which not only are increasingly conventionalized, but also legitimated by a large public on a world scale.

Critique

The universal or the transcendental? Critique is surely something that happens in thought. It integrates theory and practice. But, it is something that somehow primarily involves the dimension of thought. Critique has normally taken two forms. One is the critique of the particular through the universal. This is the sort of critique that is involved in Kant's *Critique of Pure Reason*. Or in the late Marx, in which capitalism is seen as a particular criticized from the universalism of Marxian theory. This is also the idea of critique we have in the later Habermas, in which the particularism of 'strategic rationality' is criticized from the universalism of communicative rationality. Habermas proffers critique through discourse. Through the legitimation of speech acts that are at the same time validity claims, through a set of legitimating arguments. This type of discourse is difficult in the information age because of the very speed and immediacy of socio-cultural processes. Universalism involves very much the opposite of the information age's space-time compression. It involves instead the furthest possible spatio-temporal, not compression, but 'extension', taking the form 'inter alia' of metanarratives. The information age compresses even narratives, which have some temporal extension, let alone metanarratives.

The more widespread notion of critique is not of the particular by the universal. It is the critique of the universal-particular couple itself. Here reason or thought becomes something that evades the logic of universal and particular, i.e. that moves outside of propositional logic. It rejects propositional logic as the space of 'the same', and operates instead from a critical space of 'the other'. Thus Kantian critique most importantly establishes limits for the operation of pure reason. The sphere of pure reason, of logic, is the sphere of necessity. It is here that we have understanding of nature. Outside of the limits of this realm and the condition for its possibility is the realm of practical reason, the sphere of freedom. Its rules are not at all the rules of logic. Inside the sphere of pure reason, the laws of nature, of necessity – cause, effect, syllogism, identity are operative. Outside there is the unknowability of the moral law, of freedom, of God, infinity and of things in themselves. We can know things, said Kant, according to the above stated laws of nature, but we cannot know them as they are in themselves. We cannot know things according to their own ontological structures. All this takes place in the sphere not of theoretical understanding but of praxis, of practical reason.

This is the dominant notion of critique from which the critical social and human sciences come. The logic of necessity, of pure reason is also for Kant and later Hegel, the logic of instrumental reason, in which nature becomes a means not an end. It is also positivism, hence the uncomfortable positivist echoes in the late Marx and late Habermas, something not present in the Habermas of *Theory and Practice* or Marx's earlier writings. Thus basically for Hegel, reason is only in its first beginnings identified with the sort of knowledge from mathematics and physics of Kantian pure reason. For Kant the concepts of understanding (Verstand) had to do with things such as the knowledge of nature which derive from mathematics and physics, while the ideas of reason (Vernunft) were the ungraspables through the logic of freedom, infinity, and things in themselves. Hegel started his Encyclopaedia thus with nature (i.e. the understanding and pure reason) before moving to mind, which needs to be otherwise explored and finally on to the state, religion, art and philosophy. Reason thus ultimately points less to science than to the critique of science.

Descartes bequeathed to us – in place of religion and the ancient regime – the centrality of the subject, of subject-object thinking. The Enlightenment extended this to the moral and political realm in which science – on a natural science model – would be the universalist motor of history on the way towards the good society, morally and politically. For his part, Kant, an 'Aufklärer', was as importantly a critic of the Enlightenment. He wanted to preserve a very important place for reason. Kantian critique is a critique in the first instance of the ancient regime, speculative reason, and of Humean skepticism to establish a sphere of reason as knowledge on the model of physics, mathematics and logic. But more importantly this critique established the critique of instrumental reason. The morality and politics involved here, unlike the Enlightenment (and the late Marx, Durkheim, etc.) do not have to do with the application of science to existing particulars. But with the moral law, something that lies outside of the knowable, of the understanding, outside of the relationship at all of universal to particular.

Aporetics and dialectics Subsequently we have had two traditions of critique. One of dialectics and the second of aporetics. Dialectics comprises most of the German tradition from Hegel to early Marx to Lukacs to Adorno, Marcuse and the young Habermas and now for example Seyla Benhabib. Aporetics comes from Kant and informs Heidegger and most of the French post-structuralist tradition. Aporetics speaks of an 'aporia of reason'.

This pertains to Kant's distinction between two types of reason. One is pure reason, meaning the understanding, science and logic. The other is 'pure practical reason', focusing on the moral law, the condition of possibility of moral action. The first sphere is the sphere of 'the same' and instrumental rationality. The second, the 'outside', though it governs the sphere of practice and relations between humans, is more than just this. It includes God (religion), noumena (i.e. the knowing of things, not according to the principles of science (nature), but in-themselves, according to their own ontological structures), infinity (including death) and finally the aesthetic. Some critical theorists have understood this 'sphere of freedom' in terms of not instrumental but substantive rationality. In any event, not just the inside is reason, but so is the outside. The outside, the realm of practical/substantive reason is somehow more fundamental (more 'primordial') than the inside (Heidegger, Levinas). It is the condition of possibility of the inside. Enlightenment as distinct from the Enlightenment and surely critique began to be primarily identified with this 'outside'. These two types of reason underlie the subsequent battles between positivism and hermeneutics (interpretative social science) in sociology, where critical sociology is always a sort of 'left hermeneutics'.

This Kantian distinction between the two spheres of reason, in which the second is defined by a major dimension of unknowability, underlies both dialectic and aporetic traditions of critique. The 'aporetic' tradition speaks of irreconcilables, whereas in 'dialectics' there is either a resolution or at least an interpenetration of the two spheres. The best of dialectics has little to do with the 'resolution' of the particular into the absolute, whether the latter is the Prussian state or Philosophy, and a lot more to do with a correction of the unhappy abstraction of aporetics. The best of dialectics is not about reconciliation or absolutes but a recognition that the way we lead our lives – cultural experience, ethical activities, social relations, relations to place, the way that we live our bodies – cannot be approached through such abstraction. Hence most of Hegel's *Philosophy of Right* is addressed not to resolution in the absolute, but to the necessary appearance of the moral law (i.e. the sphere of 'the other', of freedom, of substantive reason) in the grain of social life in 'the same'. This is not a relation between universal and particular, but between the 'transcendental' and the particular. Between the way that the Other (or Being) manifests itself in the particular.

Kantian aporetics would have ontology, on the one hand, and things, on the other, as unbridgeable antinomies. Thus if Husserl and Heidegger can talk of the ontological structure of things, in this sense they are on the side of dialectics. Heidegger has no notion of ultimate resolution. Similarly Adorno's negative dialectics wants to understand the aesthetic in a much more grounded way than Kantian aesthetics, in terms of the materiality of art. Yet also for Adorno this transcendental moment grounded in the particular does not lead to any kind of reconciliation. Thus should be understood also Gillian Rose's and Seyla Benhabib's excursions into critical theory. Again there is no necessary reconciliation. But the transcendental moment of reason or 'being' is manifested in the conventions of everyday moral practice (Benhabib) or in the law, love and religion (Rose).

Informationcritique But what I am arguing is that both German dialectics and French post-structuralism are legitimate heirs to the mantle of critical theory. Both aporetics and dialectics are legitimate critique. What is clear is that both dialectics and aporetics, both forms of critical theory are based in a fundamental 'dualism', a fundamental binary, of the two types of reason. One speaks of grounding and reconciliation, the other of unbridge-ability. But both speak in terms of such a fundamental dualism. Both presume a sphere of transcendence. Now as sociologists, we need to be able to situate these philosophers. We need to understand this dualism as socially or socio-culturally constituted. We need to notice that it has to do with the rise, challenge (by the working class and intellectuals) and then decline of the national manufacturing society.

In critique, what is compelling is that it is 'thought', whether philosophic, sociological/ hermeneutic, whether manifested in art, cinema, or the novel, that occupies this transcendental realm. But as long as we have a transcendental realm of thought, and this transcendental realm is identified with truth, being, the primordial and the like (and this goes for Heidegger as well as Marx, for Gadamer as well as Habermas), we are still in the realm of 'Ideologiekritik'. For his part Derrida too works in the medium of a transcendental space of 'differance'. This ideologycritique has been incredibly effective. But it is suited much better to the constitutive dualisms of the era of the national manufacturing society. The problem is that the global information culture tends to destroy these dualisms, tends to erase the possibility of a transcendental realm. 'Informationcritique must be critique without transcendentals.' It tends to destroy the fiber of the ground as we are lifted out from the grain of social relations into networks. It tends to erase main differences between the same and the other, as national boundaries are questioned and the boundaries between humans and non-humans challenged. Within an age of general informationalization of not just culture but nature.

Ideologiekritik and Informationcritique are both first and foremost questions of thought. And what happens to thought in the information society? As transcendentals disappear, thought is swept up into the general plane of 'immanence' with everything else. In the information age, cultural experience is transformed from the previously existing transcendental dualisms of the reader and the book, the concerto and the audience, the painting and the spectator. Cultural is displaced into an immanent plane of actors attached or interfaced with machines. Now we experience cultural things not as transcendental representations, but instead as immanent things: as objects, as technologies. In this generalized immanence super-structures collapse as the economy is collateralized, informationalized.

The older manufacturing capitalism was very much driven by the contra-diction between use value and exchange value, in which use value occupied the space of 'the transcendental' (substantive/practical reason) and exchange value the space of 'the empirical' (instrumental rationality). The couple use value/exchange value is the instantiation of the transcendental/empirical pair in goods. Manufacturing capitalism was driven by the logic of commodification (exchange value) and its critique (use value). Sometimes it looked like commodification would completely subsume critique (Marcuse) and sometimes not. But the logic of informationalization is altogether different. Unlike the logic of commodification it is not dualist. It is an immanentist logic. It explodes and partly marginalizes the exchange value/use value couple. In its place is an immanent plane of actor networks: of humans and non-humans of cultural objects and material objects, that are generally disembedded and not at all necessarily re-embedded. The actors, the networks the non-humans, the interface of humans and machines are disembedded. The information is disembedded. This is a society of the 'and', not a society of 'the there'. A society of the 'conjunction', not of the 'adverb'. Ideologiekritik, as Cartesian critique of the ancient regime foregrounded a problematic of the 'I', of the substantive, of the subject on the one hand and object on the other. This was a problematic of beings, of the proper noun. Ideologiekritik as critique, not of the ancient regime, but of instrumental reason, posits a problematic of 'the there' (world or life-world), of the adverbial. But now we have the network society, the society of the 'and', defined as Deleuze noted by neither noun, nor adverb but the conjunction. How can critical theory work here?

How does critical theory work in this general informational immanence in which there is no outside any more? In which nothing is the primordial or transcendent condition of possibility of anything else? This general immanence of informationalization is not the old 'same' of instrumental rationality and the commodity. As it erodes the transcendent it also erodes the instrumental (empirical). It is instead something else entirely. The old 'same' presumed the 'other' of critique and practical reason. All this disappears now. Without an other there is no same. Everything that used to be in the other is now part and parcel of this informationalized and networked general immanence. Even death. Even what Max Weber called theodicy. And for that matter 'life'.

So which way for informationcritique, for critical social science in the information age? First it is only we, i.e. critical social science who will even 'think' the information age. While the philosophers, anthropologists and aestheticians will speak in absolutes, ignoring the centrality of socio-cultural change. The understanding of social change, and the transition to the global information culture is the proper study of sociologists. Second, we need to break with the dualist notions of critique. And here, we might turn for inspiration to Nietzsche. To Nietzsche's idea of 'amor fati'. To embrace your fate means to no longer deal with the dualism of necessity and freedom, but with the much more primordial fate. It is not to live fate like habit, but to seize it and run with it. For Nietszche all dualisms (from Plato to Christian spirit and matter to Kant's aporia and logically on to Adorno, Hegel's and Marx's dialectics as well as Heidegger's unbridgeable 'ontological difference' of beings and being) are constitutively 'slave moralities'. Truth on the other hand is immanent. Truth is neither 'out there' nor 'in here'. But the 'out there' and 'in here' no longer make sense in such a Nietzschean problematic of immanence. Of generalized immanence, of the actor-network society of the information age.

The information age opens up new problematics of power and inequality, alluded to above. It opens up as well infinite opportunities for a whole array of innovations and creativities. Any critical theory, which will have more in common with 'amor fati' than with traditional notions of critique in the information age, must deal with these emergent constellations of power and inequality. But perhaps most important is that 'in the age of general informationalization, critique itself must become informational'. There must necessarily be an informationalization of critique. This is a lot different than the older Ideologiekritik. Ideology critique had to be somehow outside of ideology. With the disappearance of a constitutive outside, informationcritique must be inside of information. Hence it must be a question of 'amor fati'. There is no outside any more. Critique, and the texts of critical theory must be part and parcel of this general informationalization. Here the critical theory text becomes just another object, just another cultural object, consumed less reflectively than in the past, written (and often not just written, as CD-ROM, installation and Web presentation become increasingly prevalent) under conditions of time and budget constraint much more than in the past. Informationcritique itself is branded, another object of intellectual property, mechanistically mediated. Through your laptop, palm pilot, your movement from interface with auto and mobile phone to airplane to television to pager to the new 'worn technologies' on your set-top box and refrigerator. Texts of informationcritique are part and parcel of the flows, the 'economies of signs and space'. Perhaps with a bit more duration, a bit more time for reflection, but nonetheless part of the global information and media 'scapes'. To be anything less would render critical theory all too irrelevant in the information age.

A final caveat however. One that leads us back to today's most influential Critical Theorist, not Adorno or Marcuse, and surely not Habermas, and not even Foucault but of course Walter Benjamin. Benjamin's work was always double edged. On the one hand he embraced (amor fati) the age of mechanical reproduction. He discerned the cutting edge in commodified and popular culture, the importance of information age in the newspapers. He knew that there was no going back. That there was no separate space for critique. But Benjamin's angel of history, while being dragged forward at a tremendous speed was at the same time facing backwards. Facing the past, he was always and necessarily a melancholic. In a similar fashion it seems to me informationcritique itself must be melancholic. While realizing the inescapability from the information and communication flows, it must remember to bury its dead. It must live with the ghosts of Kant, Hegel, Marx, Adorno, Heidegger and for that matter Max Weber. It must live with, mourn and not forget the ghosts of ideology critique. Though informationcritique of necessity occupies the new 'scapes' and flows of intellectual property, post-national rights, object and installation art, multimedia, the proliferation of interfaces and the like, it must not forget that it stands on the shoulders of giants.

Walter Benjamin –
Looking at the Dream-Side of the
City **Dieter Hassenpflug**

In the present debate concerning the future of the European city, the work of Walter Benjamin enjoys extraordinary attention. Ever more frequently he is quoted in seminars, lectures, and publications. So it is no accident that the conference Cities in Transition II dedicated a Workshop to only one thinker explicitly: Walter Benjamin! How can we explain this interest of theorists of architecture, urban developers, urban sociologists and art historians in a social-philosopher who studied the city of the 19th Century – an object, that was already historical to him? From a European point of view, two reasons seem to justify this elevated attention.

The first and most immediate reason has to be seen in the present boom of dome-constructions, galleries and arcades inside and outside the cities. This post-industrial glass, textile and plastic architecture for entertainment and leisure facilities, theme parks, city centers and malls refer to the present renaissance of synthetic pleasure and symbol worlds. Apparently, urbanists hope to get support from the author of the Arcades Project for a better socio-cultural understanding of postmodern synthetic worlds and for a better interpretation of places, where private and public space interfere, communicate and clash. The second, more important reason is to be seen in the disintegration of the European cities, urban and urbane lifestyles. New ideals of social- and nature-romantic provenance like the garden city, the anti-civil big-city enmity of the national-socialist movement in Germany and the 'Fordist'-oriented treatment of cities, transforming them by functional differentiation, efficiency, acceleration and automobilism into soulless machines, have already largely destroyed the integrity of the urban and rural space. Today the public space as arena, medium and symbol of civil society is severely threatened.

Apparently, the need for reformulating the lost urban and rural 'composition' incites the interest of the 'experts of space' in authors like Walter Benjamin. At least his œuvre offers a fascinating method to read the city and to understand its idea. It is an aesthetic semantics of the urbane text. In the figure of the 'flaneur' he gives a real metropolitan organ to this semantics. By choosing the flaneur as reception-organ of the 'capital of the 19th century', Paris, he makes the city readable, an awareness and knowledge of the city by and through itself.[1]

---

1 Unfortunately Benjamin's Arcades Project is often regarded only as a mere collection of hints, ideas and quotations without any structure. Llovet is right at first glance, resuming: 'Benjamin's analyses or mere hints about the city of Paris seem merely a conglomerate of separate observations, an accumulation of sketches taken from nature, and, above all, a collection of other people's quotations. However, all these elements can never consolidate as a text with narrative aspects, and they do not attain that discursive organization that Benjamin's first, academic essays possess... Nothing in the Arcades Project can be subsumed in the category of anatomical discourse or indicates the structured composition of a mosaic; it consists only of a string of "disjecta membra".' Jordi Llovet, 'Benjamin Flâneur: The Arcades Project' in: Ingrid and Konrad Scheurmann (ed.), **For Walter Benjamin**, Bonn 1993. It is an issue of this essay to show that the Arcades Project hides a strongly structured, coherent epistemology of city-analysis – a kind of perception that should be of very high interest to all 'urbanists'.

Walter Benjamin
– Looking at the
Dream-Side of the
City

History and analysis of expression   The flaneur's

urban perception first refers to a peculiarity of Benjamin's theory of history. In this theory, the past admittedly has influence on the present – without determining it. 'It is not so, that the past illuminates the present or the present illuminates the past, but image is when the past meets the present in a flash-like constellation.' (GS V 1, 576 and 578)[2] Therefore the past (the 'gone by') is a stratum of the present. The present is memory. It is filled with memory. But simultaneously the remembered reaches through the present into the future. In this respect imagination, the spiritual draft of the future, is nothing other than the reformulation of the remembered with the methods of the present. Benjamin himself marked this connection of the past, present and future in the medium of the dream as 'Copernical revolution in the historical view'. (GS V 1, 490 ff and GS V II, 1057) This revolution runs through his work like a thread and is condensed in his eighteen theses 'On the Idea of History' (GS 1, 2, 691 ff) to a manifesto.[3]

In his philosophy of history Benjamin frequently uses the idea of the 'aura' which he made famous. Aura means the presence of an uncertain but emotionally powerful distance in the temporal and spatial proximity of things. Aura is a counter notion to 'trace': 'The trace is the appearance of a proximity, so distant that it may be what is left behind. The aura is the appearance of a distance, so near that it may be what is evoked. Through the trace, we get the thing into possession; through the aura the thing takes hold of us.' (GS V 1, 560) The auratic dimension of an object is what touches us emotionally. Also, the aura is an aspect of its recognizability. 'Each present is determined by those pictures that are synchronic with it. Each here and now is the here and now of a certain recognizability.' (GS V 1, 578)

To things aura is what subconscious is to human beings (or creatures). Also aura is a construction of the recognizing, perceiving, sensually noticing subject. It originates in dialogue, emerges when there is communication

---

2 All quotations from the German **Gesammelte Schriften** (GS) edited by Rolf Tiedemann and Hermann Schweppenhäuser, Frankfurt/M. 1974/82/91.

3 'Little methodical proposition concerning the dialectics of the history of culture. It is easy to get busy on dualisms for every sphere of each epoch, so that you have on one side the fertile, future providing, vivid, alive and on the other the futile, backward, dead part of that epoch. You can even contrast the outlines of this positive part only by profiling them against the negative part. But on the other hand each negation has its value only as a basis for the outlines of the alive, the positive. So it is of great importance to apply this negative part separately before a new division is created. By moving the perspective (not the measures!) again something positive arises which is not the same as before. And so on ad infinitum, until the whole past has been introduced to

between subject and object. Aura is a component of atmosphere. However, to be open to this atmosphere, to get it, it is necessary to have a special, dream-work trained organ of reception. With a point of view taught by Georg Simmel and led by Charles Baudelaire Benjamin finds this talent in the figure of the flaneur.[4] He possesses the organ to read the colorful, living reverse of the urban phenomenon. The high position that Benjamin gives to the flaneur in his literary and scientific work is due to this gift. So, if a particular epistemology of expression-analysis is to be found in the work of Benjamin, then this epistemology has its roots in the sophistication of the 'lonesome in the crowd' and in his 'pathos of proximity'.(GS V 11, 1015)

Finally, Walter Benjamin is not interested in strictly causal-analytic explanations of social developments. In this respect, Benjamin does not place himself in the Neo-Marxistic tradition of the 'critique of political economy'. He interprets social phenomena by means of expression analysis.[5] Facing the expression and form analysis of civil society the city as its materialization inevitably comes into sight. Whoever has read Benjamin's studies of Baudelaire or some sections of the 'Arcades Project-Torso' has experienced the lucid magic of his aesthetic method of sociology: the 'sensitive knowledge'. (GS V 11, 1053) Sensitivity as medium of knowledge – originally 'aesthetics' means nothing else – is a subject of interest to architects, urban developers and urban designers as the 'professional aesthetes'. And their interest increases the more they suffer from the anti-urban ugliness and malfunction of 'Fordistic' modernity.

To find the traces of the expression-context as realized in the big city, Benjamin uses, as already mentioned, the flaneur. He represents the dream-side of the metropolis. He is that gray and bored appearing sleeper, who opens its case (or 'sheathe'), to be at home in its hidden 'arabesques'.(GS V 11, 1054) This method has nothing to do with transcendental philosophy. It is neither about platonic ideas nor about a historic a priori of the urban.[6] The method of the flaneur deals with the acquisition of the urban potential of imagination and myth. It deals with the studies of that urban stock of images that connects the past with the future. This stock of images is singular. It forms uniqueness and through that, local relationship and identity.

the present by a historical apokatastasis.' (GS V I, 573) 'That is the only possibility to understand why modern times are permanently quoting primeval history.' (GS V I, 55)

4 The fascination that Baudelaire holds for Benjamin is not least caused by the fact that Baudelaire was the very first author who used a genuine urban treasure of words in poetry. (GS I 2, 603)

5 'Marx describes the causal relationship between economy and culture. Here the relationship of expression is relevant. Not the economic reasons of culture but the expression of economy in culture has to be described.' (GS V I, 573 f.)

6 Similar to his brother in mind, Georg Simmel, Benjamin is not a paradigmatic thinker. See: Adorno, Theodor W., **Philosophische Terminologie**, Bd. 1, 62.

Walter Benjamin
– Looking at the
Dream-Side of the
City

The flaneur The flaneur is a creature of the big city, especially a creation of Paris. (GS V II, 1053) To him the city is at the same time land-scape and living room. (GS V I, 525) He perceives streets as interiors. He experiences the city as a world that attracts and also repels him. He refuses the crowd. (GS I 2, 627) He is the individual and the lonesome in the crowd – and he knows about his isolation and loneliness. (GS I 2, 626) 'The passerby wedges himself into the crowd, while the flaneur needs space and time and will not miss his way of privatizing.' (GS I 2, 627)

The Flaneur is a master, a priest of the big city. He is at home in the Parisian jungle of houses and streets. He possesses its arcanum, the secret of its wild and labyrinthic landscape.[7] His urbanistic authority is grounded in his particular way of looking. It is that of a child. The childlike percep-tion can add the new to the mythology, to the timeless and universal treasure of images of humankind. 'It is the task of childhood', Benjamin says, 'to introduce the new world into the space of symbols. What the adult is absolutely not able to do, the child can: it is able to remember the new.' (GS V I, 493, 576; GS V II, 1024)

However, for adults there seems to be a possibility to recapture this per-ception. The medium for this regaining is ecstasy. The Flaneur, Benjamin says, passes through the city 'in an anamnetic high'. (GS V II, 1053) For him 'each street is steep', for each street leads him into a past that is actually the time of youth. He resembles 'the hashish consumer, conquers the space like him'. (GS V II, 1009) This conquest is carried out by means of 'super-imposition'. (GS V I, 526) Superimposition is a kind of space-perception, which connects the sensations of the new with the return of the everlasting (or eversame).[8]

As much as the flaneur is a modern, metropolitan appearance, he orients himself according to the past. He is a conservative rebel against modern times, against labor division, acceleration and meaningless accu-mulation. For example, he celebrates his conservatism in the odd fashion of taking turtles for a walk in the arcades. (GS V II, 1054) Quoting Benjamin: 'About 1840 it temporarily was good style to take turtles for a walk in the

---

7 See GS I 2, 687 f. 'The city is the product of the old human dream of the labyrinth. Without knowing it he follows this reality.' (GS V I, 541)
8 GS V II, 1023. With this reception the flaneur anticipates the reception of the film too – long before the film was invented. (GS V I, 135)

arcades. The Flaneur liked them to dictate his speed. To him, (technical) progress should learn this pace.' (GS I 2, 557) 'In the figure of the flaneur the idler returns, which Socrates found as a partner for conversation in the marketplace of Athens. However, Socrates does not exist any more and so the flaneur remains undiscovered.' (GS I 2, 685) 'The idleness of the flaneur is a protest against labor division.' (GS V 1, 538) 'Flânerie is a result of the idea, that the profit of idleness is much more valuable than that of labor.' (GS V 1, 567) However, if one wants to connect idleness with a form of labor the best would be the connection with gathering. The flaneur is a collector (GS V 11, 969), who roams the countless streets for botanical studies. (GS I 2, 538)

As far as idleness is a forerunner of the diversion organized by the amusement industry, the flaneur is also a pioneer of modern consumerism. In him curiosity celebrates its earliest triumph. (GS I 2, 572) While in his perception the city is both landscape and room, the big department stores stage landscape and room to make roaming usable for merchandise turnovers. (GS V 1, 54) The flaneur himself 'takes the category of venality for a walk'. The department store is 'his last game (or streetwalk)'.(GS V 1 562)

Arcades

For Benjamin there exists not only this urbanistic dream analysis as method of urban perception but also the physical manifestation of the dream. The arcades are such a demonstration or 'estuary' of the dream dimension of Paris, Benjamin says. 'Each epoch has this dream-side, this child-side. As to the previous century, the arcades clearly carried it out.' (GS V 1, 490) The facades of the arcade-houses are turned into an outside that is simultaneously inside. They are 'houses, corridors without outside – like dreams'. (GS V 1, 513; V 2, 1006) At another point he says: 'In old Greece places were shown with openings leading down to the underworld. In the same way our awakened existence is a country, where at hidden places paths lead down to the underworld, with invisible places into where dreams lead. During the day, we unsuspectingly pass by. However, when sleep comes, we quickly grope our way back to them, getting lost in the dark corridors. During the light of day the labyrinth of houses in the big city is like the consciousness. By this time the arcades (the galleries, which lead into the past of the city) lead unnoticed into the streets. But at night their more compact darkness stands out of the darkness of the ocean of houses...' (V 2, 1046)

The Parisian arcades of the first generation were built between 1822 and 1837 – before the metropolitan transformation of Paris by Baron Haussmann. To Benjamin they are the

Walter Benjamin
– Looking at the
Dream-Side of the
City

urban subject for showing his aesthetical expression analysis, his flaneur perception method and his interconnected theory of history. The arcades he comprehends as built intersection of past and future. Their understanding claims a competence of realizing the simultaneity of all tempi, a kind of 'transparency of passing through and superimposing' as it is only suitable to the flaneur. (V 2, 679) Looking through his eyes the arcades grasp deeply into the past – and far into the future. So they are 'the mold forming the picture of the future'. (GS V II, 1045) They are the new that constantly exists. They are also bewitched and weird places, where even 'false colors' (GS V I, 235) are possible: 'fairy-palaces'. Therefore, they are consequently 'the birthplaces of surrealism'.[9]

The particular magic of the arcades is at least based on the 'ambiguity' (GS V II, 1050) of the space produced by them. Benjamin describes them for example as a strange 'mix of house and street' (GS V II, 1041; GS I 2, 539), as products of a hybrid space, which is public and private too. While the present-day galleries are without exception private places faking public spaces, the early arcades are public areas, staging private spaces.[10] 'The flaneur experiences the arcades as an ecstatic penetration of public street and private home.' (GS V I, 524)The triumph of the urban streetlight is due to the living-room character of the Parisian arcades. The first gas lamps of the world were placed here. (GS I 2, 552 ff) Their light has illuminated the epoch of the flaneur. The gaslight gives the streets the magic he needs for his city-reception. 'The appearance of the street as interior, in which the phantasmagoria of the flaneur is summarized, cannot be separated from the gaslight.' (GS I 2, 552) The introduction of the electric light and the realization of broad sidewalks by Baron Haussmann was the beginning of the decline of the first-generation arcades. (GS V II, 1001) Haussmann also destroyed several arcades. Their end however meant the end of the flaneur. (GS I 2, 553) But who nowadays is able to use the method of the flaneur, who is still able to understand the quotations of the past in the present? (GS V I, 55)

9 GS V II, 1054, 1057. In the arcades the first panoramas were to be found. These arrangements announced a revolution in the relationship between art and technique. 'They tried hard to make the panoramas locations of a perfect mimesis of nature.' (GS V I, 48) The same way the reception of the flaneur anticipates that of the film viewer (auditor), the panoramas anticipate the film. As the panoramas try to generate changes of their staged nature that look remarkably similar to real nature, they point to film and acoustic film – going beyond photography (GS V I).
10 This does not affect the fact that the early passages, i.e. the glazing and wood of the city streets were the results of private engagement. The streets remain public space.
11 GS V II, 1061. This seems to be a parallel to early industrialization. There was a lack of local free energy (technological aspect) and a political hegemony of the guilds in the old cities

In retrospect and referring to Sigfried Gideon, Benjamin defined the arcades as 'the most important architecture of the 19th Century'. In his opinion the main reason for that is the 'introduction of the constructive principle into architecture' through the application of iron. The separation of art and architecture and of artist and engineer starts here. (GS V 1, 46, 48) With the invention of the arcades iron-construction begins and with iron the first artificial construction material appears in architecture. (GS V 1, 46; GS V II, 1061) In covered markets, railway stations and exhibition pavilions iron soon finds new fields of application. The most lasting expression the new architecture admittedly gets is through the Crystal Palace of Paxton, built for the first World's Fair of 1851 in London. (V 1, 239, 247) Like this palace, the arcades refer to the coming Fordist epoch where the worker and the engineer are the main socio-cultural representatives of industrial-modern times. (GS V 1, 572) Not accidentally the avant-garde socialist Charles Fourier suggested arcade-like buildings as homes for his perfect utopian community of tomorrow. His Phalanstères are, as Benjamin says, 'nothing else but cities made of arcades'. (GS V 1, 47) If the street is a 'home of the crowd', then the arcade is the 'palace of the collective'. (GS V II, 1052)

The arcades are at least 'a newer invention of industrial luxury' (GS V II, 1044), 'hoary streets of business' and therefore something like 'very early landscapes of consumption, landscapes of the last existing dinosaurs of Europe: the consumers'. As 'glass and iron that have come too early' (V 2, 1052 and V 1, 211 ff), they precede the big department stores of the future. (GS V II, 1061, GS V 1, 87, 90) 'With these galleries the emergence of the big department stores begins, the most revolutionary of which, the Bon Marché, was a building by the architect of the Eiffel tower.'[11] And: 'With the foundation of the department stores for the first time in history the consumers feel as a mass (in former times only misery teaches people to feel as a mass). That is the reason that the circensic and show element of the trade starts to boom exceptionally.'[12]

The arcades and glass-palaces of the advanced industrialized nations are certainly the predecessors of the present postmodern synthetic worlds, of the theme parks, malls, galleries etc. They all aim at generating spectacular atmospheres. The Crystal Palace of Paxton was already a synthetic world[13], which anticipates the actual consumption, event and leisure parks in various senses. Like today, show-qualities were generated by atopian

(socio-cultural aspect). So industry had to take a detour around the country (home industry, coal industry, manufactory). Finally, under conditions of the steam engine and the republican order it succeeded in reaching the city. The department store too did not emerge directly from the transfer of a weekly market into a building or from a so called evolutionary growing of a former little store. The invention of the gallery or mall needed the detour of the public street, which stages private space.

12   GS V I, 93. Richard Sennett pays attention to the 'Fordistic' aspect of this evolution. In this respect the theatrical and circensic is related to the market place. The invention of the big store house and the introduction of fixed prices bring the end of the theatrical in the arena of public space. Richard Sennett, **The Fall of Public Man**, New York, WW Norton and Company, 1974.

Walter Benjamin
– Looking at the
Dream-Side of the
City

arrangements, by simulation, quoting or fictionalization of distant or imagined places and pictures. 'The feathered palms of the south are mixed with the treetops of five-hundred-year-old elms and the main products of the arts, statues, big bronzes and the trophies of free artwork were placed in this magic forest. In the middle of it is a mighty fountain made of glass-crystals. To the right and left people find the galleries where they can stroll from one nation to the other and so the whole appeared as a marvel that moved imagination even more than mind. (GS V I, 248)

According to Benjamin the world fairs are the only festivities originally invented in modern times. Especially the world fairs of Paris had a big influence on urban design. (GS V I, 268) National shows of the industry preceded the world fairs. They aimed at amusing the working class. The amusement industry gradually developed along with the emergence of the world fairs. (GS V I 50 and 267; GS V II, 967)

City and country

'City' is more than and different from the 'idea of the city'. Cities are nature too, a specific landscape, a kind of countryside. This point of view emerges inevitably from the epistemology of Benjamin. 'Country' is not only the condition or prerequisite of 'city'. It is also a part of the city, is incorporated, transformed and permanently invented anew by the city. Moreover, the idea of the city cannot be separated from the idea of the country. Both need each other. Even more: The flaneur reads the city by means of a rural dispositive. Refusing the banalities of modernity as such, he shows his unique modernity. How else could his interpretation of the city as wilderness[14] or landscape, his staging of slowness, his mistrust of the new and his weakness for the panoramas be understood? By means of the panoramas, the city-dweller, 'whose political superiority over the country finds its strong expression during the century, tries to introduce the country into the city. In the panoramas the city expands to landscape, as it does in a more subtle way for the flaneur'. (GS V I, 48)

Rural and urban spaces mark two ideal space-personalities. Their rela-

---

13 According to Benjamin, 'experience' is an impression which is so strong that it cannot immediately be managed psychically (GS V I, 500).
14 GS, I 2, 541 544, 565, 630. Benjamin quotes Valéry: 'The inhabitant of the big urban centers declines to the condition of wilderness, that is loneliness.' (GS, I 2, 630) Quoting Baudelaire: 'What are the threats of the forest and the prairie in comparison to the daily shocks and conflicts in the civilized world?' GS, I 2, 541

tionship is that of image and counter-image. They need each other and produce each other reciprocally. This is valid as much in a diachronic, i.e., historical, as in a synchronic, i.e., topical perspective. The tension between 'urban' and 'rural' (of 'society' and 'community') characterizes human history throughout. However, their cultural weight has changed repeatedly. It has to be left open whether a general trend of the dominance of the urban can be proved. In any case, even the modern big city (metropolis) was unable to uncouple the urban population completely from the 'rural pole' of its existence. In the Arcades Project we find a remarkable hint on this subject. The typical inhabitant of Paris does not look at himself as a big-city dweller. He is an inhabitant of his quarter or arrondissement, in other words an inhabitant of a village in the city: Quoting Benjamin: 'With a shrug the real Parisian (...) refuses to be home in Paris. He inhabits the treizième, or the deuxième or the dix-huitième – not Paris. Nevertheless, he lives in his arrondissement – in the third, seventh or in the twentieth – and that is province. Maybe, here the secret of the mild hegemony of the city over France is to be found: it owns in the heart of its quarters... more provinces than France possesses in the whole. (...) Paris has more than twenty arrondissements and is full of cities and villages.' (GS V II, 999) Villages, meaning the quarters, are elements of the city. However, the city is something else than the sum of its quarters. It emerges from its quarters with its own qualities and the manifestations of these qualities are the public spaces.

Citytainment: the city as 'kitsch'   According to Benjamin solely aesthetical and analytical thinking does not guarantee the truth-ability of criticism. The dialectical method inalienably and inevitably is part of that. Here, in the art of dialectical reflection, we find another fascinating aspect of Benjamin's thinking. Whoever reads his books will discover a dialectical, non-instrumental epistemology of life and dialogue – a method far beyond the teleological constructions of Hegelian and Marxistic theory of history. Let me briefly explain this phenomenon – referring to the present crisis of the city:

The disintegration of the old European city is only one side of a process, the other side of which is the raising, or better: the reinvention of the city as a fiction of itself. Following the example of the theme parks of Walt Disney – all around the globe malls and big fun-shopping centers were built that fake urban qualities through main streets and small

Walter Benjamin
– Looking at the
Dream-Side of the
City

facades. Referring to Benjamin, you can call this phenomenon the revival of the city as kitsch: Quoting Benjamin: 'Kitsch is the attempt to impress forms of art on urban or industrial techniques.' (GS V I 186) That is the reason why Benjamin judges Jugendstil (art nouveau) as kitsch.

One has to take kitsch seriously. Whoever doesn't will dig an insurmountable ditch between kitsch and art. Left to itself kitsch remains a kind of 'cold' art, an art with a 'hundred percent, absolute and momentary use value'. On the other hand art that is freed from social limitations and responsibilities cannot be good (high) art. It then becomes arrogant art. But arrogant art is only the reverse of kitsch and as such an expression of conceit and irresponsibility. Benjamin says: 'Really growing, alive forms carry inside something warming, usable, finally making happy. They incorporate kitsch dialectically and by that they surmount it and reach the people anyway.' (GS V I, 500) One has to return to this point of view to find a productive access to the current phenomenon of citytainment and disneyfication surrounding us.

The Benjamin art of rescuing, mediated through the look of the flaneur, is required today more than ever before. It is necessary to find the traces of dreams and visions making people roam and drift around. Ernst Bloch, contemporary and friend of Benjamin and philosopher of the real utopian 'not yet' puts the 'decoding' or 'deciphering' of the dream-side of things – from the industrial mass-product over art up to architecture – in the context of an obligation to the telos of history, that can only be achieved in a collective revolutionary action. On the other hand the decodings or decipherings of Benjamin aim at the individual, who alone carries the load of historical responsibility. For in it a sly (nomothetic) logic of progress is not available. Benjamin has taken Nietzsche seriously and lost the belief in progress of the socialistic movement. Progress, taken absolutely, is the catastrophe. Or better: Progress is the contemporary, individual and artistic reformulation of the 'ever the same'.

The reinvention and improvement of the city are in a certain manner the tasks of adults who have preserved their ability to look at things like a child.

'The Arcades and the glass-palaces of the advanced
industrialized nations are certainly the predecessors
of the present postmodern synthetic worlds,
of theme parks, malls and galleries. They all aim
at generating spectacular atmospheres.'

Ideologies of Media and the Architecture of Cities in Transition K. Michael Hays

The most theoretically aware of contemporary architects have rejected the most important operative concept of architecture theory at the moment of its re-foundation in the 1970s: namely, the aspiration to an autonomy of disciplinary forms and techniques as a way of creating and measuring the distance between a critical practice and the degraded status quo of consumer culture. Over and against resistance and autonomy – or better, resistance 'through' autonomy – recent design theories of various stripes have tended to take an affirmative position with regard to their cultural sponsors and accept a certain determination by cultural forces outside architecture (information and entertainment technologies, in particular), over which, it is assumed, architecture has no control. While I am not yet able to fully account for this new attitude, I wish to briefly reflect on it and the ideologies it has replaced. I shall proceed historically, sketching in some of the major markers for a still faint and incomplete narrative.

1 While the ideology of autonomy is properly part of the legacy of high modernism, the concept still had enormous resonance in the formation of architecture theory after 1968 (especially, perhaps, in the United States and Italy), at a time when architecture as traditionally practiced saw itself threatened by technological optimization and utilitarianism, by the demands placed on it as a service industry, as well as by the positivist inquiries of the behavioral sciences, sociology, and operations research. Architecture theory drew on various models in an effort to think architecture back into its own as a discipline, a practice, and an irreducible mode of knowledge and experience. In particular, there was developed a theory of typology, which allowed the resolution of the contradictory desires for autonomy, on the one hand, and an architectural representation of the city, on the other. Autonomy provided a way for architecture to intervene in culture negatively, through the effort 'not' to collapse into some other discourse, to be a medium different from all others. This, for example, is from Massimo Scolari, speaking for the architecture of the Fifteenth Triennale in Milan in 1973, the so-called 'Tendenza':

The new architecture's 'renunciation' is actually a full historical awareness...For the Tendenza, architecture is a cognitive process that in and of itself, in the acknowledgement of its own autonomy, is today necessitating a re-founding of the discipline; that refuses interdisciplinary solutions to its own crisis; that does not pursue and immerse itself in political, economic, social, and technological events...but rather desires to understand them so as to be able to intervene in them with lucidity.[1]

1   Massimo Scolari, 'The New Architecture and the Avant-Garde' in K. Michael Hays (ed.),
Architecture Theory since 1968, Cambridge, MIT Press, 1998, pp.131-132.

Ideologies of Media
and the Architecture
of Cities in Transition

There are two sources I detect in the autonomy-typology thesis that are worth pointing out. First, the notion of typology entails a realist discourse based on a reading of Georg Lukács that seeks an architecture whose very 'authenticity' paradoxically depends on its reiterability – that is, an architecture whose success at evoking and recollecting solid, concrete memories depends on its repetition of an already iterable code. What is more, the interactive subject of any type is just the city itself, understood as a whole, whose nature is induced from its architectural elements (the 'ontology of the city'). The city is responsible for the isolation and fragmentation of architecture down into constitutive parts (hence the importance of Piranesi for an architect like Rossi or a historian like Tafuri) but the city also simultaneously extends its logic uniformly over every patch of the cultural fabric so that in each isolated type the entire genetic code of the city, as it were, can be found.

Rossi's Modena cemetery, for example, seizes on this idea and derives its poignancy from the constructed interaction of the fragments tomb, house, cemetery, and city. Within each of these primary types are insinuated obliquely, anamorphically, all the others, producing a kind of overprinting of types and a conceptual pass through different registers of analogous moments. In typological thinking the relentless fragmenting of everything, what Lukács called reification (Verdinglichung), continues to be felt. And yet typology is the power to think generally, to take up the fragments and organize them in groups, to recognize processes, tendencies, and qualities where reification allows only lifeless quantities.

At a different level of the autonomy thesis there appears a key concept from Louis Althusser, that of the 'semi-autonomy' of 'levels' or 'instances' within an ideological field – the economic, political, juridical, cultural, aesthetic levels, and so on. The autonomy of each disciplinary level allows the development and advance of that discipline's particular techniques. But each level also feels pressure from all the others and exerts pressure on all the others. What results is a set of insides and outsides that are reciprocally constituted and related by way of their ultimate structural difference and distance from one another rather than their identity, all held together by the 'structural totality' of a social formation. Some version of this Althusserian model, I think, helps explain Scolari's otherwise contradictory assertion of autonomy and lucid intervention: architecture's autonomy must be understand as a relational concept, not as a mere isolationist position; if architecture looses its autonomy, it looses the specificity of its cultural response.

While Tendenza's model of autonomy seems powerful and, in its basic contours, still correct, what was missed by its arguments is that the very conditions on which its 'ontology' depends – namely the traditional European city – had, by the time of this theorization, already disappeared as a contemporaneous object of experience. For by the mid 1960s it was no longer the city in 'this' sense that was primarily operative but rather the suburbs, edge city, exurbia.

Or perhaps it wasn't missed. For, while Rossi's typological obsessions seem to be a way of constantly confirming the determinate presence of the traditional European city – refracting its historical logic of form through a neo-Enlightenment lens in contingent, contradictory, and quasi-surreal ways – their peculiar mnemonic function also makes it possible to see in them a new beauty in precisely what is vanishing. The originality of Rossi's work may well be its capacity to convey, alternately with melancholy or unblinking disenchantment, that the traditional European city – which in some sense means architecture itself – is forever lost. As Manfredo Tafuri insisted, in a direct response to what Scolari called a re-founding of the discipline: The thread of Ariadne with which Rossi weaves his typological research does not lead to the 'reestablishment of the discipline', but rather to its dissolution, thereby confirming 'in extremis' the tragic recognition of Georg Simmel and György Lukács.[2]

What is more, this revelation of loss follows, I believe, from the Lukácsian moment in Rossi's thesis, for the one form of experience that concretely represents the force of reification is crisis – when, in the present case, the mnemonic function is just about to fail, when the memory banks become so compartmentalized and arid that they will hold nothing other than the most bleached out of material. Thus does Rossi's architecture historicize itself to a certain extent, place itself and reflect on itself before the historian or critic ever arrives; thus, too, the palpable sense in his work of a historically determined melancholy.

---

2   Manfredo Tafuri, 'L'Architecture dans la Boudoir' in Hays, p.155.

Ideologies of Media
and the Architecture
of Cities in Transition

2   Looking now for the terms on which the traditional city was disappearing and a new suburbanism was emerging, one remembers Thomas Pynchon's 1966 novel, *The Crying of Lot 49*, when the protagonist Oedipa Maas looks out from her Chevy Impala across California's private property developments (which Pynchon called San Narciso) and sees them as a printed circuit communicating to her – not communicating directly but in textural patterns or, as Pynchon says, in 'a hieroglyphic sense of concealed meaning, of an intent to communicate. There'd seemed no limit to what the printed circuit could have told her … So in her first minute of San Narciso, a revelation also trembled just past the threshold of her understanding.'[3] What is striking here is not only that this veil of hieroglyphs is the suburban form itself, but also that the opposing terms of this new system are, first, the development of electronic technology – represented here by the printed circuit – and, second, communication, the intent to communicate, which must be understood as contradictory vis-à-vis the new technology, since new technologies tend to be illegible, lying 'just past the threshold of her understanding'. But this contradiction is resolved by the third term we now know as media, that is, by the technology of communication itself.

We need not rehearse the ways in which media changed the very nature of the experience of public space during this time except to recall that advertising media joined with the extensive development of buildings on the outskirts of the city and the new distribution of services to suburban commercial zones, and made the control of the quality of urban space through traditional tectonic and typological means more difficult. Venturi, Scott Brown, and others seized on this new perceptual convention. Visual reception challenged the tactility of objects and the perception of architectural surfaces began to overtake the experience of urban space in the traditional sense. Image consumption began to replace object production and the sheer heterogeneity of images exploded any single, stable, typology of the city. Public meaning was now to be found in the signs and perceptual conventions forged in a pluralist, consumerist, suburban culture. Consequently a split was felt to open up between the European typological

3   Thomas Pynchon, **The Crying of Lot 49**, New York, Harper & Rowe, 1966, p.24.

tradition and the everyday world of the American popular environment, a split that was fundamental to theoretical debates of the 1970s.

What is further suggested here (and completely understood by the Venturist) is that the semiotic surface of architecture, understood as a displacement of the older, volumetric, type form, is entirely adequate to – entirely conforms to – the new terms of media. Henceforth the social system will be inconceivable without a concept of media and its two constituents – electronic, consumer technology and heterogeneous communication – as, right up to our own time, media becomes the spontaneous solution to architecture's representational problem.

In an early study of film, Fredric Jameson suggested that in our present social system, a media term is always present to function as what Sartre called an 'analogon', or term of external mediation, for one or another more directly representational form, or term of internal mediation.[4] In our present case, it is helpful to think of the semiotic surface of architecture (the flattened out surface of Venturi's decorated shed) as the internal, architectural mediation. To conceptualize how the semiotic surface can represent the (ultimately unrepresentable) 'real' of suburban consumer culture, we must interpose the external term of 'media' (in the historically specific sense of electronic circuitry and the advertising images of suburban appliances and services) as an interpretant of the content of that culture itself (as Pynchon also does in our example). What must be underscored is that the very possibility of this mechanism of indirect representation is projected out of the total system (suburban consumer culture and electronic communication) that it can then, in turn, claim to represent.

3   And so it is a mutation of this second paradigm (the second city in transition) and the architectural production adequate to it that must concern us now. The examples I could draw from are growing almost daily,[5] but I have in mind recent theoretical and architectural projects of Greg Lynn, Lars Spuybroek, and Kas Oosterhuis, among others. In general, I have in mind the attempts to shift our thinking about architectural forms and functions from either a model of disciplinary autonomy and typology *or* of communication and heterogeneity of the semiotic surface to one that affirms the smooth fusion of relations among digitally synthesized images of diverse origins. For its internal mediatory term this new architecture employs the metaphor not of a typological object or a semiotic surface but of computer software itself, which coordinates multiple entities

4 Fredric Jameson, 'Class and Allegory in Contemporary Mass Culture' (1977), now in **Signatures of the Visible**, New York, Routledge, 1990.
5 See, for example, **Folding in Architecture**, ed. Greg Lynn, London, Academy Editions, 1993, **Hypersurface Architecture**, ed. Stephen Perrella, London, Academy Editions, 1998 and **ArchiLab,** Orléans, Blanchard, 1999.

Ideologies of Media
and the Architecture
of Cities in Transition

in a smooth, frictionless flow. As a corollary, this position also affirms a unity of techniques from different disciplines and cultural regions – architecture, physics, chemical engineering, computation, biology, and the flows of capital itself. One might characterize this shift as one away from the autonomy of the object, through the heterogeneity of the collaged, semiotic surface – both of which dramatize formal disjunction – toward the production of a new whole through the liquification of boundaries and the radical mixing of not only forms but of materials and concepts from different disciplines.

This is architecture's full entry into the new communications and entertainment technologies and, with that, a breakdown of the once fiercely defended autonomy of the architectural object and irreducibility of the architectural experience. Feeling increasing pressure from other forms of contemporary image culture that would displace architecture's collective communicative-symbolic function, it seems that architecture has reacted by trying to 'become' just those things – a multimedia fusion of graphic devices collected on an animated, alloyed surface of texture and pattern that can be scanned for information, that seems to send out references, at one scale, to the molecular, biological, informational system of DNA and, at another scale, to the global urbanization of the planet, and to join those two poles with an image, a look, that I have previously referred to as an architectural (and ideological) 'smoothness'.[6]

But the slackening of specificity and the de-differentiation of practices seem also to have produced an architecture whose function and visage can drift and expand in culture in unprecedented ways, spreading laterally in a stretched-out mixed-media experience. The production of this architecture explicitly refuses any craven professionalism or disciplinary partitioning; its techniques are the generic ones of 'design' as can be applied to Audi TTs and iMacs as much as to buildings. The perception of the architecture thus produced is woven into the same fabric as the latest high-tech gadgets, video games, and televisual leisure. Architecture is now just part of the smooth media mix and yet, in all of this, the architecture strives to play a crucial cultural role. What I want to suggest is that the precise nature of

6 See K. Michael Hays, 'Architecture Theory, Media, and the Question of Audience', **Assemblage** 27, August 1995.

its cultural vocation relates this recent stance back to the previous two paradigms we have mentioned.

The architectural surface is still important in this third category, and this is evidence that it builds on the accumulated techniques and effects of the second. But notice, for one thing, that this new surface no longer corresponds to a particular social public or locale – the street, the strip, Las Vegas, or Levittown – with the same immediacy as, say, Venturi's populism.[7] This seeming lack of a locale is, I think, partly what gives these projects their faint air of unreality, but it is also what attests to the global ambitions of this new architecture. Second, the disjunctive heterogeneity of the earlier surface is now collapsed into the singularity of a complex whole. This new surface is not made up of semiotic material that has been sampled, as it were, from popular culture; but, nevertheless, the surface is modulated through procedures that trace certain external sociological or technological facts more directly, perhaps even more literally, than the first two paradigms. These traces appear in our reading of the architecture as doing the double duty of articulating the surface, implying differentiated possibilities for occupation, and encoding phenomena outside the object that cannot, in their very nature, be represented directly (patterns of origination and destination in Lynn's New York Port Authority Gateway, for example). They effectively expand the space of the project to include a range of institutional, legal, technical, and cultural arrangements that precede, determine, and exist beyond the architectural object.

A new kind of reception is suggested here in which the sensory, the aesthetic, is somehow mingled with the theoretical (on the model, say, of minimalism) as the surface asks to be read as a registration of the discursive practices that shape the object and make possible what can become visible within it, and simultaneously, as a diagram of potentials for occupation, a 'dispositif' or distribution apparatus for other practices that it, in turn, enables. As an explanation of this latter diagrammatic function, Greg Lynn gives the example of a boat hull: 'Although the form of a boat hull is designed to anticipate motion, there is no expectation that its shape will change … The particular form of a hull stores multiple vectors of motion and flow from the space in which it was designed.'[8]

As for the discourse of type, we can see a development out of the vertical imitation or repetition of presumably timeless precedents toward a different kind of repetition, that of a complex series of parts that exist in a continual process of differentiation. Lynn, for one,

---

7 In the aforementioned article, I suggested that the 'proper' audience for this architecture is the generation of baby boomers and their just younger siblings who, through historical circumstance and class alliance, have developed a highly paradoxical mode of perception that one might call specific generalization, in which the distinctions between previously distinct modes of cultural expression are liquified and liquidated into the new generic smoothness.
8 Gregg Lynn, **Animate Form**, New York, Princeton Architectural Press, 1999, p.10.

Ideologies of Media
and the Architecture
of Cities in Transition

is explicit about the fact that his reiterative, interconnective 'blobs' are themselves deviations out of typology's formal logic. 'Typological fixity... depends on a closed static order to underlie a family of continuous variations. This concept of discreet, ideal, and fixed prototypes can be subsumed by the model of the numerically controlled multi-type that is flexible, mutable, and differential.'[9] From my perspective, what seems to have happened is a de-differentiation at the level of typological technique as well, such that now a single, generic, fluid form supercedes the already limited field of types. To use Lukácsian language: where reification had already hollowed out Rossi's typological shells, fragmenting them into disenchanted objects, now reification extends its power so absolutely that an object as such is no longer possible. But this should not be understood as entirely negative, for where the disjunctive object has disappeared there is now a new whole, a surface or a field, that now describes the space of propagation, the space of effects.[10]

Though one would not think to associate the realist, narrative ambitions of the Tendenza with this new architecture, there is still a historically aware, totalizing impulse in its practice, evident in the attempt to give form to the effective elements of a new posturban condition and a globalized media technology, that is, to make the 'system' of city and media the subject and the problem of the work of design. I do not believe the representational project of this new architecture has been successful yet; it is more the case, as I say, that the representation has arisen spontaneously from the software. But it is the aspiration to represent the (always absent, unrepresentable) totality that I find important. Posturbanism itself – edge cities, suburbs, the 'thick two-dimensions' of Asian cities, and the whole docket of the emergent posturban life that has heretofore seemed unmappable and unmanageable – is the most obvious manifestation of the sort of distribution apparatus that this architecture seeks to both represent and become: an enormous deterritorialized plane, its boundaries contingent on a particular geography and topography (stopped by a river or mountain range or an arbitrarily legislated property line), reterritorialized by any of various patterns (grids, patchworks, mosaics, and the like), some of which are inscribed on the

9 Ibid., 13.
10 It should be pointed out that a fuller account of the narrative I am sketching here would have to include a passage through the work, most importantly, of Eisenman and Tschumi, but also, as Robert McAnulty has pointed out in conversation, through the work of Diller and Scofidio as well, with their use of television as both appliance and surface or screen. The present emphasis, however, is on the paradigmatic changes due to changed conceptualizations of the city (cities in transition), which, it seems to me, yields a slightly different story.

ground, many of which may lie beneath the thin, occupiable surface, insensible yet controlling – infrastructural points and lines of force whose positions and relations have been determined by a notational language with translation rules conventionally understood by the multiple agents responsible for putting them in place. As much as by the partitioning off of areas, the type and intensity of activity on the surface is regulated by a kind of rheostat apparatus below that also senses changes on the surface it now charges (we need more cable here, another transportation tunnel there). The bodies on the surface are so many metal filings on a plate, forming patterns (flocks, swarms, neighborhoods), which are also charged with group alliances and specific cognitive and practical ways of negotiating the templates that enable possible performative events.

If globalized posturbanism and information technology have replaced both the traditional city and the suburbs along with their earlier technologies, and if the architectural representation or term of internal mediation seems to have been given by the media itself, our problem now is to determine what is the 'external' term of mediation – the analogon – that might allow us to complete the theorization of this paradigm in relation to the previous two. What is the structural nexus in our viewing and aesthetic decoding apparatus that would allow us to conceptualize the experience of the unrepresentable real of posturbanism and information technology in a similar way that advertising media allows us to conceptualize the semiotic surface of architecture in relation to the earlier consumerist suburb?

I am not the first to suggest that such an analogon will turn out to be something like what 1970s video theorists called 'total flow': the constant emission of generic but constantly changing bits of information that we move in and out of in a kind of ultimate suture between time and space.[11] Interestingly enough, total flow has its roots in the pop culture and media experience of our second paradigm, but its time-space is volatilized far beyond anything that the term 'heterogeneity' describes. In fact, the emissions from the video screen (and the computer terminal with which it will eventually merge) neutralize psychic energy and homogenize experience into a kind of all pervasive liquid force in such a way as to make it a logical candidate with which to theorize the newer work in question. What is more, the deregulation of television, or, at least, the possibility of 'surfing' across hundreds of channels whose broadcasts never stop, is a suitable analogue for the sort of spontaneous occupation desired by recent architecture, but also for its complex eco-

11   See, above all, Raymond Williams, **Television: Technology and Cultural Form**, London, Fontana, 1974.

Ideologies of Media
and the Architecture
of Cities in Transition

nomic ties to multinational capital and entertainment technologies.

A further advantage of the notion of total flow is that it has as its distant relative nothing less than distraction itself, which, of course, Walter Benjamin saw as the architectural mode of perception 'par excellence'. And surely the random succession of serialized images presented by the new architecture – which one attends to in varying degrees, pulling in and out of the frame of one's conscious attention – is very like the experience of video. And, too, total flow helps to model the way in which this new architectural practice is able to debit a wide range of sources for its cultural credit, and make use of a variety of modes of dissemination, from journals and exhibitions to web sites and DVDs. By weakening disciplinary autonomy, by de-differentiating procedures of design and dissemination, by dissolving the very distinction between the architectural representation and the larger world of image-spectacles, this architecture paradoxically (or dialectically) produces a link between the spatial experiences it enables and the abstract global system of late capitalism; but more: the link is made in terms of social space, the architecture constructed to locate subject positions in that space, and the actual experience of that space.

I would like to insist upon this last point and return here to Jameson's sketch of the Sartrean analogon, for Jameson suggests that this sort of triangulation (that is, the triangle of the unrepresentable real, the internal mediation, and the external mediation) is historically specific (to what he calls postmodernism) and that its terms are themselves 'unconscious structures and so many afterimages and secondary effects of some properly postmodern cognitive mapping [an instance of what I am here calling representation], whose indispensable media term now passes itself off as this or that philosophical reflection on language, communication, and the media, rather than the manipulation of its figure'.[12]

The development of this work should be seen according to a double movement of, first, internal transformations out of 1970s typology and the semiotic surface and, second, a shifting and transitory mapping of those external determinations of urban or posturban life under capitalism. Certainly those who defend this new architecture would want to pass off

12   Fredric Jameson, **Postmodernism, or, The Cultural Logic of Late Capitalism**,
Durham, Duke University Press, 1991, p.417.

its media term as a theoretical reflection as well as a manipulation of form. The vestiges of the raw material of media remain visible within these projects, inevitably, and this work finds its representational endeavor severely constrained. At the same time, however, the transmutation of the datascape of capital can be understood to continue architecture's vocation to represent (or aspire to represent) totalities. Perhaps, then, we have here a rather extraordinary condition in which a mutant form of reification continues its work of leveling out disciplinary techniques, de-differentiating across previously distinct practices, erasing the specific traces of production, and homogenizing particular experiences into one generic experiential flow, and yet, 'at the same time', does not eradicate the architectural impulse but rather is paradoxically pressed into service of altogether new ones adequate (just maybe) for our present.

Thanks to Jeffrey Kipnis and Robert McAnulty for helpful discussions of this material. Special thanks to Arie Graafland for the extraordinary conference at which it was first presented.

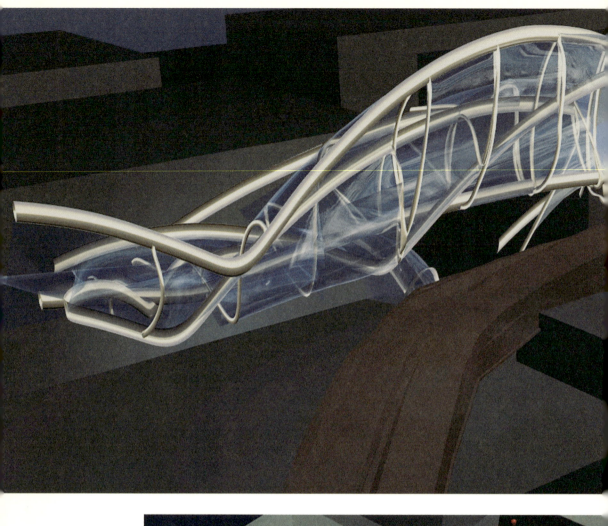

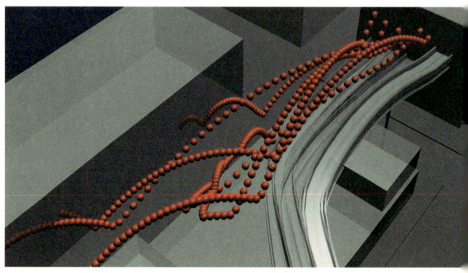

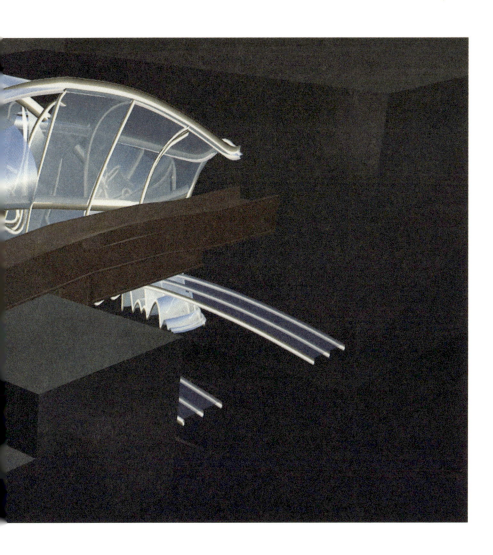

Gregg Lynn, New York Port Authority Gateway

MEDIATIONS in Architecture and in the Urban Landscape

Ignasi de Solà-Morales Rubio

For some time past the street lamps outside my house have been decked with banners advertising an interesting new local television channel. BTV, Barcelona Television, is the name of this channel, which combines information and entertainment with a significant dose of experimentation, in an intelligent and innovative way.

The channel's advertising features the ambiguous image of an eye that looks like the lens of a camera, or vice versa, deliberately confusing the 'natural' gaze of the human eye with the 'artificial' vision of the televisual eye.

The text which accompanies this advertising image is also deliberately ambiguous. It is in Catalan, and reads *El que passa a Barcelona, passa a* BTV. In English, the direct translation, 'What happens in Barcelona, happens on/appears on BTV', does not have the significant ambiguity of the original Catalan. The first use of the word 'passa' in Catalan is in the sense of what 'happens', what 'takes place'. It refers to events, which it is supposed, 'happen in reality'. The ambiguity lies in the second sense of the word passa. 'Passar a BTV' also means to happen, to occur, on the screens of BTV television, thanks to the capacity of television to reproduce, to repeat. There would be something like 'primary', 'de facto', 'real' events, which would also be accessible by means of a 'secondary' mechanism of reproduction, of transmission, facilitated by the technology of television.

But in Catalan, as also in Spanish, the expression 'pasar a, passar por', has a sense of inescapable necessity. 'Passar en, pasar por' is not only a process of passing on but also the condition necessary for the event to be produced in full. In other words, events only really exist, socially, informatively, etc., if they are communicated through or by means of the vehicle, the technology that causes them to be passed on, to be put across; in short, to exist socially and culturally.

This apparently innocuous reference serves to exemplify the question I would like to engage with in the pages that follow.

During at least three decades, from the years immediately after the Second World War up until the end of the sixties, the urban and the architectural landscape were conceived as the series of 'places' in which urban life was 'lived', 'existed', 'occurred'.

On the basis of an existential notion of experience it was thought that there were places because there was direct, physical, contiguous experience, a relation between places and our perception of these.

The representations we can make of these places, graphic, literary, photographic, etc., etc., are approximations, imitations, reproductions 'of the things themselves' or 'of the facts themselves' as these are and really occur in the place where they actually are.

Nothing can fully replace life itself in its scenarios. Every process of representation is a second version, a substitute imitation.

But there is a place for a different conception of our experiential and cognitive relationship with what is outside of ourselves. Perhaps the veracity that we can concede to the media by means of which we have knowledge of architectures and urban landscapes makes those media inescapable, necessary data in our approximation to this reality.

Gilles Deleuze has said that knowledge advances by way of the 'establishing of fictions in science, art and philosophy'. For the French thinker there is no aesthetic, scientific or philosophical experience without mediation and mediators.[1] In the same way that theoretical hypotheses are an instrument of mediation for the production of scientific or philosophical knowledge, so too in artistic creation, places, stories or images do not exist in themselves, waiting only to be revealed, but are pro-posals, positions prepared in advance, for the production of a given experience and thus of a particular knowledge, architectural, landscapist, literary or pictorial.

The media frame the turbulent flow of reality, cut it out and pro-pose it as a possibility of intelligible hypothesis. Reality does not exist in advance, waiting for us to come along and contemplate it, but is a product of the media we construct in order to engage with it. The production of the medium and the production of the experience are two facets of the same process. Architecture and the urban landscape are at one and the same time both the medium and the result of this mediation that makes non-places, places; makes the formless, form; makes the unintelligible, intelligible; makes the fluid, solid.

Thus not only does our access to the experience of places necessarily pass through the media that make them accessible to us, but this mediation is architecture itself. In other words, what I am attempting to explain is not only the necessity of mediation but also the mediatic condition, the establishing of fictions, that is intrinsic to architecture and the urban landscape.

1   Gilles Deleuze, **Différence et répétition**. P.V.F., Paris, 1968, p.3. (Spanish trans., **Diferencia y repetición**, Ediciones Jucar, Madrid, 1988, p.33).

Intentions   The western architectural culture of the middle of the 20th century has rested on theoretical hypotheses derived from phenomenology. The positivist empiricism, which underpinned architectural theory between the wars, was succeeded by the overwhelming rise of phenomenology in the task of defining the architectural specific.

The thought of Heidegger and of Merleau-Ponty were especially favored when it came to structuring a whole theory of architectural experience based on the Husserlian engagement with things in themselves.

What was regarded as abstract thought had to be replaced by a direct upheaval produced by the effort of engaging with objects, places, and spaces.

Architecture as a totality could not be dissected in its functional, technical or formal aspects. Instead, it was necessary to dive down to more profound depths where it was possible to perceive architectural totality as an essential synthesis and as the origin of meaning.

The influence of Heidegger, through his well-known texts on the subject of architecture, has been far-reaching, and we can see traces of his inspiring genius in, for example, the texts of J. Rykwert, E.N. Rogers, K. Frampton, or C. Norberg-Schultz. The last-named is a prolific author who may be said to have developed an extensive theoretical literature that defines what I have elsewhere called architectural existentialism, as a way of explaining the essentials of architecture on the basis of the notion of intentionality elaborated within the phenomenological tradition by the disciples of E. Husserl.

It is no accident that Norberg-Schultz's first attempt at formulating a complete theory of architecture was in the book *Intentions*, published in 1961.[2] If phenomenology sees the action of consciousness as realizing itself intentionally in the world (Brentano), for architecture this becomes intelligible as 'lebenswelt', as the existential space in which our being-in-the-world unfolds. No logic, no form, no economy is capable of explaining the lived, existential, direct experience of the places forged by architecture. Life as totality is brought together in spaces and places which are accessible to us through our experiencing them, through our living them.

In his most important books, Norberg-Schultz has elaborated key notions that have gone on to become conventional commonplaces for explaining the architectural essential.

The notion of space forged by the pure-visualist tradition from Riegl to Frankl and from Wölflin to Giedion is reformulated with phenomenological co-ordinates such as 'existential space', while 'gestalt psychology' moves in the direction of investigations into the dynamic structural psychology of Piaget and the phenomenology of perception of M. Merleau-

---

2   Christian Norberg-Schultz, **Intensjorner i arkitekturen** (Intentions in Architecture) Universitetsforlaget, Oslo, 1967. (Spanish trans., Intenciones en Arquitectura, Gustavo Gili, Barcelona, 1979). See also **Existence, Space and Architecture**. Studio Vista, London, 1971, and **Genius Loci**, Electa, Milan, 1979.

Ponty. The house, the city and the landscape are spaces to be lived, in which the experience of being and our relation with the world take place.

The notion of place does not designate simple photographic or geometrical determinations but the setting in which there is produced the encounter with a world inhabited by meanings, by memories, by divinities. The Latin notion of 'Genius Loci' serves here as a common term with which to designate experiences of revelation and encounter by means of which the constructing, the making of architecture constitutes an authentic act of initiation, single and unique in space and time.

The evident quasi-religious archaism, which accompanies the construction of these notions, is of course, linked to Heidegger's metaphysical reflections and the possibility of the ground which his philosophy proposes as its primordial objective.

The phenomenological-existential way of thinking has had a great number of consequences, not only in the way we understand architecture and our experience of it, but also in the modes of its representation.

To move forward in this consideration of the wide-ranging work of C. Norberg-Schultz, we must now turn our attention to the physical and visual construction of his books. The author is not only the author of a text but of a narrative in which the images – schematic, diagrammatic and, above all, photographic – are essential.

Given that the experience of architecture is existential, lived, the photographic images that show us this learning to live the architectural landscape have to derive from an experience that is temporal, in movement, not exempt from chance, as an event that takes place at a precise biographical moment in our personal experience.

In common with other masters of the exercise of looking at architecture in a certain way, Norberg-Schultz has often illustrated his own texts. A careful and 'intentional' photographer, the images which illustrate the majority of his books are carefully chosen – and in more than 50% of cases, taken – by the author himself in the course of his direct personal experience of places, of landscapes, of buildings.

These images are characterized by their indifference to history, thanks to which the essential experience of the architecture takes place in architectural scenarios of any age, period, geographical area, style, etc., etc. The camera, the eye of the observer, seems to move at a leisurely walking pace, without shunning the presence of the passers-by or those anecdotal details we always encounter when we come to look at any place.

The photography of a reporter, of an attentive and curious traveler, documented yet unburdened with singular points of view, seems to be the 'modus operandi' of this testimony of the experience, on the edge, irreplaceable.

The existentialist images, the phenomenology photographic, are primarily reports which invite us to share in the experience, the journey, the living contact with the thing itself.

Mediations   The characteristic quality of the modern vision is that of being an external and indirect construction.

The illusion of existentialist phenomenology consisted in supposing an essential, stripped-down gaze, capable of making possible the direct contact between the subject and the world.

Since the 18th century at least, visual culture has constructed the mechanisms with which to organize the gaze and with which to mediate, to make possible, in a certain way, the gaze organized by means of the apparatus.

The first engagement with the 'natural' landscape on the part of the picturesque painters made use of mechanisms such as that known as Claude's mirror: a little glass which the 'plein air' painter would use to paint what could be seen in the limited frame of the mirror, which in this way mediates between the boundless natural landscape and its representation on the canvas of the picture.

The panorama, the camera lucida, the daguerreotype, the photograph and the panopticon were some of the new mechanisms which made it possible to see and fix landscapes, cities, portraits of individuals, spaces for the organization of work, etc., etc.[3]

The vision is never something that can submerge itself in the interior of a landscape, a building or a body. It is, on the contrary, something external, separate, whose capacity for apprehending reality is absolutely dependent on the medium which organizes the vision.

Of course, the vision – photographic, panoramic, panoptic, etc. – is a vision conditioned by a technical mechanism which interposes itself between an eye 'in bruto' and a reality that is in some way not directly, ingenuously accessible. The technification of the gaze and

3   Jonathan Crary, **Techniques of the Observer**, MIT Press, Cambridge, Mass., 1991.

its mediation does not involve a loss of reality, authenticity or vividness. On the contrary, it represents the concretion of our visual field and the multiplication of its possibilities.

The eye and the brain increasingly extend the realms that are accessible to them by means of prostheses which perfect and specialize different types of access to reality. Even an ordinary pair of spectacles or a microscope are clear instances of the way we engage with visual worlds not directly accessible to our eyes alone thanks to the mediation of the optical technology of these instruments. But in the modern world, technology and visual access are in a permanent process of diversification and expansion. We accumulate, reduce, expand, modify, using techniques that are completely alien to the 'natural' process of the eye, which nonetheless afford us access to visual worlds that are part of reality and on which we constantly operate.

Between the body and the visual stock of images, which we call reality, we recognize a 'naturally' unbridgeable distance. We know that we are, in some way, on the outside; we construct from an observatory that is not part of the interior of things in themselves.

In contrast to the realist illusion of the phenomenological tradition there is a long tradition centered on the advances of science and technology which explains the fact that in the modern world the appropriation of sights, sounds and perceptions of all kinds is produced through phenomena of mediation, and that this mediation always has a technical format which characterizes it and differentiates it from other possible mediations.

The action of art, in the figurative realm, like the action of thought in the conceptual, is that of constructing forms and concepts capable of organizing the formless on the basis of a certain strangeness and a certain necessity.

In the ocean of perceptions and information, every constructive operation consists in the production of landscapes and of architectures. In the beginning there is disorder and the informal. The mediatized construction of gazes and perceptions, seductive with some stamp of necessity however provisional and ephemeral, is that which produces the transfer from pure navigation to the definition of those meshes and relations, stable or labile, by means of which reality is wrapped up in new packages, given new features.

Gilles Deleuze said that he was not interested in self-portraits – a pretension incapable of establishing the features that define a subject, an in-itself – but only in the traces, the tracks, the images by means of which we receive successive waves of information structured in relation to a particular concern.[4]

The exercise of practices that structure provisional, successive, multiplied images is a non-essentialist way of understanding the practice by which landscape and architecture are deliberately and consciously a production of externalities, a pouring forth of images in which each one of the necessary hypotheses to which we have alluded above constitutes a contingent and discrete (in the sense of separate, discontinuous) way of showing, in a mediatized fashion, the surface of things.

'I have no other substance than my appearance', Baltasar Gracian declared in *El Criticón*.[5] Baroque wisdom, disillusioned and artful, saw only possibilities of hold or leverage in the discredited world of appearance. All of the essentialist discourses have rejected the apparent for the substantial, the image for the essence. Landscape and architecture, too, have repudiated appearances, images, the spectacle in the name of the essential, the profound, the permanent.

A mediatic conception of these realities moves, in contrast, along a totally different conceptual path. The media – multiple, interposed, technical – are the means of access – partial, provisional, conditioned – to these external worlds to which there is no access by any other way.

A theory of the urban landscape today has to be a theory of the media, free of any fears or anxieties that we are propagating multiple procedures deficient in rigor and permanence.

The introduction of contingency and permanent operability into the formless is a much closer approximation to our methods of definition of the urban and architectural form than the pursuit of the essential, minimal or existential. To think of landscapes and architectures as provisional packages is not to renounce tension, energy and invention but merely to orient our efforts in the only possible direction: that of the mediatized production of forms, images, simulacra as part of a contingent in which the distinction between real and virtual no longer has a metaphysical significance, but becomes instead a permanent challenge to the productive imagination.

4   Mireille Burdens, 'La forme devorée. Pour une approche deleuzienne d'internet',
in Thierry Lenain, ed., **L'image. Deleuze, Foucault, Lyotard**, Vrin, Paris, 1997.
5   Quoted by Mireille Burdens in Lenain, **op. cit.**, p.62.

Coda: Jean Baudrillard. Photographies

In January 1998 Jean Baudrillard published a small book with the title *Photographies. Car l'illusion ne s'oppose a la realité...*[6] This consists of a short but intense essay on photography, accompanied by a hundred or so photographic images taken by Baudrillard himself. The book is a kind of catalogue, produced at the suggestion of the Musée Nicéphore Niépce in the town of Chalon-sur-Saône.

The critic of the society of simulation and appearance retraces his steps and reflects on a practice with which he is familiar from his own experience: photography. Here he is not the sociologist-anthropologist launching apocalyptic diatribes against the society of the spectacle but the photographer who seeks to understand the relations that obtain between what he has seen with his own eyes and what is shown by the photographic images.

'To photograph is not to take the world as object but to construct it, to make it become, by means of a thousand facets' (mil feuilles), Baudrillard writes.

Photography, a technical mechanism characteristic of the modern gaze, is a partial, elaborated, technical construction capable of affording us access to other strata of reality, to different levels, none of which can claim to capture the totality or the essential. The very expansive, multiplied condition of the photographic images supports the idea that there is no one, single image but approximations, segments of a discontinuous appropriation of which the separation of the photographic images is an evident proof.

Every photographic image is a story, at once insufficient yet real, a take, a discharging on something that does not allow itself to be used up once and for all because it will always retain its fleeting, ungraspable condition.

'But this construction neither sets itself up against reality nor exhausts it. The fact is that the illusion does not oppose itself to reality; it is rather another and subtler reality, which envelops the first with the sign of disappearance.' Baudrillard does not set up in opposition here, as in other earlier texts and in the best tradition of Situationism, the fiction of the world of the technological images and some vanished Arcadia in which the relationship between the image and the object would constitute a permanent reflection.

6 Jean Baudrillard, **Photographies**, Descartes & Cie., Paris, 1998.

The redemption of the world of the image photographic, of its solitude and its silence, does not inevitably come into conflict with its condition as ephemeral, reproducible, manipulable, contingent. On the contrary, photography presents itself to us as the technology of vision capable of embracing this other aspect of reality, its hidden face, its absent presence.

In the same way as Siegfried Kracauer noted in the thirties the capacity of photography to 'freeze' the world, to reveal it as fragmented and the bearer of another historical time different from the time of the actual experience, Baudrillard remarks in his introductory text on the capacity of photography to constitute registers of the 'disappeared', of the tracks of the things that are inaccessible to us or which we can only recover through the 'apparition' or appearance of the images.[7]

But photography is also a way of operating on reality, fundamentally exorcizing it.

For Baudrillard, primitive societies flee from the phantoms of memory and fear by means of the mask. The creation of an artificial, caricatured face is the mechanism through which anguish is distanced and powers conjured up.

Bourgeois society, in contrast, has made the mirror the paradigm of its image. Reflecting itself, seeing itself, copying itself, imitating itself, bourgeois art and architecture close the circle of the world on themselves, making this self-absorption their protection and their strength.

However, in the post-industrial society the conjuration, memory and exorcism are produced by means of images. A limitless, expansive universe, constantly open to reformulation, creates the galaxy not of Gutenberg but of Eidos. Our universe is icon-dependent to such an extent that our communication systems are unthinkable without the inexhaustible iconology of which we constantly make use and in the interior of which we move.

It may be that architecture and the urban landscape can no longer serve as the mask that protects us neither with its theological horror, nor as the safe and pacified reflection of an image of an order constructed to our own scale.

The world that we narrate with the images of landscape and of architecture; but also the architecture and landscape mediatized by its images: these are, at the present time, the possible wrapping of our crowded solitude.

To put it in the celebrated words of one of the most famous photographic documenters of contemporary society, 'we must catch people in their self-rapport, in their silence'.[8]

7   Siegfried Kracauer, 'Photography', in **The Mass Ornament. Weimar Essays**,
Harvard University Press, Cambridge, Mass., 1995, pp.47 and 55.
8   Henry Cartier-Bresson, quoted in Baudrillard, **op. cit.**

[1]

[2]

Recipiente ambiental

Recipiente de plástico transparente, inflado y con aire
acondicionado, en forma de cúpula.

[4]

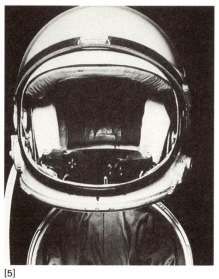

[5]

[8]

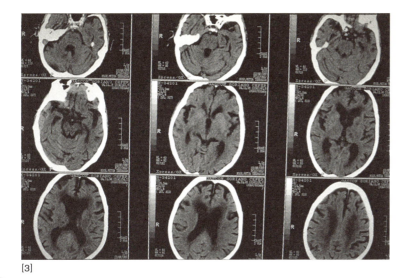

[3]

[6]

[7]

1 Advertisement flags of Barcelona TV
2 UMBO Autoportrait, 1948
3 Brain scan
4 On-house 1965, Reyner Banham
5 Apollo XV Suit and helmet for the space traveller
6 Jean Baudrillard, sociologist and photographer, New York 1988
7 Jean Baudrillard, sociologist and photographer, Toronto 1994
8 Diller and Scofidio, Broadway sport hall installation, 1997

Of Time and the Fetishization of the Built City **Peter Marcuse**

This paper deals with three related issues:

- *Layering*, as a way of making essential but invisible aspects of the city visible;
- *Time*, as a necessary dimension of spatial analysis, design, and planning;
- *Fetishization* of the built environment, as a danger for spatial analysis, design, and planning.

The argument is simple: ignoring the dimension of time and the layering of social uses leads to a fetishization of the built environment, of the city as a physical form, which supports a rigid, one-dimensional view of the city, tending if a basis for policy to solidify the tendencies towards segregation and hierarchization to which capitalist economies, particularly in an age of globalization, are pushed.

To begin with an analogy from geographical information system programs: every GIS system today calls for one map as a base layer, and then permits information to be added in successive layers on top of the base. Typically, the base map will be of street patterns, perhaps with lot lines showing ownership, perhaps with legal boundaries or geomorphological features, perhaps with transportation routes. In practice, it will generally be limited to physical features.

Suppose we conceptualize the bottom layer of a city in all its complexity as the built environment, and then overlay it with the social characteristics of space.[1] Again, there is nothing unusual in the technique. One can use standard indicators, usually including income, education, occupation, rent or housing cost, household composition, often 'race' and/or ethnicity, possibly car ownership, type of utility service, communication equipment. One might hypothesize (I have hypothesized[2]) that a picture of a quartered city would result:

- a luxury city, made up of the mansions and well-located plush apartments of the very rich, scattered over substantial sections of the center city and the ex-urbs;
- a gentrified city, occupied by professionals, technicians, managers, located in select areas near the central business district, or, for those with children, in outer suburbs;
- a suburban city, the communities of the middle class whose location will depend on household composition, but will form sizable and relatively homogeneous neighborhoods;
- a tenement city, housing the working class, both blue and white collar, largely but not only rental, in older sections of the central city and (largely in the Third World) in older settlements of often self-built housing;

1   Part of this discussion builds on Marcuse, Peter, 'The Layered City,' in Peter Madsden, **Copenhagen and New York: A Comparison**, (tentative title), forthcoming. See Marcuse, Peter. 1989. '"Dual City": a muddy metaphor for a quartered city.' **International Journal of Urban and Regional Research**, vol. 13, no. 4, December, pp.697-708.

■ an abandoned city, in which those excluded from the benefits of participation in the mainstream economy are relegated, sometimes in
excluded ghettos, sometimes (in the Third World) in squatter settlements
on the fringes of the city.

One might call the resulting pattern the residential class layer of the city.

But there are many other possibilities for the formulation of the resulting patterns. The approach permits a spatial analysis of the extent of
polarization, the nature of the lines of division, the relevance of individual
facts such an education or 'race' to such divisions, and a substantial body
of work has begun to tease out the details. One can, for instance, examine
the development of spatial configurations such as citadels, ethnic enclaves,
edge cities, etc.[3] And the results can be revealing: Christine Boyer, for
instance, speaks of 'scenic enclaves' designed for tourists, which 'eventually
reduces the city to a map of tourist attractions',[4] and the producer of a
best-selling three-dimensional tourist map of New York City carries out
the thought (unconsciously, we suppose) by simply blanking out the areas
of the tenement and the abandoned city on its map; they do not exist, the
producers of the map assume, for the average tourist.

We might then speak of this map of the tourist city as a layer placed over
the physical and residential class layers with which we are familiar. But
a problem then develops. The tourist city is not a permanent feature of the
landscape: it will be different in the summer than in the winter, it will be
different at night from its configuration in the daytime, and its locations
will certainly not be exclusively tourist. If one mapped the locations of
theater workers, for instance, they would substantially overlap the locations
relevant to tourists, as would the locations of restaurant service workers,
hotel services workers, etc. It is not surprising, of course, that differently
defined layers of the city will overlap with each other; what is relevant for
the point here is that they overlap in 'time' as well as in space. Those who
clean the hotel rooms come after the guests have left, and leave when

2 See Marcuse, Peter. 1989. '"Dual City": a muddy metaphor for a quartered city.' **International Journal of Urban and Regional Research**, vol. 13, no. 4, December, pp.697-708.
3 My own most recent contribution is in a book co-edited with Ronald van Kempen of Utrecht,
entitled **Globalizing Cities,**, to be published shortly by Blackwell.
4 Boyer, Christine. 1992. 'Cities for Sale – Merchandising History at South Street Seaport.'
in Michael Sorkin, ed., **Variations on a Theme Park**, p.192.
5 'The built environment of the City may therefore be seen as a series of overlapping texts in
which previous layer of meaning are overlain with new meanings which strengthen, succeed or
disrupt earlier meanings.' McDowell, Linda. 1998. **Capital Culture: Gender at Work in the
City.** London: Blackwell, pp.53-54.

they return; the cooks are up early in the morning to buy fresh provisions, while those who enjoy the results of the labors only arrive in the evening. Without reference to the dimension of 'time', the information provided by the static layers of physical and social development and use are incomplete.

It is not simply that, in other times, there were other spaces or other objects, that spaces have history and changed their appearance and their meaning over time;[5] this is a well-known, if not an always respected, point. One might refer to this element of time as 'historical time', and I will return to it later in speaking of the fetishism of the existing built. It is time seen 'vertically', looking at the past of a given space. What is meant here is something different, what one might call 'contemporary time', the difference in the function of the existing environment today, at different times, different days, and different seasons. It might be called 'horizontal' time, what happens at a fixed period in historical time. Vertical time is permanent, frozen, even if understood differently in different times; horizontal time is dynamic, fluid, malleable.[6]

The importance of contemporary time issues can be illustrated through four examples.[7]

A project in which we have been engaged in various forms has been examining economic development issues in central Harlem in New York City, perhaps the most famous ghetto in the United States. It has focused on the impact of recent Empowerment Zone legislation, legislation that is really all there is of a national urban policy in the country today. The legislation concentrates tax incentives and social service programs in particular zones, selected for the high level of poverty within them and the plans for their development. A central provision of the legislation provides tax incentives for employers to hire empowerment zone residents – but only for employers with jobs 'within' the empowerment zone. We have been critical because the best jobs are not within the empowerment zone, within the ghetto, but outside it, in the Manhattan case largely within the central business district. The issue is that raised by William Wilson: that conditions within the ghetto are poor, but that there are restrictions on the access of the ghetto poor to jobs outside the ghetto. To demonstrate this, it would be useful to show, not only where people in New York City live, but also where those same people work; in other words, to show where they are, where each group is, not only at night but also during the day. That requires a set of maps with layers organized by 'time'.[8]

---

6 Richard Sennett's phrase, 'places full of time,' illustrates the difference. He properly critiques Battery Park City in New York City as being all of one time, the present, despite its attempts at diversity. What is missing is historical time; it is quite possible (although I doubt it) that in fact Battery Park City would 'contain' more layers of contemporary time than many a historically preserved setting. Sennett, Richard. 1990. **The Conscience of the Eye: The Design and Social Life of Cities.** New York: Knopf, p.193.
7 The market of course takes the layering of time regularly into account: not only in the more recent practice of time-sharing, as for vacation homes, but also in the old Anglo-Saxon law of property with its life estate and fees tail, as well as in commercial transactions.

The second example of the importance of layering in contemporary or horizontal time is an elaboration of an account Saskia Sassen frequently gives. She describes the occupancy of a downtown skyscraper during the day: dominated by men, overwhelmingly white, with ties and jackets, doing high finance, giving orders, communicating all over the world. But at night these men all leave, and an entirely different occupancy takes place: the cleaning crew comes in, janitors and cleaning ladies, often immigrants, in overalls or smocks, poorly paid, taking orders, not giving them. So a class map of the building at night would show an entirely different configuration from what appears during the day. Both layers in time are needed for a meaningful picture. Ignoring this, for instance in transportation planning, seeing a need for access from the suburbs or the citadels but not from the ghettos or the tenements, can have disastrous social results. The same split in occupancy within the 24 hours of the day has traditionally been true for factories: blue collar workers are there for two or three 8 hour shifts, while white collar and managerial employees work 9 to 5; layers pictured at different times would give very different pictures. While, of course, the building and the machinery are there all the time.

An example from Johannesburg, South Africa, makes the same point at a slightly different scale: one varying not only by hour of the day, but day of the week. When we were mapping segregation in Johannesburg at the time of the ending of Apartheid, we got a peculiar result: for working class areas, there was a sharp separation between African and white (and Indian and colored) residences, but for middle class residential areas, despite strict laws, there always appeared to be a significant number of Africans there. The explanation of course is that the Africans were there as domestic servants, living in the residences (usually in fact in outbuildings in the back yards) of their employers. So if you drove down the streets of a middle class area or went into a supermarket at midday in Westdene, where we lived, you would see almost as many blacks as whites: domestics doing the

8 It would, incidentally, show a quite different class configuration than that of residential space. In some cases, the spatial organization of work will be largely congruent with the spatial distribution of residences, e.g. in the citadel or the ghetto (see Marcuse, Peter, 1999, 'Conclusion: No New Spatial Order,' in Marcuse and van Kempen, eds. **Globalizing Cities: A New Spatial Order,** London: Blackwell), but in many other instances, classically in the suburban city, the spatial organization of work and of residence will be very different.
9 The picture was probably truer in earlier periods with fewer women in the active paid labor force, but it remains true in many suburbs today.
10 At a cruder level, it could also be used to describe many claims in the growing field of environmental simulation, e.g. the argument of Peter Bosselman, director of the Environmental

shopping, Africans delivering goods, children living with mothers employed as domestics and hustling on the streets parking cars for a little change. But if you went on a weekend, you would see almost no black faces. A layer during one day of the week would look very different from a layer on another day.

That argument can of course be extended dramatically when looking at vacation areas, areas where work is seasonal, areas with annual migratory patterns, from itinerant farm workers to 'snow birds' in the United States living in Florida in the winter and in the northern states in the summer. Layers at different seasons will produce very different patterns of occupancy.

Consider a fourth problem with a static presentation of space, ignoring time. Feminist writers have brought home the point that different spaces have different impacts on women than on men. Much of that difference has to do with time. Dolores Hayden among many others has addressed the change in the occupancy of the suburbs during the working day and in the evenings and weekends: in the middle of the day, you find only women and children there; in the evening, the men come home from work.[9] Or the question of safety on the streets: there is in effect a wall of time on the other side of which, in many quarters, it is unsafe for a woman to be on the street. The same was true for many areas in apartheid South Africa, and remains true in parts of many cities in the United States today: an African American in a white neighborhood after dark is likely to arouse suspicion if not direct harassment.

Linking the conceptualization of layers of time with layers of space has other implications: it inhibits the tendency to fetishize space.

Fetishization is a clumsy, but appropriate, term for what is here involved.[10] Marx used the term to describe the transformation that occurs when produced objects are viewed as commodities, characterized by their relation to each other, their uses and prices determined by the objects themselves, concealing the fact that their creation and use is entirely the result of relations among people. Freud used the term in a somewhat similar way, to speak of the patterns of behavior that view things – generally parts of the body – as having a value, an attraction, in themselves, instead of as a part of the deeper relations among full persons. In the same way, space, the built environment generally, can be seen as exerting an influence in and of itself, as a thing, rather than as the product of people and given

Simulation Laboratory at the University of California at Berkeley, who gives the aim of his work as being to provide representations of reality that are 'complete, accurate, engaging, detailed and true to the sense of those who will experience the designs once they are built' — fetishization of a picture on a computer screen? Bosselmann, Peter. 1998. **Representation of Places: Reality and Realism in City Design:** Berkeley: University of California Press, p.199. See the excellent review by Kevin R. McNamara, posted on compurb-l@ssc.wisc.edu.

meaning only as a social production. Fetishization of space is not quite the same thing as environmental determinism, for environmental determinism generally assumes it is the physical characteristics of an environment that determine its impacts; I mean rather to emphasize the view that the social characteristics of an object, a space, are an attribute of the space itself, rather than the results of any present human agency. Historical time can be traced back through an exploration of the history
of an object; its present meaning is not embedded in that object itself, but is given it by the way it is handled in the relationships among persons, the meaning socially constructed for it in contemporary time.

Consider Linda McDowell's description of a new international style office building in the City in London:

'…the new City landscapes of power reflect a revolution in workplace technologies and in their glass and steel towers… they distill … a singular image of international dominance, remnants of past socio-spatial practices remain in internal spaces. In anomalous boardrooms and private dining rooms, oak-paneled and beamed, often a careful pastiche constructed from fragments saved in the demolition of older structures…'[11]

Not anomalous at all, it is as if the fetishized oak of the boardroom walls gives a historical legitimacy to the power of its current, sometimes upstart, wielders – an attempt to merge two periods of time and two sets of social relations by means of an architectural ruse. No physical characteristic
of the oak, of course, defines the status of those within its walls, but the historical time presently recalled – whether accurately or not makes no difference – and imposed on it as its characteristic. Not environmental determinism, but fetishization.[12]

The issue is one that runs through the entire historic preservation movement: how to deal with the relationship between present interests and needs and the choice of what 'history' to preserve. It is too complex to be dealt with here. I would simply argue that the present effect of any preservation action and its differential impact on persons in the here and now must be considered as well as the preservation of a physical object in its

11 Supra, p.60.
12 The examples of course could be multiplied indefinitely. Curiously enough, postmodern architecture, for all its faults, can be viewed as countering this tendency to see forms developed in the past as having that past embedded in them, precisely negating the fetishism criticized here, although at the same time it may try to create a new form of fetishism by so doing.

state as of some historical time. It is, after all, not some objective 'history' that is usually in question for preservation, as a fetishist would contend, but layers of past time viewed in contemporary time. Accretion, the recognition of layers of use and of time, is probably in most cases a better solution than the preservation/reconstruction of what might have been in some particular layer.

And a final layer that I think is in some ways the most important of all: the layer of time 'in the future'.

Robert Musil, the great Czech novelist, once said that the man who, when he looks, sees only what is there now, and not what could be there, does not see at all.

Particularly for those of us in professions dealing with the built environment, with issues of planning and design, if our values tell us that our task is something more than simply preservation of the status quo, it is this layer of the future, the alternatives, the possibilities, and the roads to them, whose presentation is really our most important responsibility. We cannot afford to fetishize history in built objects, we cannot afford to ignore the multiple layers of space spread out over contemporary time, and we must keep a focus on the layer of time ahead.

Traffic in Democracy **Michael Sorkin**

A few months ago, Mayor Giuliani closed the 50th Street crosswalks at Fifth and at Madison Avenues. The reason was to combat 'congestion' in midtown Manhattan (of course, what he meant was automotive congestion). Preventing walkers from crossing the street enabled cars to turn right or left onto the opposing one-way avenues without having to worry about negotiating with pedestrians.

In the Mayor's scheme, pedestrians are inconvenienced to convenience cars. As a result, 50th Street has become a contested zone in the fight over the right to move: crossing the street is now an act of civil disobedience. Reflecting this proscription, a policeman has been installed on each corner to assure compliance. Although this breaches the historic understanding between New York pedestrians and police that jaywalking laws are ridiculous and will therefore be ignored, it is consonant with the mayor's (the ex-prosecutor's, the urban disciplinarian's) penal comprehension of time and space. A prison, after all, is built on the abstraction of every dimension of time but length and on the devolution of spatial choice to a clockwise or counter route around the exercise yard.

The mayor's strictures against crossing derive from a desire to enhance the 'flow' of traffic. Flow seeks to increase speed (and save time) by prioritizing the faster means of movement. Safety is often foregrounded as the reason for this system of preferences; the potential for danger, confusion, and slow-down resulting from the undisciplined mix gives rise to elaborate structures for vetting what traffic engineers call 'conflict' between modes. Typically, this means slower vehicles yield to faster ones and pedestrians to all, walkers deferring to cars, cars to trains, trains to planes, and so on.

Modern city planning is structured around an armature of such conflict avoidance. Elevated highways, pedestrian skyways, subway systems, and other movement technologies clarify relations between classes of vehicles for the sake of efficient flow. This traffic strategy is mirrored in (and derived from) the idea of zoning by use, another gambit based on the idea of separating 'incompatible' activities and persons. For both, the segregating clarity of the movement hierarchy is presented as evidence of the 'rationality' of the system.

Chandigarh, the north Indian city designed by Le Corbusier – modernity's leading enthusiast for the city of efficient flow – is perhaps the most elaborate and self-conscious example of this type of traffic 'zoning'. Here, seven categories of road traffic are distinguished – based on speed – and the city is designed efficiently to separate them. Likewise, in a kind of nightmarish Taylorization of caste, the city distributes residents of various income levels among more than a dozen different income-based housing types.

The result is a city altogether different from the older Indian cities with their indigenous styles of motion that so appalled the fastidious Corbusier. Typically, Indian traffic is completely mixed up, a slow-moving mass of cows and pedicabs, motor-rickshaws, trucks and buses, camels and people on foot, the antithesis of 'efficient' separation. Motion through this sluggish maelstrom does not proceed so much by absolute right as through a continuing process of local negotiation for the right of passage.

There's something deeply satisfying about the movement through these old cities, not only because everyone is obliged to slow down but because this slow-down is the material basis for the tractability of the system. A student of mine who recently studied traffic patterns in Istanbul observed that its glacial pace guaranteed the safe and convenient crossing of pedestrians. In this decelerated system, slow may not become fast, but it does become fast for pedestrians.

Traffic codes and historic laws of rights of way codify urban styles of deference in motion. These rules of accessibility form criteria for determining who may go where and when. As such, these rights of way – which grant temporary permission to use private or public property for passage – structure a primal rite of giving ground and can thus serve us here as a concrete, that is, physical, exemplum of the deference to one's neighbor that urban existence daily demands. The homey concreteness of this instance should not, however, trivialize it or turn it into some plodding metaphor for more 'abstract' instances of giving way. For, though speed – and indeed almost instantaneous 'movement' – is now conceived as the determining factor of our new global economic and political order, the slower, physical flow of vehicular and human traffic remains a neglected issue. Not only is it true that it is primarily information and capital that travels at lightning speed and crosses all territorial barriers while the diaspora of despised peoples moves at a much slower pace and while strictures against movement – set up by inhospitable nations and opportunistic corporations – increase, it is also the case that urban density and movement through it has to be thought through politically, in these terms, rather than approached as merely a set of technical problems.

Growth complicates matters by introducing a vector of continuous transformation into the general pattern of urban distances. Under the contemporary regime of growth, this relationship has escaped rational management. The typical American – and increasingly global – result has been sprawl without end, the rapid outward movement of the urban periphery. As stable adjacencies and proximities are disrupted by the growth of the edge and the resultant transformation of the center, the system has produced its characteristic form: the 'edge city' in which uses are continuously relocated to reestablish proximity both by introducing new lateral relations oblivious to the center and by creating a physical texture in which hierarchies are highly repetitive and places increasingly indistinguishable.

There is a potentially ethical relation between speed and purpose, a system of rights that awards access to speed (and space) differentially. This demands a nuanced – and contested – ethics of privilege in a complex system that must weigh the rights of ambulances and strollers against more general rights of way and place. Such an ethics can derive from a very large number of criteria which – taken altogether – describe the politics of urban circulation. Indeed, the negotiated character of any urban spatial encounter begs an ethical reading of all of its components.

Energy, for example, is needed to produce motion. The ethics of energy expenditure – which is today articulated largely on the side of conservation – could arguably be invoked in defense of either side of the pedestrian/automotive question. On behalf of cars, the argument would come from their greater momentum (derived from both greater mass and greater speed), from the idea that their efficiency derives from smooth and speedy operation. The economy of stop and start opposes – in its inefficiency – the conservation of automotive energy.

The counter-argument is that cars are intrinsically wasteful of energy. This is a large claim, based on a global paradigm of conservation, not just a local one. Here, pedestrians become the alpha-means of low-energy travel, the ideal movers. This hierarchy puts walkers at the top, followed by human-powered transport – such as bikes, and so on down the line – the criterion being that the more energetic always yields to the least, reversing orthodox priorities. Of course, the moment the rising curve of teleological privilege crosses the sinking curve of energy output, the whole becomes impossible.

This mathematical system defines walkers as energyless movers, as 'O'. Once their actual expenditure is introduced into the equation, a difficulty arises. On the one hand, it's clear that the expenditure of aerobic energy by the organism increases (or at least conserves) the potential for further expenditure. This is called exercise. On the other hand, this calculation is based on individual potential and thus on the difference between old and young, disabled and fit, and so on. The collision is between life conceived as pure physiology and life conceived in human terms (in which pleasure and convenience play important roles).

By identifying this priority of individual benefit (vs. the class benefits of traffic), the way is open to a system that offers preferences based on the ability to derive benefit from locomotion. This would be based on a blending of physiological issues (whose ambulatory efficiency would be most increased by a given expenditure of energy) and human purpose (whose functioning arrogates the highest degree of necessity). While the road to the absurd is opened up by this calculation, it remains true that systems of traffic must be based on precepts beyond pure speed, on ideas about the distribution of rights.

The politics of traffic derives from the degree of access to the malleability of – the right to – time, the ability to speed up and slow down at will as well as the general enjoyment of the right of way. This right is ultimately to entropy since the individuation of desires tends (in a condition of freedom) to an increase in variation, a chaos of happiness. Under such a system, older folks, disabled people, and the encumbered would – in order to enjoy temporal parity with other citizens – be the first candidates for the allotment of the energy that would become the means for a fair distribution of time.

Propinquity – neighborliness – is the ground and problem of democracy. Agnes Heller has described politics as the concretization of the universal value of freedom. The city – because of its intensity – is the privileged place of this politics of freedom, if not of freedom itself. The old Hanseatic maxim, 'city air makes people free' was based on the liquidity of association that characterizes urban life. City politics is deeply inscribed in questions of propinquity and access, in the legibility and tractability of routines of circulation and contact: the currency of propinquity is exchange, the most vital measure of the city's intensity.

The public spaces of the city are preeminently the spaces of circulation and exchange, overwhelmingly streets and sidewalks. We judge the good city by the quality of its public life and hence of its public space, yet the very idea of public space is now under siege. Formerly, attempts to limit it hid behind expressions of fear of its decline, but this disguise is now unnecessary. The notion of public space is attacked outright as itself a mask. The forces arrayed against public space come from a number of different and even opposed directions: from economic and social drives toward privatization; identity politics; communitarianism; from sprawl and the resulting growth of cyburbia, that pale blue zone of connectivity without place. As the idea of a universal public is supplanted by a desire for and embrace of multiple publics, traditional formulations of physical consent are becoming strained.

While the notion of public space was never meant to refer exclusively to a geographically delimited space that was open to all, it seems indisputable that the broader notion cannot dispense with such spaces. It is most likely, because public space is so often and so readily conceived as dependent on a decorporealization of its citizenry – a demotion and even denigration of the particular and the physical – that the notion of public space has become so abstract, so divorced from any theorization of physical locations. This is also why notions such as the 'electronic town hall' have been so easy to sell, as though its very incorporeality guaranteed its publicity. Public space never comes down to a social abstraction from the individual body (in a famous quip, Marx mocked the naiveté of such formulations: 'I have never encountered an abstract man, only concrete men'), it is rather, a matter of reconfiguring the individual citizen's relation to his or her body and to those of other citizens.

What must be acknowledged and understood is the enormous anxiety that marks the decline of space as the primary medium of urban exchange. This need not take place on the terrain of nostalgia, as a simple mourning of the loss of once-familiar, now disappearing forms of human contact. It is a matter of grasping the consequences of – and often altering – the ways in which contemporary strategies of the virtual compete with historic ideas of location as the basis of propinquity. We've got to watch out: the fundamental epistemology of the city – the way it constructs its meanings – is being transformed as physical presence ceases to be the privileged means of participation and enjoyment of urban life.

The human character of cities begins with face-to-face interactions. From the city's styles of intensifying such intercourse descends any description of the urban economy and its politics. Traffic is one medium of this commerce, the sum of those instrumentalities of motion by which propinquity is engineered, the means by which we are enabled physically to encounter different circumstances within the city. While no mode of movement will make a difference if the character and variety of places between which we travel fail to reflect a sufficient range of differences, the dialogue of intersection between public and private is mediated and – in part – invented by the available means of circulating between them.

The relationship between propinquity and publicity begins with this statistical necessity: democratic deliberation is only possible in an environment that conduces both consensus and accident. This continual potential for conflict is vital to deliberation and marks the vigor of difference within culture. The design of urban systems demands a beautifully negotiated balance between the predictable and the unexpected, in order to produce the largest number of accidental discursive events.

Accidental encounter is produced by the character of urban access. One of the by-products of density and adjacency in cities is a continual testing of access. Propinquity – the ongoing legibility of adjacencies – always harbors a testing function and the power to reveal the limits of urban boundaries. This is analogous to the 'testing' of public accommodation that was part of the civil rights movement's strategy in the early 1960s, when groups of blacks would seek to be served at restaurants, hotels and other 'public' sites in order to establish the facts of discrimination as antecedent to legal intervention. An older form of such testing is the continuing and systematic use by walkers in England of historic 'rights of way' across private property, a form of close reading and measurement of the health and dimensions of the public environment and a means for setting the algorithms of territorial convenience.

While metropolitan citizens may choose to ignore what they happen to see in the city, their physical presence at the scenes of urbanity assures the likelihood of direct observation of the sites of stricture, conflict, conversion, appropriation, and other negotiations. The approaching US census is now raising a procedural question which is, in fact more than that: should we continue to take the national census by a door-to-door head count or should we rely on statistical information to arrive at a determination of our numbers? We have been repeatedly told that statistics makes visible the individuals who once composed an invisible feudal mass, but it is more than clear that statistical calculations bring into being new classes of the uncounted whose invisibility is perhaps more profound for being now disavowed. Urban ghettos are fast becoming not only the blind spots in the modern game of statistics, but areas we would just as soon see burned to the ground as see.

Founded on the rule of law, democracy demands the continual application of legality as well as the continual review of the nature and quality of the justice that inheres in the system of legal sanction. The functioning of that system is, in turn, contingent on presence, on the drawing in of citizens to the rites and routines of adjudication so that the plurality and variety of citizen-observers produces another guarantee of fairness via the statistical likelihood that urban encounters will often include – if only at their periphery – substantial numbers of disinterested parties.

Of course, this idea of constant encounter inevitably produces friction, the simple result of rubbing subjects together. (It's no accident that frottage is the 'classic' urban perversion.) Urban friction is the signal of boundary and a symptomatic constituent of urban social gradients. Such friction – by signaling difference – locates the internal edges of the city as well as potential sources of conflict. Yet, the very idea of accommodation is produced by such conflict, heightened by the physical character of urban life. It is no tautology to suggest that the only training for living together is living together. Racial tolerance is never concretized in the absence of the other, which is why anti-Semitism, and racism of all forms, thrives where there are no Jews, no racial others, in sight.

The city thus produces citizenship through the repetitive confrontation of citizens with an environment that organizes its prejudices and privileges physically, which is to say measurably. Unfortunately, traffic today is never thought against the background of these concerns; it is approached as merely a technological problem and thus is saddled with the myths of technology, pinioned between visions of tractability and autonomy. Traffic engineers seek utopian solutions and fear 'Frankenstein-ian' rebellions, see-sawing on the only two possibilities offered by technology and its discontents.

Modernist urbanism collapsed as the result of its blind thrall to such scientism, whether in the form of its devotion to technology and the social 'sciences', or in its dreary mimesis of tech-forms. When – in reaction to this – cities ceased to be planned in the old physical sense, the prerogatives of planning activity were taken over by 'infrastructure', by something supposed to be underneath, invisible, common, neutral. This, of course, is simply modernism stripped of its iconic veneer. Traffic planning was quickly subsumed under this logic, becoming the favored visibility of planning, the thing that could tolerably be seen.

The foregrounding of the means of motion in city planning has proved disastrous. Cities have historically been obliged to play catch-up with existing transportation technologies, successively refitting themselves with systems that do not love them; urban space has been rent and scarred by railways and freeways, clogged and scored by pollution and metal. Yet the appeal of motion-based urbanism is rendered 'obvious' by discourses that effectively substitute the freedom to move unobstructed and in isolation for freedom of association. To the list of freedoms we have added the freedom of speedy disassociation.

Modern movement culture is increasingly serviced by capsules of intermediacy, by trains, planes, automobiles, and elevators. These instrumentalities now make time for sitting in front of the video and computer screens with which they are being fitted. Just as the view from the railway car window forever altered not simply the landscape but our fundamental perceptions of time and space, so the window of the monitor represents a shift in our perceptual and psychical relationship to exteriority. Virtual travel embodies a remarkable economy of energy as the experience of motion is efficiently stripped from actual mobility.

Walter Hudson is this virtual dream turned flesh. At the time of his death on Christmas Eve 1991, he weighed 1,125 pounds, down from the 1400 pounds that had established his Guinness-certified record as the world's fattest human. Hudson was so large that when he died a wall of his house had to be demolished to permit the removal of his body by a forklift. This body was towed behind a hearse to the cemetery where his piano-case coffin was buried in a double plot.

What made Hudson truly exemplary, though, was not his bulk but his immobility: except for a tragically brief period of slimming, Hudson never left his house, unable for years to rise from his specially-constructed bed. Sustained by a high-tech personal 'existenzminimum' of computer and television, toilet and refrigerator – a Big Mac in one hand the remote control in the other – he led his contracted life.

Hudson's heft was both the medium of his immobility and the reason for his celebrity. Although his baroque corpulence bespoke spatiality (his achievement, after all, was to have occupied more space than anyone in history), his presence on the world stage was pure mediation. Hudson managed – without ever being present – to be incredibly visible, lavishly attended to by the media who made him a poster child for America's prurient obsession with the consumption of space. Hudson represented the flip side of anorexia – the spatial neurosis of the age – and evoked the nation's prurient censure of overweight, a moral failure that infringes on the rights of the rest of us to space and aesthetic conformity.

On the other hand, Hudson's 'luxurious' occupation of physical space bore a striking resemblance to the delimiting privileges of the global elite, who circle the globe with effortless efficiency immobilized in their business-class seats, strapped and wired in, stuffed like Strasbourg geese. As they cruise through the ether on the way to a distant place that they are increasingly at pains to distinguish from the one left twelve hours ago and half a world away, questions of status and comfort are reduced to a consideration of the extra inches they occupy for the duration.

This global movement system trades access for privacy: constant surveillance is the price of 'freedom' of movement. Ironically, this surveillance is at its most Draconian for those with the greatest 'rights'. World travelers, for example, are subject to microscopic attention, their activities recorded, correlated, and made available to an enormous invisible government of customs authorities, shadowy credit agencies, back-office computer banks, market research firms, private security companies, advertisers, data-base gatherers, and an endlessness of media connections. Pull out your Amex card and we know exactly where you are. Turn on your home security system and we know you've left. Order a special meal and we know there's a non-smoking Muslim in seat 3K.

The most dramatically efficient solution to the traffic problem is elimination of the reasons to move, whether through Walter Hudson-style immobility or the suppression of evocative qualities of difference in the environment. Location today is under intense competition from position, that is from location emptied of locality, proximity defined through virtual relations with other entities around the globe and with others living life on the net. Location more and more rules at the expense of place. A tremendous rescaling is under way and with it a fattening culture of post-adjacent propinquity, configured at global scale.

Traffic – at whatever scale – is defined by the relationship between speed and flow, a quality that has by now obtained a quasi-metaphysical status. Like the circulation of capital, the circulation of traffic is most perfectly efficient when it attains the status of a constant – perpetual motion. But, while stasis is the enemy of a flowing system of perfect efficiency, it is also indispensable to its functioning: flow needs nodes.

The node is the corollary of flow, implying not simply centrality (and therefore directionality) but cease, the place where motion stops, enabling transfer (to foot, to another means, to another purpose). Flow imposes its own idea of efficiency, always calibrated to keeping going, not stopping, overcoming impedance and resisting inertia. The consequences are dramatic: nodal architecture subsumed by strategies of flow is predominant in the American landscape: the strip, the shopping mall, the suburbs, the edge city. Walter Hudson was a living node.

In America, the car is the main means for activating this landscape, for a variety of reasons, few of which are functional. It is well-observed that cars, in America, are idealized objects of identification and desire ('I love my Buick'). We hold the right to bear arms and own a car most dear. This auto-eroticism is responsible for the exponential enlargement of America's pavement – over one third the total area of Los Angeles, for example, is devoted to the car. Indeed, no longer content to ply the confines of the pavement, the largest growth sector in the American automobile market is for off-the-road vehicles and for space-aggrandizing, home-surrogate, minivans.

Because the car seeks to optimize both speed and flow it looks for a conflict-free environment. In a mixed system, this means that either traffic must be separated strictly or a hierarchy must arise. Stop signs and traffic lights (as well as pedestrian barricades and cops on the corner) are means for sorting out this conflict. Traffic lights, which are meant to increase the efficient utility of the street, are, however, designed from the position of the car, directed primarily at resolving potential conflicts among vehicles. By any measure, pedestrians are disadvantaged: the space of the car, which predominates, is always a danger to them. Although the ideal for traffic is an easy mingling, we only produce technologies predicated on separation. The automobile system seeks invariably to exclude other modes that might come into conflict with it.

Los Angeles is the omega of the spatial city and the prototype of the city of the edge. Los Angeles – and cities like it – seeks to create a consistent culture of the particle, in which an ostensibly egalitarian set of property relations is matched to a similarly conceived strategy of circulation. The experiment conducted with the use of cars in Los Angeles succinctly recapitulates Thomas Jefferson's Cartesian fantasy of the organization of American space. The grid – the instrument of an equality achieved by the surrender of difference in space or rather by the reduction of the arena of difference to a rigidly circumscribed territory – functions only if there is an even distribution of use, or if it runs like 'clock work', no caesura, no surcease, and if there are no intersections. This was Jefferson's fundamental error: he saw the grid as constituted purely of the aggregated surfaces of infinite squares, their boundaries immaterial, pure edge.

The Jeffersonian grid, however, generates both territories and interstices. Each square contains not simply its own surface but also four extra-territorial intersections, which must be shared through negotiation. The conundrum is that an intersection is both a deterrent to flow and a necessity for contact. As a practical matter, the grid system only works at very low loadings where the possibilities of conflict are extremely reduced. As anyone who has driven the LA grid late at night knows, this kind of geometrical freedom – in which one encounters public space as almost purely private – can be exhilarating. At higher rates of utilization, though, contact becomes impediment.

In cities like Los Angeles, the loadings on the grid are thrown into disequilibria by the inequalities of use that culture imposes on the system. Zoning by class and by function, as well as the extremely uneven distribution of energy and motion over the diurnal cycle, distort the stable, static, relationships that are at the core of the Cartesian fantasy: Thomas Jefferson never imagined the rush hour. Planning in Los Angeles is a history of successively failed panaceas for this problem. Coordinated traffic signals (traffic timing being the bedrock of the fantasy of flow) is one strategy for introducing hierarchy, great blocks of traffic shifted around the gridded zones, like trains of space in a synchronicity of flow. Urban expansion is another, but such growth – that old frontiersperson's hankering after infinity – reaches its limits in LA, the edge of the continent. Thus, the classic LA solution was to introduce the next order of physical gridding: the freeway.

Freeways are a symptom of both the spatial and temporal disequilibria of real life, a mismatch of a technological fix with a conceptual difficulty. Freeways understand the city from the position of the car. Like other concentrating styles of motion, they try to reconcile the actual nodality of the system (the exits are discrete, if not the communities) with the fantasy of a continuous fabric of equalized relationships. Los Angeles traffic effectively models the condition of American democracy with its inherent conflicts between an egalitarian model of social relations and a rapidly expanding system of privileges increasingly at odds with it.

America's national book of virtues celebrates the frontier and locates our autonomy in property, the literal possession of space. On the frontier, the quality of space lies in its boundlessness and our share must thus also share in this infinitude. In a system of generous dimensions – the mile-square grid, for example – privacy can be both elective and absolute. After all, if our neighbor is always invisible, our domain will appear unbounded: American polity is not founded on the fantasy of collectivity but on the right to be left alone. The contemporary fight over immigration reflects this anxiety over the loss of space and the excess visibility of the other. Where Alberti famously conceived the city as a magnified house, the American house summarizes the nation, the family isolated in its dominion of space. Such a vision is reread back onto the body of the city itself whether in conversions of territory directly to value or, more darkly, in the strategies of enclaving and exclusion that dominate so much contemporary place-making.

Disneyland – the objective correlative for everything – is a time-space bordello. With its carefully marked 'photo opportunities' and its scrupulous control of the marketing of its images, it is the high-capitalist field of seeing. At Disneyland, the stroll – slowed to a tortoise creep in the form of lines – is the means of circulation between attractions that are themselves based on a kind of pure interior speed, roller-coasting in the dark. All other means of motion offer no benefit in convenience or time. The wait on line precedes a brief burst of speed on a journey to nowhere, a potlatch of haste aestheticized. High speed is totally decoupled from convenience and transferred to the territory of pure – if highly marketable – enjoyment.

It's no coincidence that Disneyland first appeared in – or rather near – Los Angeles and represents a world's fair model 'solution' to the problem of the city. Viewed as a critique of modern urbanism, it is remarkable for its reestablishment of a version of pedestrian morality. Disneyland, located at a site that exists only because of the conjunction of freeways, forsakes the grid for the node. The huge, warped, point-grid of freeway nodes raises the grid a notch, finding its curves at topographic scale. But again, like the city itself, the system feels intermediate. There is a dialectic of distortion produced by the relationship of the efficient placement of freeway exits and the prior claims of the existing condition – farms, forests, houses, towns, and so on. Unlike the Jeffersonian grid which seeks to organize nothingness into a map of potential, the freeway grid is predicated on the prior existence of places of value and therefore lacks the geometric rigor of its Jeffersonian counterpart, reversing its priority of dispersal by searching out the already existing intersection, seeking concentrations or their potential. And, another notch on, Disneyland constructs a cultural grid. In its juxtapositions of simulated versions of different historical and cultural moments, Disneyland adds the fourth dimension to the grid – another substitution of location for place – and thus harbingers in the physical the possibilities now everywhere actualized by strategies of the virtual.

Disneyland is a playground of mobility, it entertains with pleasure-motion. For all its depredations, regimentation, surveillance and control, part of what is experienced as enjoyable at Disneyland really is the passage through an environment of urban density in which both the physical texture and the means of circulation are not simply entertaining but stand in invigorating contrast to the dysfunctional versions back home. One thus extracts from Disneyland a shred of hope, the persuasive example that pedestrianism coupled with short distance collective transport systems can be both efficient and fun, can thrive in the midst of an environment completely otherwise constituted, and that the space of flow sufficiently decelerated can become the space of exchange. But only if we're not just passing through. The paranoiac privatized space of Disneyland could never make itself home to any but the most abstract – that is, monetary – exchange.

Democratic traffic de-privileges unimpeded flow and favors concrete exchange. To promote the enabling deceleration, cities need to adopt supply-side transport management strategies. This will not necessarily be easy. Our culture – nursed on advertising round the clock – makes a fetish of demand: the whole system thrives on spurious need. But this is no signal of the autonomy of our desires, these, rather, are the sounds of their silencing and reveal how thoroughly entrapped we have become in someone else's entrepreneurial dream.

To begin again will mean reconsidering the place of the body in democracy. For the most part, democracy does not traffic in bodies; it is theorized instead in terms of disincorporation, the beheading of the monarch, the emptying out of the central place of power, the establishment of body-blind tribunals of public justice, and so on. Yet, as I argued earlier, it is a mistake to take this disincorporation literally, as the mere excision of the physical body from space, for what democratic theory actually represents is a radical clearing of old notions of the body and an invitation to invent it anew.

The grid prefers a movement monoculture, and monoculture is tyranny. Uniform transit helps produce uniform neighborhoods. Conversely, it seems clear that the ability of neighborhoods to act autonomously is enhanced by their accessibility. Indeed, the solution to the traffic problem is not continuously to model its operations at larger and larger scales but radically to disconnect locality from larger systems which, on balance, ill serve it. For many places, the only way to come to terms with the hegemony of the automotive system is to secede from it. In inner city areas, starved for useful public space and clotted with traffic, the most logical and effective step is to reduce the physical area actually available to the car. Roadways constitute the major portion of the commonly maintained public realm in cities. Cars have been given an enormous franchise on the use of this space – public property – for both circulation and storage.

Recently, working on a plan for East New York, a poor neighborhood in Brooklyn, I wondered what a minimum intervention might be that would begin to recapture the order of the neighborhood from motor traffic, promote greening, and reinforce new patterns of relative self-sufficiency and local autonomy. The answer, I decided, was to plant a tree in an intersection. Several consequences were anticipated. First, the space devoted to the automobile would be reduced by the instant creation of four dead-end streets: the tree would oblige traffic either to find collateral means of circulation or keep out. Second, the quieted zone would permit dramatic alteration to the ratios of green and built space with accompanying possibilities for new agricultural activities and architectural types. Finally, I hoped that street-life – its sparse commerce having been attenuated into useless, center-crushing linearity – would be densified in a series of locally-scaled commercial and social centers that would restore legibility, convenience, and conviviality to a place ragged, over-large, and devoid of all character.

Accident demands the retention of urban difference, not its reduction to a series of empty, abstracted, visual distinctions. But if not by abstraction, how should the city be divided? In the age of identity politics, what is the meaning and purchase of the ghetto? While we think of it as primarily carceral, we know it can breed great dynamism. Common experiences and common cause produce sometimes a variety of solutions and goals. The ghetto begs the question of the boundary, of the morphology of difference. In a city dedicated to free circulation, how is it possible to construct the boundaries that will make variety both legible and accessible?

The antidote to the ghetto would be the neighborhood, a place of social and physical semi-permeability, if it were not for the fact that the notion of neighborhood is now often appropriated by those who conceive it as a fortress against 'neighborliness' in all its properly vexatious and thus productive aspects. For these people, the neighborhood is little more than an inverse ghetto – that is, elective and privileged. It is time to reinstate a notion of neighborhood that is simultaneously bounded and open. To achieve appropriate legibility, and to engender productive rates of and settings for accidental encounter, neighborhoods must be secured to the body, to both its scale and constraints. Thus, a neighborhood must be meaningfully physical, configuring the blend of the social and the dimensional.

It is necessary to bear in mind, however, that the constraints, and even the scale, of the body are not what they were in the classical age when Aristotle famously called for a limitation of the agora to the space of a shout. We can hear and see much farther now than then, the result of a myriad of prosthetic devices of our own invention. It is easy to say – and so it often is said – that these prostheses have annulled, or alienated us from, our bodies. The truth, I believe, is more complex: the body itself is not what it once was. With the rise of capitalism it acquired the potential of a tool, something that could be used. What has never been adequately dealt with by urban theorists or planners is the effect this redefinition of the body has on the notion of neighborhood. If public space, the agora, was defined by Aristotle through the imprinting of the capability of the body on it, this is because incorporation was the metaphor by which the alien – the foreign – difference could be accommodated without threatening its integrity and autonomy. Once the notion of body changed, once it became conceivable as a tool, the notion of incorporation was replaced by that of assimilation and the foreign came under increasing pressure to surrender its difference in favor of some unqualified substrate.

No modern neighborhood – inasmuch as it is home to computers, televisions, phones, faxes, and so on – will ever be as small as the agora of antiquity; it is thus impossible to return to this scale in some real sense. Nor is it possible voluntarily to return to the older metaphor of incorporation, since our bodies and our conditions are materially different. But it is possible – and indeed necessary – to think and construct our cities in a way that binds them to the body and what it can do. For the modern body has, it turns out, redoubled and contradictory functions: it serves not only as a tool but as that which incarnates the accident as such. That is, whereas in antiquity accidents had a place and thus a body could expect to meet with them, in modernity accidents are not given a place and thus a body could only be one. The body now bears the burden of being the only place where the accident resides. In other terms, only the body – through work – can introduce difference into an otherwise uniform system.

Consumer research and focus groups, the media of planning not only for Disney's town of Celebration but for many of our global cities, are busy designing urban environments suited to the programmable body-as-tool. The question is what place the other modern body – the body-as-accident – does and might occupy in the global city. Against all the arguments about the dematerialization attendant on our 'information age', it seems important to recognize that the modern body has the impossible role of giving a place to place. Neither nostalgic nor humanist, this recognition stresses the historical novelty of this role and the radical impossibility that conditions it. That is to say, what is at issue here is not an argument for an urbanism that would allow the body to develop its full potential. Cities must make room not for what is possible but for what is still impossible. This latter never wears a human face, which is the source of a great deal of difficulty, the major urban difficulty we now confront.

This essay has appeared as the introduction to *Giving Ground* edited by Joan Copjec and Michael Sorkin, Verso 1999.

Walter Benjamin and some Aspects of Today's Urbanity **Michael Müller**

Distant view and social engagement   Talking about Walter

Benjamin's influence on contemporary urban studies or concepts we shouldn't have or produce any illusions. In the seventies and eighties I tried to work out – with regards to Benjamin – a critical, dialectical understanding of the historical avant-garde in architecture.[1] I wondered whether there were radical aspects in the programmatic and practice of avant-garde strategies in comparison with and different to the moderate modern architecture? Whether there was something, which anticipated more than the forthcoming Fordism and the permanent repetition of standard and type.

I hoped that such a view on the aesthetic and social meaning of the avant-garde would be accepted as something that can help us to find the right questions in the architectural and urban debate. We all know quite well that postmodernity did not concern itself with such questions. However, interestingly enough, in the recently published edition of the German architectural magazine, *Arch+*[2], on modernity, Nikolaus Kuhnert and Angelika Schnell say that it is now time to remember these very questions and to open this debate. I mention this because I doubt that we can really speak about a specific and representative influence Benjamin's work has had on contemporary urban studies or concepts. I refuse to accept that what happens today i.e. in Berlin – the roll-back to the Gründerzeit, or expressed with more consideration, to the urbanity of the 19th and early 20th century – has anything in common with Benjamin's interest in the 19th century as the beginning of modernity. And also the often cited and fashionable figure of the 'flaneur' does not suffice in finding bridges to him. As an intellectual construction this masculine dominated gaze might give us the feeling of controlling and estimating the otherwise incoherency of city life. The flaneur as a more or less nostalgic, voyeuristic matrix to look at, but also to live in? The flaneur has always been an ambivalent figure, not only captivated by the movement and excitement of the modern urban crowd but also terrified of being swallowed up by the masses. As Steve Pile mentions, the flaneur 'is in the streets, but not of the streets'.[3] As a spectator who distances himself from the spectacle, the flaneur can never become an engaged figure in the chaos of his surroundings.

For that very reason I decided not to look at these influences but instead, to introduce aspects of Benjamin's thinking, which I try to confront with the actual urban situation.

Transformation   I begin with something general: that is the obvious transforma-

tion of the city and its images: The city as a place and matrix for consumer culture. In sev-

1   Michael Müller, **Die Verdrängung des Ornaments. Zur Dialektik von Architektur und Lebenspraxis**, Frankfurt/M., 1977; ders., **Architektur und Avant-garde. Ein vergessenes Projekt der Moderne?**, Frankfurt/M., 1984.
2   Nikolaus Kuhnert, Angelika Schnell, 'Die Moderne der Moderne', in **Arch+** 143, October 1998, p.17.
3   Steve Pile, **The Body and the City**, London, 1996, p.230.

Walter Benjamin
and some Aspects
of Today's Urbanity

eral of his essays Walter Benjamin has often expressed his positive attitude towards the new production of cultural symbols in the urban context. Here, more than the traditional language of architecture, he favored the signs and images of low culture. To Benjamin the forms of art in connection with architecture have always been very important. Looking at the actual situation he says architecture would have become the carrier of advertising. And the reception of distraction would become one of the most significant agents in advertising. Important elements of art – so Benjamin continues – like the graphics of advertising, the advertisement and radio publishing are connected with the interests of capital. But that's not only bad because advertising should be seen as an example for the transformation of the reception of art by the masses, but as a consequence it doesn't make any sense to fix the border between art and advertising.[4]

For it is also a fact that the images in the city and the meaning of cultural signs and symbols have changed, and hence also what Marshall Berman[5] so enthusiastically identified in Baudelaire's description of city life, especially in the 'petits poèmes', as paradigmatic of modern life, namely the 'here-and-now' of everyday life and the impossibility of understanding and portraying in its inter-relatedness what Baudelaire, in the introduction to 'Le Spleen de Paris', described as the chopped fragments of modern life.[6]

The signs and symbols of the present-day urban world are universal and have remained homogeneous. In recent decades this world of symbols has infiltrated and taken possession not only of the local spaces of the centers, but also of the peripheral areas, in what appears to be a natural process. It is not only signs but also attitudes and gestures that bind people to these signs, which are strangely indifferent to the geographical sites that are as indispensable as ever for representation. Whereas in civil society the cultural symbols, marks of distinction and the interests of power in the modern city were constituted in a cultural space that was largely identical with the concrete location of its reification, a difference now seems to have arisen between 'space' and 'location'. Neither cultural production nor the city as a source for cultural production remains untouched by this development.

4   Walter Benjamin, **Gesammelte Schriften**, Bd. I, 3, Frankfurt/M., 1974, p.1043f.
5   Marshall Berman, **All That is Solid Melts Into Air**, New York, 1993, p.131ff.
6   Charles Baudelaire, **Gesammelte Schriften** Bd.4, Dreieich 1981.

As late as the 1920s, one could still have the impression that the avant-garde's heterogeneous text of the city was read, aesthetically processed and understood in that day and age, for all its fascination, oscillating between destruction and construction, for the fragmentary, the dissolving of boundaries, the vague and the contradictory, but also in terms of fears and despairs. But this is not quite true. We should not forget that the nontransparency and incomprehensibility of the city in those days was already a common complaint in the conservative critique of culture and civilization. For the latter it was an acknowledged fact that the internationalism of New Architecture was progressively marginalizing the solid 'localness' of the urban environment.

The illegibility of the text of the city also has less impact, therefore, than the mounting impression of its deeper dimension as it becomes increasingly lost. This is problematic because the circulation of the signs is causally linked to the decentralized structure of economic power. The reference here is not to the old iconology of power, for that has meanwhile been covered over in the cities by the iconology of mobility, of communication and consumption (and thus appears more public, but, in each of its forms of individual appropriation, essentially private). A center – be it that of a city, or a cultural institution – that could organize and give structure to a field of meanings no longer exists in this conventional sense. The perspective that tolerates and appreciates this today is an aesthetic perspective through and through. This is basically nothing other than the temporary, mass-cultural zenith of the distanced reception characterizing modernity. However, this view no longer sees any background and, as Christine Boyer[7] once put it, has changed into a perspective void of critique or opposition. What it sees is a space filled with public dreams, defined by private enterprises.

Aestheticization and the urban

To Benjamin, aestheticization as well as the special meaning of perception in connection with architecture is of major importance. But aestheticization is a very contradictory category, which appears in his famous Kunstwerk-essay as the fascist variation of what he calls the aestheticization of politics in opposition to the politicization of the aesthetic. Distraction (Zertreuung) – another favored term – has become a dominant form of perception in consumer-culture society and is based on a universal form of aestheticization that the urban space reflects.

In this sense I would name 'museumification' and 'mediation' (or 'mediatization' – in German we would say 'Musealisierung' and 'Mediatisierung') as currently two identical

---

7   Christine Boyer, 'The Return of Aesthetics to City Planning' in **Society**, 25 (4), 1988, p.51.

Walter Benjamin
and some Aspects
of Today's Urbanity

and interwoven strategies for transforming urban spaces. Both strategies interfere with the traditional structures of public and private spaces, imbuing them with new meanings, replacing and redesigning them afresh. The common denominator of both strategies is their method, namely 'aestheticization', which they also share with other forms, such as self-staging, lifestyle, advertising, and fashion. What distinguishes them from the latter, for all the similarity of objectives, is the impact they have in the production of virtuality through the conscious simulation of real spatial situations and the actions that occur in them.

It is no coincidence that museumification of urban space conjures up associations with museums as such. On the contrary; new thinking in the mid 1970s about the purpose of the museum and its 'postmodern' architectural redefinition as an 'event space', has led to this locus of exclusive aesthetic experience being transformed into a space for multicultural involvement. The dissolution of traditional spatial boundaries here, and the projection of the aesthetic perspective of the concrete world and its history into the urban space, in which historical and traditional narratives congeal into aesthetically frozen images, is paralleled by the urbanization of the museum. One function within this process is the mediation of museum space as one of many spaces within a universal media network. Think about the museum shops where you start your visitor's tour and where you are already confronted with the museum's masterpieces
on T-shirts or teacups, the CD-ROM rooms, the immense space in new museums for events like eating, drinking, games and – of course – the presentation of the architecture itself.

Alongside new forms of museum design (Groningen is the extremity in this respect), even museums, once imbued with local distinction and with firm, characteristic contours, have meanwhile dissolved into dynamic spaces that no longer draw their cultural energies from the traditional features of the specific location. One can certainly observe the same tendencies in all large and medium sized European cities, namely the dissolution of traditional spatial structures in favor of what we call 'liminal space'.[8] This is particularly the case for economic spaces and cultural spaces, which

8   Sharon Zukin, **Landscape of Power. From Detroit to Disney World**,
Berkeley: University of California Press, 1993, p.28.
9   Franz Dröge, Michael Müller, 'Museum als urbaner Raumknoten' in
Werk, Bauen+Wohnen 12, Zürich, December 1997, pp.6-21.
10   Sharon Zukin, **Landscape of Power. From Detroit to Disney World**,
Berkeley: University of California Press, 1993, p.28.
11   Franz Dröge, Michael Müller, 'Museum als urbaner Raumknoten' in

involves more than mere commercialization. A symbolic space, such as the museum, is a good example.[9, 10, 11]

And what about Walter Benjamin? The museum is not one of his favorite topics, for, as discussed above in terms of 'low art', it no longer played such an important role. The concept of the 'destruction of aura' did not foresee that its privileged and constituting place, the museum, would re-invent the brightness of auratic experience in the field of urban transformation at the end of our century.

As far as 'mediation' is concerned, we need to take at least three dimensions into consideration. Firstly, the new urban transformations, especially those in the inner-city areas, present themselves as the 'postmodern', aestheticized mediation of contemporary interpretations of the objective world. Secondly, and corresponding to these, there is an underlying, invisible mediation that privatizes formerly public events and which may even be removed increasingly from public and democratic control. It is within this context that the twin aspects of modern electronic media come to the fore – the congealing of mass and individual communication made possible through the construction of unitary (digitalized) networks means the disappearance within them of commercial and political decision-making processes, especially at local community level. Thirdly, since the industrialization of mass-circulation newspapers and the early days of cinema and electronic media, we are now witnessing a process in which the political public aspect of urban spaces is being substituted by the mass media to an ever-increasing extent, thus becoming superfluous or dysfunctional in its traditional form. The transitory and the conservative character of the city or: the difference between place and space.

In his 1929 written essay on *Surrealismus* Benjamin talks about two forms or experiences of liberation: it is the opposition of the subject against the traditional rules of an overall controlled and regulated life and it is the revolution, what he also calls the constructive. In this connection Benjamin asks the question: 'How do we have to imagine an existence, completely oriented on the Boulevard Bonne-Nouvelle, in rooms designed by Le Corbusier and Oud?'[12] What Benjamin brings together are two experiences of aesthetic modernity: the constructive and the dadaistic, the surrealistic.

If we forget for a moment Benjamin's emphatic belief in the necessity of a revolutionary transformation of civic society and the opposition between the surrealistic dream and the rationality of the constructive, we are also confronted with two other different forms of

Werk, Bauen+Wohnen 12, Zürich, December 1997, pp.6-21.

12   Walter Benjamin, **Gesammelte Schriften**, Bd. II, I, Franfkurt/M. 1977, p.307.
See also Heinz Brüggemann, 'Walter Benjamin und Sigfried Giedion oder die Wege der Modernität' in **Deutsche Vierteljahresschrift für Literaturwissenschaft und Geistesgeschicht**, H.3, 1996, pp.443-474.

Walter Benjamin
and some Aspects
of Today's Urbanity

experience: 1. that of a subject-oriented experience of the local and 2. that of the transitory character of architecture, which transforms the local or the place into space. So, what is the condition today? Has the Boulevard Bonne-Nouvelle been transformed more generally into the conservative or nostalgic aspect of the local and its specific experience of time, that we insist that the place is important for our everyday life? And as for the former transparency of the constructive? Has it been transformed into what I before tried to describe as mediatization, the new role of space and its specific time-experience?

We can conceive of the city as a cultural superstructure undergoing a permanent process of development. And indeed: today, this structure is located within the contradiction of place and space. With regard to regional and town planning, we can draw the conclusion that the modern city has long since expanded its economy beyond its own borders, and has now become a spatial entity. However, this says nothing at all about its internal structure. Socially and culturally, it appears to remain a local entity, due to the reinforcing factors contained within these two dimensions, a local entity that still blocks itself off to a large degree from its actual or potential and perhaps necessary spatial orientation, despite verbal declarations to the contrary.

It is unclear in this connection what the categories of place and space have actually come to mean. With the decline of the urban bourgeoisie in the first half of the 20th century and its transformation chiefly into a clientele of property owners with substantial interests in land speculation, the identification of many urban dwellers with their city disintegrates. The 'identity leadership' of the bourgeois class, so to speak, sinks along with it into the ashes of its cultural and political bankruptcy. According to Richard Sennett, the sense of location among the intellectually leading sections of the modern city, in other words the conceptualizing ideologists of its culture, is shrinking to the tribalist mechanics of antiquarian residential quarters. Anyone who walks attentively through restored and gentrified old areas will corroborate this. Cities are breaking up culturally and politically through the growing dissociation in society, even if this has not yet produced such dramatic segregations in Germany or the

Netherlands as in the cities of America, England or France, countries in which cities (usa) or suburbs (France) mark the segregation of ethnic boundaries. If the signs are not deceiving us, this development will also occur in other eu countries. The reintegration of cities is thus becoming a political problem, but one which is to be solved not by political means or with social welfare policy, but with cultural policies. Despite these internal structural problems of virtually all major cities, they are the place, the location of cultural sedimentation. This is due above all to the conservatism of urbanity, which reacts to only a limited extent to the continual destruction of urban structures and which demonstrates little flexibility.

This conservatism is primarily attributable to its material roots in what could broadly be thought of as two cultural complexes. One is the longevity of buildings. Depreciation periods may be declining, especially for the commercial buildings, the offices and business premises that constitute the bulk of inner-city architecture, but they still have by far the longest life-cycle of all modern commodities. Moreover, there are effectively no more architectural ensembles that are homogeneous in terms of their period of origin. In most cities, they display temporal layers that extend over several generations to the nineteenth century, sometimes to early modernity or even further back. Restorers or decorators inspired by tourism and people responsible for protecting the architectural heritage are working hard to preserve this intergenerational architectural ambience. The evolutionary time-span of the city has coagulated in the longevity of its buildings, and has shed the annual rings of its past cultures. Some of these may no longer be accessible to present day city dwellers, but they are still connected at least to their reflected, nostalgic glory. The city's evolution cannot easily be broken up architecturally or even replaced by instantaneous time, in which the buildings would be made flexible in the same manner as their human counterparts so that the new economic environments could be either adapted in the short term without further ado, or simply demolished and rebuilt.

From this is derived a second context for urbanity's conservatism. Further developments of the urban environment are always linked to experience in the handling and criticism of the respective models that exist and the spatial designs on which they are based. One can view this fact as the 'power of imagination' that is exerted by existing urban designs. Above all, it has ensured so far that the continual change of urban culture is not excessively fragmentary, with all too radically alienating impacts. The power of imagination is thus the

Walter Benjamin
and some Aspects
of Today's Urbanity

power of the old narrative backed up by the power of its urban design, which is always the current narrative of practical value in life. What pain is inflicted among those concerned when, for example, in accordance with the bureaucratic ritual of a redevelopment plan, the bulldozers come and tear down a residential quarter because the history of a quarter, its collective practices and its cultural context are destroyed? The pain is the impact of that part of the old narrative that was authoritative for the inhabitants' social perception and experience of space, which was their continued actual narrative.

Two forms of time

The two forms of time, evolutionary and instantaneous time, which, according to the two English social scientists Lash and Urry[13], shape in their contradictoriness the modes of production in the post-Fordist society and lead to enormous tensions, clashing directly against each other in the contemporary city. This clash occurs in the city, which embodies the evolutionary mode in its material architectural form and which articulates it in narrative form. The city is under economic pressure to modernize and must at the same time implant instantaneous time in the form of new information and communications technologies, in particular digital networking, i.e. the ramps leading to and from the global information highway. The interface of these time worlds is certainly not an abstract one. It has its locations in the city, where the terminals are, where the new information workers sit and conduct financial transactions in the Antipodes, where designers create new prototypes and interact with factories in India, and where 'creative' individuals develop advertising campaigns in and for three world regions all at the same time. This interface produces flexibility in and through 'real time', because everybody moves as a physical being in both time modes, and produces special mentalities.

A curious fascination for architecture emanates from the media, which appear to offer the possibility of doing away with the temporal aspect of urban longevity and hence with urbanistic conservatism. It then seems as if the city can be conveyed into the simultaneity of functions and form, into the instantaneous time mode. Two possibilities have been envisaged for this pathway: one is the mediation of the optical appearance of the

13   Scott Lash, John Urry, **Economics of Signs & Space**, London, 1994.

architectural object through its facade. The other consists in the abandonment of the city in favor of cyberspace, because all architecture is already functionally obsolete and can only be pulled down again as a result of the incessantly changing demands for a totally flexible economy in the time interval between the granting of an order and the completion of a building. This view is advocated by the architect and architectural critic Martin Pawley[14], who generously projects the over-dimensioned office planning of the London Docklands area onto the whole city and its residential areas. Because people of the post-modern age are totally mobilized as appendices of the economy (for this medial theory of architecture they are quite obviously no more than this, in any case they have no independent right of existence, never mind right of housing or abode), the only edifices which could give the city of the future its appropriate pattern are mobile camps, such as camping grounds, hostels for long-distance lorry drivers and similar transient structures. The architect Lev Manovich[15] agrees with this analysis, but he improves the proposal by offering agglomerated quarters of the cheapest variety, a kind of barrack settlement, in order to free up investment capital for cyberspace.

One the one hand, it is astounding how pretentiously authoritarian the reflective weaknesses of so-called experts are revealed, particularly in view of the dictatorially defined needs of residential populations. On the other hand, beyond such euphoric naivety, the city as a cultural sediment and with its sheer longevity is increasingly a provocation for architects because they are no longer able to formulate modernity in the language of architecture. Logically enough, they can no longer accept the neo-historicism of post-modernity, and instead are seeking refuge in the instantaneous time mode of the digital media.

The role of public space or: the opposition between the street and the interior
The experience in the Boulevard Bonne-Nouvelle reflects the idea of cross-boarding (enclosing) which is the perception of the flaneur; a cross-boarding of space- and time-perception, which gives the old world of commodities the capacity to speak, to tell stories. Its appropriate space in the city is the passage. The opposite is transparency – what Benjamin calls penetration (what the Futurists called 'compenetrazione') which Benjamin, in the *Surrealismus* essay, connected with the work of Le Corbusier. But in the vision this master-architect has of the ideal city and street-life by segregation, this new perception of transparency as a main formula of the aesthetic

14 Martin Pawley, 'Architektur im Kampf gegen die neuen Medien' in **Iglhaut, Stadt am Netz**, Mannheim, 1996, pp.27-38.
15 Lew Manovich, 'Avant-garde, Cyberspace und die Architektur der Zukunft' in **Iglhaut, Stadt am Netz**, Mannheim 1996, pp.39-40. The original English text is available at http://jupiter.uscd.edu/~manovich/cyberspace.txt.

Walter Benjamin
and some Aspects
of Today's Urbanity

modern, is reduced into an urban space where narration has no chance and urban cross-boarding no longer exists. Is it not the drama of city-life that is eliminated by the perception of transparency? The urban space today is no longer a 'kolportage-roman' and the place for the flaneur.

For that reason, it is not possible to give a simple and immediate answer to the perennial question of whether nowadays the public spaces of the contemporary city, its streets and squares, can be conceived as the social background for a revitalized radical mass culture in the face of the aestheticization strategies of museumification and mediation. The signs and symbols of the urban space are without doubt multicultural in origin. Streets, too, will not cease in the foreseeable future to be places for demonstrations. But they are also very often a place for nothingness and loneliness, for aggression or even the simulation of all this. And they are no longer what Walter Benjamin once called – in opposition to the interior – the adequate place for the cultural life and the interests of the masses.[16] The space of the street as a symbol for the transformation of bourgeois culture: the street as the enemy of privacy and as a public space that confronts and organizes the masses.

On the other hand, of course, this transformation has actually occurred[17], but only to the extent that the cultural symbolism dominating the urban space of the streets embodies the end of civil society and its culture. Museumification and mediation subvert the virulent contradiction in civil society between public and private by removing the boundaries between the spheres. Viewed in this way, the space of the streets – what used to be public space – is no longer the enemy of the private, just as the traditional values of the private have largely disappeared. Jameson is right to point out that we would no longer approach the masses with the fear that the internalized bourgeois individual used to feel.[18]

In everyday practice this does not come about of its own accord, because the strategies of museumification and mediation are still reliant, increasingly so, on security measures, and/or articulating new distinctions in the luxurious shopping paradises, office centers and cultural establishments in such a way that all the undesirables do not even attempt to call the dissolu-

16   Walter Benjamin, **Gesammelte Schriften**, Bd.III, Frankfurt/M., 1972, pp.194-199.
17   Franz Dröge, Michael Müller, op. cit.
18   Fredric Jameson, **The Seeds of Time**, New York, 1994, p.158.
19   Mike Davis, **City of Quartz**, Berlin/Göttingen, 1994, p.262.
20   Fredric Jameson, op. cit., p.145ff.
21   Ibid., p.159.
22   Michel de Certeau, **The Practice of Everyday Life**, Berkeley and Los Angeles, 1984.

tion of boundaries into question.[19] In fact, we can now observe a double planning strategy that disintegrates into an inner and an outer dimension – the de-problematizing of public space through aesthetically produced private atmospheres, on the one hand, and its intensification through exclusion and surveillance of the homeless and poor on the other. In both cases, the public space disappears in the perception of the citizens.

If the opposition between private and public is to be eradicated, then, following Jameson's cue, we would have to try and elaborate a theoretical explanation for the spaces and zones of the street and everyday life as a 'candidate for such an intermediary position'. The spaces proposed by Jameson[20], who is impressed by the contextualism of 'dirty realism', involve risks – a kind of 'no-man's land', spaces in which neither private ownership nor public law exists. His examples are literary fictions and anything but encouraging – Chandler's description of a police station as 'a space beyond the law', or one of John Le Carré's novels, where the characters meet in a space near the Berlin Wall, 'a space beyond all national or political jurisdiction, in which the worst crimes can be committed with impunity and in which the very social persona itself dissolves'.[21]

This is a quite different aspect of Benjamin's transformed experience of the Boulevard Bonne-Nouvelle: It is not the conservative, nostalgic place of museumification. Even more so, the way we use the term 'dirty realism', it is a new field on which to project our fantasies. As a cultural production this projection has much in common with Michel de Certeau's[22] image of a city which has an unconscious life, where administrative rationality struggles to impose an order on people's everyday urban spatial practices. And it is linked with Foucault's concept of physical space as 'Heterotopia', where the experience of disturbing interruptions dominates and stops words in their tracks. Here we are confronted with an area in which our thought encounters objects or patterns that it can neither locate nor order.[23] Henri Lefebvre's 'thirdings'[24] and Edward Soja's 'Thirdspace'[25] give us – with all their differences – also an idea of this new experience.

The empathy for such more or less uncontrolled and sometimes risky (the Jameson version) spaces, suggestive of a somewhat diffuse emotional attitude, as 'bearers of hope' in the midst of desolate urban wastelands is somewhat problematic, of course. Mike Davis warns here, not without justification, that we should be aware of falsely celebrating the myth of paradigmatic postmodern and/or post-Fordist cities and shouldn't make the mistake of tending to reduce history 'to teleology' and therefore glorifying the very reality that is supposed to be deconstructed.[26]

23   Michel Foucault, 'Of Other Spaces' in R. Ritter, B. Knaller-Vlay, **Other Spaces. The Affair of the Heterotopia**, Graz, 1998, pp.22-37; and the introduction by the editors, pp.8-19.
24   Henri Lefebvre, **The Production of Space**, Oxford/UK and Cambridge/MA, 1991.
25   Edward W. Soja, **Thirdspace. Journeys to Los Angeles and other Real-And-Imagined Places**, Oxford/UK and Cambridge/MA, 1996.
26   Mike Davis, op. cit., p.107.

The Impact of the New Technologies and Globalization on Cities **Saskia Sassen**

Telecommunications and globalization have emerged as major forces shaping the organization of urban space. This reorganization ranges from the spatial virtualization of a growing number of social and economic activities to the reconfiguration of the geography of the built environment for these activities. Whether in electronic space or in the geography of the built environment, this reorganization involves a repositioning of the urban and of urban centrality in particular.

The growth of global markets for finance and specialized services, the need for transnational servicing networks due to sharp increases in international investment, the reduced role of the government in the regulation of international economic activity and the corresponding ascendance of other institutional arenas, notably global markets and corporate headquarters – all these point to the existence of a series of transnational networks of cities. We can see here the formation, at least incipient, of transnational urban systems. To a large extent it seems to me that the major business centers in the world today draw their importance from these transnational networks. There is no such thing as a single global city – and in this sense there is a sharp contrast with the erstwhile capitals of empires.

These networks of major international business centers constitute new geographies of centrality. The most powerful of these new geographies of centrality at the global level binds the major international financial and business centers: New York, London, Tokyo, Paris, Frankfurt, Zurich, Amsterdam, Los Angeles, Sydney, Hong Kong, among others. But this geography now also includes cities such as Bangkok, Seoul, Taipei, São Paulo, Mexico City. The intensity of transactions among these cities, particularly through the financial markets, trade in services, and investment has increased sharply, and so have the orders of magnitude involved. At the same time, there has been a sharpening inequality in the concentration of strategic resources and activities between each of these cities and others in the same country.

Cities, particularly the major cities in the developed world, are production sites for the leading information industries of our time. This entails a whole infrastructure of activities, firms and jobs, which is necessary to run the advanced corporate economy. These industries are typically conceptualized in terms of the hypermobility of their outputs and the high levels of expertise of their professionals rather than in terms of the production or work process involved and the requisite infrastructure of facilities and non-expert jobs that are also part of these industries. Emphasizing place, infrastructure and non-expert jobs matters precisely because so much of the focus has been on the neutralization of geography and place made possible by the new technologies.

The concept of the city is complex, imprecise, and charged with specific historical meanings. A more abstract category might be centrality, one of the properties cities have historically provided/produced. The effort here would not be on matters such as the boundaries of cities or what cities actually are. These are partly empirical questions: each city is going to have a different configuration of boundaries and contents. The question is, rather, what are the conditions for the continuity of centrality in advanced economic systems in the face of major new organizational forms and technologies that maximize the possibility for geographic dispersal at the regional, national and indeed, global scale with simultaneous system integration? Historically centrality has largely been embedded in the central city. One of the changes brought about by the new conditions is the reconfiguring of centrality: the central city is today but one form of centrality. Important emerging spaces for the constitution of centrality range from the new transnational networks of cities to electronic space.

1 Worldwide networks and central command functions

The geography of globalization contains both a dynamic of dispersal and of centralization, the latter a condition that began receiving recognition only recently (See e.g. Sassen, 1991; Castells, 1989; Friedmann, 1986; Knox and Taylor, 1995; Frost and Spence, 1993; *Le Debat*, 1994). The massive trends towards the spatial dispersal of economic activities at the metropolitan, national and global level which we associate with globalization have contributed to a demand for new forms of territorial centralization of top-level management and control operations. The rapid growth of affiliates illustrates this dynamic. By 1998 firms had about half a million affiliates outside their home countries. The sheer number of dispersed factories and service outlets that are part of a firm's integrated operation creates massive new needs for central coordination and servicing. Thus the spatial dispersal of economic activity made possible by telecommunications and the new

---

1 A central proposition here, developed at length in my work (e.g. Sassen, 1991-2000), is that we cannot take the existence of a global economic system as a given, but rather need to examine the particular ways in which the conditions for economic globalization are produced. This requires examining not only communication capacities and the power of multinationals, but also the infrastructure of facilities and work processes necessary for the implementation of global economic systems, including the production of those inputs that constitute the capability for global control and the infrastructure of jobs involved in this production. The emphasis shifts

legal frameworks for globalization contributes to an expansion of central functions if this dispersal is to take place under the continuing concentration in control, ownership and profit appropriation that characterizes the current economic system.

Another instance today of this negotiation between a global cross-border dynamic and territorially specific sites is that of the global financial markets. The orders of magnitude in these transactions have risen sharply, as illustrated by the 75 USD trillion in turnover in the global capital market, a major component of the global economy. These transactions are partly embedded in telecommunications systems that make possible the instantaneous transmission of money/information around the globe. Much attention has gone to the capacity for instantaneous transmission of the new technologies. But the other half of the story is the extent to which the global financial markets are located in particular cities in the highly developed countries; indeed, the degrees of concentration are unexpectedly high, a subject I discuss empirically in a later section.

Stock markets worldwide have become globally integrated. Besides deregulation in the 1980s in all the major European and North American markets, the late 1980s and early 1990s saw the addition of such markets as Buenos Aires, São Paulo, Mexico City, Bangkok, Taipei, etc. The integration of a growing number of stock markets has contributed to raise the capital that can be mobilized through stock markets. Worldwide market value reached over 20 trillion dollars in 1998. It also is reflected in the growing numbers of non-national firms listed in most of these markets (see Table 1). This globally integrated stock market which makes possible the circulation of publicly listed shares around the globe in seconds, is embedded in a grid of very material, physical, strategic places – that is, cities belonging to national territories (See Table 1).

The specific forms assumed by globalization over the last decade have created particular organizational requirements. The emergence of global markets for finance and specialized services, the growth of investment as a major type of international transaction, all have contributed to the expansion in command functions and in the demand for specialized services for firms.[1]

By central functions I do not only mean top level headquarters; I am referring to all the top level financial, legal, accounting, managerial, executive, planning functions necessary to run a corporate organization operating in more than one country, and increasingly in

to the 'practice' of global control: the work of producing and reproducing the organization and management of a global production system and a global marketplace for finance, both under conditions of economic concentration. The recovery of place and production also implies that global processes can be studied in great empirical detail.

Table 1 Select Stock Exchanges: Market Size, 1990 and 1997 (USD millions and number)

1990

City	Market Value		Listed Companies (N)	
	Domestic	Domestic+Foreign	Domestic	Foreign
New York	2692123	2819778	1678	96
Tokyo	3416495		1627	125
London	921583	1037531	2006	553
Frankfurt	383823		649	555
Paris	342948		873	231
Zurich	172709		234	245
Toronto	233752	585637	1127	66
Amsterdam	153144	323	240	
Milan	133506		229	
Sydney	120888	170212	1089	33
Hong Kong	126921		284	15
Singapore	196868		163	166
Taiwan	110454		199	
Seoul	122937		669	

1997

City	Market Value		Listed Companies (N)	
	Domestic	Domestic+Foreign	Domestic	Foreign
New York	6595209	9413109	2691	356
Tokyo	2321928		1805	60
London	2049459	1879137	2465	526
Frankfurt	855689		700	1996
Paris	696765		727	172
Zurich	578232		216	212
Toronto	586698	917484	1362	58
Amsterdam	570943		332	179
Milan	352323		209	4
Sydney	337777	578059	1149	70
Hong Kong	413670		638	20
Singapore	332825		303	181
Taiwan	314668		404	
Seoul	74624		776	

Notes For Australia 1997, the number of listed companies is from 1996; when only domestic is listed, it represents the total market value.
Source Based on Meridian Securities Markets, World Stock Exchange Fact Book, 1998.

Table 3 Top 5 Global Command Centers Based on Corporations, Banks, Stock Markets and Advertising Agency rankings, 1996 and 1997 (numbers)

Rank	City[1]	Corporations 1997	Banks 1996	Stock markets (1996)[2]	Advertising agencies 1997
1	**Tokyo**	1	1	3	2
2	**New York**	2	6	2	1
3	**London**	6	4	1	3
4	**Paris**	3	2	5	5
5	**Frankfurt**	11	3	4	11

Notes
1 Cities ranked within the top 20 in the corporation (based on Fortune's Global 500) and bank tables, within the top 5 stock markets and within the top 17 advertising agencies.
2 Based on the number of listed companies (domestic and foreign).
Source Short, J.R. and Y.H. Kim, Globalization and the City, 1999, p.36.

Table 2 Location of Top Banking, Industrial, and Commercial Firms by City, selected years, 1960-1997

City, country[a]	1997	1990	1980	1970	1960
Tokyo, Japan	18 (5)[b]	12 (2)	6	5 (1)	1
New York, USA	12 (1)	7 (5)	10 (4)	25 (8)	29 (8)
Paris, France	11 (1)	5	7 (2)	0	0
Osaka, Japan	7 (3)	2 (1)	1	1	0
Detroit, USA	4 (2)	2 (2)	2 (2)	3 (3)	5 (2)
London, UK	3 (1)	7 (2)	8 (3)	7 (3)	7 (3)
Chicago, USA	3	2	4 (2)	5	6 (2)
Munich, Germany	3	2	1	1	1
Amsterdam, Netherlands	3	0	0	0	0
Seoul, South Korea	3	0	0	0	0

Notes
a After ranking cities according to the number holding the world's 100 largest corporation headquarters, the list was trimmed to the top 40 cities of which 10 are listed in the table above;
b the figure in brackets gives the number of the world's top 20 corporations for that city.
Source Short and Kim, Globalization and the City, 1999, p.26.

Table 4 International Bank Lending by Country, selected years, 1980-1998 (percentage, USD trillions)

	1980	1991	1998
Japan	6.2	15.1	19.8
Germany[1]	4.0	6.1	16.5
France	9.4	6.6	11.3
United States	9.4	9.4	11.2
Switzerland	3.4	6.3	8.4
United Kingdom	26.2	16.3	6.1
Luxembourg	5.6	5.0	0.9
Other	35.8	35.2	26.0
Total	100.0	100.0	100.0
Total in USD trillions	1.89	6.24	9.03

1 1980 figures based on West German reporting banks and institutions.
Source Based on data from the Bank for International Settlements, 62nd and 69th Annual Reports (Basel: B.I.S., 1992 and 1999).

Table 5 Foreign Exchange Turnover by Country, Daily Averages, 1989 and 1998 (USD billions and percentages)

	1989		1998	
	Daily Average (USD bn)	% of 'net-gross'	Daily Average (USD bn)	% of 'net-gross'
United Kingdom	184.0	25.630310628	637.3	32.33384069
United States	115.2	16.046803176	350.9	17.803145611
Japan	110.8	15.433904444	148.6	7.5393201421
Switzerland	56.0	7.8005293216	81.7	4.1451040081
Singapore	55.0	7.6612341552	139.0	7.0522577372
Hong Kong	48.8	6.7976041231	78.6	3.9878234399
Australia	28.9	4.0256303106	46.6	2.3642820903
France	23.2	3.2316478618	71.9	3.6478944698
Sub-total for listed countries	621.9	86.62766402	1554.6	78.873668189
Total 'net-gross' turnover	717.9		1971.0	

Source Based on data from the Bank for International Settlements, Central Bank Survey, April 1998 (Basel: B.I.S., 1999).

several countries. These central functions are partly embedded in headquarters, but also in good part in what has been called the corporate
services complex, that is, the network of financial, legal, accounting,
advertising firms that handle the complexities of operating in more than
one national legal system, national accounting system, advertising culture,
etc. and do so under conditions of rapid innovations in all these fields.
Such services have become so specialized and complex, that headquarters
increasingly buy them from specialized firms rather than producing them
in-house. These agglomerations of firms producing central functions
for the management and coordination of global economic systems, are
disproportionately concentrated in the highly developed countries –
particularly, though not exclusively, in the kinds of cities I call global cities
(see Tables 2 and 3). Such concentrations of functions represent a strategic
factor in the organization of the global economy, and they are situated
right here, in New York, in Paris, in Amsterdam.

National and global markets as well as globally integrated organizations
require central places where the work of globalization gets done. Finance
and advanced corporate services are industries producing the organizational
commodities necessary for the implementation and management of global
economic systems. Cities are preferred sites for the production of these
services, particularly the most innovative, speculative, internationalized
service sectors. Further, leading firms in information industries require
a vast physical infrastructure containing strategic nodes with hyperconcen-
tration of facilities; we need to distinguish between the capacity for global
transmission/communication and the material conditions that make
this possible. Finally, even the most advanced information industries have
a production process that is at least partly place-bound because of the
combination of resources it requires even when the outputs are hypermobile.
   Cities have historically provided national economies, polities and
societies with something we can think of as centrality. In terms of their
economic function, cities provide agglomeration economies, massive
concentrations of information on the latest developments, a marketplace.

The question how economic globalization and the new technologies alter the role of centrality and hence of cities as economic entities becomes pertinent. Centrality remains a key feature of the global information economy, but it can assume several spatial correlates, ranging from the Central Business District to a new global grid of cities.

2 New forms of centrality

Today there is no longer a simple straightforward relation between centrality and such geographic entities as the downtown, or the central business district. In the past, and up to quite recently in fact, the center was synonymous with the downtown or the CBD. Today, the spatial correlate of the center can assume several geographic forms. It can be the CBD, as it still is largely in New York City, or it can extend into a metropolitan area in the form of a grid of nodes of intense business activity, as we see in Frankfurt and Zurich (Keil and Ronneberg, 1993; Hitz et al., 1996). The center has been profoundly altered by telecommunications and the growth of a global economy, both inextricably linked; they have contributed to a new geography of centrality (and marginality). Simplifying one could identify four forms assumed by centrality today.

First, while there is no longer a simple straightforward relation between centrality and such geographic entities as the downtown, or the central business district as was the case in the past, the CBD remains a key form of centrality. But the CBD in major international business centers is one profoundly reconfigured by technological and economic change.

We may be seeing a difference in the pattern of global city formation in parts of the United States and in parts of Western Europe (Hall, 1988; Kunzmann and Wegener, 1991; Sassen, 1994; Keil and Ronneberger, 1993). In the United States, major cities such as New York and Chicago have large centers that have been rebuilt many times, given the brutal neglect suffered by much urban infrastructure and the imposed obsolescence so characteristic of US cities. This neglect and accelerated obsolescence produce vast spaces for rebuilding the center according to the requirements of whatever regime of urban accumulation or pattern of spatial organization of the urban economy prevails at a given time. In Europe, urban centers are far more protected and they rarely contain significant stretches of abandoned space; the expansion of workplaces and the need for intelligent buildings necessarily will have to take place partly outside the old centers. One of the most extreme cases is the complex of La Défense, the massive, state of the art office

complex developed right outside Paris to avoid harming the built environment inside the city. This is an explicit instance of government policy and
planning aimed at addressing the growing demand for central office space
of prime quality. Yet another variant of this expansion of the 'center' onto
hitherto peripheral land can be seen in London's Docklands. Similar
projects for recentralizing peripheral areas were launched in several major
cities in Europe, North America, and Japan during the 1980s.

Second, the center can extend into a metropolitan area in the form of a
grid of nodes of intense business activity. One might ask whether a spatial
organization characterized by dense strategic nodes spread over a broader
region does or does not constitute a new form of organizing the territory
of the 'center', rather than, as in the more conventional view, an instance
of suburbanization or geographic dispersal. Insofar as these various nodes
are articulated through cyber-routes or digital highways, they represent
a new geographic correlate of the most advanced type of 'center'. The
places that fall outside this new grid of digital highways, however, are
peripheralized. This regional grid of nodes represents, in my analysis, a
reconstitution of the concept of region. Far from neutralizing geography
the regional grid is likely to be embedded in conventional forms of
communications infrastructure, notably rapid rail and highways connecting
to airports. Ironically perhaps, conventional infrastructure is likely to
maximize the economic benefits derived from telematics. I think this is
an important issue that has been lost somewhat in discussions about the
neutralization of geography through telematics.

Third, we are seeing the formation of a transterritorial 'center' constituted via telematics and intense economic transactions (Sassen, 1991;
Castells, 1989; Graham and Marvin, 1996). The most powerful of these new
geographies of centrality at the inter-urban level binds the major international financial and business centers: New York, London, Tokyo, Paris,
Frankfurt, Zurich, Amsterdam, Los Angeles, Sydney, Hong Kong, among
others. But this geography now also includes cities such as São Paulo and
Mexico City. The intensity of transactions among these cities, particularly
through the financial markets, trade in services, and investment has

increased sharply, and so have the orders of magnitude involved.[2] At the same time, there has been a sharpening inequality in the concentration of strategic resources and activities between each of these cities and others in the same country. For instance, Paris now concentrates a larger share of leading economic sectors and wealth in France than it did fifteen years ago, while Marseilles, once a major economic hub, has lost its share and is suffering severe decline.

In the case of a complex landscape such as Europe's we see in fact several geographies of centrality, one global, others continental and regional. A central urban hierarchy connects major cities, many of which in turn play central roles in the wider global system of cities: Paris, London, Frankfurt, Amsterdam, Zurich. These cities are also part of a wider network of European financial/cultural/service capitals, some with only one, others with several of these functions, that articulate the European region and are somewhat less oriented to the global economy than Paris, Frankfurt, or London. And then there are several geographies of marginality: the East-West divide and the North-South divide across Europe as well as newer divisions. In Eastern Europe, certain cities and regions, notably Budapest, are rather attractive for purposes of investment, both European and non-European, while others will increasingly fall behind, notably in Romania, Yugoslavia, and Albania. We see a similar differentiation in the south of Europe: Madrid, Barcelona, and Milan are gaining in the new European hierarchy; Naples, Rome, and Marseilles are not.

Fourth, new forms of centrality are being constituted in electronically generated spaces. Electronic space is often read as a purely technological event and in that sense a space of innocence. But if we consider for instance that strategic components of the financial industry operate in such space we can see that these are spaces where profits are produced and power is thereby constituted. Insofar as these technologies strengthen the profit-making capability of finance and make possible the hyper-mobility of finance capital, they also contribute to the often devastating impacts of the ascendance of finance on other industries, on particular sectors of the population, and on whole economies. Cyberspace, like any other space can be inscribed in a multiplicity of ways, some benevolent or enlightening; others, not (see Sassen, 1998: chapter 9). My argument is that structures for economic power are being built in electronic space and that their highly complex configurations contain points of coordination and centralization.

---

2 The pronounced orientation to the world markets evident in such cities raises questions about the articulation with their nation-states, their regions, and the larger economic and social structure in such cities. Cities have typically been deeply embedded in the economies of their region, indeed often reflecting the characteristics of the latter; and they still do. But cities that are strategic sites in the global economy tend, in part, to disconnect from their region. This conflicts with a key proposition in traditional scholarship about urban systems, namely, that these systems promote the territorial integration of regional and national economies.

In the next sections I discuss various aspects of these four forms of centrality, focusing particularly on cities as a way of showing the logic that produces centrality in a global information economy.

A Concentration and the redefinition of the center: some empirical referents
The trend towards concentration of top-level management, coordination and servicing functions is evident at the national and international scales in all highly developed countries. For instance, the Paris region accounts for over 40% of all producer services in France, and over 80% of the most advanced ones. New York City is estimated to account for between a fourth and a fifth of all US producer services exports though it has only 3% of the US population. London accounts for 40% of all exports of producer services in the UK. Similar trends are also evident in Zurich, Frankfurt, and Tokyo, all located in much smaller countries.

Elsewhere (Sassen, 2000), a somewhat detailed empirical examination of several cities serves to explore different aspects of this trend towards concentration. Here there is space only for a few observations. The case of Toronto, a city whose financial district was built up only in recent years, allows us to see to what extent the pressure towards physical concentration is embedded in an economic dynamic rather than simply being the consequence of an inherited built infrastructure from the past, as one could think was the case in older centers such as London or New York. But the case also shows that it is particularly certain industries that are subject to the pressure towards spatial concentration, notably finance and its sister industries (Gad, 1991; Todd, 1995).

In the financial district in Manhattan, the use of advanced information and telecommunication technologies has had a strong impact on the spatial organization of the district because of the added spatial requirements of 'intelligent' buildings. A ring of new office buildings meeting these requirements was built over the last decade immediately around the old Wall Street core, where the narrow streets and lots made this difficult; furthermore, renovating old buildings in the Wall Street core is extremely expensive and often not possible. The new buildings in the district were

3 Furthermore, this unchanged level of concentration has happened at a time when financial services are more mobile than ever before: globalization, deregulation (an essential ingredient for globalization), and securitization have been the key to this mobility – in the context of massive advances in telecommunications and electronic networks. One result is growing competition among centers for hypermobile financial activity. In my view there has been an overemphasis on competition in general and in specialized accounts on this subject. As I have argued elsewhere (Sassen, 1991: chapter 7), there is also a functional division of labor among various mostly corporate headquarters and financial services industry facilities. These firms tend to be extremely intensive users of telematics, and the availability of the most advanced forms typically is a major factor in their real estate and locational decisions. They need complete redundancy of telecommunications systems, high carrying capacity, often their own private branch exchange, etc. With this often goes a need for large spaces. For instance, the technical installations backing a firm's trading floor are likely to require additional space equivalent to the size of the trading floor itself.

The case of Sydney illuminates the interaction of a vast, continental economic scale and pressures towards spatial concentration (Brotchie et al., 1995). Rather than strengthening the multipolarity of the Australian urban system, the developments of the 1980s – increased internationalization of the Australian economy, sharp increases in foreign investment, a strong shift towards finance, real estate and producer services – contributed to a greater concentration of major economic activities and actors in Sydney. This included a loss of share of such activities and actors by Melbourne, long the center of commercial activity and wealth in Australia (Daly and Stimson, 1992).

At the international level, the case of the leading financial centers in the world today is of continued interest, since one might have expected that the growing number of financial centers now integrated into the global markets and the enormous increase in volumes would have reduced the extent of concentration of financial activity in the top centers.[3] Yet the levels of concentration remain unchanged in the face of massive transformations in the financial industry and in the technological infrastructure this industry depends on.[4] One indicator of this combination of growth in volumes and unchanged levels of concentration can be found in the evidence on international bank lending and foreign exchange turnover (see Tables 4 and 5). While these data are for countries, other evidence makes it clear that it is generally the major financial centers of these countries that handle much of the international lending and foreign exchange transactions.

In brief, with the potential for global control capability, certain cities are becoming nodal points in a vast communications and market system. Advances in electronics and telecommunication have transformed geographically distant cities into centers for global communication and long-distance management. But centralized control and management over a geographically dispersed array of plants, offices, and service outlets does not come

major financial centers. In that sense we can think of a transnational system with multiple locations.
4 Much of the discussion around the formation of a single European market and financial system has raised the possibility, and even the need if it is to be competitive, of centralizing financial functions and capital in a limited number of cities rather than maintaining the current structure in which each country has an international financial center.

about inevitably as part of a 'world system'. It requires the development of a vast range of highly specialized services and of top-level management and control functions.

3 The intersection of service intensity and globalization

To understand the new or sharply expanded role of a particular kind of city in the world economy since the early 1980s, we need to focus on the intersection of two major processes. The first is the sharp growth in the globalization of economic activity; this has raised the scale and the complexity of transactions, thereby feeding the growth of top-level multi-national headquarter functions and the growth of advanced corporate services. It is important to note that even though globalization raises the scale and complexity of these operations, they are also evident at smaller geographic scales and lower orders of complexity, as is the case with firms that operate regionally. Thus while regionally oriented firms need not negotiate the complexities of international borders and the regulations of different countries, they are still faced with a regionally dispersed network of operations that requires centralized control and servicing.

The second process we need to consider is the growing service intensity in the organization of all industries. This has contributed to a massive growth in the demand for services by firms in all industries, from mining and manufacturing to finance and consumer services.[5] Cities are key sites for the production of services for firms. Hence the increase in service intensity in the organization of all industries has had a significant growth effect on cities in the 1980s. It is important to recognize that this growth in services for firms is evident in cities at different levels of a nation's urban system. Some of these cities cater to regional or sub-national markets; others cater to national markets and yet others cater to global markets. In this context, globalization becomes a question of scale and added complexity.

The key process from the perspective of the urban economy is the growing demand for services by firms in all industries and the fact that

---

5 We can think of the producer services, and most especially finance and advanced corporate services, as industries producing the 'organizational commodities' necessary for the implementation and management of global economic systems. Producer services are intermediate ouputs, that is, services bought by firms. They cover financial, legal, and general management matters, innovation, development, design, administration, personnel, production technology, maintenance, transport, communications, wholesale distribution, advertising, cleaning services for firms, security, and storage. Central components of the producer services category are a

cities are preferred production sites for such services, whether at the global, national, or regional level. As a result we see in cities the formation of a new urban economic core of banking and service activities that comes to replace the older typically manufacturing oriented core.

In the case of cities that are major international business centers, the scale, power, and profit levels of this new core suggest that we are seeing the formation of a new urban economy. This is so in at least two regards. First, even though these cities have long been centers for business and finance, since the late 1970s there have been dramatic changes in the structure of the business and financial sectors, as well as sharp increases in the overall magnitude of these sectors and their weight in the urban economy. Second, the ascendance of the new finance and services complex, particularly international finance, engenders what may be regarded as a new economic regime, that is, although this sector may account for only a fraction of the economy of a city, it imposes itself on that larger economy. Most notably, the possibility for super-profits in finance has the effect of devalorizing manufacturing insofar as the latter cannot generate the super-profits typical in much financial activity.

This is not to say that everything in the economy of these cities has changed. On the contrary, they still show a great deal of continuity and many similarities with cities that are not global nodes. Rather, the implantation of global processes and markets has meant that the internationalized sector of the economy has expanded sharply and has imposed a new valorization dynamic – that is, a new set of criteria for valuing or pricing various economic activities and outcomes. This has had devastating effects on large sectors of the urban economy. High prices and profit levels in the internationalized sector and its ancillary activities, such as top-of-the-line restaurants and hotels, have made it increasingly difficult for other sectors to compete for space and investments. Many of these other sectors have experienced considerable downgrading and/or displacement, as, for example, neighborhood shops tailored to local needs are replaced by upscale boutiques and restaurants catering to new high-income urban elites.

Though at a different order of magnitude, these trends also became evident during the late 1980s in a number of major cities in the developing world that have become integrated into various world markets: São Paulo, Buenos Aires, Bangkok, Taipei, and Mexico City are only a few examples. Also here the new urban core was fed by the

range of industries with mixed business and consumer markets; they are insurance, banking, financial services, real estate, legal services, accounting, and professional associations (for more detailed discussions see, e.g. Noyelle and Dutka, 1988; Daniels, 1991; Veltz, 1996; Sassen, 1991: chapters 2-5).

deregulation of financial markets, ascendance of finance and specialized services, and integration into the world markets. The opening of stock markets to foreign investors and the privatization of what were once public sector firms have been crucial institutional arenas for this articulation. Given the vast size of some of these cities, the impact of this new core on the broader city is not always as evident as in central London or Frankfurt, but the transformation is still very real.

A **The new marginality** The new growth sectors, the new organizational capacities of firms, and the new technologies – all three interrelated – are contributing to produce not only a new geography of centrality but also a new geography of marginality. The evidence for the US, Western Europe and Japan suggests that it will take government policy and action to reduce the new forms of spatial and social inequality.

The new marginality has several components: the inevitable 'creative destruction' that is part of growth; losses due to international and national competition; insufficient quality in factors of production; redundancy or excess capacity; and others.

One critical component, not sufficiently recognized and where government policy could make a difference, is the misunderstanding that seems to prevail in much general commentary about what matters in an advanced economic system, the information economy, and economic globalization. Many types of firms, workers, and places, such as industrial services, which look as if they do not belong in an advanced, information-based, globally oriented economic system, are actually integral parts of such a system. They need policy recognition and support: they can't compete in the new environments where leading sectors have bid up prices and standards, even though their products and labor are in demand. For instance, the financial industry in Manhattan, one of the most sophisticated and complex industries, needs truckers to deliver not only software, but also tables and light bulbs; and it needs blue-collar maintenance workers and cleaners. These activities and workers need to be able to make a decent living if they are to stay in the region (see e.g. *Social Justice*, 1994; *Competition and Change*, 1995; King, 1996).

Yet another dimension not sufficiently recognized is the fact of a new valuation dynamic: the combination of globalization and the new technologies has altered the criteria and mechanisms through which factors, inputs, goods, services are valued/priced. This has had devastating effects on some localities, industries, firms and workers. Thus salaries of financial experts and the profits of financial services firms began to grow sharply in the 1980s while wages of blue-collar workers and profits of many traditional manufacturing firms sank. We can expect more of this. At times the devastation hits sectors that are part of a well-balanced economic system and hence it becomes counterproductive for economic growth.

B The formation of a new production complex According to standard conceptions about information industries, the rapid growth and disproportionate concentration of producer services in central cities should not have happened. Because they are thoroughly embedded in the most advanced information technologies, producer services could be expected to have locational options that bypass the high costs and congestion typical of major cities. But cities offer agglomeration economies and highly innovative environments. The growing complexity, diversity, and specialization of the services required have contributed to the economic viability of a freestanding specialized service sector.

The production process in these services benefits from proximity to other specialized services. This is especially the case in the leading and most innovative sectors of these industries. Complexity and innovation often require multiple highly specialized inputs from several industries. The production of a financial instrument, for example, requires inputs from accounting, advertising, legal expertise, economic consulting, public relations, designers, and printers. The particular characteristics of production of these services, especially those involved in complex and innovative operations, explain their pronounced concentration in major cities. The commonly heard explanation that high-level professionals require face-to-face interactions needs to be refined in several ways. Producer services, unlike other types of services, are not necessarily dependent on spatial proximity to the consumers, i.e. firms, served. Rather, economies occur in such specialized firms when they locate close to others that produce key inputs or whose proximity makes possible joint production of certain service offerings. The accounting firm can service its clients at a distance, but the nature of its service depends on proximity to specialists, lawyers, programmers. Moreover, concentration arises out of the needs and expectations of the people likely to be employed in these new high-skill jobs, who tend to be attracted to the amenities and lifestyles that large urban centers can offer. Frequently, what is thought of as face-to-face communication is actually a production process that requires multiple simultaneous inputs and feedbacks. At the current stage of technical development, immediate and simultaneous access to the pertinent experts is still the most effective way, especially when dealing with a highly complex product. The concentration of the most advanced telecommunications and computer network facilities in major cities is a key factor in what I refer to as the production process of these industries.[6]

Further, time replaces weight in these sectors as a force for agglomeration. In the past, the pressure of the weight of inputs from iron ore to unprocessed agricultural products, was a major constraint pushing toward agglomeration in sites where the heaviest inputs were located. Today, the acceleration of economic transactions and the premium put on time, have created new forces for agglomeration. This is increasingly not the case in routine operations. But where time is of the essence, as it is today in many of the leading sectors of these industries, the benefits of agglomeration are still extremely high – to the point where it is not simply a cost advantage, but an indispensable arrangement.

This combination of constraints suggests that the agglomeration of producer services in major cities actually constitutes a production complex. This producer services complex is intimately connected to the world of corporate headquarters; they are often thought of as forming a joint headquarters-corporate services complex. But in my reading, we need to distinguish the two. Although it is true that headquarters still tend to be disproportionately concentrated in cities, over the last two decades many have moved out. Headquarters can indeed locate outside cities, but they need a producer services complex somewhere in order to buy or contract for the needed specialized services and financing. Further, headquarters of firms with very high overseas activity or in highly innovative and complex lines of business tend to locate in major cities. In brief, firms in more

---

6 The telecommunications infrastructure also contributes to concentration of leading sectors in major cities. Long-distance communications systems increasingly use fiber optic wires. These have several advantages over traditional copper wire: large carrying capacity, high speed, more security, and higher signal strength. Fiber systems tend to connect major communications hubs because they are not easily spliced and hence not desirable for connecting multiple lateral sites. Fiber systems tend to be installed along existing rights of way, whether rail, water or highways (Graham and Marvin, 1996). The growing use of fiber optic systems thus tends to strengthen

routinized lines of activity, with predominantly regional or national markets, appear to be increasingly free to move or install their headquarters outside cities. Firms in highly competitive and innovative lines of activity and/or with a strong world market orientation appear to benefit from being located at the center of major international business centers, no matter how high the costs.

Both types of firms, however, need a corporate services complex to be located somewhere. Where this complex is located is probably increasingly unimportant from the perspective of many, though not all, headquarters. From the perspective of producer services firms, such a specialized complex is most likely to be in a city rather than, for example, a suburban office park. The latter will be the site for producer services firms but not for a services complex. And only such a complex is capable of handling the most advanced and complicated corporate demands.

C The region in the global information age The massive use of telematics in the economy and the corresponding possibility for geographic dispersal and mobility of firms suggest that the whole notion of regional specialization and of the region may become obsolete. But there are indications that, as is the case for large cities, so also for regions the hyper-mobility of information industries and the heightened capacity for geographic dispersal may be only part of the story. The evidence on regional specialization in the US and in other highly developed countries along with new insights into the actual work involved in producing these services point to a different set of outcomes.

What is important from the perspective of the region is that the existence of, for instance, a producer services complex in the major city or cities in a region creates a vast concentration of communications infrastructure which can be of great use to other economic nodes in that region. Such nodes can (and do) connect with the major city or cities in a region and thereby to a worldwide network of firms and markets. The issue from the regional perspective is, then, that somewhere in its territory the region connects with state of the art communication facilities which connect it with the world and which brings foreign firms from all over the world to the region. Given a regional grid of economic nodes, the benefits of this concentration in the major city or cities are no longer confined only to firms located in those cities.

Secondly, given the nature of the production process in advanced information industries, as described in the preceding section, the geographic dispersal of activities has

the major existing telecommunication concentrations and therefore the existing hierarchies.

limits. The importance of actual face-to-face transactions means that a metropolitan or regional network of firms will need conventional communications infrastructure, e.g. highways or rapid rail, and locations not farther than something like two hours. One of the ironies of the new information technologies is that to maximize their use we need access to conventional infrastructure. In the case of international networks it takes airports and planes; and in the case of metropolitan or regional networks, trains and cars.

The importance of conventional infrastructure in the operation of economic sectors that are heavy users of telematics has not received sufficient attention. The dominant notion seems to be that telematics obliterates the need for conventional infrastructure. But it is precisely the nature of the production process in advanced industries, whether they operate globally or nationally, which contributes to explain the immense rise in business travel we have seen in all advanced economies over the last decade, the new electronic era. The virtual office is a far more limited option than a purely technological analysis would suggest. Certain types of economic activities can be run from a virtual office located anywhere. But for work processes requiring multiple specialized inputs, considerable innovation and risk taking, the need for direct interaction with other firms and specialists remains a key locational factor. Hence the metropolitanization and regionalization of an economic sector has boundaries that are set by the time it takes for a reasonable commute to the major city or cities in the region. The irony of today's electronic era is that the older notion of the region and older forms of infrastructure re-emerge as critical for key economic sectors. This type of region in many ways diverges from older forms of region. It corresponds rather to the second form of centrality posited above in this paper – a metropolitan grid of nodes connected via telematics. But for this digital grid to work, conventional infrastructure – ideally of the most advanced kind – is also a necessity.

4 Implications for architecture and urbanism

There is a specific kind of materiality underlying this world of new business activities even if they take place partly in electronic space. Even the most digitalized, globalized and dematerialized sector, notably global finance, hits the ground at some point in its operations. And when it does, it does so in vast concentrations of very material structures. These activities inhabit physical spaces, and they inhabit digital spaces. There are material and digital structures to be built, with very specific requirements – the need to incorporate the fact that a firm's activities are simultaneously partly deterritorialized and partly deeply territorialized, that they span the globe and that they are highly concentrated in very specific places. This produces a strategic geography that cuts across borders and across spaces yet installs itself also in specific cities. It is a geography that explodes the boundaries of contextuality.

One question I would have is whether the specific kind of materiality underlying this interface economy carries implications for architecture, rather than simply 'building'. There would seem to be three issues here. One is the particular type of subeconomy this is: internally networked, partly digital, mostly oriented to global markets and to a large extent operating out of multiple sites around the world. The second is a more elusive, and perhaps purely theoretical issue – though I do not think so – which has to do with the point of intersection between the physical and the digital spaces within which a firm or, more generally this subeconomy operates. The third is the matter of contextuality in architectural practice. The particular characteristics of this networked subeconomy (partly deeply centered in particular sites, partly deterritorialized and operating on a global digital span) would seem to unbundle established concepts of context, the local setting for building, etc.

A **Networked subeconomy** To a large extent this sector is constituted through a large number of relatively small, highly specialized firms. Even if some of the financial services firms, especially given recent mergers, can mobilize enormous amounts of capital and control enormous assets, they are small firms in terms of employment and the actual physical space they occupy compared, for example, with the large manufacturing firms. The latter are far more labor intensive, no matter how automated their production process might be, and require vastly larger amounts of physical space. Secondly, as developed earlier, specialized service firms need and benefit from proximity to kindred specialized firms-financial services, legal services, accounting, economic forecasting, credit rating and other advisory services, computer specialists, public relations, and several other types of expertise in a broad range of fields.

Physical proximity has clearly emerged as an advantage insofar as time is of the essence and the complexity is such that direct transactions are often more efficient and cheaper than telecommunications (it would take enormous bandwidth and you would still not have the full array of acts of communication – the shorthand way in which enormous amounts of information can be exchanged). But, at the same time, this networked sector has global span and definitely operates partly in digital space, so it is networked also in a deterritorialized way, one not pivoting on physical proximity.[7]

5 The intersection between actual and digital space

There is a new topography of economic activity, sharply evident in this subeconomy. This topography weaves in and out between actual and digital space. There is today no fully virtualized firm or economic sector. Even finance, the most digitalized, dematerialized and globalized of all activities has a topography that weaves back and forth between actual and digital space.[8] To different extents in different types of sectors and different types of firms, a firm's tasks now are distributed across these two kinds of spaces; further the actual configurations are subject to considerable transformation as tasks are computerized or standardized, markets are further globalized, etc. More generally, telematics and globalization have emerged as funda-mental forces reshaping the organization of economic space.

The question I have for architects here is whether the point of inter-section between these two kinds of spaces in a firm's or a dynamic's topography of activity, is one worth thinking about, theorizing, exploring. This intersection is unwittingly, perhaps, thought of as a line that divides two mutually exclusive zones. I would propose, again, to open up this line into an 'analytic borderland' which demands its own empirical specification and theorization, and contains its own possibilities for architecture. The

---

7 I examine some of these issues, particularly the future of financial centers given electronic trading and the new strategic alliances between the major financial centers, in **Foreign Affairs** January 1999 – in a non-specialist version.

8 Another angle into these issues came out of last year's Aspen Roundtable on Electronic Commerce (Aspen, Colorado, August 21-23, 1997), an annual event that brings together the CEOs of the main software and hardware firms as well as the key venture capitalists in the sector. See **The Global Advance of Electronic Commerce. Reinventing Markets**,

space of the computer screen, which one might posit as one version of the intersection, will not do, or is at most a partial enactment of this intersection.[9]

What does contextuality mean in this setting? A networked subeconomy that operates partly in actual space and partly in globe-spanning digital space cannot easily be contextualized in terms of its surroundings. Nor can the individual firms. The orientation is simultaneously towards itself and towards the global. The intensity of its internal transactions is such that it overrides all considerations of the broader locality or region within which it exists. On another, larger scale, in my research on global cities I found rather clearly that these cities develop a stronger orientation towards the global markets than to their hinterlands. Thereby they override a key proposition in the urban systems literature, to wit, that cities and urban systems integrate, articulate national territory. This may have been the case during the period when mass manufacturing and mass consumption were the dominant growth machines in developed economies and thrived on the possibility of a national scale.

But it is not today with the ascendance of digitalized, globalized, dematerialized sectors such as finance. The connections with other zones and sectors in its 'context' are of a special sort – one that connects worlds that we think of as radically distinct. For instance, the informal economy in several immigrant communities in New York provides some of the low-wage workers for the 'other' jobs on Wall Street, the capital of global finance. The same is happening in Paris, London, Frankfurt, Zurich. Yet these other zones and other workers are not considered to be part of the context, the locality, of the networked subeconomy I have been speaking of – even if, in my reading, they are.

What then is the 'context', the local, here? The new networked subeconomy occupies a strategic geography, partly deterritorialized, that cuts across borders and connects a variety of points on the globe. It occupies only a fraction of its 'local' setting, its boundaries are not those of the city where it is partly located, nor those of the 'neighborhood'. This subeconomy interfaces the intensity of the vast concentration of very material resources it needs when it hits the ground and the fact of its global span or cross-border geography. Its interlocutor is not the surrounding, the context, but the fact of the global.

I am not sure what this tearing away of the context and its replacement with the fact of the global could mean for architecture. The strategic operation is not the search for a connection with the 'surroundings', the context. It is, rather, installation in a strategic

Management and National Sovereignty, Washington D.C., The Aspen Institute, Communications and Society Program, 1998.
9 The work by John Seely Brown (Xerox Parc) on the space of the screen is among the most sophisticated and promising.

cross-border geography constituted through multiple 'locals'. In the case of the economy I see a re-scaling: old hierarchies – local, regional, national, global – do not hold. Going to the next scale in terms of size is no longer how integration is achieved. The local now transacts directly with the global – the global installs itself in locals and the global is itself constituted through a multiplicity of locals.[10]

6 Conclusion

Economic globalization and telecommunications have contributed to produce a spatiality for the urban that pivots on cross-border networks and territorial locations with massive concentrations of resources. This is not a completely new feature. Over the centuries cities have been at the crossroads of major often worldwide processes. What is different today is the intensity, complexity and global span of these networks, the extent to which significant portions of economies are now dematerialized and digitalized and hence the extent to which they can travel at great speeds through some of these networks, and, thirdly, the numbers of cities that are part of cross-border networks operating at vast geographic scales.

The new urban spatiality thus produced is partial in a double sense: it accounts for only part of what happens in cities and what cities are about, and it inhabits only part of what we might think of as the space of the city, whether this be understood in terms as diverse as those of a city's administrative boundaries or in the sense of a city's public imaginary. What stands out, however, is the extent to which the city remains an integral part of these new configurations.

---

10 I also see this in the political realm, particularly the kind of 'global' politics attributed to the Internet. I think of it rather as a multiplicity of localized operations, but with a difference, they are part of the global network that is the Internet. This produces a 'knowing' that re-marks the local. See the chapter 'Electronic Space and Power' in **Globalization and its Discontents**, New York, New Press, 1998.

Select bibliography

Brotchie, J. and M. Barry, E. Blakely, P. Hall, and P. Newton (eds.), **Cities in Competition: Productive and Sustainable Cities for the 21st Century**, Melbourne, Longman Australia, 1995.

Castells, M., **The Informational City**, London, Blackwell, 1989.

Cohen, Michael A., Blair A. Ruble, Joseph S. Tulchin, and Allison M. Garland (eds.), **Preparing for the Urban Future. Global Pressures and Local Forces,** Washington D.C., Woodrow Wilson Center Press, 1996, distributed by The Johns Hopkins University Press.

Daniels, Peter W., 'Producer Services and the Development of the Space Economy' in Daniels, Peter W. and Frank Moulaert (eds.) **The Changing Geography of Advanced Producer Services**, London/New York, Belhaven Press, 1991.

Le Debat. Le Nouveau Paris, Special Issue, Summer 1994, Paris, Gallimard.

European Institute of Urban Affairs, **Urbanisation and the Functions of Cities in the European Community: A Report to Commission of the European Communities Directorate General for Regional Policy (XVI)**, Liverpool, Liverpool John Moores University, April, 1992.

Fainstein, Susan, **The City Builders**, Oxford, Blackwell, 1993.

Fainstein, S., I. Gordon, and M. Harloe, **Divided City: Economic Restructuring and Social Change in London and New York**, New York, Blackwell, 1993.

Frost, Martin and Nigel Spence, 'Global City Characteristics and Central London's Employment', **Urban Studies**, Vol. 30, No. 3, 1992, pp.547-558.

Futur Anterieur, special issue **La Ville-Monde Aujourd'hui: Entre Virtualité et Ancragé**, (Edited by Thierry Pillon and Anne Querrien), Vols. 30-32, Paris, L'Harmattan, 1995.

Gad, Gunter, 'Toronto's Financial District', **Canadian Urban Landscapes-1**, 1991, pp.203-207.

Garcia, Linda, 'The Globalization of Telecommunications and Information' in Drake, William J. (ed.) **The New Information Infrastructure: Strategies for US Policy**, New York, Twentieth Century Fund Press, 1995, pp.75-92.

The Journal of Urban Technology, special issue, **Information Technologies and Inner-City Communities**, Vol. 3, no. 1 (Fall), 1995.

Graham, Stephen and Simon Marvin, **Telecommunications and the City: electronic spaces, urban places,** London, Routledge, 1996.

Gravesteijn, S.G.E., S. van Griensven, and M.C. de Smidt (eds.), **Timing global cities, Nederlandse Geografische Studies**, 241, Utrecht, 1998.

King, A.D. (ed.), **Representing the City. Ethnicity, Capital and Culture in the 21st Century**, London, Macmillan, 1995.

Kloosterman, Robert C, 'Double Dutch: Polarization Trends in Amsterdam and Rotterdam after 1980', **Regional Studie**, 30, 5, 1996.

Paul L. Knox and Peter J. Taylor (eds.), **World Cities in a World-System**, Cambridge UK, Cambridge University Press, 1995.

Kowarick, L. and M. Campanario, 'São Paulo: the price of world city status', **Development and Change**, 17(1), 1986, pp.159-74.

Noyelle, T. and A.B. Dutka, **International Trade in Business Services: Accounting, Advertising, Law and Management Consulting**, Cambridge MA, Ballinger Publishing, 1988.

Olds, Kris, Peter Dicken, Philip F. Kelly, Lilly Kong, and Henry Wai-Chung Yeung (eds.), **Globalization and the Asian Pacific**: **Contested Territories**, London, Routledge, 1999.

Peraldi, Michel and Evelyne Perrin (eds.), **Réseaux Productifs et Territoires Urbains**, Toulouse, Presses Universitaires du Mirail, 1996.

Petz, Ursula von and Klaus M. Schmals (eds.), **Metropole, Weltstadt, Global City: Neue Formen der Urbanisierung**, Dortmund, Dortmunder Beitrage zur Raumplanung, Vol. 60, Universitat Dortmund, 1992.

Pozos Ponce, Fernando, **Metropolis en reestructuracion: Guadalajara y Monterrey 1980-1989**, Guadalajar, Mex, Universidad de Guadalajara, con apoyo de El Fondo para la Modernizacion de la Educacion Superior, 1996.

Sachar, A, 'The global economy and world cities' in A. Sachar and S. Oberg (eds.) **The World Economy and the Spatial Organization of Power**, Aldershot, Avebury, 1990, pp.149-60.

Santos, Milton, Maria Adelia A. De Souze, and Maria Laura Silveira (eds.), **Territorio Globalizacao e Fragmentacao**, São Paulo, Editorial Hucitec, 1994.

Sassen, Saskia, **Globalization and its Discontents**, New York, New Press, 1998.

Sassen, Saskia, **Cities in a World Economy**, Thousand Oaks, Pine Forge/Sage Press (New updated edition), 2000.

Sassen, Saskia, **The Global City: New York, London, Tokyo**, Princeton University Press, 1991.

Stren, Richard, 'The Studies of Cities: Popular Perceptions, Academic Disciplines, and Emerging Agendas' in Cohen et al. (eds.), op.cit, 1996, pp.392-420.

Simon, David, 'The world city hypothesis: reflections from the periphery', In Knox and Taylor (eds.), op. cit., 1995, pp.132-155.

Todd, Graham, '"Going Global" in the semi-periphery: world cities as political projects. The case of Toronto', in Knox and Taylor (eds.), op. cit., 1995, pp.192-214.

Wentz, Martin (ed.), **Stadtplanung in Frankfurt: Wohnen, Arbeiten, Verkehr**, Frankfurt am Main/New York, Campus, 1991.

Veltz, Pierre, **Mondialisation Villes et Territoires: L'Economie d'Archipel**, Paris, Presses Universitaires de France, 1996.

The Past which **Is**: The Present that **Was** Benjamin and the Bergson trajectory

Deborah Hauptmann

1   Walter Benjamin, 'Some Motifs in Baudelaire' in: **Charles Baudelaire, a lyric poet in the era of high capitalism**, Verso, 1997. First published in English as 'On Some Motifs in Baudelaire', **Illuminations**, edited by Hannah Arendt, Harcourt Brace Jovanovich, New York, 1968. The original essay was written in 1939 in response to a critique by Theodor Adorno on **The Paris of the Second Empire in Baudelaire** completed the previous year.

2   By current society I mean not only that carried with the names of 'high modernity' (Habermas, Giddens) or 'post modernity' (Harvey, Castells) but that considered most broadly under the discourse supporting the critique of 'information society'. And with this I include such writers as Deleuze, Virilio and Haraway, Lash, Douglas Rushkoff, and as predecessor to these late 20th century thinkers, I enter this discussion with Benjamin.

Resonance   In the opening line of *On Some Motifs in Baudelaire* Benjamin writes: 'Baudelaire envisaged readers to whom the reading of lyric poetry would present difficulties.' He goes on to question whether lyric poetry remained capable of resonating with the masses, with their experience of modernity. Benjamin continues: 'If conditions for a positive reception of lyric poetry have become less favorable, it is reasonable to assume that only in rare instances is lyric poetry in rapport with the experience of its readers. This may be due to the change in structure of their experience.'[1]

Consistent with Benjamin, writers of the late 20th century have problematized questions of *experience* in terms of space and time, and it is to the furthering of this query that this paper will address the constituent elements of experience as they were brought forward in Benjamin's essay; these elements include primarily a discussion on memory and perception and these as they are related to the domains of time and space. For perhaps by examining these structures of experience as Benjamin approximated them in terms of modernity we may better address the constituents of experience, as they exist in our current society.[2]

Bergson's trajectory   In order to address the 'problem of experience' Benjamin suggests that we must look to philosophy and the philosopher he turned to was Henri Bergson. He begins his discussion on Bergson by challenging his philosophical notions with the literary work of Marcel Proust; he further argues that an understanding of Baudelaire must include a reading of Proust. And just as Benjamin constructs a trajectory which links these thinkers of Modernity, it is conceivable that we too can imagine such a course. One which will also pass through Bergson on a journey towards thinkers such as Virilio, Haraway, Rushkoff, and Lash and of course, Deleuze.[3] And most importantly, passing through Bergson forces us to reconsider our use of the terms so freely applied in discussions over 'time' and 'space'. In terms of architecture and urbanism this is an especially difficult task, to ask that we apprehend our language from within a discourse, which for such obvious reasons, privileges space over time. Even Virilio, who with amazing acumen and fluency of thought, almost makes us believe that the immediacy of time has superceded mediations on space, continues to beg the question 'where did the *here* of the here and now go?'

---

3   See: Gilles Deleuze, **Bergsonism**, Zone Books, New York, 1988. Originally published, **Le Bergsonisme**, Presses Universitaires de France, 1966. In the afterword of **Bergsonism** Deleuze suggest an extension of Bergson's project in terms of three primary concepts: **Intuition** – as a method which utilizes the means of differentiation on one hand and convergence on the other, 'the two successive turns in experience', in establishing true and false problem statements. **Metaphysics** – in relation to immanence and duration '… a metaphysical image of thought corresponding to the new lines, openings, traces, leaps, dynamisms discovered by molecular biology… new linkings and re-linkings in thought.' And **Multiplicities** – which he distinguishes in terms of the spatial and temporal, the actual and the virtual, 'this is perhaps one of the least appreciated aspects of his thought – the constitution of a logic of multiplicities.'

Perception of memory/memory of perception

Benjamin begins his discussion on Bergson by questioning memory as
both an element within and a condition of Proust's work. He suggests that,
with memory, we witness in Proust 'an attempt to produce experience
synthetically… under today's conditions in for there is less and less hope
that it will come into being naturally.'[4] In this he is referring to Proust's
lament over the inability of the intellect to summons the past upon will,
within the 'mémoire volontaire'. What Proust then terms 'mémoire
involontaire' is subjected to chance encounter. Proust writes that the past
is 'somewhere beyond the reach of the intellect, and unmistakably present
in some material object… As for that object, it depends entirely on chance
whether we come upon it before we die or whether we never encounter it.'[5]
Of course Proust is here referring to the material object which acts as
trace, which triggers a recall of a past image, a moment in time actualized
if not realized and either way a moment that has a form of objective
existence on a time trajectory which moves in a direction from this
moment *back* towards moments past. The past so understood constitutes
the entire of our history. Of course, when Proust recalls a 'moment' it may
take him ten pages of written description in order to detail the moment
with all its nuances and significance, thus we see not the compression of
time and space (into an instance, an event) but the absolute extension of
time through space (spatializing all emotion, feeling and sensation so that
it transcends the moment into the finitude of the infinite). Nevertheless,
what remains is the fortuitous dependency on chance which allows for
the breach between one's past and one's present, between tradition and
progression; as Benjamin writes, according to Proust 'it is a matter of
chance whether an individual forms an image of himself, whether he can
take hold of his experience.'[6]

Benjamin parallels Proust's mémoire involontaire to Bergson's concept
of 'mémoire pure' yet he does not elaborate their difference. For the pure
memory of Bergson must be described in subtly, yet fundamentally,
different terms.[7] To begin with, 'pure memory' must be understood as

4 'Some Motifs in Baudelaire', p.111.
5 Ibid. p.112.
6 Ibid. p.112. Further, Benjamin's work on Kafka is perhaps especially relevant to this breach
between progress and tradition, as is his oft-cited critique of Klee's '**Angelus Novus**', which
might, while utilizing a critique of Bergson, allow us to imagine the angel's face not turned only
to the past but also to the future.

having an intimate and immediate relation with the present, while constituting the whole of the past; as with Proust this includes history and pre-history, both personal and collective. It acts in terms of 'movement', it does not collect itself in terms of 'moments'. Further, its movement is continuous and fluid – in terms of time; not contiguous and contingent – in terms of space. Bergson's pure memory is to time what perception is to space and further, perception itself would be impossible without it. Memory as such is not a memory of a perception to be recovered as a *remembrance of things past*, nor is it a vague notion of a lost instance or distant image (as representation) which can be called forward and re-lived; for it *is*-lived, and it is of the essence of time, in that which Bergson terms 'durée' (duration): a concept which we will return to later.

Simply stated, in the terms of Proust, it is through our present, through our accidental encounter with objects that we may, or may not, recover our past. In the terms of Bergson it is by virtue of the past that we are able to actualize our present.

For now however, we must return to Proust for it is necessary to ask how it is that man can become dependent on a 'chance encounter' with his past in order to 'take hold of his experience'. Benjamin argues that it is because man is becoming isolated from his ability to 'assimilate the data of the world around him by way of experience'.[8] Modern man, (his very consciousness) had become alienated from his neighbor, his city, his own identity lost in the masses (struggling in the breach between tradition and progress). But moreover, he had become isolated from his very relationship to 'things'; for Bergson this would include the entire of *matter and memory* itself. The example that Benjamin draws on to explain this is mass media: where it is the intention of media to present the 'information of the day' in a manner that above all allows the reader to dis-associate himself from even the possibility of an engagement with the 'events' being delivered. Further, that the structure of this media itself follows this principle of dis-association by avoiding any links, or affinities, to be established with the various articles of news. In other words, it is non-narrative, it has no need for memory, for the past, but is attempting to present only the 'present' – it is, in this sense, pure stimuli, in fact, synthetic. How then was modern man supposed to recover, much less to recall, himself in this flux, within this barrage of meaningless, non symbolic images and information? And if he had become disassociated from experience then how was he to reflect upon the consequences of his actions? Again,

7 Benjamin cites form: Henri Bergson, **Matière et Mémoire, Essai sur la relation du corps à l'esprit**, Paris, 1933.
8 'Some Motifs in Baudelaire', p.112.

the point is worth reiteration, not merely alienation – the recognition of one's 'otherness'; but absolute isolation – the realization of one's inconsolable, if not irreconcilable, 'absence'. In this sense it is not so difficult to see why terms such as 'shock', 'horror' and 'revulsion' were so commonly used by writers from Baudelaire, Poe, and Kafka to Engels and Freud to describe modern man's encounter with the density of the nameless crowd as it manifested a change in the 'structure of experience'.

Stimuli/hide & seek In part III of *Some Motifs on Baudelaire*, Benjamin turns in the direction of Freud and his 1923 essay *Beyond the Pleasure Principle*. What is important in this excerpt on Freud is not to follow the structural categories or logic of the original work (although it is relevant to note that for Freud memory and consciousness operate in mutually exclusive systems) but to draw upon it in order to introduce the idea of unmediated stimuli resulting in 'shock'. For consciousness, which is disassociated from memory, does not act as the perceptive receptor of memory (nor as the actualization of perception through memory), it is not, in other words, the awareness of a present moment on a trajectory directed to the past. Its function, following Freudian theorists, is not to process but to protect, to intercept, to deflect, and guard man from the ever-present threat of (un-assimilated) stimuli. Benjamin writes that the unique achievement of the shock defense 'may be seen in its function of assigning to an incident a precise point in time in consciousness at the cost of the integrity of its contents.' He continues, saying that 'this would be a peak achievement of the intellect; it would turn the incident into a moment that has been lived' and even further, as an incident which, 'at its most powerful and enduring never actually enters consciousness'. A virtual condition which never actually *actualizes*; 'without reflection there would be nothing but the sudden start, usually the sensation of fright…' [9]

This sensation of fright, so described, becomes a state of being in Baudelaire. Manifested externally in the form of his mannerisms (body/matter), and internally in the nature of his personality (spirit/memory), in short, his

9   Ibid., p.117.
10   This is perhaps why the great quantity of work produced by contemporary critique on the subject of Baudelaire's 'flaneur' is beginning to tend towards conceptual redundancy.

entire being. But more importantly, it is a state which he negotiates in order to both engage the city (within space) and simultaneously distance himself from the crowd (within time). In other words, he contracts the space of the incident and time of the lived to the point where they cross trajectories, neither one or the other, but the both/and of the virtual, not on its way to action but in the self-preserving necessity to elude realization. This 'shock' as it is absorbed (contracted) by Baudelaire both reveals and re-veils itself by virtue of the hidden figure of the crowd; but it is interesting to note that both the crowd, and the city that contains it are only rarely actualized, either in terms of space or time, in his work.[10]

Benjamin writes: 'the masses had become so much a part of Baudelaire that it is rare to find a description of them in his works. His most important subjects are hardly ever encountered in descriptive form… it is futile to search in 'les Fleurs du mal' or in 'Spleen de Paris' for any counterpart to the portrayals of the city which Victor Hugo wrote with such mastery. Baudelaire describes neither the Parisians nor their city. Forgoing such descriptions enables him to invoke the one in the form of the other.'[11] Neither the mass nor the city is described, but each is called upon, one in the figure of the other. In other words, they are 'present without being represented': 'It is true that an image may be without being perceived – it may be present without being represented – and the distance between these two terms, presence and representation, seems just to measure the interval between matter itself and our conscious perception of matter.'[12]

If, as suggested above, a stimulus evades the deflection of consciousness and is recorded directly in 'conscious memory' then, according to Benjamin, 'It would sterilize this incident for poetic experience'. I am reminded of a favorite passage in the Artist's Confiteor of *Paris Spleen*: '… These thoughts, whether they come from me or spring from things, soon, at all events, grow too intense. Energy in voluptuousness creates uneasiness and actual pain. My nerves are strung to such a pitch that they can no longer give out anything but shrill and painful vibrations.' Thus, if a stimulus gets past the barricades of consciousness it would be neutralized into the non-actualized experience. And this suggests precisely the problem of lyric poetry for 'how can it have as its basis an experience for which the shock experience is the norm.'[13] How can a representational form based on metaphoric narration resonate with the masses when the structure of experience has shifted to a theory based not in recognition, but in deflection? Of course, Benjamin alludes to this in his embrace

11 'Some Motifs in Baudelaire', p.122.

12 Henri Bergson, **Matter and Memory**, Zone Books, New York, 1988, p.35.
Authorized translation, Nancy Margaret Paul and W. Scott Palmer, London, 1911.
(Originally published as **Matière et Mémoire**, Presses Universitaires de France, 1896).
It should also be noted that any reading of Bergson on the topics cited in this essay
should include his **Time and Free Will** of 1889.

13 'Some Motifs in Baudelaire', p.116.

of the technological invention of cinematic film. Where he speaks of the 'new and urgent' need of the masses for stimuli. Where in film, 'perception in the form of shocks was established as a formal principle.'[14]

When shock becomes a formal principle, when it has been incorporated into the body of our desires, the notion of 'stimuli' becomes a different matter altogether: what before could be seen as a new product of consumption, witnessed critically by the advent of film; today can be witnessed, for instance, in urbanism's focus on the 'event', and further on architecture's reliance on the object of presentation, not the (Proustian) image of representation. Stimuli, as seen today, in the simple form of presence, of image as (already neutralized) information to be individually appropriated and culturally acquisitioned. Further, and importantly, stimuli which are already beyond mass media theories of ideological consciousness (Enzensberger) and self-conscious reflection. According to Freud, when shock has been incorporated by memory, it manifests itself in trauma; but if we begin, as Bergson does, with memory then it is perception which buffers us in the form of the virtual. For in Bergson, only when a virtual action – and all objects, all images exist as virtual bodies in space – moves into a determinable proximity with our body, are we compelled towards action, and with action the virtual passes to the real. That which we may be missing in our current understanding of stimuli, as a (less-threatening) condition of information flow, is precisely Bergson's notion on the image as that which lies between representation and the 'thing' in itself. He writes: '…my perception is outside my body and my affection within it… so my affective states are experienced where they occur, that is, at a given point in my body.'[15] It is interesting to note that 'of all the experiences that made his life what it was, Baudelaire singled out his having been jostled by the crowd as the decisive, unique experience.'[16]

The body as conscious experience, not only consciousness as a mental state, as the last line, the last site of resistance.

14 ibid., p.132.
15 **Matter and Memory**, 1988, p.57.
16 'Some Motifs in Baudelaire', p.154.

The past 'is'/The present 'was' Now, if we return to this idea of disassociation as that which not only estranges modern man from his own identity, but from the space of his own occupation within the world where he performs, we will find that in contemporary society it is precisely a new form of 'disassociation', of distancing as a self-conscious (self-actual-izing) act of appropriation which accommodates a new form of 'associative' experience.

Douglas Rushkoff writes on a current manner of processing stimuli into information, and of information into knowledge under the terms of 'recapitulation'. He distinguishes the presentation of information directed at knowledge from that of data directed at the accumulation of information into categories of storytelling: 'instructional' (real-life exchange of experience as a survival method in pre-history – literal), 'metaphorical' (narrative exchange or experience which functions with the 'like me' recognition of similarity through empathetic recognition – symbolic) and 'recapitulation' (the intentional distancing from emotional reality through 'self-conscious awareness' – non representational). Of course, it is the last which interest us here for it addresses the 'change in experience' which today constitutes our memory and perception, the virtual and the real, the actualized and the lived.

The play within the play compels the 'self-conscious' recognition of the 'self-similar', not the 'like me reflection' of parable, but the 'actuated me' of recapitulation. Benjamin writes: 'The so-called immortal works just flash briefly through every present time. Hamlet is one of the very fastest, the hardest to grasp.'[17] Rushkoff too points to Shakespeare; but also to Brecht, as one of the first 'moderns' to realize the necessity of recapitulation with the technique which he developed and called the 'alienation effect'. With this Brecht attempts to draw the viewer into the play by rearranging the structure of the role oppositions of actor/audience. He disabled the pause of the curtains draw between acts, he pulled the audience into the entire production and thus created plays within plays – one of the story being told, the other of the action of telling it. Forcing the audience to be constantly aware both of the self-conscious position of the actors on stage and of their own self-conscious involvement with the issues, with the message, which the play itself performed. As Rushkoff writes, 'Instead of looking within the context of the play on stage for the answers that Brecht's tragic characters could not find, we look outside the theater into our very real world.'[18]

---

17 Walter Benjamin, **Selected writings, vol. II**, Cambridge, London, 1999, p.285 (fragment written circa 1929).
18 Douglas Rushkoff, **Children of Chaos**, Harper Collins, London, 1997, p.224.

Recapitulation as it acts today allows for an immediate engagement with media, with the flow of images and information which are ever present, ever ready to flood over us with a rush which, without an effective manner of processing, could serve further to alienate us from our selves, conflate our own identities, to disassociate us further from our societies with an effect beyond the traumatic and bordering, no less than, on the schizophrenic. When there is no time for reflection, no time even for reflexivity, we are forced to engage in the action as actors and this form of recapitulated engagement is the only thing which sustains our sense of agency, and further, allows for us to experience a sense of commonality, of community. 'Why is recapitulation necessarily more advanced or better than literal or metaphorical understandings of our world? Because it is capable of representing our chaotic cultural experience in a manner that allows us to relate to it. It gives us an insight into how nature works, and motivates us to become more fully conscious and self-determining.'[19]

The processing of information streams has passed through the objectivity of 'reflection', through the subjectivity of the 'reflexive' to a form of a-subjective 'recapitulation'. Virilio too writes of recapitulation as a '… pure phenomenon of speed, a phenomenon on the way to the realization of its absolute essence.'[20] What is interesting in Virilio is that we see not merely the presence of immediacy but that of the instantaneous. The instantiation of time within space, not the immediacy of space within time. And it is precisely this inversion, this apparent privileging of time over space which gives to his work the sense of the loss of human agency. In Bergson this idea of the 'instantaneous' is understood as a mechanistic, or reflex reaction whereby time is forcibly 'sectioned' off as if its composite properties were similar to those of space. Whereas subjectivity (as I am describing in terms of the immediate, a-subjective) is 'affectivity' itself, externalized in image, and internalized as memory. Although these terms as they are used by Virilio and Bergson are the same, what they denote is exactly inverted. Nevertheless, it is precisely this 'illusion of loss' within the sense of the non-mediated and instantaneous, that we should work through to form

19 Ibid., p.228.
20 Paul Virilio, **The Aesthetics of Disappearance**, Semiotext(e), New York, 1991, trans. Philip Beitchman, p.44. (originally published in 1980).

a more critical position in our search for the condition – the 'structure of experience' – in which man now appears destined not only to 'react' but to 'act'. These notions lead Bergson to advance the conclusion that the past should be referred to as that which 'is' while the present must be always understood as that which 'was'.[21]

Multiplicities of Immanence/Sites of Transcendence

In 1918 Benjamin writes that the 'task of coming philosophy can be conceived as the discovery or creation of that concept of knowledge which, by relating experience *exclusively* to the transcendental consciousness, makes not only mechanical but also f-religious experience logically possible.' And he continues: 'With a new concept of knowledge, therefore, not only the concept of experience but also that of freedom will undergo a decisive transformation.'[22]

In part X of *Some Motifs on Baudelaire* Benjamin, like Proust, summoning time, brings forward Bergson's concept of durée. He suggests that Bergson's durée is essentially a-historical; that it functions to isolate man from history, and from ritual. Some readers of Bergson may take issue with this interpretation as a misapplication of his metaphysics, however, the position he draws from it remains relevant; for in this we must imagine that he understood duration as absolute presence, presence without the structural trajectory of memory (perhaps what we refer to too carelessly today as 'real time'). He cites Horkheimer who writes that 'Bergson the metaphysician suppresses death.' And Benjamin continues that the durée 'from which death is eliminated has the miserable endlessness of a scroll. Tradition is excluded from it. It is the quintessence of a passing moment that struts about in the borrowed garb of experience. The *spleen*, on the other hand exposes the passing moment in all its nakedness.'[23] The pure presence of time is understood here not as a condition to be valued as pure experience of the present, but as an eradication of experience, an annihilation of being. And in this, though he allows for the poetic surrender of Proust to this 'new structure of experience' he maintains the quality of transcendence in Baudelaire.

Proust also writes that time is 'peculiarly chopped up in Baudelaire', and Benjamin continues, 'they are days of recollection, not marked by any experience… (they) stand out from time.'[24] As such, they are days of waiting, of passing moments standing as segments

---

21 See: **Matter and Memory**, 1988, chapter 1. And Gilles Deleuze, **Bergsonism**, Zone Books, New York, 1991, trans. Hugh Tomlinson, chapter 3 (originally published as **Le Bergsonisme**, Press Universitaires de France, 1966).

22 Walter Benjamin, **Selected writings, vol. I**, Cambridge/London, 1996, p.105. From the essay 'The Coming Philosophy' (which contains primarily a neo-Kantian critique of transformations regarding the domains of knowledge and experience).

23 'Some Motifs in Baudelaire', p.144-145.

they can only occupy space: the space of the day in wait of transcendence. How much more incompatible could this be with Bergson's multiplicities of flow, with his process of perpetual becoming. Benjamin's understanding of days which cannot be lived, but only thought; in the Deleuzian sense become days which cannot be thought but only lived. With Deleuze we see Bergsonism brought forward into the lived experience, into a multiplicity of planes of immanence: the radical immanence of the process of perpetual becoming. The 'embodied intensity... a process of approaching what we are, that is to say reducing oneself to the naked bone of one's speed of rememoration, one's capacity for perception, one's empathy for and impact on others.'[25]

For Bergson the most common error of philosophy is that it confuses matters of degrees with matters of kind: domains of space (fundamentally homogeneous, quantitative and extensive) with those of time (essentially heterogeneous, qualitative and intensive). Space as extrinsic and mediated (perception) and time as intrinsic and immediate (memory). He understands movement (time) as the fundamental principle of life, motion as the essence of existence, continuity and heterogeneity as the two fundamental characteristics of duration. Duration is always seen as the process of continual changes in kind, not in degrees, it is *transition* in its purist form.

The activity of transcendence, which always alludes to the spatial domain of experience in terms of a passage from one realm (the unperfected of the lived, the body) to the next (the perfected of the absolute, the spirit) thus establishes itself in a domain which can only admit to differences of degrees when in fact, the discussion must revolve on distinctions in kind.[26] And even then, when it does address time, it poses itself within the logic of linear time as that which can be somehow apprehended (further compounded by the mechanical ability of the cinematic freezing of movement thus constructing the illusion of sequential and spatial delineation). Immanence, on the other hand is understood as the simultaneous unfolding of multiplicities both physical and spiritual, both matter and memory at

24 Ibid., p.139.
25 Rosi Braidotti, **Meta(l)morphosis**, cited from conference proceedings, **The Politics of Gilles Deleuze**, Amsterdam School of Cultural Analysis (ASCA), Amsterdam University, April, 1999.
26 Bergson regularly points to what he sees as this 'confusion of composites' within the work of other philosophers, Kant and Hegel amongst them.

once, it cannot be apprehended but only approximated in movement, it can never be fixed for motion itself is molecular. Thus we find one of the basic rules of Bergsonian logic – 'all problems related to subject and object must be stated in terms of time rather than space.'[27]

The city *in* 'transition', in immanent and perpetual flows; not the city undergoing transition, in transcendent structural change (i.e. modern consciousness to post-modern condition to techno-informational flux). Perhaps the distance which separates modernity's interpretation of Bergson from contemporary interpretation is precisely this: the search for transcendent states of being, over and against the immanence of the subject embodying the process of becoming; the need for reflection over and against the necessity of recapitulation; and the confusion of domains of space with those of the experience of time. And thus the dilemma of architects and planners who, despite their rhetoric on 'flexibility' and 'spaces of flow', are equivocally addressing problems of heterogeneous flow with incompatible answers in terms of homogeneous spatial fixity.

27 **Matter and Memory**, 1988, p.71. 'Subject and object would unite in an extended perception, the subjective side of perception being the contraction effected by memory, and the objective reality of matter fusing with the multitudinous and successive vibrations into which this perception can be internally broken up… Questions relating to subject and object, to their distinction and their union, should be put in terms of time rather than space.' Also, **Bergsonism**, p.31 (cited as the third rule of the 'intuitive method').

The Gentle Way of Reading and the Montage of the Masses
Franziska Bollerey

Benjamin calls himself a 'ragman'.[1] He writes in his essay on Baudelaire: Ragman or poet – both are concerned with refuse, both jointly follow their profession... even their style is identical. Nadar calls it 'pas saccadé', that is the poet's step who hunts for rhyme-prey in the city. It also has to be the poet's step, who stops in his tracks every other moment.[2] 'Promeneur' constitutes another concept; 'Flaneur' is the most common. In the figure of the flaneur, the delight in looking on, triumphs as a process of concentration on pure observation.

The flaneur's conquest of the street is not a phenomenon of the early 19th century. Critics speak of 'reports written with his legs', when referring to Louis Sebastian Mercier's wanderings through the great city in the middle of the 18th century. Like a lighting technician, he allows his beams to glide over the city, bringing material together for more and more articles, in his 'pictures' of Paris. He was on the go day and night driven by insatiable curiosity.[3] Around 1840 it was fashionable to parade turtles on a leash in the galleries (that Benjamin emphasizes in his title *Passagenwerk*). 'The flaneur willingly adopted the animal's speed as his own. Had he his will, progress would have had to learn it as well. But this was not the last word. It was Taylor who made "down with the flaneur" his slogan, as Georges Friedmann remarks in his *La crise du progès*.'[4]

There is no room for the flaneur in Taylor's age – or should we have one? Wim Wenders with his plea for 'optical breathers' seems to hint at it.

Instigated by Benjamin's literary-philosophical approaches (Bloch calls it 'Passagen-Denken') of the concepts of 'isolation and multitude' I would like to discuss two thematic topics: 'the gentle way of reading' and 'the montage of the masses'. I do this as a historian, to whom the narration of history is intended to give physiognomies to datas. With Benjamin this means: 'to articulate the past as historical is not understanding, "what actually happened" (Leopold von Ranke). It means taking possession of memory, as it has its epiphany in a moment of danger.'[5] 'Only the narrator of history has the ability to kindle a spark of hope in the past' (*Berliner Kindheit um 1900*).[6] According to Benjamin's materialistic way of narrating history the past is not completed, is not a fixed unchangeable part of tradition, but carries the demand for redemption, by some historical index, which we have to find out.

'Cities do not tell a story. But they can tell us a lot about history. Cities can carry their

1 Benjamin, Walter, **Charles Baudelaire. Ein Lyriker im Zeitalter des Hochkapitalismus**, re-issued with an afterword by Rolf Tiedemann, Frankfurt am Main, 1974, pp.17ff.

2 Op. cit., p.79.

3 Mercier, Louis Sebastian, edition: Hamburg/Neuchâtel 1781, Volume 2, Amsterdam, 1782-1788, Paris, 1947 (Ausz.) Translations: **Paris ein Gemählde**, B.G. Walch, Leipzig, 1783-1784, Volume 8; **Schilderung von Paris**, S. G. Bürde, Breslau 1785; **Neuestes Gemählde von Paris für Reisende und Nichtreisende**, H.A.O. Richard, Leipzig, 1789-1790. Volume 2; **Paris, Vorabend der Revolution**, G. Metgen, Karlsruhe 1967 (with foreword). Editions used; Mercier, Louis Sebastian: Tableau de Paris ou explication de différentes figures, gravées, a leau forte, pour servir au differentes éditions du tableau de Paris, Yverdon 1787, German edition: **Bilder der Großstadt in**

The Gentle Way
of Reading and
the Montage
of the Masses

history in themselves and they can show it, they can make it visible, or they can hide it. They can open eyes, just as films can, or they can close them. They can speak out, or they can nurture the imagination' according to Wim Wenders.[7]

'Gazers' allow cities to speak for themselves in that they represent the cities with their respective media, without violating them. Their 'second-hand reality' – that of the gazers – presents itself in order to stir emotions, associations, fantasies. Their perception of the cityscape triggers the creation of new images. The affirmative must be alien to them, since it closes the door on understanding and interpretation. And these are precisely what constitute the material of films, paintings, novels and poems. Gentle exploitation is the polar opposite of aggressive exploitation. Therefore Benjamin defines the power of imagination as 'the gift to interpolate in the informatively small, to supply every intensity as extrusive phenomenon with a new, compressed plenitude, in short, to take every image, as if it were one of a folded fan, which breathes only when unfolded'.

And this is what Wim Wenders gives voice to in the cautious warning that ends his paper *The Urban Landscape*, presented to Japanese architects in Tokyo in 1991: 'I ask you to view your work differently for just one moment, as an exercise in providing future children with a place of origin, cities and landscapes that will form the visual worlds and imaginative powers of these children. And I want you to take into consideration the opposite of what is by definition your work: not only the construction of buildings, but the creation of spaces, so as to preserve emptiness, so that the FULL will not block out our view and so that an emptiness, in which to pause, can be conserved.'[8] Like Sten Nadolny who declares war on speed as the so-called efficient relation to time with *Die Erfahrung der Langsamkeit*[9] (The Experience of Slowness), Wim Wenders pleads for stasis; that is not to say city repair at any price: contemplative rather than affirmative planning corresponds to his ideal vision of the city. There must be room for pauses,

Radierungen von Balthasar Anton Dunker. Nebst Erläuterungen, die auf die nämlichen Kapitel im Werk von Louis Sebastian Mercier verweisen, Neuauflage Berlin, 1989, re-issued by Paul Thiel.

4 Friedmann, Georges, **La crise du progrès. Esquisse d'histoire des idées 1895-1935**, second edition, Paris, 1936, p.76, as quoted in Benjamin, Walter: op. cit., p.53.

5 See also: Benjamin, Walter, **Über den Begriff der Geschichte. 18 Theses auf elf Seiten**, written in 1939 at the earliest, more likely early 1940, published posthumously in 1942. This final completed work of Benjamin examines the relationship of theology to historical materialism, like the critique of progress and historicism.

6 Benjamin, Walter, **Berliner Kindheit um 1900**. Prose by Walter Benjamin, begun in 1932/33

pauses for an optical breather, for reflection, for making sense, for digestion, for suggestion.

Here we are dealing with a cityscape whose meaning is not nurtured merely by its many monuments, nor by its one unmistakable monument, but rather by an image that is an exercise in reading: 'The wall that speaks.'

'I do not know if I have already said that I mean this wall', writes Rainer Maria Rilke in *Aufzeichnungen des Malte Laurids Brigge*:

'One saw its inner side. One saw the walls of rooms on different stories, with wallpaper still clinging to them, here and there the beginning of a floor or ceiling. Next to the walls of the rooms there was a dirty space still running the whole length of the wall, and through this space the open rust spotted conduits of the toilet pipes snaked with an ineffably revolting wormy and at the same time digesting motion. Dusty traces remained near the ceilings that marked the path taken by the pipes for lighting gas, bending here and there in unexpected directions and then around and into the colored wall, into a hole that had been ripped out blackly and carelessly. But the walls themselves were the most unforgettable thing of all. The tenacious life of these rooms had refused to be trodden down. It was still there, hanging onto the remaining nails, standing on the hand span of floorboards still left, creeping into the remnants of corners where a little of the inside of the rooms persisted. One could see that it was in the color that had changed slowly, year by year: blue to moldy green, green to gray and yellow, to an old stale white that now rotted. But it was also in the fresher places that had been conserved behind mirrors, pictures, closets; for it had drawn and traced their outlines and it had also lived there, in hidden, dusty spidery places that now lay bare. It was in every stripe that had been worn away... In it were the noons and the sicknesses and the exhalations and the age-old smoke and sweat that breaks out under the arms and makes clothes heavy, and the staleness of mouths and the rotgut smell of fermenting feet. In it was the sharpness of urine and the burning smell of soot and the gray steam from boiling potatoes and the flat heavy smell of lard going off. The long sweet smell of neglected suckling infants and the smell of fear from children on their way to school, and the damp smell from the beds of mannish boys. And all of this had been joined by what had come up, evaporating, from underneath, from the gully of the alleyway, and yet more had come down trickling with that rain which is never clean over cities.'[10]

as a reworking of the Berlin Chronicles (published 1970 posthumously), 1932 in the **Frankfurter- und Vossischen Zeitung**, first full collection issued 1955. See also: Benjamin, Walter, **Gesammelte Schriften**, Volume 7, re-issued by Rolf Tiedemann and in collaboration with Theodor W. Adorno and Gershom Scholem, Frankfurt am Main, 1991.

7 Wenders, Wim, **The act of seeing. Essays, Reden und Gespräche**, Frankfurt/Main, 1992, p.124.

8 Wenders, Wim, op. cit., p.128.

9 Nadolny, Sten, **Die Entdeckung der Langsamkeit**, Munich, 1983.

10 Rilke, Rainer Maria, **Schriften in Prosa**, Volume 2. Die Aufzeichnungen des Malte Laurids Brigge, Leipzig, 1930, pp.57-59.

The Gentle Way
of Reading and
the Montage
of the Masses

Next to this city seen with the help of the gentle way of reading we find the portrait of the loud, obtrusive city: the city of quantities, of speed, of meaninglessness, of noise, of light, of piercing sounds, of competing images and signs. Michel Butor, for example, speaks of the 'city as a buildup of text': 'In some big streets there is an accumulation of huge, showy, dazzling, flashing signs that praise this or that thing in familiar or unfamiliar, bright or dark letters. There are signs indicating the prices, quality and origin of goods in shop windows; there are menus in restaurants; there are long commentaries in the museums. Wherever I stop I find myself surrounded and closed in by text, and certain books can help to put me right inside this mass, books that give me an analysis of the outer qualities of the whole, often with the aid of maps, plans and surveys; these allow me to become part of the traffic, to move from one point/handhold to another: I then know which area is meant by a particular name, what it is like, the possibilities it offers, its special features and points.'[11]

Piccadilly Circus, Times Square and the crowded signs of Tokyo are the 'pars pro toto', the way in which the city screams itself into the consciousness of the inhabitant. 'Just as the pictorial world which surrounds us becomes ever more cacophonic, disharmonious, louder, multiformed and showy, so too the cities become more complex, dissonant, louder, complicated and overwhelming. Images and cities go well together. Just look at this overwhelming crowd of city-images: traffic signs, huge neon signs on the rooftops, the advertising hoardings and posters, the shop windows, the video walls, the newspaper stands, the automats, the 'messages' on cars, trucks and buses, all of the visual information on taxis and subways: every plastic bag has something printed on it, etc. etc.', states Wenders.[12]

The masses, accumulation, speed, incongruence, simultaneity, density, chaos: these are all nouns describing the large city. They have always provided a stimulating and fertile soil for artists and writers, and what these latter evoked led to the creation of ever-newer cityscapes. Masses of

11   Butor, Michel, **Die Stadt als Text**, translated from the French (**La Ville Comme Texte**) by Helmut Scheffel, Graz/Vienna, 1992, p.9.
12   Wenders, Wim, op. cit. p.120.
13   Piranesi, Giovanni Battista, **Invenzioni Capric di Carceri**, ca. 1745; –: Antichità Romane, 4 vols., Rome, 1756; –: Il campo Marzio dell' Antica – Rome, 1762.
14   Musil, Robert, **Der Mann ohne Eigenschaften**, 1930. Re-issue by Alfred Frisé, Reinbek bei Hamburg, 1978.
15   Döblin, Alfred, **Berlin Alexanderplatz. Die Geschichte von Franz Biberkopf**, Berlin, 1929.
16   Mann, Thomas, **Der Zauberberg**, Volume 2, Berlin, 1924.
17   Johnson, Uwe, **Jahrestage. Aus dem Leben von Gesine Cresspahl**, Volume 4,

humans, of stone, masses of images, noise, light, and atmosphere, and their domestication using the media of collage or montage. As far back as 1740 Giovanni Battista Piranesi had searched for an artistic medium, a method of representation that would dominate these superimpositions, the simultaneity, massiveness and density. His 'Antichitá di Roma', his 'Carceri' are an expression of the intermeshing of the coexistence of stone, history and life. They are attempts to conquer the labyrinth of the city. Piranesi goes beyond collage-like interweaving in his engravings of the 'Campo Marzio'. Here he assembles the edifices of ancient Rome in a montage of the ideal city spaces of a new metropolis.[13]

Exactly two hundred years later montage became the artistic medium 'par excellence' for making films out of single images and actions.

Abundance and the masses are handled in montages of chains of associations. Robert Musil in his novel *The Man without Qualities*[14] as well as Alfred Döblin in his *Berlin Alexanderplatz*[15] use montage as a principle of technical production in that they include news and newspaper cuttings into the text without any sort of break, as Thomas Mann does with lexical sources in *The Magic Mountain*[16] or Uwe Johnson in *Jahrestage*[17] with reports from the *New York Times*.

Art attempts to put the industrial world, with its altered processes of production, in its place by using its own methods; it relegates the alien to a new context through alienation by means of a montage[18] of heterodox elements. At the same time art, in this connection, requires of anyone approaching it the readiness and the effort required by a new way of reading. What is aimed at here is an effect of discontinuity, a granting of meaning which tears materials which do not go together from their original and functional relationships in order to unite them in a new entity by means of an artistic treatment which is then in a position to make statements about the original context. Montage techniques do not of course only find expression in the above-mentioned novels, in James Joyce's *Ulysses*[19] or John Dos Passos' *Manhattan Transfer*[20]; they are a part of many photographic books and theatre stage designs of the twenties. I am referring as much here to the pure collages of the Dadaists and El Lissitzky's photo collages as to Láslo Moholy-Nagy and Walter Mehring's joint work on *Der Kaufmann von Berlin*[21] and Heartfield's satirical critical work for Kurt Tucholsky's *Deutschland, Deutschland über alles*[22] and to Paul Citroën's famous collage *Metropolis* of 1923.[23]

Frankfurt am Main, 1970-1983.

18 See also: Schneider, Peter Paul, 'Montage-Zeit' in Schneider, Peter Paul et al. (re-issue), **Literatur im Industriezeitalter**, Ausstellungskatalog des Deutschen Literaturarchivs im Schiller Nationalmuseum, Marbach am Neckar, 1987, pp.731-759.

19 Joyce, James, **Ulysses**, Paris, 1922.

20 Dos Passos, John, **Manhattan Transfer**, Boston, 1925.

21 Moholy-Nagy, Lászlo, Berlin. Projektionsphotomontage für ein Bühnenbild zu Walter Mehrings **Der Kaufmann von Berlin,** Brom Silber Mattglanz, 25.8 × 38.0 cm an. 1929.

22 Tucholsky, Kurt: **Deutschland, Deutschland über alles**. Ein Bilderbuch von Kurt Tucholsky und vielen Fotografen. Montiert von John Heartfield, Berlin, 1929.

The Gentle Way
of Reading and
the Montage
of the Masses

Walter Ruttman's *Berlin, Sinfonie der Großstadt*[24] (1927) is not only a classic work of cinema art, but also an exemplary montage film. The film was so popular as an unusual attempt to capture the essence of the metropolis that it was followed by a series of imitations: *Symphonie urbaine*, Mexico 1929 and *Symphonie d'une metropole*, Tokyo 1929. *42nd Street*[25], the portrait of New York so often mentioned in this respect, does not bear comparison. It is a revue film. The only montage element here is the skyscraper architecture that alternates with the ballet dancers, stylized as building-like figurines that sway to and fro on the steps of the stage.

Ruttman's film is remarkable not only for its montage technique. Over a space of twenty-four hours he turns his attention to a very wide variety of social classes. The unemployed, workers, idlers, bank directors and chairmen of boards symbolize at the same time the shadowy and sunny sides of the metropolis and they fire the imagination of painters, poets, photographers and filmmakers just as much as the phenomenon of the masses.

Georg Simmel sets out the psychological and physiological conditions of the big-city dweller in his essay *Die Großstädte und ihr Geistesleben*[26] (The Metropolis and Mental Life). The human reactions to such existential conditions are not so much, in his opinion and in open contradiction to the cultural critiques of the nineteenth century and the cultural pessimism of the early twentieth century, a question of deformation as of survival techniques. 'The psychological foundations (and this is especially true of writers, painters and filmmakers) on which typically metropolitan traits are built involve the increase of nervous life that results from the rapid and continuous changing of internal and external impressions. The human being is a distinguishing being, in other words, its consciousness is excited by the distinctions between present and previous impressions; persistently occurring impressions, with negligible differences between them, and with habitual regularity in their course and their contrasts, demand, so to

23   Paul Citroën. **Metropolis**, 1923, collage, 76.1 × 58.4 cm, Universiteitsbibliotheek Leiden.
24   **Berlin, Sinfonie der Großstadt**, Germany, 1927, directed by Walter Ruttmann.
25   **42nd Street,** USA, 1933, directed by Lloyd Bacon.
26   Simmel, Georg, 'Die Großstädte und das Geistesleben' in **Die Grosstadt**, Dresden, 1903.

speak, less consciousness than the sudden rushing together of altering images, the harsh contrasts marking what can be seen in a single glance, the unexpectedness of oncoming impressions. In that the big city creates these psychological conditions with every step taken across the street, with the speed and variety of commercial, professional, social life, it establishes in the material foundations of mental life, in the quantity of consciousness it demands from us because of our organization as distinguishing beings, a profound contrast to small-town or country life with the slower, more routine, steadier flowing rhythm of its material and mental life. Thus the intellectual character of big city life begins to be comprehensible.'[27]

Or expressed in Benjamin's words: 'Haptic sensations were augmented by optical observations like the advertising sections of a newspaper' – here I refer to Michel Butor's words: 'these allow me to see the city as a building up of text.'[28] To move in a big city means a series of shocks and collisions for the individual. At dangerous crossings impulses flash through him like the current of an electrical battery. So technology forced human sensations to undergo a complex training process. There came a day when movie pictures formed an analogy to a new and urgent desire for sensations. In movies shock-like reception establishes a formal principle. What at the assembly line determines the rhythm of production forms in the medium of film – today that would be the silver or other screens – the basic fundament of reception.

Today the amount of changing internal and external impressions has even grown compared to Simmel's and Benjamin's time and they are paralyzed by the virtualization of the world. And as Benjamin and Simmel analyze the specific psychological conditions of city dwellers they are not denying the necessity of contemplation and gentle perception. The gentle way of reading asks for undetermined spaces. Heidi Lüdi, the scenographer of Wim Wenders speaks of the 'calming uselessness', of places that have 'yet to be commercialized by aggressive exploitation'.[29]

Is discussion restarted, again and again, of the concept of modernism with its yearning for the latest sensation as opposed to the parallel a-historic nostalgia for the eternal return of the identical?

It seems fitting to use Wenders' words again: 'When I was shooting *The Wings of Desire*, I noticed that I was constantly looking for these open expanses, these no man's lands.

27 Op. cit., p.188f.
28 See note 11.
29 Lüdi, 'Toni und Heidi: Räume für den Film' in **Archithese** 5/92, p.47.

The Gentle Way
of Reading and
the Montage
of the Masses

I had the feeling that this city could define itself much better through its empty places than through its full ones... Berlin has many open spaces. One sees houses that are completely free on one side because the neighboring building was destroyed or never built. The desolate sidewalls of such houses are called "fire walls" (Brandmauern). And they are rarely found in other cities. These empty surfaces are wounds, and I like the city for its wounds. They communicate history better than any history book or document.'[30] On another occasion he says: 'I am sure that these fire-walls have a much stronger effect on the memory than the painted facades. The "broken" engraves itself on the mind much more clearly than the "intact".'[31]

30   Wenders, Wim, op. cit., p.123
31   Ibid., p.145.

'Les passages', the realm of the flaneur

1 Entrance of the Galerie Vérot Dodat, Paris ca. 1830

2 Galerie Vérot Dodat, Paris, 1826. [photo: Bollerey, '99]

It was Taylor, who made 'down with flaneur' his parole.

3 Portrait of Louis Lozowick. [photo: Ralph Steiner, '30]

4 Gerald Murphy: **Watch**, 1925. Dallas Museum of Art

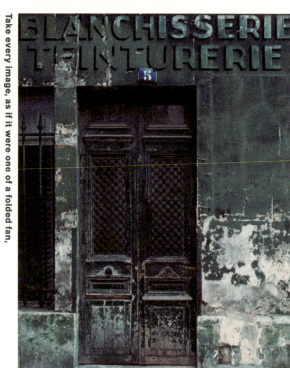

Take every image, as if it were one of a folded fan, which breathes only when unfolded

5 Berlin-Prenzlauerberg. [photo: Bollerey, '86]

6 Paris-14ième arr. [photo: Bollerey, '99]

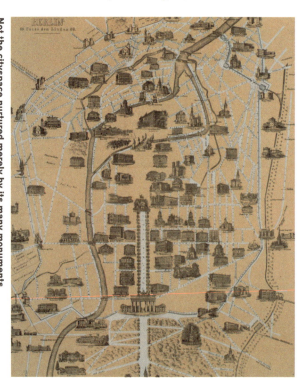

Not the cityspace nurtured merely by its many monuments

7 Plan monumentale Paris, 1867
8 Plan monumentale Berlin, Carl Glück, 1860

9 Berlin-Mitte. [photo: Bollerey, '97]
10 Paris, 13ième arr. [photo: Bollerey, '99]
11 Paris, 13ième arr. [photo: Bollerey, '99]

The wall that speaks

The city of quantities

12 Paul Citroën, Photocollage: **Metropolis**, 1923

Creating a new context through alienation by means of montage

The way in which the city screams itself into the consciousness of the inhabitant

13 El Lissitzky, Photomontage: **The Runners**, 1930

14 Nikolaus Braun, **Streetscene Berlin**, 1930s

A method, to dominate super impositions, simultaneity, mass and density

15 Giovanni Battista Piranesi, Frontispiece: **Antichità**, 1756

An exemplary montage film

16 Scene from Walter Ruttmann's film: **Berlin, Sinfonie der Grossstadt**. Berlin. Symphony of a big city, 1927

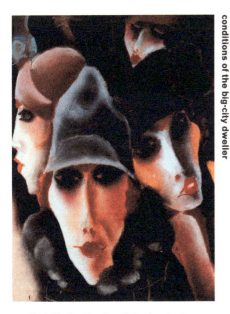

The psychological and physiological conditions of the big-city dweller

17 Erich Ziegler: **Vor dem Schaufenster/**
In front of the shopwindow, 1927

The 'broken' engraves itself on the mind much more clearly than the 'intact'

18 Paris, 6ième. arr. [photo: Bollerey, '99]
19 Berlin-Wedding. [photo: Bollerey]
20 Berlin-Prenzlauerberg. [photo: Bollerey, '93]

Part IV

Urbanism

Chaos behind the Sea Wall:
Interview with Dirk Frieling **Peter Brusse**

Maps on his wall, utopia in his mind. The professor concerns himself with the reorganization of the Netherlands. Provincial towns should become world-class cities. The Westland will become an area full of splendor. Pastures are allowed to disappear, dunes may remain, and Rotterdam, well… 'Rotterdam is the sick man of Holland'. The great rebuilding by urban studies professor, Dirk Frieling.

'When I think of Holland I see…', wrote the poet; and Dirk Frieling does so constantly. He thinks; of Holland, about Holland and observes that the country 'is becoming visibly uglier'. But declaring the Green Heart untouchable is something that makes him livid. 'Why exactly the Green Heart? And that HSL tunnel (high-speed rail) under the pastures, isn't that simply decadent? Why can't we enjoy a view as travelers?'

His eyes twinkle in angry amusement. 'If you were to ask me: what makes Sammy run? Well, that's it. The fixation on the Green Heart as if there are no other areas, even more important, that will be lost because of the Green Heart.'

Frieling, professor of urban studies at Delft and chairman of the foundation 'The Metropolitan Debate', keeps hearing everywhere that the Netherlands is at the dawn of a 'great rebuilding', comparable to what took place in the second half of the nineteenth century, when King William I, followed by Thorbecke, furnished the young kingdom with new waterways, railway lines and industry. 'It will happen, but we have no idea which direction it is headed. Until now, it has been only a loose collection of projects.'

The system of decision-making irritates him especially. 'It is completely shoddy. Everybody in the Netherlands knows that it doesn't work. The Betuwe Rail, the HSL, the expansion of Schiphol, the procedures of these projects serve only to clarify that it cannot go on like this. The projects become far too expensive, the procedures are infinitely delayed, lead to irrelevant discussions at the wrong time and offer poor solutions that satisfy no one. They are solutions befitting an incidental policy that hasn't been examined against a few scenarios for the future of the Netherlands.'

As an aside, he notes: 'The representatives are out of touch with what the people think. Of course, the gap between citizens and politics has always existed, but it has increased because political parties don't really exist anymore. They no longer have any members. In Almere, where I live, a city of more than one hundred thousand residents, I would guess that the PvdA (the labor party) has around five hundred members, half of whom are over sixty years old.'

In a speech recently, Frieling called the political parties 'the thoroughly petrified remains of the columns that once carried the proud temple of democracy'.

Frieling himself, just under sixty, is also a member of the PvdA party and continues to believe in and hope for 'the renaissance of politics as an expression of a lively social discussion'.

But, I ask, what exactly was wrong with the discussion on the HSL?

Frieling responds laconically: 'The discussion was about the route itself, while I believe it should have been about the stations.'

Please explain, I ask him in confusion.

'It was a technocratic discussion, not a political one. I think Rotterdam and Amsterdam are good choices. But why those cities were chosen was not discussed. Of course, a connection to the international network. But still…'

He reseats himself and begins almost mischievously: 'There was a different option, namely Antwerp, Breda, Utrecht and Amsterdam. Timewise, it would have even meant saving about fifty minutes. The north and east would have fared better. It was quite a serious option. The economic base is gravitating towards the middle of the Netherlands. And the funny thing is, it was never seriously discussed. It did not fit within the cabinet's scenario to help Rotterdam recuperate no matter what the cost. That is a great risk, which I do believe they had to take. Seriously, I hate the competition between Amsterdam and Rotterdam. But regrettably, to be blunt: Rotterdam is the sick man of the Netherlands.'

And all of a sudden he seems like the nice doctor explaining an unpleasant diagnosis. 'Rotterdam has suffered heavily under the changes in the Ruhr area, where the iron and steel industries have virtually disappeared. In volume, Rotterdam has remained the largest harbor in the world, which is an enormous achievement, but the hinterland has changed. Rotterdam lives off of massive transshipments, shall we say heavy and stupid work. While Amsterdam, since the Golden Age, has concentrated on expensive goods such as coffee, quinine and tobacco.'

And marijuana.

'Of course, things that weigh next to nothing and that people trade and earn good money with. The harbor of Antwerp processes only a third of the volume that Rotterdam does, but offers the same level of employment, because people actually do something with the goods there.'

But the Rotterdam harbor still needs to expand, doesn't it?

'The bulk of the money is not earned in transport, but in trade. In this trade, banks and information-based companies play a central role. They are all concentrated around Utrecht and Amsterdam. The HSL via Utrecht was not just a silly infatuation.'

Frieling explains that at the beginning of the previous century Amsterdam was still described as 'a dead city on the Zuiderzee' in travel guides. Little was left of the Golden Age, but the trade houses reappeared thanks to the North Sea Canal; this prosperity lasted until the economic crisis of the thirties. Then the Second World War began and Dutch India was lost. To Amsterdam, that was a blow equal to the one Rotterdam received twenty years later from the Ruhr area.

Frieling names the 'psychological, structural and strategically important initiatives' to transform Rotterdam from a port city to a city with a great variety of activities: the university, the museums, a beautiful and dynamic new city center, and the leap to the Kop van Zuid (southern tip) with 'that beautiful bridge'.

So in Rotterdam, they are managing to create what didn't happen in Amsterdam. There is a Kop van Zuid, while the IJ-banks are not being developed.

Frieling nods, but with some hesitation. 'Yes', he says, thinking, 'but the center of Amsterdam with its centuries-old canals remains strong, even though the IJ-banks project was discontinued. The same thing that has been forced in Rotterdam with much financial vigor is happening naturally around Schiphol, like the growth of Hoofddorp, of Schiphol itself and the enormous pressure on the Southern Axis of Amsterdam (the area around the RAI, VU – free university, and WTC – world trade center, ed.). In today's information society, the airport is much more important than the seaport. Rotterdam is still suffering from the trauma of the bombardment and has thus lagged far behind.'

Referring to a large map of the Benelux countries which hangs on the wall, he mumbles, 'How will Rotterdam and Amsterdam develop within Europe? Charles de Gaulle spoke of the Europe of the fatherlands. If the American critic Jane Jacobs is right, then it will become a "Europe of the mother cities", perhaps a variation on the "Europe of the regions". I think that it is all about the cities that offer their energy to the surrounding regions. The creative centers where economics and politics go hand in hand with science and the arts.'

According to Frieling, the question is whether Holland – the square area between the North Sea, the North Sea Canal, the Holland Waterline (Muiden, Utrecht, Gorcum) and the Upper-Merwede, Old Maas, Nieuwe Waterweg – will, can or may become one of these European mother cities.

Five million people live here in an area twice the size of Paris, which also has a population of five million. 'You would think that Rotterdam and Amsterdam are the two magnetic poles of the Randstad. But on the map, the Randstad is still only a loose concentration of provincial towns.'

Compared to Copenhagen, Hamburg, Marseilles or Milan, even Amsterdam and Rotterdam are still 'slightly larger provincial cities'. Can they continue to compete within Europe?

'Somehow we always think that we live in the same little provincial town, whether it's called Meppel or Amsterdam. To the Christians, the big city was a festering pool of evil, while the socialists believed in the equal rationing of prosperity: if there is something beautiful in Amsterdam, then Zwolle should have the same. Keep them down over there in Holland.'

But Frieling believes the map is misleading. In fact, the Randstad can already be seen as a kind of Los Angeles. In that case, you could definitely speak of a metropolis; a metropolis with five million people. 'That is what we are beginning to realize and that is how we are beginning to build. All of a sudden. Until a few years ago, Amsterdam held on to the city center for dear life, as if it were the only real thing in the city. What happened outside of that was either opposed or ignored. Nobody had ever heard of Hoofddorp, and Amstelveen was not really there. Almere was only a residential area and Amsterdam Southeast with its hundred thousand residents did get a shopping mall, but was prevented from acquiring its own nightlife, cafes and restaurants.'

He talks about his becoming president of the steering committee for the renovation of the Bijlmermeer in 1991, and explains how the steering committee held a plea for their own cultural center. '"Give them a new center, with its own regional attractions," we said. "Give them their own image, that's the best way to integrate the residents." That was not an option. There are about thirty religious groups, so we said, "Give them churches." That was still no option. Now suddenly everyone thinks their own center is the most normal thing in the world. Own center, own identity.'

Frieling notes that the former suburbs should actually be allowed to lead their own lives, like young shoots on a tree. He talks of the Olympic rings that interlock. 'No longer a loose collection of provincial towns, but a cohesive whole. No longer either-or, but a museum in Amstelveen that stimulates visits to the Stedelijk Museum.'

He is a strong supporter of a new 'internal' high-speed railway on the HSL line between Amsterdam, Rotterdam, 's-Gravenhage, Utrecht and Schiphol (the so-called ARGUS). If these cities are connected to each other, he thinks, it can be nothing but good for the local markets, just like the European Union increases trade between its members. 'The top will pull up the bottom.'

When I ask if the Randstad should become a municipality or a city-province he says: 'I don't know. I don't think that it's particularly important one way or the other. I don't really care and the citizens don't see the relevance. Managerial organization is not a condition but a consequence. When coherence has been reached, we'll see how to deal with the rest.'

Frieling, formerly the project leader for the construction of Almere, believes that the old and new centers in the large Randstad will reinforce their own specific character, just like the large scale of Europe forces a small-scale soul-search on culture and identity. 'The Rotterdammer will become more Rotterdammer, the Amsterdammer more Amsterdammer. Even the neighborhoods and districts are looking for their own character. I have no problem with a Turkish district or a black city. I actually still hope that the Bijlmermeer will become the first black anytown in the Netherlands.'

Den Haag will remain the Court city with the royal palace, the parliaments, representatives and lobbyists. When Europe integrates, more activities will be shifted to Brussels. Den Haag will then become the capital of the province The Netherlands, as Haarlem is currently the capital of the province North-Holland. 'Nothing is wrong with that, Haarlem is a prospering, industrious city. And the squabbling about whether or not to connect Den Haag to the international HSL line is ridiculous, of course. Representatives and politicians can take a cab, can't they? That's the way it should be. On the scale of Europe, Den Haag is the suburb of Rotterdam.' He hopes the greenhouses of the West-land will disappear to a better place, and it would be good if the Westland became a new

Wassenaar. 'Such a large European city could use a few glamorous residential areas.'

Oscar Wilde once said that any map without Utopia is pointless. 'Yes', Frieling says, 'if the provinces outside of Holland continue to, as the saying goes, "act normal and you'll stand out enough already" – and that is a good Dutch saying – well, then we won't manage that green metropolis Minister De Boer talks about.'

He is silent for a moment, then asks: 'But what then? Can we still play on an international level then? Can we offer something on the world market that nobody else has? And what is that specifically Dutch added value, that cultural identity? Can a society retain its culture if it is destroyed economically?'

But it is also part of the Dutch culture to follow the highly praised equality principle and not desire anything grand. A painful paradox. If the Randstad seems to be 'too much of a good thing', then Frieling can imagine the northern flank, Amsterdam-Utrecht, as the next best thing for now. As the engine for it all.

'Utrecht is growing incredibly quickly, is modern and contemporary with its computer companies, the information centers; it has a central location, with an excellent connection to Germany, has a pleasant city-center with a good cultural position.'

What if that doesn't happen either? There is another possibility: 'If we want, everyone in the Netherlands can have a house with a garden. There is enough space. But then we would continue to translate societal "equality", a good principle, into spatial mediocrity. Then we would have McDonald's everywhere. I have nothing against McDonald's but it does become a bit boring. The same things, the same density everywhere.'

This is not the best solution in his opinion. He would prefer creating green cities to putting everyone in the same green countryside. The northern provinces are slowly emptying out and Frieling considers that a good development. 'The minister of VROM [De Boer] dislikes the retired population moving to Drenthe. What is she talking about? It's fantastic. Offer the older population the opportunity to move away from the Randstad with its stress, smell and noise. Not everyone will want to leave, but others would like peace and beautiful nature in their old age. Life is also cheaper there, allowing them to retain the same standard of living on the pension they have earned in the Randstad. This way, the prosperity of the west will also reach the north. I wish they would understand that.'

The beauty of the countryside is a wonderful and expensive thing. 'The polders are unique, the dunes are extremely special, but due to the Green Heart, Leiden has no place to go. The city is not allowed to expand towards Alphen, so now you see the pressure building towards the interior dune wall, southward towards Valkenburg and Wassenaar, and northwards towards the Flower area.'

The professor squeezes his fists and lets his head hang. 'I went for a drive through the Green Heart on one of those beautiful Sundays in September. There are gorgeous areas, but also expanses with no qualities whatsoever. Nothing. But you cannot touch them.

'That is why companies are finding it necessary to fan out towards the unprotected nature in North-Brabant and Gelderland. It's a terrible shame. We should be much more careful with the river landscape, the forests and fens on the Brabant sandgrounds. And those high-visibility sites along the highways, like at Veenendaal in the Gelderland valley. Or near Nijkerk, along the Veluwe. It is all terribly ugly, but it shows the costs of the scenario: Holland is full, go to Gelderland.'

He returns to the HSL, and the Betuwe-rail: 'the irritating endless whining and finally throwing around money to force a compromise. Not to make a good project even better, but to patch up a bad project. That 900 million extra for the HSL tunnels could have been put to much better use. For example to construct a nature reserve in the Green Heart like the Oostvaardersplassen. But then at twice the size somewhere near Alphen. That would have been good. We talk about the Green Heart all the time, but because of Gelderland the Betuwe-rail cost five billion more; in other words, twice the amount that has been reserved for the improvement of the nature in the Green Heart over the next ten years. Unbelievable. It was not even considered.'

Once again, Frieling stares at the map on the wall. The professor is not satisfied. 'We will have to better our lives, create order in the chaos.'

Together with five other professors in Delft and Amsterdam, Frieling started the foundation 'The Metropolitan Debate' in 1995. The first task was the inventory of all plans, notes and discussion pieces, because you could 'no longer see the forest for the trees'. After that the future projections were put in the same category, because friend and foe, everyone, consciously or unconsciously, offered sectored, single-sided visions and thus an incomplete representation of things. The six creators of order began to see that the economic battle will be fought between concentration in the Randstad and diffusion over the 'Zandstad' (sand cities: Brabant and Gelderland), as they put it so visually. And furthermore, whether the Randstad and Zandstad should have large cities (fusions) or not. Even the professors of the Metropolitan Debate hold different views on this. In this way they promote the objectivity of the debate, or so they hope.

'The coming discussion about the new airport will be the first big test, in which the political parties will finally get another chance to engage the public debate in relation to their own scenarios for the Netherlands. They will have to regain the terrain from action groups and interest groups that justifiably jumped into the hole left by the political parties.'

'The future of the Netherlands concerns everyone, the parties will have to offer their conception of its organization and according to Frieling the question is not: are you for or against Schiphol? But: is it desirable or necessary for our country that the current volume of forty million air travel passengers per year declines, increases or stabilizes. Only when that is clear, only when we know what the Netherlands wants and can do in Europe, will we be able to decide in a follow-up discussion where the national airport should be situated. 'That does not have to be Schiphol. If the Netherlands does not believe in a strong Randstad, it may well be better to choose the airport Volkel in the Zandstad.'

This interview was published in the Newspaper *de Volkskrant*, January 18, 1997.

Dirk Frieling is Professor in Urban Planning, Faculty of Architecture, TU Delft and Director of the Research School for Design and Computation.

Recent Transformations
in Urban Policies
in the Netherlands Hugo Priemus

Introduction   This contribution offers an overview of recent transformations in urban policies in the Netherlands, especially in the four major cities: Amsterdam, Rotterdam, The Hague and Utrecht.

The intention of this paper is to make clear the changes that took place in urban policies in the 1960s, both as a result of changing national policies and of changing local policies. It will be argued that 'building for the neighborhood' was the dominant approach in the 1970s to improve the housing situation of mainly low-income inhabitants in cities. Urban renewal appeared to reduce urban housing problems, but in the same time to sharpen labor market problems in the cities. In the 1990s strengthening of the economic vitality of cities was the main goal of city-oriented national policies. As a result a new generation of urban investments policy developed in the second half of the 1990s, not aiming at social housing but at gentrification of housing areas, dominated by social rented housing, and also at restructuring business parks, and stimulating urban employment in general.

In the second part of the paper a historical overview regarding the redefinitions of urban problems since the 1960s is presented. This overview will be elaborated by a number of quantitative sections: one, on demographic and housing changes in Dutch cities, another on economic stagnation of these cities and a third on the mismatch between urban housing markets and urban labor markets. Finally, we introduce the recent urban investment policy, developed by national government to pave the way to an increasing economic vitality of cities.

Historical overview: redefining urban problems since the 1960s

Inner city problems were first spotlighted in the Netherlands in the 1960s. The construction of large numbers of homes on the outskirts of towns, or in so-called growth poles, continued to be the main priority of housing policy, but plans were also made for renewal of old residential neighborhoods just outside town centers. The primary strategy to improve these neighborhoods was demolition followed by new construction. In Rotterdam, and especially Amsterdam, residential neighborhoods were to undergo a transformation to commercial areas with bigger factories, office blocks and facilities for cars such as motor-ways and car parks. Neighborhood communities, supported by student protesters, vehemently opposed these plans. Trade and industry with its car-dominated traffic

Recent Transforma-
tions in Urban
Policies in the
Netherlands

infrastructure was seen as the enemy and the communities fought to keep neighborhoods residential. The quality of living did have to be improved, but for the locals themselves not for people from elsewhere. This was called 'building for the neighborhood'. After heated political debates and municipal elections, Rotterdam (alderman Van der Ploeg) unequivocally decided in favor of building for the community. Amsterdam (alderman Schaefer) later followed suit. Major subsidies provided by national housing policy enabled the construction of affordable rental housing in the social housing sector and affordable high-quality renovations.

In several pre-war neighborhoods (Crooswijk, Feijenoord, Dapperbuurt, Kinkerbuurt), there was a proliferation of new social housing, and private rentals were bought up and thoroughly renovated. The business community accepted the political decisions and moved its economic activities to the outskirts of town, or even further afield. Thus Heineken brewery discarded all its plans for expansion and modernization of the Crooswijk factory, closed it down and built a new modern factory in the small (commuter) town of Zoeterwoude. According to Hessels (1992), the shift of employment opportunities away from the town centers to the outskirts has been a general trend in and around Dutch cities these last few decades. In Croos-wijk, the livestock market (Veemarkt) and slaughterhouse (Slachthuis) made way for large social housing estates. With them, the network of bars, meeting places and suppliers around Veemarkt and Slachthuis, which were so typical of Crooswijk, also faded into history. Only later did people realize that the conventional urban renewal approach as realized in Croos-wijk might have improved the locals' living situation but it also drove employers – and jobs – out of the neighborhood.

Urban changes in Amsterdam and especially Rotterdam were largely a consequence of changes in the cities' harbor areas in the seventies and eighties. Large ocean freighters could not be loaded and unloaded in city docks, so large ports were built close to the North Sea for this purpose. The explosive growth in container transports also contributed to this development. There was no room in the city for transferring and stacking containers, and this activity moved west to mostly new, modern docks where space was not a problem. The economic boost it gave to the Waterweg and North Sea Canal regions was enormous, but within the city limits, progress showed its dark side in the huge brownfield sites along the Nieuwe Maas and the IJ. Harbor companies had abandoned the cities, but the polluted soil they had caused stayed behind and would cost the public authorities many millions to clean up.

Initially, Rotterdam and Amsterdam intended to use generous national subsidies to build affordable, no-nonsense social housing estates on the newly vacated land. A number of pioneer projects were actually realized this way, such as new construction in Feijenoord designed by Bureau Henk van Schagen and the Peperklip by Carel Weeber. In the late 1970s however, in the face of the most severe recession since the Second World War politicians were forced to redefine social problems and seek new solutions. From 1978 to 1982, the nation, and large cities in particular, struggled to cope with ever-higher unemployment rates. The economy started to recover in 1982. Though the economy in the cities improved too, it structurally trailed behind the overall pace of recovery. Van der Vegt and Manshanden (1996) made a study of economic development in Dutch cities and boroughs in the period 1970-1995. Their conclusions were unequivocal: employment opportunities, growth of gross regional product and population development were way behind in the cities as compared to the surrounding regions. The four largest cities suffered the greatest in this respect. And the economy in the southern wing of the Randstad (Rotterdam and The Hague) developed much more slowly than in the northern wing (Amsterdam and Utrecht).

By this time, the nation's number one political priority of the 1960s and 1970s to alleviate the housing shortage was losing momentum. Unemployment, the environment and law and order were considered much more pressing social issues. In the 1980s, public support waned for the 14 billion guilders which the government annually spent on housing. Drastic cuts in housing expenditure were called for and this meant a major turnaround in housing policy (Heerma, 1989). In the late 1980s, new policy was proposed in which the financial risk was shifted to local authorities and housing corporations, tenants' housing costs were raised and housing subsidies were slashed.

From then on, most new houses were to be built by the private sector, preferably for owner occupation and preferably not for people in the lowest income brackets. The latter had little other choice in housing than the existing housing supply. High subsidies to

Recent Transforma-
tions in Urban
Policies in the
Netherlands

make new housing units available to low income households were no longer considered necessary.

In 1990, locations for new housing development were laid down in the Fourth Spatial Planning Memorandum Extra (VINEX). Locations were selected within city limits as much as possible. At least 50% (urban VINEX locations) or 70% (VINEX development areas outside the city) had to be developed by the private sector without subsidies. This was a break with growth poles policy, in which large-scale areas consisting mostly of social rental housing were developed at some distance from the city (Priemus, 1998).

In Rotterdam, this policy has prompted the development of Kop van Zuid, an extensive parcel of land in the inner city, formerly used for commercial purposes, where most new housing will provide for the private market rather than social housing. IJburg, to be built on a number of man-made islands, is a major VINEX location in the city of Amsterdam.

In 1995, the national government and local governments signed regional VINEX implementation covenants. These covenants dictate the number of dwellings to be built, the quantity of space for businesses, the required infrastructure and subsidization in the period 1995-2005.

Not until the government had already decided on a new market-oriented housing policy (Heerma, 1989) and new spatial planning policy (Ministry of Housing, Spatial Planning and the Environment, 1990) did people begin to realize that large-scale housing development at VINEX locations outside the cities would prompt a long series of selective moves from the cities to the urban fringe. Further, that this could negatively impact on the livability of certain, less popular inner-city urban neighborhoods and make it harder for housing corporations to get tenants for social housing in these areas. Subsequently, the Ministry of Housing, Spatial Planning and the Environment presented a Memorandum on Urban Renewal in 1997. The Memorandum contained new policy for restructuring city neighborhoods, in particular homogeneous post-war neighborhoods where the government hopes to raise housing and environment quality and increase the diversity of the housing supply. The government has thus recognized that it needs to invest in socially vulnerable city neighborhoods as well as in VINEX locations.

1.85 Billion guilders has been set aside for urban renewal from 1999 to 2010. The 1998 coalition agreement adds another 2.25 billion to this sum. The money is to be supplied by the Economic Structure Improvement Fund, as the government has determined that improving the housing and neighborhood quality of cities is a requisite for a strong economic structure in the Netherlands. In addition, it is now generally recognized that the economic performance of Dutch cities is poor and that urban economies sorely need a boost, on the one hand by improving housing and neighborhood quality and on the other by directly restructuring former business areas and improving accessibility.

Demographic and housing changes in Dutch cities In the past, the major cities in the Netherlands were regarded as propellers of the economy, but for more than a quarter of a century now, this description has been anything but apt.

Development in population rates As Table 2 shows, the population of each of the four major cities has declined steadily since 1965 while in the same period the total Dutch population has grown considerably. In thirty years, the three largest cities have lost about 150,000 inhabitants each. In Utrecht, the population dropped by only 30,000. In general, the urban population is expected to stabilize over the next fifteen years: a slight drop is predicted for Rotterdam and The Hague and a slight increase for Amsterdam and Utrecht. Population growth for all of the Netherlands is estimated to be 6% from 1997 to 2010, only a little higher than the expected growth of the urban population. These estimates suggest that the trend in which urban populations declined while the population in the whole country grew, is expected to be brought to a halt.

Population composition As in the past, the composition of the urban population deviates from the national standard. In 1982, 29% of households in the four major cities consisted of families with children, while nationwide this was 45% (SCP, 1996a: 566). Ethnic minorities made up 6.9% of the population in the four cities in 1982; the national average was only 2.2%. The concentration rates in Table 3 show how different population groups are over-represented or under-represented in the four major cities in comparison with the national average (the Netherlands=100).

Table 1 Housing construction activities in the metropolitan areas of the four major cities, according to the VINEX implementation covenants, 1995–2005

	no. of dwellings, 1995–2005
Greater Amsterdam	100,100
Greater Rotterdam	53,000
Greater Haaglanden	
(The Hague and surroundings)	42,500
Greater Utrecht	31,600
Other urban areas	236,500
Total	463,700

Source VINEX implementation covenants

Table 2 Population dynamics in the four major cities, 1965–1995 (measured) and 1997–2010 (prognoses), absolute numbers (×1,000) and index rates for the periods 1965–1995 and 1997–2010

	1.1.1965	1.1.1995	1.1.2010	Index for 1965–1995 (1965=100)	Index for 1997–2010 (1997=100)
Amsterdam	866.3	722.1	750.1	83	105
Rotterdam	731.6	598.2	577.0	82	98
The Hague	598.7	442.9	414.2	74	94
Utrecht	267.0	235.6	237.8	88	102

Source CBS/Focus/Priemus et al., 1998: 1–11.

Table 3 Over-represented and under-represented population groups in the four cities compared to the national population composition in early 1982 and 1994, respectively (concentration rates: the Netherlands =100)

Type of household	early 1982	early 1994
singles and couples <25 years	131	147
singles 25–64 years	174	172
singles >65 years	147	125
families with children	64	58
couples 25–54 years	91	88
couples >55 years	116	74
single parent families	117	135
Ethnic background **of head of household**		
Suriname and Netherlands Antilles	350	380
Turkey and Morocco	313	518
Southern Europe	225	300
Total	313	422
Income distribution		
1st quartile (low income)	124	136
2nd quartile	109	117
3rd quartile	85	79
4th quartile (high income)	82	68

Source CBS (WBO '81/82 and '93/93) SCP analysis: SCP, 1996a: 566.

Table 4 Net domestic relocations to (+) and from (−) the four major cities, 1989−1993[b] and expected net relocations to and from the four cities in the next two years[b] (in percent, per population group)

Type of household	Net relocations 1989−1993[c]	Expected net relocations in next two years[d]
singles and couples < 25 years	+0.7	+4.8
singles 25−64 years	−0.1	+0.8
singles > 65 years	−2.2	−0.9
families with children	−9.3	−2.7
couples 25−54 years	−14.5	−5.1
couples > 55 years	−3.5	−2.5
single parent families	−0.8	+1.0
Total	−4.0	−0.8
Ethnic minorities	−1.5	−0.3
Income distribution		
1st quartile (low income)	−0.8	+1.7
2nd quartile	−0.3	−0.8
3rd quartile	−5.0	−3.2
4th quartile (high income)	−17.4	−3.1
Total	−4.0	−0.8

a Realized relocations
b Intended relocations in 1994 and 1995
c The net relocation rate in relation to the size of the population group concerned in 1990.
d The net relocation rate in relation to the size of the population group concerned in 1994.
Source CBS (WBO '93/94) SCP analysis: SCP, 1996a: 568.

Table 5 Total housing supply, rate of owner-occupied dwellings and rate of pre-war housing in the four major cities, 1 January 1996

	Housing supply (no. dwellings)	% social rental	% owner-occupied	% private rental	% pre 1945
Amsterdam	358,489	13.0	23.7	63.3	51.2
Rotterdam	279,811	18.4	21.9	59.7	38.1
The Hague	206,632	32.5	28.8	38.7	49.4
Utrecht	100,094	36.3	13.3	50.4	43.1

Source Priemus et al., 1998: 1−23.

Table 6 Development of job opportunities in the four major cities in index rates and mean annual growth in percent, 1980−1995

	Index 1980−1995 (1980=100)	Mean growth 1980−1995	Index 1990−1995 (1990=100)	Mean growth 1990−1995
Amsterdam	118	1.1	104	0.8
Rotterdam	108	0.5	98	−0.5
The Hague	102	0.1	98	−0.5
Utrecht	131	1.8	109	1.7
Total 4 major cities	113	0.8	101	0.2
Total 27 other cities	131	1.8	107	1.3
The Netherlands	145	2.5	114	2.7

Source CBS/Priemus et al., 1998: 1-65.

Recent Transforma-
tions in Urban
Policies in the
Netherlands

The data in Table 3 clearly shows how certain population groups increasingly dominated the urban landscape in the period 1982-1994. The number of ethnic minorities, strongly concentrated in cities, continued to grow. In Amsterdam, ethnic minorities made up 6% of the population in 1975 and 32% of the population in 1995. In the same period, the immigrant population in Rotterdam grew from 6% to 29% (Tesser et al., 1995). The cities especially have high rates of Turkish and Moroccan inhabitants. The number of low-income households in the cities also grew while more and more high-income households (fourth quartile) moved away.

The concentration index of families with children dropped from 64 to 58 and the proportion of singles and young couples under age 25 rose. Although the proportion of singles between 25 and 65 years in the cities is higher than the national average, their relative number did not increase during this period. The proportion of retired singles (over age 65) declined during this period, but they are still over-represented in the cities.

The proportion of single-parent families in the cities also grew between 1982 and 1994. Interestingly, couples over age 55 were over-represented at the beginning of this period, but by the end their proportion in the urban population was less than the national average: a clear sign that the cities are now rejuvenating. Generally speaking, there is a growing concentration of low-income households, singles, young people, single parent families and, especially, ethnic minorities in the cities. Moreover, high-income households and families with children are becoming scarce in the urban landscape.

Not all of these developments should be viewed with alarm. Immigrant populations in cities do not by definition pose a problem. In fact, cities and immigrants are inextricably connected. For example, both Amsterdam's golden age in the 17th century and New York's present day economic recovery can be attributed for a large part to the activities of immigrants in these cities (Waldinger, 1996).

Naturally, immigrant populations vary in their size as well as in their ability to stabilize and integrate in their new societies (Kloosterman, 1996). This is certainly the case in the Netherlands where Turkish and Moroccan immigrants continue to have major difficulties finding employment, despite the fact that job opportunities have grown quite steadily since 1985. Their situation contrasts strongly with falling unemployment rates in Antilles and Surinamese immigrant populations (SCP, 1996b).

The ethnic population in the three largest cities together grew by 24% between 1975 and 1995 (from 6% to 30% of the total population of the three cities). In Utrecht, ethnic minorities made up 21% of the population in 1995, compared to 5% in 1975 (Tesser et al., 1995: 56).

Housing supply The increasingly distinct composition of the urban population is closely linked to the distinct characteristics of the urban housing supply. The urban housing supply consists mostly of rentals, both in the social and commercial sector, small dwellings, cheap dwellings, multi-family estates and pre-war housing. Renewal policy is aimed at increasing the share of owner-occupied dwellings, increasing the number of dwellings tied to land, increasing the number of large dwellings and improving overall housing and neighborhood quality.

Economic stagnation in Dutch cities

Employment Table 6 shows how urban employment rates have lagged behind the national employment rate since 1980. This applies most strongly to the four major cities. Specifically, unemployment is greater in the southern part of the Randstad (Rotterdam, The Hague) than in the northern part (Amsterdam, Utrecht). In fact, Rotterdam and The Hague experienced a net loss of jobs between 1990 and 1995.

In 1995, average unemployment in all cities together (10%) was almost 2% higher than the national average (8.1%). The unemployment rate of the four major cities was higher again (12%). Rotterdam's unemployment rate was particularly alarming. Utrecht seems to offer its inhabitants better employment perspectives; in fact, its unemployment rate beats the national average.

Table 11 sketches the urban and national employment structure that is the relative number of jobs in the different sectors. In some cases, the urban job structure differs from the

Table 7 Registered unemployment in percent of total working population and W/P ratio in the four major cities in 1995 (W/P = working population/population 15–64 years)

	unemployment rate (%)	W/P ratio
Amsterdam	12.0	0.74
Rotterdam	16.0	0.74
The Hague	10.0	0.67
Utrecht	7.0	0.97
Total 4 major cities	12.0	0.75
Total 27 other cities	10.0	0.70
The Netherlands	8.1	0.58

Source Priemus et al., 1998: 1–71.

Table 8 Distribution of population and employment per type of municipality in the Randstad and the Ruhr area, 1970–1990

	Randstad		Ruhr area	
	distribution 1990 (%)	increase 1970–1990 (%)	distribution 1990 (%)	increase 1970–1990 (%)
Population				
city centers of major cities	4	-14	18	-12
suburbs of major cities and suburban cities	46	-1	43	0
towns	20	+23	27	-2
rural community; country	30	+13	22	+20
all areas	100	+8	100	+2
Employment				
city centers of major cities	14	-12	17	-6
suburbs of major cities and suburban cities	44	+26	38	0
towns	19	+29	26	-3
rural community; country	23	+52	19	+39
all areas	100	+24	100	+3

Source Jansen, Hilbers, Wilmink, 1998:11.

Table 9 Growth of the Gross Regional Product in the 4 major cities, the surrounding regions and the entire greater metropolitan regions in the Netherlands, 1970–1995

	City % per year	Surrounding region % per year	Entire greater metro area; % per year
Amsterdam	1.4	4.3	2.4
Rotterdam	1.4	3.1	2.0
The Hague	0.9	4.0	2.2
Utrecht	2.4	4.5	3.6
26 urban regions	2.0	3.7	2.8
rest of the Netherlands			3.2
total the Netherlands			2.8

Source Van der Vegt & Manshanden, 1996: 31; see also Priemus et al., 1997: 54.

Table 10 Job growths in the cities and in the surrounding regions, as a result of increased production, increased productivity and increase in full-time and part-time positions, respectively, 1970–1995 (%)

	City					Surrounding region				
	GRP	job prod.	full-time	part-time	jobs	GRP	job prod.	full-time	part-time	jobs
Amsterdam	1.4	2.2	-0.8	0.4	0.4	4.3	2.6	1.7	0.4	2.1
Rotterdam	1.4	2.2	-0.7	0.4	-0.3	3.1	2.5	0.7	0.4	1.1
The Hague	0.9	2.1	-1.2	0.5	-0.7	4.0	2.4	1.7	0.4	2.1
Largest 3	1.4	2.2	-0.8	0.4	-0.4	3.8	2.5	1.3	0.4	1.7
Utrecht	2.4	2.0	0.4	0.4	0.8	4.5	2.4	2.1	0.4	2.6
Other cities	2.6	2.2	0.4	0.4	0.8	3.7	2.8	1.0	0.4	1.4
Other NL						2.7	2.2	0.5	0.5	1.0
Netherlands						2.8	2.3	0.5	0.4	0.9

GRP = Gross Regional Product
Source Van der Vegt & Manshanden, 1996: 60; see also Priemus et al., 1997: 58.

Table 11 Employment in 1995 per economic sector in the four major cities (percentage of total employment)

	Industry	Construction	Trade and catering	Transport and communication services	Financial and professional services	Government and other services
Amsterdam	7.3	2.9	19.8	7.3	28.3	33.5
Rotterdam	11.4	4.8	16.5	13.7	23.0	29.5
The Hague	4.3	3.4	13.2	18.4	23.8	45.2
Utrecht	5.1	3.2	15.5	10.2	26.5	38.1
Total 4 major cities	7.6	3.6	16.9	9.8	25.6	35.3
Total 27 other cities	16.5	4.3	17.6	5.5	19.9	35.2
The Netherlands	18.2	6.2	19.7	6.6	16.7	32.6

Source CBS/Priemus et al., 1998: 1–68.

Table 12 Job commuters in the four major cities, 1975 and 1995 (×1000 persons)

	1975	1995
Amsterdam (city)		
total employed	445	451
number of commuters	178	211
Rotterdam (city)		
total employed	340	333
number of commuters	137	181
The Hague (city)		
total employed	244	226
number of commuters	102	124
Utrecht (city)		
total employed	142	178
number of commuters	68	131

Source CPB et al., 1998.

Recent Transforma-
tions in Urban
Policies in the
Netherlands

average Dutch situation. Most strikingly, industry only accounted for 7.6%
of total jobs in the four major cities in 1995, while 18.2% of jobs in all of the
Netherlands were in the industry sector. Also, fewer construction jobs were
to be found in the four major cities (3.6%) compared to the Netherlands as
a whole (6.2%).On the other hand, the cities have a greater share of jobs in
the sectors 'transport and communication', 'government and other services'
and 'financial and other professional services'. This last category is a particularly good source of employment in the four major cities (25.6% of all
jobs compared to 16.7% in the Netherlands as a whole).

Table 10 shows how the number of jobs increased in the cities and the sur-
rounding regions from 1970 to 1995. Again, The Hague, Amsterdam and
Rotterdam score poorly for overall job creation: there is a net loss of jobs.
A good number of jobs were however created in the immediate vicinity of
Utrecht, Amsterdam and The Hague. Job growth in the Rotterdam region
was less high, but still exceeded the average Dutch rate. Table 10 confirms
Hessels' proposition (1992) that employment has shifted from the cities
to the regions directly surrounding the cities, and that job growth in the
region more or less fully compensates for the loss of jobs in the cities.

Gross Regional Product   The growth of the Gross Regional Product (GRP)
between 1970 and 1995 is depicted in Table 9 for the surrounding regions
of the four cities and for 22 medium-sized cities. Economic growth in
the largest three cities trailed behind the average GRP growth nationwide.
On the other hand, Utrecht experienced outstanding GRP growth.

The relatively poor economic performance of the Netherlands' largest
three cities has affected economic growth in the Randstad as a whole.
Over the last decades, growth here has fallen behind national economic
growth by a full percent per year. In particular, fewer jobs were created here
than in the rest of the country, which seems to contradict the government's
view (in the Fourth Memorandum on Spatial Planning) of the Randstad
as an internationally focused core economic area.

Van der Vegt and Manshanden (1996) showed that the bigger the city, the smaller its growth rate in production volume. This is illustrated for the period 1970-1995. The Hague's economic performance was particularly weak during that period as that city was unable to expand beyond its city limits.

Mismatch between urban housing markets and urban labor markets Starting in the 1970s, the rise of suburbs and sleeper towns and the decline of city centers in the Randstad followed a far more rapid course than in the Ruhr area of western Germany. Jansen et al., 1998, showed that there has been a strong peripheral movement of both the population and employment opportunities in the Randstad in recent decades (Table 8).

The Randstad had a much higher total job growth between 1970 and 1995 (27%) than the Ruhr area (3%). At the same time, the residential function of the city centers in the Randstad declined more (-25%) than in the Ruhr area (-8%). Most population growth in the Randstad occurred at more than 5 km from city centers and the greatest growth occurred at more than 30 km from city centers.

The number of daily commuters to jobs in the cities has grown strongly in recent decades, with commuters coming from outside the greater metropolitan regions accounting for the greatest growth. Currently, half of all urban jobs are held by employees who do not live in the city (Table 12).

In general, the cities have relatively high unemployment rates. Jobs at the lower end of the scale are particularly scarce. The higher an employee's level of education, the more likely he or she is to be a commuter and the further his or her commute. To balance things out, lower income households should have easier access to housing in the regions surrounding the cities and the urban housing supply should include more dwellings which cater to the taste and needs of higher income households.

Urban investment policy: paving the way to an increasing economic vitality of cities The data presented above have convinced both the national government and local authorities that the major cities sorely need an economic boost. Since its inception in 1994, Major Cities Policy has focused on improving employment opportunities, improving health care and education and boosting livability and security. The 1994-1998 coalition government appointed a state secretary for policy for the major cities (Kohnstamm); now, for the first

Recent Transforma-
tions in Urban
Policies in the
Netherlands

time, the new government has made this a ministerial post. Mr. Van Boxtel
has been appointed Minister for the Major Cities and Integration Policy
for the period 1998-2002. Aside from recognizing the need for policy
specifically for the major cities, politicians have also been quick to grasp
the importance of urban investment policy in boosting cities' economic
vitality and improving their accessibility, social cohesion and sustainability.
Prime Minister Kok's second coalition government has vowed to invest
NLG 28.5 billion between 1999 and 2010 to reinforce the spatial-economic
structure of the Netherlands. Some of this additional investment will be
crucial to the realization of major cities' policy.

NLG 8.8 billion (+PM) is by no means enough to enable the cities to fulfill
all their ambitions (Priemus et al., 1998). Nonetheless, the coalition
agreement drawn up by the second government under Mr. Kok (1998) is a
launching pad for further urban investments. Urban councils have been
asked for their views on where investments should be made; this knowledge
will form the foundation of a multi-year investment program. The national
government's contribution is intended to stimulate private investment. City
councils will be responsible for directing spending, making priorities and
developing concrete plans in cooperation with the private sector, housing
corporations and neighboring municipalities. Public support is crucial in
this process. Once investment policy has been developed, additional means
will probably be required for its implementation.

The future will teach us how effective this new urban investment policy
will be in strengthening the economic vitality of cities. In any case it seems
that central government has found the right diagnosis for some persistent
urban problems, and has an open eye for the opportunities of the urban
economy. The future of Dutch cities seems promising, now that central
government has decided to support the cities in their endeavors to improve
their economic vitality.

References

Centraal Planbureau (CPB), Rijksinstituut voor
Volksgezondheid en Milieu (RIVM), Sociaal en Cultureel
Planbureau (scp) & Adviesdienst Verkeer en Vervoer (AVV),
Kiezen of delen: ICES-maatregelen tegen het licht, The
Hague, CPB, 1998.

Heerma, E., **Nota volkshuisvesting in de jaren negentig**,
The Hague, Sdu, 1989.

Hessels, M., **Location dynamics of business services, an
intrametropolitan study on the Randstad Holland**,
Netherlands Geographical Studies 147, Utrecht, 1992.

Jansen, G.R.M., H. Hilbers and I. Wilmink, **Transport net-
works and mobility: a comparative analysis of the
Randstad, the Rhein-Ruhr Area and the Antwerp-
Brussels-Ghent region**, paper presented at the 4th NECTAR
Euro Conference 'Sustainable transport: Europe and its sur-
roundings', Tel Aviv, April 1998.

Kloosterman, R.C., 'Mixed experiences; postindustrial transition
and ethnic minorities on the Amsterdam labor market', **New
Community**, 22 (4), December 1996, pp.637-653.

Kok, W., 'Brief van de formateur aan de voorzitter van de
Tweede Kamer der Staten-Generaal' supplement
Regeerakkoord 1998, Tweede Kamer 1997-1998, 26.024,
no.120, The Hague, Sdu, 3 August 1998.

Ministry of Housing, Spatial Planning and the Environment,
Fourth Spatial Planning Memorandum Extra, The Hague,
Sdu, 1990.

Ministry of Housing, Spatial Planning and the Environment,
Nota Stedelijke Vernieuwing [Memorandum on Urban
Renewal], The Hague, Ministry vrom, 1997.

Priemus, H., E. Kalle and R. Teule, **De stedelijke investering-
sopgave: naar vitale, ongedeelde en duurzame steden in
Nederland**, Delft, Delft University Press, 1997.

Priemus, H., 'Contradictions between Dutch housing policy and
spatial planning', **TESG Journal of Economic and Social
Geography**, 84, no. 1, 1998, pp.31-43.

Priemus, H., R.C. Kloosterman, B.W. Lambregts, H.M.
Kruythoff and J. den Draak, **De stedelijke investeringsop-
gave 1999-2010 gekwantificeerd. Naar economische
vitaliteit, bereikbaarheid, sociale cohesie en duurza-
amheid**, Delft, Delft University Press, 1998.

Sociaal en Cultureel Planbureau (scp), **Sociaal en Cultureel
Rapport 1996**, Rijswijk, 1996a.

Sociaal en Cultureel Planbureau, **Rapportage minderheden;
Bevolking, arbeid, onderwijs, huisvesting**, Rijswijk, Sociaal
en Cultureel Planbureau, 1996b.

Tesser, P.T.M., C.S. van Praag, F.A. van Dugteren, L.J. Herwijer
and H.C. van der Wouden, **Rapportage minderheden 1995.
Concentratie en segregatie**, Rijswijk/The Hague,
SCP/VUGA, 1995.

Vegt, C. van der, and W.J.J. Manshanden, **Steden en stads-
gewesten: economische ontwikkelingen 1970-2015**, The
Hague, Sdu, 1996.

Waldinger, R., **Still the Promised City? African-Americans
and New Immigrants in Postindustrial New York**,
Cambridge/London, Harvard University Press, 1996.

Between Port and City   **Stefano Boeri**

The Italian port cities continue to be subject to the effects of a phase of re-launching maritime transport in the Mediterranean basin. A propelling force that has been flanked of late by phenomena of lesser impact, such as the growth of Mediterranean and European cruise traffic (also marked by the entry of US liners into the basin), together with a widespread upsurge in industrial and shipbuilding activities. Even though this phase of expansion is due to outside factors and has no secure future (due largely to events in the Asian markets), there can be no doubt that the Italian port cities have had to deal with a new brand of problems over recent years. These consist above all in the emergence of a primary issue: that of 're-identification' of their essence as urban areas furnished with an important port basin.

The issue could be posed through a paradox: the main Italian port cities whose 'body' discloses the history of a profound and inextricable bond of direct contacts between historic urban zones and port quaysides, are often today also dual-fronted territories where not only are a noble urban identity and a strong port identity not integrated, but they often do not even succeed in cohabiting. In other words, when faced with a geographical situation which may force urban port activities and coastal residential zones to cohabit and bear the costs of this obligatory cohabitation (for the city congestion, environmental pollution, inaccessibility to the seafront; for the port lack of areas for expansion, limited mobility of goods, local, institutional and social confliction), a culture persists based on the assumption of a clear separation of interests between port and city. A regressive and punishing culture that has accompanied these last decades marked by a crisis in the large Italian port areas, and that today – in a contrasting expansive phase – must be overcome if the important possibilities for competition in the maritime markets of the Mediterranean and Europe are not to be lost.

The issue is clearly complex and long-standing and cannot be solved either with recip-rocal declarations of good intention, or with legislative solutions in that it highlights the lack of a substantial culture of managing the urban transformations relative to a territory (that of the city-port) that should be considered as a single whole area. In this regard, and with special reference to the Italian urban port areas, several points for reflection emerge.

The Italian port areas – and more generally those of Mediterranean Europe (Barcelona, Marseilles, Genoa, Naples, Trieste, Piraeus, Thessaloniki...) have three unusual characteristics.

The Mediterranean ports are, above all, 'multi-functional'. Different landscapes and environments co-exist: the commercial zones, the tourist areas, the productive areas, the large open areas for handling goods and passengers but also niches of residential space, meeting places, areas for recreation. This range of spaces inside a closed perimeter, in combination with the layout of the Italian coast that often compresses the historic city onto port areas preventing their shift to external areas (unlike the situation in northern European ports), means that the ports belonging to the large cities of southern Europe are inextricably inter-connected with their cities. Like the cities that gave rise to them, the Italian and Mediterranean ports are tolerated and are 'mixed blood' areas, capable of hosting a remarkable variety of types and spaces within a compact, coherent and distinct environment.

In Naples, Genoa, Palermo, Marseilles or Thessaloniki, transiting from the medieval center to the port means traversing in a matter of meters, a rapid succession of radically different urban landscapes that always contain a wealth of variety. This characteristic, genetic code of the large port cities of southern Europe, is a theme worthy of careful study.

The second characteristic of the ports – not only those in the Mediterranean – is their intrinsic 'centrality'. The port is not envisaged as an extension of the city on water, as a waterfront (a hypocritical and distracting term if referred to port areas), but as a halfway place between water and urban land; an essentially 'intermediate' place that entertains relationships with both the landscapes that border it, on the sea and land sides. The flow of goods and passengers from the latter come together on the quayside – which are vast open fluid spaces, by no coincidence – and determine the centrality of the port. In other words the port is the artificial place of a mobile 'centrality' where the goods that occupy quaysides and wharves are exchanged and circulated. The area has clear rules and principles, and the open spaces are more stable and important than the building-containers. This 'mobile' centrality is one of the most interesting themes in planning design for urban port areas, because on one hand it conflicts with the static centrality of the historic city, while on the other it stimulates it.

In conclusion, the third characteristic of the Italian and southern European ports concerns their remarkable 'mobility'. The ports are subject to continual change in terms of parts, areas, corridors, which also makes them unpredictable. Designing a port area means learning to deal with the issue of uncertainty and the unforeseeable nature of the future of an urban coastal area. This future is often dictated by choices and strategies that take place tens of thousands of kilometers away, for instance in the office of a foreign company or on the bridge of a large container ship at sea. The lack of reliable predictions about the economic scenario and the market often forces port operators to take direct responsibility for intervention strategy. There may be no scenarios that require an action, which may be wholly intentional, or 'political', to be discussed without resorting to the use of deductive reasoning.

In terms of these unusual characteristics that clearly distinguish the ports from the neighboring historic city centers while also revealing their common history, it is essential for the hypocrisy of false promises of 'integration' between port and city to be avoided. Requesting 'integration' often means suggesting that the distinguishing features of one or both be partly or wholly cancelled, as happened for the wharves monopolized by container traffic as well as with the large-scale recreational/commercial projects that – based on the North American model – have colonized and thus brought to an end many 'mixed blood' urban areas of the Mediterranean cities (as for example has been partly the case for the Barcelona seafront). From this viewpoint, the landscapes of Italy's historic port cities, namely Genoa, Naples and Trieste, are a rare resource worthy of conservation. At stake here is a radical alternative to the model of the great US and eastern ports, where it is a matter of alternating immense plazas destined for container handling and freshly spruced-up wharves for groups of tourists, with fast food outlets with figureheads, waiters with cummerbunds, theme parks and car parks.

The relationship between port and city in the Italian coastal cities – often the cause of bitter conflicts and misunderstandings – must be dealt with while avoiding the opposing trends towards rigid separation (as happened in the past) and mechanical integration of the two territories (an attitude that often conceals the claims for authority each exerts on the other). 'Co-habitation' between the two territories, and their reciprocal grafts instead are possible only when the 'differences' are clarified, as well as their similarities and 'harmonies' matured over decades of cohabitation and common use of infrastructures. These differences are physical, spatial, cultural and social in nature; and derive from a different political and economic management of the territory, as well as from the inertia of two different image systems.

The great Mediterranean port cities – Genoa, Naples, Athens, Thessaloniki, Barcelona and Alexandria – can and must avoid the arrogant monotony of this comparison because they are still complex and composite sites, where work mingles with leisure, cars with containers, liners with historical palaces. They are still places where architecture can be surprising, entailing changes in scale and consonance between different and distant spaces.

The forthcoming master plans for the Italian port cities will thus be greeted by a complete vision of city, not a legislative obligation.

Two recent projects in the port areas of Genoa and Naples have been conducted on the assumption that an increase in the port activities and a substantial opening of the docks to the city can take place simultaneously only if work is done to define the differences between port and city. Recognizing the specific identities of these areas, and recognizing that for each individual port city these are made up of an interactive reciprocal relationship, are two essential conditions for planning the future of a city/port.

In Genoa the new Port Master Plan (recently adopted after approval by the City Council) stood for the first Italian experiment for 'concerted' planning in port areas. It is an articulated instrument with the purpose of solving problems concerning the coastal belt with the inclusion of the city's 'viewpoint'. A plan that has entailed co-operation with the City Council right from the start and that – despite a long tradition of non-communication – has constructed a shared scenario on the future of the city/port. It is also innovative in terms of methodology: considerable effort is made to involve those who operate in the sector and make exploratory use of architectural projects, developed as 'designed concepts' as the plan was being drawn up; a plan with new original work lines in both procedural terms and concerning the legal 'form' of the text.

In Naples on the other hand, the 'Study for the Regeneration of the

Tourist-Passenger Hub' is an attempt to deal simultaneously with the city's necessity for expansion and the need to boost the port, through a project with various planning and work levels. The preliminary project and its architectonic preview on the Molo Beverello – demolition of part of the wall that still separates port and city and the construction of a temporary platform as an intermediary between the wharves and the urban space – point to the possibility of responding simultaneously to the urgent needs of the city and its port even when they appear to be irreconcilable, as when faced with the request to make better use of scarce disputed property such as wharf space.

The idea of a great port park, a large-scale public promenade that allows the city to approach a working port (whose performance is then augmented) is the result of careful consideration of the needs of the two bodies and the opportunities offered by the coastal belt.

Cities in Transition and the Urban-Architectural Project   **Yorgos Simeoforidis**

The new urban landscape seems to be the focus of the community of architects and urbanist seeking those tools for approaching, understanding and describing which could render effective different processes of spatial interventions. It may be a coincidence, however this attention to the new urban landscape is not accidental and unrelated to the primacy that spatial issues acquired in the nineties. In fact, as Edward Soja has put it 'since the beginning of the nineties, we have also undergone what I perceive as the first significant trans-disciplinary spatial turn – a turn to new ways of thinking in which space occupies a central position as a form of analysis, critical inquiry, practice, theory-building, politics.'[1]

Architecture and urbanism, as spatial disciplines 'par excellence', are radically affected by this spatial turn which offers a new modality of space; besides spatial practices or – according to Lefebvre – 'perceived space' and 'conceived space' or representations of space, there is also the fully 'lived space' (respectively: Firstspace, Secondspace and Thirdspace for Soja). Soja claims that both disciplines are still bound up in First and Secondspace; however a series of events or new spatio-cultural politics bring forward issues of 'rights to city', 'civil rights', 'spatial justice' that are going to transform them. This spatial turn is not unrelated to current urban transformations over the globe – in the European, American and particularly Asiatic context – since all cannot avoid touching issues of democracy and the new political value of the urban project.

Emerging city or escaping metapolis?

The 'emerging city' is constituted on the attempt of different French researchers who focused their attention on: the decodification of current urban transformations, the suburban diffused developments; the growth of mobility and the possibilities of choice in displacements; the renewed notion of centrality through the construction of commercial and leisure centers; the new perception of urbanity; the new forms of social cohabitation; the increasing diversification between symbolic places (the historical center) and places of banal, everyday frequency in reference to the collective unconsciousness; the new relationship between nature and city, as well as between city and countryside; the significance acquired by notions such as the ephemeral and the transitory, and their implications for the architecture of the commercial centers, office buildings, restaurants and bars; the impact of information technology and the media on the public space of the city.[2]

In contrast to homogeneity and continuity, the emerging city seems to have a

1 Edward W. Soja, 'Lessons in Spatial Justice', **hunch**, the Berlage Institute report, No. 1/1999, pp.98-107. Also, **Thirdspace: Journeys to Los Angeles and Other Real-and-Imagined Places**, Blackwell, Oxford/Massachusetts, 1996.
2 **La ville émergente**, edit. Geneviève Dubois-Taine and Yves Chalas, edit. de l'Aube, 1997.

preference for discontinuity and rupture as urban characteristics par
excellence. The city-labyrinth, the city with its artificial sub-soil related to
the functionality of network infrastructures and services and the physical
city where the banal, the monumental, the well known urban figures
do not result as common references for the contemporary inhabitants
– by definition heterogeneous and diversified – bring evidence to the issue
of democracy within the framework of an new urban condition which
differs substantially from the previous ones.

In this context, the assumption as a working hypothesis, of the notion of
metapolis, indicates a reality that integrates and supersedes at the same
time the classic notion of metropolis. According to the definition of the
French sociologist François Ascher, 'a metapolis is the whole of spaces
in which the whole or part of its inhabitants, its economic activities or
the areas are integrated within the everyday function of a metropolis.
A metapolis is generally a basin of work, residence and activities. The
spaces that compose a metapolis are fundamentally heterogeneous and
discontinuous. A metapolis comprises at least a few hundred thousand
inhabitants.'[3] The fundamental difference between the two models is
that the first indicates, in urban geography, the theory of central places of
Christaller (1933), representing the spatial and hierarchical distribution
of cities; and the second indicates the emergence of a new urban system
with polarization around the metropolises acting in a network and at an
international scale with epicenters (hubs) and radians (spokes), following
the models of rapid means of transport, in particular air transport.

There is a still an open debate as to the relation of the metapolis to
the so-called post-industrial city or the post-era city, nevertheless it is
certain that the new technologies of transport and communication which
contribute to the reconstitution of urban and ex-urban spaces, do not
necessarily imply the extinction of the cities. Metropolization and the
formation of metapolises are advanced forms of urbanization processes,
which continue their rhythm, based primarily on the modes and technologies of exchanges. Metapolis is one more phase – in a process that obviously

---

3 François Ascher, **Métapolis ou L'avenir des villes**, edit. Odile Jacob, Paris, 1995, p.34.

is neither linear nor continuous – one more form of urbanization, as a result of the new techniques of communication, conservation and displacement of goods, people and information.

'This new diffused urban space, always expanding, fragmented, heterogeneous often provokes architects and urbanists as well as politicians since it does not correspond to the traditional forms of appropriation between social life and territorial rights,' claims Ascher, distinguishing at least two modes of perception and confrontation: the first is related to a will of stopping this procedure, combined with a restitution or modernization of a classical urban model; that of the traditional compact, dense and continuous European city, while the second deals with the confrontation and handling of this new modernity rather than its refusal.[4] The French sociologist observes the conversion between the urban model of the classical city and the ecological and progressive model, with the emphasis given to public transport, this new blurred alliance, without homogeneity but with a felt political and ideological weight within the European Commission, since it carries with it, rather fortuitously, the dominant slogan for sustainable development.

Beyond territorial givens and constraints, the metapolis brings a new reality: the globalization of the urban condition. It represents freedom from the pressures of history and geographical location, the diffusion of new scales and programs, the downloading of formalistic exercises, the development of entrepreneurial strategies, the abandonment of the architectural object, the hybridization of many cultural references, the development of new materials, the search for the new. Today, according to the Italian researcher Paolo Perulli, the image of the big city is that of a huge water-clock in the two poles of which we find the new professional elites and the new sectors of manual labor (incorporated in the service industry), together with unprecedented forms of poverty and social degradation, while in the center we can find the traditional productive classes, the bourgeoisie and working class).[5] In these facets of the social fabric of the contemporary city there is still work to be done, however, as any consideration, any perspective for its present and future finds itself unavoidably in a conflict with the ever changing landscape of its social structures.

Large-scale urban-architectural projects   Barcelona offers a modus operandi, for an understanding of the transition from the eighties to the nineties, from the period before the Olympic Games (1986-1992), based on the policies of 'new centrality'

4 François Ascher, 'Gia ti metapoli' (For metapolis), **Metapolis** 1/1997, p.9.
5 Paolo Perulli, **Atlante metropolitano – Il mutamento sociale nelle grandi città**, Bologna, 1992.

and 'metastasis' (that is, the diffusion of small-scale actions in the public space of the existing city, in its historical center as well as its modern periphery), to the policy of large-scale infrastructures (Olympic Ring, Villa Olimpica, Diagonal, Vall d'Hebron, the new ring roads, the new cultural interventions, the re-appropriation of the seafront as a new collective urban space). In this transition, the urban planning of the 'flexible city' differs substantially from that of the 'functional city': 'the city is not even conceived as an immense production machine, nor is there recognition for the inexorability of the plan/program/budget chain which inspired the functional planning system. Production economies do not emerge through vertical integration in large firms, but through the juxtaposition of external economies linked to the city... The movement is from an idea of hierarchically organized cities to a notion of urban networks and interaction of space...'[6]

This transition defines the context for a series of large-scale transformations which took place in many European cities during the nineties: the definition of a new centrality related to the high-speed train system in Lille; the structural changes in the former port areas of Rotterdam over the river Maas and their remodeling as new urban areas; the new water city in the abandoned area of Spandau, on the river Havel outside Berlin; the renovation of the existing railways station in London offering an answer to the crisis of the Docklands development; the new technological-education pole Pirelli-Bicocca in Milan, on the traces of the abandoned industrial sites; the radical renewal of Bilbao and its transformation into a major cultural pole; the re-appropriation of the abandoned industrial port areas in Dunkirk, as well as of the heavy industrial territories along the river Rhine in Germany, combined with the upgrading of a network of medium scale cities; the new 'green city' on the traces of the abandoned railway tracks in the Plaine St. Denis, in northern Paris; the development of a new urban sector next to the river Tagus on the occasion of the EXPO '98 in Lisbon.

In any case, regardless of the renewal of degraded districts or the

6 Joan Trullen, 'Barcelona, the flexible city', **1856-1999/Contemporary Barcelona**, CCCB/Diputaci de Bercelona, 1997, pp.244-255.

remodeling of industrial sites and their related infrastructures or even of the new forms of urbanization, one thing is clear: today, more than ever, the challenge of the city is played on the scale of large urban-architectural projects. In this direction of the 'negotiated project', certain methods of design research and action, such as experts acting as consultants, competitions of ideas or by invitation, workshops 'in situ', etc. seem to be more effective than the traditional procedures. This new emphasis on the urban-architectural project is different from the theories of 'bigness' advanced by OMA/Rem Koolhaas, although both share many points of reference to the contemporary city.

Modernization of the Greek city

The deficiency of large-scale urban renewal projects is not completely extraneous to production modes and processes in the built-up areas in Greece. However to deal with their problems, Greek cities must focus on inventive programs in order to respond to social needs for improving the quality of the urban landscape, mindful of the increasing differentiation of the social fabric, supported by the concepts of feasibility and profitability (to the extent to which project implementation poses the problem of self-funding).

Reserve is often expressed with regard to large-scale projects for Greek cities, and counter proposals are made for small interventions; it would, however, be a mistake to adopt such ideas unilaterally, with no attention to the differences between project scales, especially regarding the possibility of involving urban parts or sections, recognizing the impossibility of applying a global project or the inefficiency of isolated interventions. One fundamental question concerns the modes of project mentality that will characterize the new design of these run-down urban areas. Should we fill these spaces with new programs or safeguard them, with special attention to the unique nature of their landscapes? Should we deal with these places in terms of continuity of the urban fabric, or recognize their separate and fragmentary nature, that may lead us towards different project practices? The Greek cities – with their casual, unplanned urban growth – require work that confers order and eases congestion in the urban fabric, emphasizing public space, or perhaps rather an intensification entailing the creation of an inward-looking public space with the insertion of large-scale objects in the city.

In all probability, a similar problem directly concerns the architects and urbanists capable of dealing with the 'large scale' in terms of the project (that is to say, of the city itself), without submitting docilely to the historicist rhetoric or the beautification of the fragmentation of the urban landscape. This all has an impact on the re-visitation of the urban project and the relationship between urbanism and architecture. An urban planning policy cannot be conceived as a list of instructions for norms to be applied, but rather as an effective, immediate and practical formulation; an act motivated by systematic if undefined visions about concrete specialist actions. The experience in urban renewal projects and urban planning work developed in Europe demonstrates that the general master plan belongs to the past, though it can be reconverted in specific urbanistic studies, on the basis of the conviction that architecture has a retroactive importance in the city. The appropriate modus operandi must not mean submitting specific urban planning studies to the general master plan, but rather the contrary. Today we are traversing a phase of transition between the hierarchical mode to the negotiable model; from 'urban planning of development to urban planning of valorization'.[7]

Designing leisure or a city made from events

Moreover in order to launch a similar mechanism, a wide-reaching initial effort is needed. Several cities have been offered exogenous opportunities; events of a different order seem to be the mechanisms for large urban transformations besides the private logic of financial enterprises in the fields of commerce and leisure in particular. As European Cultural Capital for 1997, Thessaloniki for example succeeded in exploiting that initial effort to revive its urban planning in terms of the relation park-building and public space; something that has not, unfortunately, taken place – so far – in Athens. It is not a cultural capital and has no prospects for furthering its presence in the economic network of Europe: none of this aids progress of the events and destiny of the city, other than the organization of the 2004 Olympic Games – unquestionably a large-scale event; a multi-faceted initiative, with consequences on the economic, social and urban planning levels, that could offer the incentive for general reflection in the context of the city's strategic regeneration.

The consequences of the 2004 Olympic Games in Athens, especially

---

7 Bernard Reichen, 'De l'urbanisme de développement à l'urbanisme de valorization' in the volume **L'élaboration des projets architectureaux et urbains en Europe – Les acteurs du projet architectural et urbain**, Plan Construction et Architecture, Paris, 1997, pp.177-180.

the post-Olympic use of sports structures, is crucial. It is essential for time to be spent on the question of what type of city is desirable in the wake of the Games. This prospect must be of concern for the bodies responsible for the planned work. The Olympics are not a panacea but a great opportunity for reinforcing a program that can bring urban issues to the forefront through works and projects to restructure its image and the urban fabric. Athens is a European metropolis that has developed and been extended in a casual manner, without a precise shape, set limits and – more seriously – without infrastructures and structured public spaces. It is also common knowledge that various ministers and appointed organizations have undertaken work in dealing with this new modernization process and have arranged for various projects scattered in the metropolitan territory with the aim of making Athens more sustainable. However these works are insufficient, and need to be part of a strategic project for the city.

Athens' relationship with the sea is reminiscent of the relationship of the walled city around the Acropolis with its port – Piraeus – by way of the 'long walls' that once united the two parts, and have persisted as primary signs for the landscape, set in the collective urban memory. Athens is maintaining this relationship, even without the walls, and over the 20th century has gradually been acquiring a new coastal layout from Faliron Bay to the first suburbs of Glyfada, Voula and Vouliagmeni, a relationship based on recreation, leisure, entertainment, the use of the sea for 'dolce far niente' as Ernesto Nathan Rogers referred to it in the debates of the post-war CIAMs.[8]

In the course of its development, Faliron has always been a favored place, the symbol of Athens' contact with the sea. At the 2nd Congress of Architecture held in Thessaloniki in 1962, Georges Candilis referred to Faliron as 'the balcony of Athens' towards the Mediterranean, proposing it as the site for the Urban Directional Center – in contrast to the proposal of Constantinos Doxiadis, who placed it in the northern part of the city. Later on, a series of architectonic and urban design competitions attempted to make the most of the site's latent centrality and natural beauty, with the construction of large hotels and the transformation of the coast into a pedestrian strip with facilities for athletic and bathing activities.

It is no coincidence that Candilis returned there in 1987, during the preparation of the dossier for Athens' candidature for the 1996 Olympics, held in Atlanta, USA, formulating the idea of the four Olympic Poles (the Olympic Village for the northern outskirts of

8 The Faliron Bay case was first presented in the special issue 'The Maturity of the Waterfront' of the review **Aquapolis**, 21-22/1999, pp.76-82.

Athens, the Olympic Athletic Center at Kalogresa, the historic city center as the hub for cultural events around the archaeological sites, and Faliron Bay as a pole for recreational, free time and athletic activities). However the idea was kept for the candidature for the 2004 Olympics as well, the bid now having been won by Athens.

According to the Olympic Works program, the land-filled part (100 hectares) of the bay will see the installation of beach volleyball, while the sector currently occupied by the Hippodrome (24.5 hectares) is to be moved to a different place and will host the four temporary stadiums or pavilions for volleyball, handball, judo and boxing. The current legislation governing planning for the Olympic Works (2370/1999) entails the later use of the area as a metropolitan tourist and recreational hub, with commercial activities, restaurants, coffee bars, open-air public spaces, cultural buildings, parking areas, installations and sports grounds, congress centers and marinas, but no residential sections.

The area is currently fragmented – a series of obstacles has prevented residents' access to the waterfront. These include avenue Posidonos, which functions as a high speed roadway, the landfill areas on the coast dating back to 1960, the infrastructure work under way (for a new canal to deal with the serious flooding problem and the malfunction of the existing drain beneath avenue Posidonos), and the new road hubs, especially the exit for the new Kifissos artery on the seafront (the Syggrou road node has been out of use for 20 years).[9] Having said this, the main theme to be dealt with is the refurbishment of the waterfront for the Olympics, from Faliron Bay to the Hippodrome, making the area public and accessible to the residents of the adjacent council areas as well as those from the greater city area.

The Faliron Bay workshop In order to deal with these themes, the Organizing Committee for the Olympic Games 'Athens 2004' and the Organization for Planning and Environmental Protection of Athens, have undertaken a groundbreaking initiative, inviting five leading experienced architect-urban planners to Athens (Rem Koolhaas/

---

9 In reference to the new interest in the redevelopment of the area it is worth mentioning the 'HERACLES Programme', an urban-architectural research coordinated by prof. Cesare Macchi Cassia/Milan and Dimitris N. Karidis/Athens, and sponsored by a cement industry, for five urban sites in the cities of Athens, Patras, Volos and Mitilini, including the Faliron Bay. See the volume, **Dieci progetti per la città greca**, AGET HERACLES, Athens, 1997.

Rotterdam, Josep Antonio Acebillo/Barcelona, Cesare Macchi Cassis/Milan, Bernard Reichen/Paris, Eduard Bru/Barcelona), in order to obtain a blueprint for strategic planning or a structural scheme for the area.[10] Two distinct workshops were organized in situ, coordinated by Peter Rowe/Harvard and Andreas Symeon/Athens. In the four proposals presented (Koolhaas was unable to participate in the second session), four different ideas on the city/sea relationship emerged in terms of the redevelopment for the Faliron waterfront.

The scenario from Bernard Reichen's group is based on the main idea of re-modern-ization of an urban area, Faliron Bay and the Hippodrome, taking them as an important available reserve for gradual transformation into a structured urban area for sea-related recreational activities. The proposal came as four themes: road system, land and maritime hydrology, the natural and ecological re-configuration, the layout of the constructed programs. These themes were developed separately at first, then in combination with the slogan 'four years, four building sites', pointing to a coherent urban planning procedure entailing the possibility for separation into four different actions: a) the infrastructures (changing the road system, constructing the canal, creating an 'urban forest', b) the Hippodrome (transformation of the four pavilions for the Olympic Games into congress and exhibition centers, c) the artificial island (an open area with views to the city, including three natural sites around a lagoon: the new beach, the palms, bird life resources, and d) the marina area and the aquarium (public space linked to the bay).

Josep Acebillo began with the new centrality of Faliron, viewed in terms of metropolitan geography as a connection to the port of Piraeus and the airport of Ellinikon, and as verification of the separation of the surrounding residential areas from the seafront, and produced a scenario of project gestures that focuses attention on public space: a) the new urban plaza on the Hippodrome site, as an intermediate space between the envisaged post-Olympic congress center and the new activities towards the Kallithea Council area, b) the large-scale exedra and aquatic plaza, beginning at the congress center and stretch-ing all the way to the Maritime Museum (outcome of a previous architecture competi-tion), proposed as a large public linking space, c) the linear park along the seafront, with a proposed monorail alongside a high speed road – avenue Posidonos re-designed over the canal, at a lower elevation, to enable residents to reach the new sea park, which will include the new Hippodrome and a beach.

10 The Workshop in Athens was held in two phases (September 5-7 and October 9-11). The organizers from 'Athens 2004' were Yannis Pyrgiotis, member of the company's Board of Directors, George Leventis, Managing Director of the Olympic Works, Yorgos Simeoforidis, responsible of the Workshop, and Thomas Doxiadis, group member. Those from the Organization for the Master Plan were Avgi Markopoulou, Chairman, and Stratis Koulis, head of Large-scale Works.

The scenario by Eduard Bru once again highlights the re-establishment of the equilibrium between the city's historic and geographical landscape, between the hills of the Acropolis and Lycabettus and the seafront. The success of this can be seen in the design of a new landscape for the Faliron waterfront, embracing the new canal and the existing road system, but proposing them to be re-designed in morphological and architectonic terms. Two new buildings, 'Propilea', on the Hippodrome and Flisvos site, will host the Olympic uses and the new post-Olympic uses proposed (convention and exhibition center), restructuring a new entrance from the seafront towards the urban center. The construction of light structures (open-air cinema, aquarium, museums, natural areas, restaurants) creates a monumental base for transparent containers between the hills, the city and the sea.

Lastly, Cesare Macchi Cassia also proposed re-establishing the city-sea relationship, by way of a comparison, or rather, a joint consideration of Faliron Bay as a location for the development of a new urban ecology, re-designing the coast from the urban blocks down to the sea. The scenario refers to long-term operations and structural work in terms of the area's natural assets (remodeling the road system, from the section of avenue Posidonos, draining the land and channeling the water, with no need for the new canal), and pilot work, including the transformation of the Hippodrome into a new metropolitan park and sports area, with consecutive post-Olympic uses (congress and exhibition center) in the surrounding Flisvos area.

As regards the issues of management for these operations, the scenarios of Cassia and Reichen require a decentralized procedure with a series of actions – not by stages but interconnected – to be carried out in the long run with different methods, funding and results (in this sense the 'decomposition-recomposition' of Reichen's four themes and sites may be more flexible on an operational and political level). In the scenarios of Bru and Acebillo, as per their high profile experience in Barcelona, the expected transformation of the area is obtained through the participation of public and private bodies in joint ventures; giving priority to work involving infrastructures that cannot, of course, be undertaken solely by private groups.

Paradoxically, at the close of the Workshop sessions, discussion resumed on the topic dealt with during the first session, especially the comment by Rem Koolhaas 'Who is in charge?' used in reference, after the Gordian knot of the infrastructures, to the reconsideration of the four Olympic poles and the need for a general strategy for the city – points that are unfortunately still lacking an answer. In line with the opinions of the two coordinators, it was stated that the transformation of Faliron Bay must be dealt with by a Special Agency, under the control of the Ministry of Environment, Planning and Public Works, which, in collaboration with the guest architects, will develop 'a set of planning and morphological guidelines', to lead to the necessary political commitment for the work.[11]

The Greek cities have no large abandoned industrial ports, instead they have limited areas facing or actually on the seafront, and in view of lack of public spaces, these act as collective spaces par excellence on the water or in its proximity. For these cases it may be possible to redefine a new significance for water – the sea – in the context of a society where recreation and free time take on an increasingly urban value. The vicinity or proximity of the city to water is unquestionably a cultural theme – water acquires a different role depending on the cultures and urban civilizations with which it comes into contact (I refer to the well-known difference between European, North European and American waterfronts, though I have the impression that these models can be improved by the cases of the Asian and South American cities). In the case of Faliron, the elimination of residence and the tertiary sector, irrevocably leads to a logic for development in terms of American models that define the seafront as a site for recreation with consumer points: congress center, exhibitions, aquarium, marinas (a few years ago the area of Flisvos was the 'apple of discord', with the proposal for construction of a Casino in the area blocked by the residents' protests).

Reichen's proposals, and those of Acebillo up to a certain point, deal with the transformation of the area and the role of augmenting the importance of the water – the sea – in this light: Faliron Bay is a new venue for urban leisure, and the artificial island and the marina area take on primary importance. Acebillo's and Bru's proposals entail a project for the land itself as well as architecture, a new seafront on the water; while that by Cassia is a contemporary version of a modernist logic, in consonance with the 19th century, a variation on the theme of urban coast (promenade along the waterfront).

---

11 Surprisingly enough, after the Workshop the Organization for Planning and Environmental Protection of Athens commissioned both the offices of Bernard Reichen and Josep Acebillo to produce a Master Plan for the whole area, with Andreas Symeon acting as a consultant. The Plan was presented in late February 2000 and now awaits the results of the forthcoming elections in early April to set in motion the process of a structural urban development – for the first time in post-war history.

Hybrid landscapes

In any case, if Barcelona can be held up as an excellent example of an attractive recreational space where the infrastructures are at the service of the city, Faliron Bay could be an example of another type or mode of development: of a landscape, rather than an urban space; of the hybridization of recreational and regular sports activity uses, a sort of new park flanking the sea, where existing and new infrastructures are integrated, in an excellent interpretation of a tradition of the recent Mediterranean waterfront. This seems to be the democratic challenge of the project; this is the spatial right, perhaps latent, though evident in the 'voices' of the people and the claim of the Municipalities so far, and not a well-functioning theme park.

If that is the case, Faliron Bay may then be considered a 'terrain vague', one of those 'virus areas' presently getting publicity, entering the domain of the media to claim its assumed public denominator.[12] The question is whether it will be subjugated into the consumerist system of the escaping metapolis, with a large metropolitan impact, or whether it will be able to maintain something of its erratic status and undermine the so far dominant urban symbolic places, simply by offering or even permitting a different idea of the contemporary city, based on multiplicity and heterogeneity.

12 On these questions see the texts in the volume, **Paesaggi ibridi – Un viaggio nella città contemporanea**, edit. by Mirko Zardini, Skira, Milan, 1996.

1, 2 The Faliron site in Athens. A terrain vague subject to the transformation due to the Athens 2004 Olympic Games (aerial view).
3 Josep Acebillo, urban sketch of the new waterfront.
4 Cesare Macchi Cassia, modelling the ground of the new waterfront.
5 Cesare Macchi Cassia 2, section of new waterfront.
6 Arch. Eduard Bru, perspective drawing of the new waterfront.

7, 8 Master Plan during the Olympic Games and after: architects Bernard Reichen, Josep Acebillo, Andreas Symeon, traffic engineers Constantinos ∑ekkos, John Frantzeskakis, marine engineer Andreas Nikolopoulos.
9 Aerial view of the Faliron site after the Olympic Games.
10 a+b The new urban beaches and the bathing culture in Attica during the 1960s.
a Astir Beach & Resort, Glyfada, Attica

(1957-59), arch. Emmanouil Vourekas, Periklis Sakellarios, Prokopis Vassiliadis, coll. arch. Antonis Georgiades, Constantin Decavalla (photo courtesy E. Fessas-Emmanouil Archive).
b Megali Akti Beach, Vouliagmeni (1958-1962), arch. Emmanouil Vourekas, Periklis Sakellarios, Prokopis Vassiliadis, coll. arch. Nikos Hadjimichalis (photo courtesy E. Fessas-Emmanouil Archive).

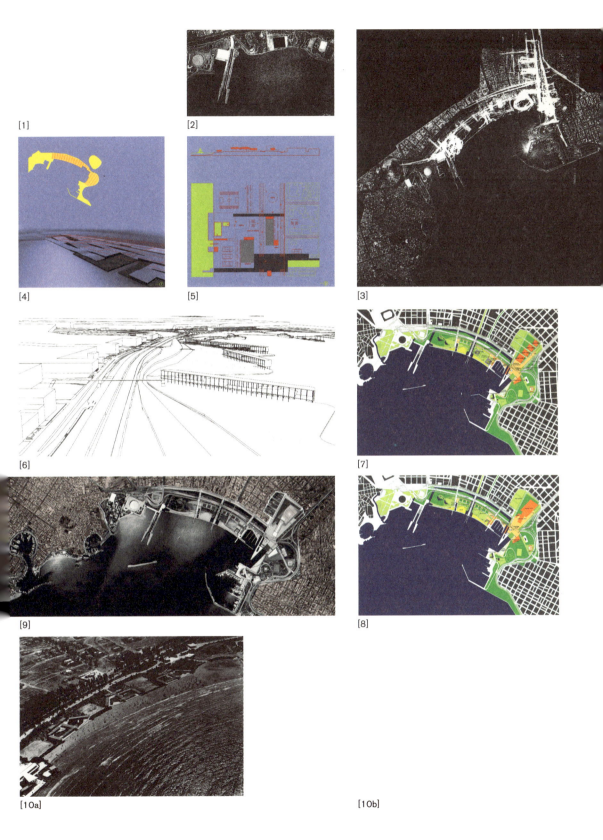

[1]

[2]

[3]

[4]

[5]

[6]

[7]

[8]

[9]

[10a]

[10b]

Meaning and Tradition **Henco Bekkering**

Modernity and tradition The designer's interpretation of the project commission forms the basis of every design process. In every urban planning assignment and even in every part of a design, it is essential that a position be taken regarding program and commission objectives. This position is not so much a question of personal opinions or preferences; it depends on the context of the commission, by which I mean the physical context as well as the extended context (social circumstances, the opinions of the client, etc.).

Until recently this critical positioning was unnecessary. During long periods in history ideas about the order of things were fixed. In architecture this was manifested in the major periods of style; and this is equally applicable to the manner in which cities were laid out, even at the time when urban planning as a discipline was completely unknown. In the Modern and Postmodern eras these kinds of certainties no longer exist, and the designer consequently feels continually under pressure to adopt a standpoint, an individual standpoint, for each specific commission. Avoiding this by assuming a 'personal style' offers a false certainty. The excessive appreciation of the 'unique result' and the 'vision' of the architect or urban planner – both within the disciplines themselves and from beyond with the clients and the public – has resulted in the present extremely multi-colored range of concepts and ideas. The paradoxical effect of scale, however, shows that excessive variation on this level irrevocably leads to monotony at a larger scale, ultimately resulting in an undifferentiated mass.

Other than the possibility of using an 'individual style' as the basis of the design of a building, a second and broader cultural mechanism, that of 'tradition', could provide a basis. The distinction between style and tradition can be made clear from a somewhat exaggerated contrast between the two: 'fixity' is advantageous to style; whilst transformation is a general social mechanism that facilitates change, albeit gradual, as regards tradition.

Studies in art history relating to style have shown that the ascent of a new style often required a break with the previous one. This was particularly true for the formative phase of 'orthodox and heroic' modern architecture, where this break with style was a consciously adopted tactic. On the other hand, tradition also makes feasible what we call historical continuity. This certainly does not imply that everything should remain as it was. Tradition should be understood as a way of doing things, focused on action. Tradition provides a basis for the manner in which a system can accommodate change without the necessity of forgetting, without 'breaking with the past'.

By far the majority of our cities were designed not so much as an entirety according to one given style, but more so as a sequence of components created according to a series of traditions, where the ideas of the time were applicable to the city as a whole. This suggests that historical continuity and consequently the mechanism of tradition are of special relevance to urban planning. Moreover, as urban planning increasingly involves measures in and management of existing urban areas (inner cities, post-war residential neighborhoods etc.) an understanding of tradition and historical continuity is now even more relevant. The Dutch psychologist-philosopher Willem Koerse states this in succinct terms: '... matters from the past, from the previous century or from the Middle Ages are a part of the "present", they constitute "the oldest part of the present". It goes without saying that their potential and the possible changes to them also belong to the present.'[1]

What we now experience as cohesion in our historical cities is largely the result of design and construction in accordance with tradition. Returning to Willem Koerse: 'There is no present that will benefit from the wish to resurrect a past, but nor should it wish to break free from it – because then it robs itself of an essential dimension. That is why the past must be revered: not to resurrect it, nor to repeat it or to copy it, but to use it as a multiple source.'[2]

Take, for example, the surroundings of Chedworth Forest in Cotswolds, or the annexes of Gouchester Cathedral, in a typically English landscape. (I have chosen examples from England, as it is the country of tradition 'par excellence'.) The landscapes keep their character, even though the scale of agriculture has increased. Their meaning and significance are still visible. In the restoration of monuments the history of changes and additions is left intact. Cathedrals for instance sometimes look not like one but several buildings that exist within the same structure at the same time.

Cohesion, fragmentation and networks Cohesion
on one scale is a precondition for the recognition of a unit on a larger scale.

1 W. Koerse, 'Een kwestie van tijd II – De stad en gelijktijdigheid', **De grenzeloze stad**, Thoth, Bussum, 1997, p.66.
2 Ibid. 'Een kwestie van tijd I – Naar behoud van heden', p.69.

This implies a formal hierarchy; it is unavoidable. The advocates of urban fragmentation consider this hierarchy to be reprehensible. This rejection has a moral undertone, because hierarchy suggests inequality, and consequently power. And in these times of heterogeneous equality this is of course no longer considered to be politically correct, especially in the ever-tolerant Netherlands. But formal hierarchy need have nothing to do with power; it refers to 'significance', legibility and comprehensibility. It does not refer to how people act towards 'each other', but how they act towards their 'surroundings'. This, by the way, acknowledges that all significance is linked to a context.

Fragmentation as a consequence of interruptions and sudden transitions has now become an undeniable fact in our cities and their peripheries. In the twentieth century, discontinuities have been admitted as an aesthetic category in our appreciation, following their glorification by the Modernists. They are now defended by terms such as 'innovation', the effects of 'contrast', and 'alienation' in modern art. This has become a widely based and deeply rooted attitude in our culture.

According to thinkers like Arendt, Berman and Sennett, 'being modern' presumes being prepared for disengagement from an existing concept, being prepared to renounce one's own past and identity. However, this very loss of identity now evokes reactions from society. Clients offering commissions for urban transformation now consider the maintenance or recovery of identity to be one of the most important items in their program.

Nevertheless, the mechanisms of modernity have consequences for the way in which contemporary society is organized, which in turn results in urban fragmentation. But this does not imply that the urban planner no longer has to design comprehensible and accessible surroundings. As long as architecture and particularly urban planning can be seen as expressions of society – whether or not consciously formulated or designed as such – attention 'should' be given to their comprehensibility and accessibility. In 1981, Kevin Lynch gave a number of criteria for a 'good' city (when experts still dared to use such descriptions). These included: it should be sensible, identifiable, structured, congruent, transparent, legible, unfolding and significant.[3]

But it is also conceivable that the traditional design techniques, used to arrive at spatial cohesion and significance, are no longer suitable for all tasks in our cities. This means that it is important to investigate how and to what extent cohesion can be achieved by the design of the overlapping networks which determine how today's cities function:

---

3 K. Lynch, **A theory of good city form**, MIT Press, Cambridge/London, 1981, p.235.

the physical networks and the virtual networks. First, however, it will be necessary to develop a better understanding of networks and the 'network city', and to describe them. One problem yet to be understood by the discipline of urban planning is the question of the (to some extent) non-traditional connections between the spatial and functional effects of contemporary networks. Instead of endeavoring to derive significance from the existence of invisible networks as such, it would probably be more fruitful to give form to the intersections at which the exchanges between the various networks actually occur. For example at the entrances and exits of the underground infrastructure as at Blaak Station, Rotterdam designed by Harry Reijnders, where the organization and the handling of direct daylight filters down and accompanies the traveler quite physically along the way to the platforms.

Public, collective and private
The most obvious approach would be to attribute a collective nature to the manifestations of society as reflected in urban planning projects. The terms public, collective and private, though, are used rather carelessly in the urban planning debate. We make a distinction between three pairs of words:
- public – private: referring to the territorial demarcation of spaces and places
- collective – individual: referring to both the desired and engendered social and psychological aspects
- accessible – inaccessible: referring to the right of access, function and use

The idea of Manuel de Solá-Morales, that the contemporary city is strengthened by a network of connections which are created by various forms of overlapping collective use of less-accessible spaces – overlapping in terms of space and time as well as in the composition of the collective groups – constituted an addition to the manner in which, in the urban planning and social disciplines, ideas about the relationships between the city and those who live in it or use it are thought. It seems that this idea must give rise to additional possibilities for reflection on the new forms of 'significance' for life in the city and in the layout of its urban space.

Of course, the phenomenon of collectives with their own ways of using the city and their own places within it is, as such, nothing new. To a certain extent, all social and cultural institutions are constituted only by the warrant of the collective. What is new, is the abundance of differences and the relative mutual isolation of the collectives referred to by De Solá-Morales: just imagine the frequent visitors to the amusement arcade, the members of the sports school, the customers of the sitting-room restaurant, the chamber music ensemble, etc. Such diverse and specific types of collectives have become even more noticeable, as the collectives which traditionally played an important role in society are continually decreasing in size and social significance: the religious community, the residents association, the brass band, etc. Investigation is required into the way in which the form of the city can respond to these new forms of collectivism. Are new forms of public spaces conceivable which could accommodate this diversity in a different way from the central city square dating from the Middle Ages, and all the other urban elements that we think we know so well? It should be realized that we usually forget that they were generally designed for a completely different use from their current use, or were even created in response to a use that has since disappeared.

Significance This last question contains one of the central dilemmas for the theory of urban planning. When something is designed for a specific use, then it can also give an optimum manifestation of its utility: it acquires a specific significance and consequently manifests a given aspect of society. Nevertheless, it has been seen that all the important basic urban elements that have been developed in the course of history, can take on completely different functions in the course of their life span. A good example is the arrival and enormous increase in motorized traffic in the city, which has been assimilated by its public spaces in the course of the years.

The difference between the historical and the present views of the street the 'Hoofdweg' in De Baarsjes in Amsterdam from the mid twenties, gives reason to make a distinction between two kinds of significance associated with urban planning elements. The first type of significance is based on the symbolic value: the cultural consensus of what a street is or should be, which is relatively stable. The other type of significance is based on the actual use, which can change enormously in the course of time.

Society is continually changing, but the duration of squares and buildings operates on a much longer time cycle. The memories they evoke have an equally intractable constancy. That significance has become embodied in stone and is kept alive, in spite of the changes in society itself. The function of the past resulted in form, which acquired significance. The significance now associated with the form has become the function for society. If as a result of the mechanism of tradition these significances continue to play a role in the collective consciousness of society (which they do by their very definition), then an understanding of them is requisite for the discipline of urban planning. This is equally true for the design of new public spaces, for example intermediary public spaces connecting large infrastructures to urban networks.

Amsterdam, Hoofdweg

Credits

This book would not have been possible without the generous support of the Netherlands Architecture Fund, Rotterdam, the Port Authority of Rotterdam, the Van Eesteren-Fluck & Van Lohuizen Foundation, The Hague, Faculty of Architecture, Delft University of Technology, the Stylos Bookfund, Delft, and the Rotterdam Arts Council.

The Critical Landscape
Stylos Series on architecture and urbanism, Faculty of Architecture, Delft University of Technology
Series editor Arie Graafland, Delft University of Technology
Editorial board K. Michael Hayes, Harvard School of Design, USA; Michael Müller, Art History, Bremen University, BRD; Michael Speaks, Southern California Institute of Architecture, USA
Advisory board Henco Bekkering, Jan Brouwer, Jasper de Haan, Deborah Hauptmann, Jeroen Mensink, Kyong Park, Yorgos Simeoforides, Carel Weeber.

In 1996 the first volume in the series was published under the title
The Critical Landscape (ISBN 90-6450-290-0),
in 2000 the second volume was published, **The Socius of Architecture** (ISBN 90-6450-389-3).

cities in transition

Editor Arie Graafland
Guest editor Deborah Hauptmann
Translation by Lara Schrijver
Text editing John Kirkpatrick
Book design by Piet Gerards, Heerlen/Amsterdam
Printed by Snoeck-Ducaju & Zoon, Ghent

Photo credits
Winny Dijkstra 36-41, 168-177, 376-377
Freek van Arkel 42-43, 81-97
dS+V and Archives of the City of Rotterdam 115-121
MVRDV 125-127
Port Authority Tokyo 197-199
Ohno Laboratory Tokyo University 213-215
Ishida Laboratory Fukuoka Institute of Design 226-229
Franziska Bollerey 230-231, 371-373, 375